Anatomy of Film

Anatomy of Film

BERNARD F. DICK

Fourth Edition

Bedford / St. Martin's

Boston • New York

For Bedford/St. Martin's

Communication Editor: Jennifer Bartlett
Developmental Editor: Jeannine Thibodeau
Associate Editor: Sara Slawnik
Senior Production Editor: Harold Chester
Senior Production Supervisor: Joe Ford
Marketing Manager: Richard Cadman
Art Director: Lucy Krikorian
Text Design: Delgado Design, Inc.
Photo Research: Joan Scafarello
Cover Design: Paul Agresti
Cover Photo: Photofest
Composition: Huron Valley Graphics, Inc.
Printing and Binding: Haddon Craftsmen, Inc., an R.R. Donnelley & Sons
  Company

President: Charles H. Christensen
Editorial Director: Joan E. Feinberg
Publisher for History and Communication: Patricia Rossi
Director of Marketing: Karen R. Melton
Director of Editing, Design, and Production: Marcia Cohen
Managing Editor: Erica T. Appel

Library of Congress Control Number: 2001090571

Manufactured in the United States of America.

7 6 5 4 3
f e d c b

For information, write: Bedford/St. Martin's, 75 Arlington Street, Boston, MA
02116   (617-399-4000)

ISBN: 0-312-25944-1

Published and distributed outside North America by
PALGRAVE
Houndmills, Basingstoke, Hampshire RG21 2XS and London
Companies and representatives throughout the world.
PALGRAVE is the new global academic imprint of St. Martin's Press
LLC Scholarly and Reference Division and Palgrave Publishers Ltd.
formerly Macmillan Press Ltd.).
ISBN: 0-333-97348-8
A catalog record for this book is available from the British Library.

TO MY STUDENTS, PAST AND PRESENT

Preface

I t is gratifying to know that *Anatomy of Film* has been in existence for almost a quarter of a century. This is in no small part due to the instructors and students who have used this book and continue to do so. In response to their comments and feedback, I am very pleased to offer an updated and revised fourth edition.

Anatomy of Film was originally conceived as a concise introductory guide to narrative film, intended both for film students and the general reader. In subsequent editions the text responded to the changes in film studies programs. The second and third editions of *Anatomy of Film* achieved this by focusing on key elements in film and film analysis and by adding more useful features. A complete overview of film elements and film theory was added, as well as new chapters on film genres and film adaptation. The purpose of the text was redefined to provide students with the basic analytical methods and vocabulary necessary to study narrative film. By keeping the book brief, my goal was to appeal to a diverse audience in a variety of courses: those requiring a brief core text, those requiring a text that is easily supplemented with readings or other materials, those involving film and literature, and those covering film within the context of other media.

These features as well as many others were retained in this new edition. The text continues to place special emphasis on the narrative film and to examine the many ways in which the technical components of the medium all come together to produce an art form like no other. Students learn how to understand and evaluate film as a total work of art in which sight, script, and sound are all part of a whole. In addition I have retained the book's well-respected coverage of film evaluation and criticism, using an approach similar to that used in literature and art studies.

Thus, the heart of *Anatomy of Film* remains intact. What has changed is a direct result of the years that have passed since the last edition and the many different films and methods of viewing that pass before us. I have listed more specific changes below. I hope this edition of *Anatomy of Film* will continue to please all who use the text.

- **Attention to our film heritage:** In 1996, the American Film Institute (AFI) celebrated the 100th anniversary of the motion picture (1896 being the date of the first commercial showing of a film in the United States) by publishing a list of the one hundred best films made during that period, sixty-two of which are referred to and discussed in the fourth edition of *Anatomy of Film*. By calling attention to our film heritage, the AFI has indirectly called attention to movie history, which roughly coincides with that of the twentieth century. This new edition of *Anatomy of Film* acknowledges this history by including background on the origins of the narrative film, historical accuracy in movies, the documentary, the production code, visual effects, and the independent film.

  The emphasis of *Anatomy of Film* is primarily on American movies for two reasons: to provide a sense of unity in a text that by its nature must include examples of myriad techniques, and to draw on films that are frequently shown on television and can be rented or purchased. However, no one can deny the importance of international cinema, particularly anyone who came of age in the 1950s and 1960s when the European film seemed to dwarf the American product by its sheer creativity. New contemporary examples of international cinema are discussed in this edition, such as *Dancer in the Dark* (1999) and *All About My Mother* (1999).

- **More on independent films and filmmakers:** This new edition also acknowledges the contribution of contemporary independent filmmakers. When an independent film such as *Shakespeare in Love* (1998) wins Academy Awards for Best Picture, Best Screenplay, Best Actress, and Best Supporting Actress, it is time to formally recognize the great contributions the "indies" have made to motion picture art. It is difficult to imagine a major studio producing *Shakespeare in Love* without wanting "bankable" stars and a script with "accessible" dialogue, rather than the Elizabethan-sounding language that was actually used. A detailed discussion of the opening of *Shakespeare in Love* is my tribute to this film and to independent moviemaking.

- **Expanded section on genres of film:** In response to requests to expand the chapter on film genres, I have added other forms of comedy besides screwball (farce, satire, gross-out). The great success of Steven Spielberg's *Saving Private Ryan* has prompted me to include the combat film, a genre that seemed to have gone out of fashion until Spielberg revived it.

- **Expanded approach to film criticism:** The criticism section has also been expanded to include two new schools of criticism: ideological criticism and reception theory. This section discusses the impact of audience response and provides historical background on the nature of film reviewing. I have also expanded the feminist criticism section by comparing two films based on the same source—one directed by a woman, the other by a man. George Kelly's Pulitzer Prize–winning play, *Craig's Wife*, was filmed twice—once by Dorothy Arzner under the same title in 1936 and again by Vincent Sherman as *Harriet Craig* (1950). Since both versions are available on video, they deserve to be studied; the results are quite startling, even though each remains fairly close to the original.

- **Web resources now included:** Since the Internet has changed everyone's research habits, I have decided to include a list of important film Web sites. I have also added another student essay, this one on the German film *Run Lola Run* (1998), in which the author uses a Web site as a source. While the Internet enables students to access information quickly and easily, the source of that information must be acknowledged, as Paul Bell has done in his essay.

- **Updated examples throughout:** I usually hesitate to include "the latest releases" as a definitive example of a revised text. However, there have been several outstanding films of the late 1990s that merit discussion: *Shakespeare in Love, You've Got Mail, Pleasantville, The Truman Show, American Beauty, Humanité,* and *The Matrix.* Although *The Blair Witch Project* has occasioned reactions ranging from awe to contempt, the film has had a broad enough appeal to suggest that the filmmakers managed to connect with an audience looking for either a bogus thrill or the real thing. In any case, *The Blair Witch Project* deserves a hearing.

- **New Glossary:** Many instructors have asked for a Glossary, and I am happy to provide one, which includes not only definitions of technical terms but also of those used in the industry (distribution, Foley artist, preproduction, exhibition, best boy, grip, gaffer, etc.).

Although the Writers Guild of America (WGA) deplores the way directors receive possessory credit for films written by others ("a film by X director"), there are some directors (Steven Spielberg, Billy Wilder, Howard Hawks, Joseph L. Mankiewicz, Martin Scorsese, Nora Ephron, Francis Coppola, and others) who truly deserve authorial status, which I have indicated when citing their work. To avoid repetition, I am including the release date in parentheses only once—with the first mention of the film. There is a List of Films Discussed, along with their directors and release dates, in an appendix.

Finally, I would like to thank those instructors whose suggestions have aided me in preparing the fourth edition of *Anatomy of Film:* Robert J. DeSmith, Dordt College; Noreen Golfman, Memorial University; Robert Holton, Okanagan University College; Daniel M. Linton, Jr., University of Memphis; Kevin Miller, Emerson College; Paul Miller, Davidson College; Anthony Miltich, Fergus Falls Community College; Susan Scrivner, Bemidji State University; and particularly Professor Thomas Murray of Fitchburg State College for alerting me to films I would otherwise have ignored.

BERNARD F. DICK
Professor of Communications and English
Fairleigh Dickinson University
Teaneck, New Jersey

Contents

Anatomy of Film

Film, Cinema, or Movie

Understanding the Medium

*F*iction is a widely understood term; it means the invented, the imaginative, the fanciful—the opposite of fact. There is also *historical fiction*, as well as *historical drama*: terms for works of the imagination that draw on history for narrative or dramatic purposes (Gore Vidal's *Lincoln*, Shakespeare's *Henry V*). Thus, a novel or a play can still be considered fiction even though it is derived from fact. There are other forms of fiction as well—gothic, romantic, picaresque, detective, stream-of-consciousness, to name a few. *Fiction*, then, is an umbrella term—one with many different spokes.

Film is another word that means different things in different contexts: roll film, film stock, *a* film, *to* film. We were all exposed to some kind of film before we saw our first example of classic moviemaking. It may have been something we saw on television: a cartoon, a *Three Stooges* short, a *Lassie* rerun. Perhaps it was an educational film we saw in school, or a theatrical film (a film intended to be shown in movie theaters).

1

Yet, asked to define *film*, many of us would hesitate. But so would professional filmmakers. Animators, documentary filmmakers, and experimental filmmakers perceive themselves as working in the same medium—film. The films they produce, however, differ totally in look, subject matter, and style from those of mainstream Hollywood. To the general public, *film* means "movie"—a perfectly acceptable term (and one that the noted American critic Pauline Kael has always championed).

Unfortunately, *movie* suggests popular culture rather than art, while *cinema* suggests art rather than popular culture. Ironically, *cinema*, though it is a French word, is derived from the Greek *kinein* (to move); thus, whether we use *cinema* or *movie*, we are talking about an art form that was once known as "moving pictures"—appropriately named because the pictures really moved. There is nothing pejorative about the word *movie*; certainly some of the greatest examples of film art ever produced (many of which are discussed in this text) are, and always will be, movies. Although Kael finds *cinema* pretentious, it is commonly used to categorize films according to kind (contemporary cinema, world cinema) and origins (American cinema, French cinema, Third World cinema, and the like). Even so, calling a film a movie implies nothing about artistic worth.

THE DIVERSITY OF THE MEDIUM

Since there are so many different kinds of film, it is impossible to generalize about the nature of the medium. There are several ways to develop an appreciation of film diversity. The most obvious, of course, is to see as many different kinds of movies as possible. You might also read *Variety* each week and note the number of films from such countries as Hungary, China, France, Iran, and Sweden that are reviewed. If you have cable television with the Independent Film Channel (IFC) or the Sundance Channel (SUN), you will see a different kind of movie from what is shown at the multiplex or on premium channels such as HBO and Cinemax. These are sometimes called "small" films because they are not big-budget, star-driven, or special effects–filled movies, in which the characters battle nature and monsters or track down terrorists. The actors may not be household names like Tom Cruise or Julia Roberts; in fact, some may not resemble Hollywood types at all. If the sets look less elaborate than those of a major studio release, it is because the filmmakers could not afford the kind of production made possible by a $70 million budget. For example, no one could mistake *The Blair Witch Project* (1999), filmed with a 16 mm camera and a camcorder at a cost of $30,000, for a movie released by one of the major studios such as Paramount, Twentieth Century-Fox, Universal, Columbia, Warner Bros., MGM, or Disney. Ironically, *Blair Witch* grossed $140 million.

Independent film is not easy to define. Traditionally, an independent film is one that was made without a studio affiliation by producers looking to distribution companies or the studios themselves to release it. Some independent producers manage to find a home at a studio where they can make their movies without interference; in such cases, the studio is only the distributor. In the past, independent producers such as Hal B. Wallis, Sam Spiegel, and Stanley Kramer used the studios as outlets. Wallis produced such classics for Paramount as *Come Back, Little Sheba* (1951) and *The Rose Tattoo* (1955); Spiegel gave Columbia *On the Waterfront* (1954), *The Bridge on the River Kwai* (1957), and *Lawrence of Arabia* (1962); Columbia also benefited from Kramer's *Ship of Fools* (1965) and *Guess Who's Coming to Dinner* (1967), both of which he also directed. Other independent producers released through United Artists, which is often perceived as a studio but was really a distribution company founded in 1919 by three actors (Mary Pickford, Charlie Chaplin, and Douglas Fairbanks) and a director (D. W. Griffith) to produce and distribute their films and those of others. United Artists' releases are among the industry's finest: Howard Hughes's production of *Scarface* (1932), Alexander Korda's production of *The Thief of Baghdad* (1940), Walter Wanger's production of *Stagecoach* (1939), and Samuel Goldwyn's production of *Dead End* (1937), to name only a few.

At present, *independent film* has a similar meaning: a film made by someone who prefers to work outside of mainstream Hollywood rather than be indebted to a studio that could force the filmmaker to compromise his or her artistic integrity. Some "indies"—usually, those with an impressive track record—consider a studio as a base of operations: the studio provides some of the financing (the rest coming from bank loans), office space, and technical services. These indies can count on the studio to distribute their films. Others, generally the younger ones, find themselves trekking to film festivals around the world to show their films to prospective distributors.

Since the 1980s, many independent films—*The Dead* (1987), *sex, lies, and videotape* (1989), *In the Company of Men* (1997), *Boys Don't Cry* (1999), and so forth—have found such widespread acceptance that the distinction between "studio film" and "independent film" seems to be fading. Even name stars are appearing in independent films (e.g., Renée Zellweger and Morgan Freeman in *Nurse Betty* [2000], a USA Films release), thus blurring the distinction even more. Although Miramax is now a subsidiary of the Walt Disney Company, it is still considered an independent, since it is autonomous in matters of production and distribution. It can therefore pursue joint ventures with the big studios without first obtaining Disney's blessing, and enjoy the freedom that draws filmmakers to the ranks of the independents. Miramax's *Shakespeare in Love* (1998), for example, was a coproduction with Universal, which also put up some of the financing. If this seems confusing, think of the words of an executive at Artisan Entertainment, which distributed *The Blair Witch Project:* "We are all independents today, and at the same time no one is independent."[1] Every filmmaker is dependent on financing, whether it comes from a bank, a studio, or friends. A good movie is a good movie, regardless of who produced it.

Another way to appreciate the diversity of the medium is to include some international films in your moviegoing schedule. Like many independent films, international films also feature actors who are largely unfamiliar to mass audiences, yet the films themselves tend to delve more deeply into human behavior than the usual Hollywood product. Often, international films do not come to closure as American movies do. The French film, *Humanité* (1999) opens with the discovery of the body of an eleven-year-old girl who has been brutally murdered and raped. More sexually explicit than any Hollywood studio film could ever be, *Humanité* is essentially a study in bleakness, set in a town in northern France where people lead aimless lives. One could easily imagine a studio executive, too busy to read the script but intrigued by the subject matter, turning it over to an assistant and saying, "Find out who the rapist is and why he did it." The rapist's identity is discovered at the end; as is often the case, he was the character who seemed least likely to commit such an act. Yet we never discover why he did it. The film is entitled *Humanité* (Humanity), which is ironic, since the only one who seems to show any humanity is a police detective who cannot articulate his feelings. *Humanité* is a disturbing film, which suggests that the only hope for those living such empty lives is to reach out to others in whatever way they can, however basic the contact may be.

Butterfly (*La Lengua de las Mariposas* [1999]) is a Spanish film set against the backdrop of the Spanish Civil War (1936–39), a conflict that has little meaning to contemporary audiences even though it was the prelude to World War II—with the fascist nations Germany and Italy supporting the Nationalists and the former Soviet Union aiding the Loyalists, who wanted to keep Spain a socialist republic, independent of the army and the church. Although the film is intensely political, it is really about a young boy's coming of age through the guidance of a wise teacher.

These are not what, in Hollywood, are called "high concept," a misleading term for a movie that can be summed up in twenty-five words or described with familiar titles: "*Lake Placid* (1999) is *Jaws* (1975) with crocodiles"; "*Gladiator* (1999) is an R-rated *Fall of the Roman Empire* (1963) with decapitations." Many international films are not so easily classified. The best seem more like literature than movies because of their density and their imperviousness to such labels as "erotic thriller," "actioner," "chick flick," or "three-hankie movie." To sum up *Humanité* as a film about the search for a child's rapist is to minimize the real point of the film: the impact of a tragedy on people whose lives are too empty to respond to it as they should.

THE CREATION OF THE NARRATIVE FILM

We will be dealing almost exclusively with the **narrative (or story) film** or, as Pauline Kael would want us to say, with movies.

Historically, the narrative film was not the first kind of film to appear, nor was it a uniquely American creation. In 1895, the Lumière brothers, Louis and Auguste, photographed scenes of real life in France (*actualités*, as they were called): a train arriving at a station; workers at quitting time; a mischievous boy stepping on a gardener's hose, causing water to squirt into the gardener's face. Another French movie pioneer, Georges Méliès, who had been a magician, preferred to tell a story rather than record everyday life. Méliès's *A Trip to the Moon* (1902) is a series of "artificially arranged scenes," to use his phrase, that were highly theatrical (for example, a landing right in the eye of the moon) and followed each other sequentially, so that there was a beginning, a middle, and an end. The narrative film was beginning to take shape. But the best narrative is not so much sequential as causal. It is not a matter of A happening first, B second, and so forth; but, rather, A's happening first causes B to happen second, with C as the result.

Historians claim that the first narrative film was E. S. Porter's *The Great Train Robbery* (1903), which pretty much follows the situation-complication-resolution model. Outlaws enter a railroad telegraph office and tie up the operator. They board a train, rob the passengers, and run off into the woods. Meanwhile, back at the telegraph office, the operator's daughter arrives with her father's lunch and unties him. A posse is formed, and the outlaws are killed—all in less than twelve minutes. Although the fourteen episodes that make up *The Great Train Robbery* seem to unfold sequentially, cause-effect is also at work. Because the operator's daughter has brought her father his lunch, she can untie him; because the operator has been untied, a posse can be formed; and because a posse has been formed, the bandits can be tracked down.

Before Porter, going to a movie often meant going to an arcade or a kinetoscope parlor, where there were rows of coin-operated peep shows (kinetoscopes) that looked like cabinets and provided about a minute's worth of moving pictures: galloping horses, speeding trains, a couple kissing, a man sneezing, waves crashing on the beach, and kangaroos boxing. Today, such entertainment hardly seems revolutionary; in fact, kinetoscope fare does not seem like entertainment at all. However, to our forebears, whose idea of a photographed image was a picture in a family album, seeing people in motion or nature in action was a revelation.

The narrative film came about only when filmmakers discovered that the medium could do more than just record whatever was in front of the camera. The next step was not to capture the real but to re-create it: to show what could or might be; in other words, to tell a story. Train robberies were common in the early twentieth century. However, it would have been impossible to film one. So why not imagine what one might have been like in 1903? And so, with *The Great Train Robbery*, the narrative film came into its own.

NARRATIVE FILM

In attempting to define *film*, the American playwright, screenwriter, and critic John Howard Lawson wrote the following: "A film is an audiovisual conflict; it embodies time-space relationships; it proceeds from a premise, through a progression, to a climax or ultimate term of the action."[2] Note that Lawson has not described film as such; he has described one of its particular forms: the narrative film, or what is commonly called a movie.

What is a movie? To Lawson it is narrative, told through sound and image, that builds to a climax and culminates in a resolution. Note that Lawson does not make dialogue part of the definition; he merely says that a movie is audiovisual. A movie does not need spoken dialogue to tell a story. The silent films had no spoken dialogue, but they did have some kind of sound. Piano or organ accompaniment was common, and sound effects were necessary to complement the action on the screen. Even with the advent of sound, filmmakers who were truly creative knew that parts of the action could be told visually without any dialogue.

In a film, the images themselves can tell part of the story, independently of language. Some of the most unforgettable moments in film are wordless. We should not go so far as Norma Desmond (Gloria Swanson) in Billy Wilder's *Sunset Boulevard* (1950), who made only silent films and saw no need for spoken dialogue. "We had faces!" she exclaims. On the other hand, the coming of sound ushered in the golden age of the American film (roughly 1930 to the end of the 1950s), during which a vast number of classic films appeared that were the result of outstanding screenplays. Orson Welles's *Citizen Kane* (1941) would never have been the masterpiece it was without the script that Herman J. Mankiewicz and Welles created. Even contemporary filmmakers such as Woody Allen and Joel and Ethan Coen realize the paramount importance of the script. Still, there are moments when words are unnecessary because the visuals are

Bette Davis (left) as Margo Channing; Marilyn Monroe as an aspiring actress; and George Sanders as a formidable critic in *All About Eve* (1950). *(Courtesy Twentieth Century-Fox)*

doing the narrating: the burning sled in *Citizen Kane* that reveals the meaning of "Rosebud"; a man, destined to be a loner, standing in the doorway of a house that everyone enters but himself (John Ford's *The Searchers* [1956]); an astronaut clearing the window of his spaceship at the same time that his wife is looking out of the window of their home, so that it seems as if they see each other—if only in their imagination (*Apollo 13* [1995]). The great filmmakers always knew that the difference between theater and film was the difference between a play and a screenplay; the latter is precisely what the term implies: a play designed for the screen, where images can carry as much weight as words.

Joseph L. Mankiewicz's *All About Eve* (1950) and Alfred Hitchcock's *Psycho* (1960) illustrate the way images advance or enhance the action without the use of dialogue. *All About Eve* is the story of an aspiring actress, Eve Harrington (Anne Baxter), who deceives the Broadway star Margo Channing (Bette Davis) into befriending her. After she betrays Margo and becomes a star herself, Eve becomes the victim of a similar scheme: Phoebe, a starstruck student, will do to Eve what Eve did to Margo. As Phoebe stands in front of a three-way mirror, bowing to an imaginary audience as if she were accepting an award, her image is multiplied until the screen is filled with what seems to be an infinity of Phoebes. The final sequence is entirely without dialogue. None is needed; the visuals themselves make the point. As long as there are stars, there will be the starstruck, some of whom will stop at nothing to achieve fame.

Psycho will always be remembered for the shower murder of Marion Crane (Janet Leigh). The episode is completely wordless. There is sound, of course: music that really shrieks, as if anticipating the audience's reaction. As Marion prepares for a shower in her room at the Bates Motel, Norman Bates (Anthony Perkins) is in the adjacent parlor, where there's a peephole, covered by the painting *Susanna and the Elders*. Removing the

A shower about to be interrupted by a murderous intruder in Hitchcock's *Psycho* (1960). *(Courtesy Museum of Modern Art/Film Still Archive, hereafter abbreviated as MOMA/FSA)*

painting, Norman watches Marion undress. She goes into the shower, luxuriating in the spray of water. Suddenly a shadow, presumably of an elderly woman, appears against the shower curtain. The woman pulls the curtain aside and proceeds to stab Marion repeatedly, as blood mingles with the water and swirls down the drain. Although the entire episode lasts less than a minute, a great deal of information has been imparted. Hitchcock's choice of painting was not arbitrary; just as the Elders in the Book of Daniel spied on Susanna as she entered her bath, so the voyeuristic Norman spies on Marion. A shower is a place of privacy, relaxation, and cleansing. Marion's privacy has been invaded. Instead of relaxation, she experiences the repose of death. Instead of her body being cleansed, it is defiled. Actually, it is the shower stall that must be cleansed, because it has been splattered with blood.

Writing down everything that happens in that episode would take longer than it does to see it. In his *Filmguide to Psycho*, James Naremore devotes five pages to a description of those forty-five seconds of film.[3]

TIME-SPACE RELATIONSHIPS

Like any narrative, a good movie involves conflict: personalities clash, goals differ, interests diverge, characters are at odds with each other or with society. In a movie, however, the conflict is audiovisual: it is heard and seen rather than written and read. A movie "embodies time-space relationships." While a written narrative can suggest that two events are occurring at the same time and in different places, a movie can do more than suggest: it can *show* them occurring.

Time Code (2000) went beyond juxtaposing two simultaneous events. In this highly experimental film, the screen is partitioned into four parts,

Simultaneous action in *Time Code* (2000). *(Courtesy MOMA/FSA)*

so that it resembles a grid. In each part, a story about infidelity unfolds, so that the audience is able to experience four interlocking narratives on the same subject, taking place on the same day and in the same general part of Los Angeles. Since *Time Code* was never intended for multiplexes, it did not attract wide audiences. It was the director Mike Figgis's attempt to illustrate how film can depict four actions occurring at the same time without the director's having to cut from one to the other. Because it is a method that is so at odds with what the public expects of a movie, *Time Code* does not represent the wave of the future.

Yet it does illustrate a major difference between film and fiction. At the beginning of Iris Murdoch's novel *Harry and Cato* (1976), one character is pacing up and down a bridge in London "at about the hour" that another is on a jet over the Atlantic. Then Murdoch reminds us that "at about the hour" the first two characters were on their respective bridge and jet, two more were in their library, and another was elsewhere, rereading his daughter's letter. Although Murdoch manages to interweave the destinies of all these individuals, she has to keep repeating "at about the hour" until they have been introduced. A filmmaker could capture the simultaneous action of the novel's opening by turning it into a prologue,

Film, Cinema, or Movie   9

using a split screen or a gridlike screen on the order of *Time Code*, then switching to a more traditional form of narrative for the rest of the film. For the novelist, it is not so easy. Apart from splitting the page (which would alienate most readers), a novelist has no other choice but to use temporal references ("at the same time") or summary statements implying that while event A was occurring in one place, event B was occurring in another.

MOVIE TIME

Since a movie tells a story, it must do so within a certain period of time. Anyone who attends movies regularly checks the movie timetable in the newspaper. Television programmers are especially conscious of a movie's running time, since films are often cut to fit into a particular time slot. Running time, however, is real time—90 minutes, 105 minutes, and so on. Movie time is not; movie time manipulates real time, so that an event can be prolonged or shortened, and an action slowed down or sped up.

Movie time is elastic. In a movie, an entire day can be compressed into a few minutes or even seconds; likewise, a few minutes or seconds can be prolonged into what seems to be an entire day. In the famous Odessa Steps sequence in *Potemkin* (1925), the Russian director Sergei Eisenstein distorts real time. He makes the massacre seem longer than it was because he wants to emphasize the atrocities the czarist troops committed against the people of Odessa. Toward the end of the sequence, a soldier swings his saber, striking the right eye of a woman wearing a pince-nez. In reality, the soldier would have slashed her eye with one movement of his arm, but Eisenstein fragments the act. First, we see the soldier, his arm raised with the blade behind his head; then we see his savage face, but not the saber; now his face dominates the screen. Next, he shouts something as his raised arm begins to descend. Finally, we see the woman—her mouth gaping, the right lens of her pince-nez shattered, blood spurting from her eye and running down her face.

Removing a key from a key ring is a simple operation. In Alfred Hitchcock's films, however, nothing is simple. In *Notorious* (1946), Alicia (Ingrid Bergman) is an American intelligence agent whose job requires her to marry Sebastian (Claude Rains), an ex-Nazi. She has the keys to every room in their house except the wine cellar. Since her coworker (Cary Grant) suspects that the cellar contains more than wine, Alicia must remove that key from her husband's key ring while he is in the bathroom getting ready for a party they are giving that evening. To create suspense, Hitchcock prolongs the action, making the audience wonder whether she will succeed; and if she does, what will happen when her husband discovers that the key is missing—which he does when the champagne runs out and he must make a trip to the wine cellar.

In real life, a wine bottle perched too close to the edge of the shelf will simply fall and shatter. In *Notorious* a wine bottle does shatter, but first it lingers on the edge, causing us to wonder if it will fall, and if it does, what its contents will reveal. In Hitchcock, things are not always what they seem; needless to say, this wine bottle does not contain wine.

The party in *Notorious*, which lasted several hours, occupies about ten minutes of screen time. Similarly, in Frank Capra's *Meet John Doe* (1941), a cross-country political campaign occurs in a few seconds. The climax of *Nickelodeon* (1976) is the premiere of D. W. Griffith's *The Birth of a Nation* (1915). To make the premiere as credible as possible, clips from the actual film were used. The premiere is so authentic, and the audience's reaction so spontaneous, that we forget that Griffith's three-hour epic has been reduced to a few minutes. Likewise, Robert Altman's *Nashville* (1975), which runs two and a half hours, is so absorbing that we forget we have spent five days with twenty-four people, whose destinies have been interconnected.

We must observe the laws of time, but movies do not; they can expand or contract time. If the film engages our attention, as James Whale's *Show Boat* (1936) does, we are oblivious to the fact that a story that spanned three generations took only 113 minutes to tell. A few films exhibit perfect unity of time: the running time coincides with the story time. Such films, admittedly, are rare, but Robert Wise's *The Set-Up* (1949) and Fred Zinnemann's *High Noon* (1952) run seventy-two and eighty-four minutes, respectively. Clocks are important markers of time in both films; as a result, we realize that there was no difference between the time it took to see the film and the time it took for the plot to unfold.

HISTORY, THE NARRATIVE FILM, AND THE DOCUMENTARY

If film can manipulate time and space, it can also do the same with history. Historians have always been critical of Hollywood either for simplifying or falsifying history. They cite, among other examples, (1) films that are too speculative and fanciful to be trustworthy; (2) World War II movies that played on Americans' fear of invasion by depicting a United States honeycombed with enemy agents; and (3) films about historical figures in which crucial details have deliberately been omitted. Many historians were appalled by Oliver Stone's *JFK* (1991), which implicated the then vice president, Lyndon B. Johnson, the CIA, and a host of others in the 1963 assassination of President John F. Kennedy. *JFK* is a fascinating film, even though Stone's thesis is unprovable (and, to many, absurd). There was also no proof for the underlying thesis behind many of the movies Hollywood turned out during World War II, which insisted that Nazi agents were infiltrating defense plans, committing sabotage in aircraft factories, and plotting to dynamite dams, while at the same time masquerading as respectable citizens. Is Hitchcock's *Saboteur* (1942), then, to be dismissed as wartime propaganda, when all it did was reflect the existing mentality? Although it is now known that there were no acts of enemy-directed sabotage in America during World War II, that should not stop anyone from enjoying *Saboteur*, which suggests that there were. We can still marvel at the film's art, even if the film itself is historically inaccurate. The climax, in which the Nazi agent falls to his death from the Statue of Liberty, has nothing to do with history. It has a great deal to do with the art of film, particularly Hitchcock's ability to stage a confrontation between the Nazi agent and the hero in the statue's torch-bearing hand, making it look realistic even though it was filmed on a soundstage at Universal Studios.

A similar problem arises with the **biopic,** a movie based on the life of a historical figure. Although one can argue that a biography should offer a balanced account of the subject's life, the result is often the contrary; instead of fair-mindedness, there is idealization, denigration, or fabrication. The American western portrayed notorious outlaws such as Jesse James and Billy the Kid sympathetically. In *Jesse James* (1939), it seems that all the James brothers wanted was to keep the railroad from going through their property; in *The Kid from Texas* (1950), one of the many films about Billy the Kid, the outlaw–cattle rustler is just a misunderstood young man who happens to kill people.

One of the few biopics to achieve a degree of objectivity is Spike Lee's *Malcolm X* (1992), which does not skirt the topic of Malcolm's early life on the streets. If it seems that Lee does not emphasize the significance of Malcolm's pilgrimage to Mecca, one can say, in Lee's defense, that a spiritual transformation, such as Malcolm's, is difficult to portray on the screen. However, Denzel Washington is so extraordinary as Malcolm—his face glowing with the feeling of brotherhood he experiences during the pilgrimage, which he conveys in a letter to his wife—that we see and hear the effects of the transformation, which is perhaps all a film can accomplish. Unfortunately, far too many biopics are so removed from the truth that they either have to be treated as fiction or be completely dismissed. In 1946, it would have been impossible to make a movie about the life of the great composer and lyricist Cole Porter that told the truth about his homosexuality and "in name only" marriage; or, in 1948, to make a movie about the legendary team of composer Richard Rodgers and lyricist Larry Hart that acknowledged Hart's homosexuality. The question was not whether Porter was alive in 1946 (he was) or Hart in 1948 (he wasn't). The question was the Production Code, which was quite explicit about what kind of material was acceptable for the screen. And, according to the code, homosexuality ("or any inference of it") was completely unacceptable. Thus the Porter biopic, *Night and Day* (1946), and the Rodgers and Hart biopic, *Words and Music* (1948), should be considered as movies with great music but with little, if any, historical value.

But how accurate is historical writing, we might ask? In the *Poetics*, Aristotle distinguished between history and tragedy (or imaginative literature, in general, such as fiction and, by extension, film). History, he claimed, portrays the particular—what was; tragedy, the universal—what should be. However, even Greek historians did not always adhere to that distinction. Pericles never gave the famous funeral speech that Thucydides ascribed to him in his *History of the Peloponnesian War*. Thucydides, a master of language, had Pericles deliver an oration that was loftier and more eloquent than anything that could ever have been spoken. The ancient historians thought nothing of inventing speeches and conversations. Since they were conscious of being writers as well as chroniclers, they considered themselves to be not so much recorders of the past as interpreters of it, looking for a pattern to emerge from the evidence they had accumulated.

Historiography, the writing of history, gives some kind of structure to the past by drawing on an arsenal of narrative devices, such as heightened language, digressions, and re-creations of events the writer may never have witnessed. Historical novelists and dramatists do much the same thing: they shape history as if it were a plot in need of form. They omit individuals and events that seem extraneous; they rearrange incidents or make some appear more important than they were. So do filmmakers. For example, *Cleopatra* (1963) implies that the battle of Actium was a major battle, while it was really little more than a skirmish. Film, like literature, embellishes history; the point is not the drama of the battle but its significance, which *Cleopatra* does not ignore: Actium, at which the forces of Antony and Cleopatra were defeated by those of Octavian, resulted in Octavian's becoming the first Roman emperor, Augustus.

Not all films, however, are as historically accurate as *Cleopatra*, which was maligned in its time but now ranks as one of Hollywood's better re-creations of the past. *Gone with the Wind* (1939) is one of the American cinema's most honored films. However, anyone basing his or her knowledge of the Civil War on *Gone with the Wind* would conclude that plantations such as Tara represented a lifestyle—genteel, civilized, humane—that, with the war's end, was "gone with the wind"; that the only difference between African American house slaves and white domestics was color; and that cotton was picked by invisible hands. The closest the film ever gets to showing what cotton-picking does to the hands occurs after the war, when the heroine, Scarlett O'Hara (Vivien Leigh), and her sisters must do the

Elizabeth Taylor and Richard Burton as Cleopatra and Mark Antony in *Cleopatra* (1963), a movie epic that for the most part is historically accurate. *(Courtesy the Margaret Herrick Library of the Academy of Motion Picture Arts and Sciences)*

work that had once been done by slaves. While *Gone with the Wind* may strike contemporary viewers as an ode to the Old South that totally ignores the evils of slavery, it is nonetheless a brilliant example of moviemaking and an acknowledged masterpiece. It was never intended to be taken as history but as a movie in which history was a point of departure for a story about fictitious characters caught up in a real event. Trying to learn history from movies is as futile as trying to learn it from art. Paintings of historical events are works of the imagination, inspired by real incidents. One would like to think that George Washington stood in the boat as he crossed the Delaware, but that would have been extremely difficult, if not impossible.

Aristotle was right: historians tell the truth in their way; playwrights (and he would have included filmmakers) in theirs. Even the Greek playwrights treated myth—the equivalent of their prehistory—as narratives that could be altered or embellished to suit their purpose. Many Greek myths

Anatomy of Film

have alternate versions; one Greek playwright, Aeschylus, has Agamemnon sacrifice his daughter, Iphigenia; another, Euripides, follows a different account in which a stag is substituted in Iphigenia's place, and she lives.

How different, we might ask, is a **documentary** (a nonfiction film)? Documentary filmmakers may have a higher regard for truth, yet they, too, can create a version (usually their own) of it by drawing on the same techniques that moviemakers use, such as juxtaposing events that are unrelated in time and place to make them seem similar or simultaneous, and omitting opposing views in order to achieve a unified vision. Some have even gone further and included scenes from feature films for contrast or transition, employing classical narrative construction (beginning-middle-end) to allow the documentary to unfold as if it were a movie.

Hollywoodism: Jews, Movies and the American Dream (1998) opens with an enactment of anti-Semitism rather than with the usual documentary footage: we witness an attack on a Jewish family in Ukraine that has left the mother dead, and her son looking as if the incident has been forever burned in his memory—as, we are told, it was burned into the memories of the men responsible for the creation of Hollywood. Soon we see newsreel footage of the men themselves: MGM's Louis Mayer, Universal's Carl Laemmle, Paramount's Adolph Zukor, the independent producer Samuel Goldwyn, the brothers Warner, Harry and Jack. While there is no doubt that the American motion picture industry was primarily the creation of Jewish immigrants and their sons, there is no evidence that the studio heads were attracted to stories about oppression because they were haunted by pogroms they had witnessed as children, which, for the most part, would have been impossible, although they had undoubtedly heard of such atrocities.

Yet in *Hollywoodism* authentic scenes of violence against Jews are followed by scenes of frontier violence from an obscure Hollywood western, *The Kansan* (1943). However, there is an enormous difference between Cossacks rampaging through an Eastern European shtetl and outlaws terrorizing a peace-loving Kansas family and burning down their house. If the implication is that the Jewish studio heads were so conscious of persecution that they were inspired to make films about it, *The Kansan* is an odd choice, since it is simply another movie in which the hero rids a town of corruption and finds love in the process. Not only does the same plot occur in countless other westerns but also *The Kansan* was released by United Artists, which was not really a studio but a distribution company. Thus it is impossible to say what a "United Artists film" means, except that it was an independent production.

If a documentary filmmaker has a political agenda, it is bound to be reflected in the film. Ernest Hemingway, who wrote the script for Joris Ivens's classic documentary *The Spanish Earth* (1937) took the side of the

Spanish Loyalists during the Spanish Civil War, as did Ivens, who was more of a radical than Hemingway. The Loyalists were fighting to keep Spain a republic (albeit a socialist one); the Nationalists, to keep Spain from falling into the hands of what they considered to be the radical left.

Like Homer's *Iliad*, whose subject is the wrath of Achilles, not the Trojan War per se, *The Spanish Earth* seems to deal with a relatively minor event: the irrigating of a Spanish village so that food can be grown for the defenders of the Spanish republic. At the end, Ivens moves back and forth between shots of the upturned earth and those of the war-scarred streets of Madrid; and between water flowing through ditches and tanks moving across the road. Since Ivens assumes that his audience is familiar with the roots of the conflict, he neither provides background information nor offers a simplistic Loyalists (Yes), Nationalists (No) approach. Ivens does not deny that there is a Nationalist point of view, nor does he argue for the Loyalists. His politics are reflected in the images, which in themselves are neutral. Life (water) is contrasted with death (tanks); country (the village) with city (Madrid). The combination of images leads the viewer to conclude that the Loyalists were fighting to preserve a way of life exemplified by a village where people live and work together in harmony. By moving from one event (the irrigation of a village) to another (the war itself), Ivens achieves a balance that would have eluded most left-wing ideologues.

We might compare *The Spanish Earth* with Frank Capra's *Prelude to War* (1942), a CliffsNotes account of the events leading up to World War II. Capra's documentary is also constructed along traditional lines, beginning and ending with two globes—one bright, one dark, symbolizing the free and enslaved worlds, respectively. Filled with sermonizing, *Prelude to War* is so concerned with oversimplification that it presents Italian fascism, Nazism, and Japanese imperialism as identical forms of tyranny. We are told which world is the best, as if anyone with sense would prefer the world of darkness to the one of light.

Any film can be planned in such a way that it appears to be about one thing but is really about another. *JFK* purports to be a movie, with well-known actors (Kevin Costner, Kevin Bacon, Tommy Lee Jones, Sissy Spacek), but it is such an explosive mix of dramatization, actual newsreel footage, and invented newsreel footage that we either have to keep reminding ourselves that it's only a movie or dismiss it as Stone's fantasy about the Kennedy assassination, even though his "conspiracy theory" has been presented so theatrically that it could almost pass for the truth.

The Blair Witch Project (1999) goes even further; it is a mock documentary ("mockdoc") that has succeeded in convincing many viewers that it was the footage of three student filmmakers who disappeared in the Maryland woods while trying to solve the mystery of the so-called Blair Witch. The three—the producer (Heather Donaghue), the cinematogra-

Heather's confession into the camcorder in *The Blair Witch Project* (1999). *(Courtesy MOMA/FSA)*

pher (Josh Leonard), and the sound person (Mike Williams)—embark on their project, armed with a 16 mm camera and a camcorder. *Blair Witch* begins like a documentary, with Heather speaking directly into the camera ("Hi, this is my home, which I am leaving the comfort of for the weekend, to explore the Blair Witch"). The interviews with the locals sound so authentic; the photography (mostly color but occasionally black-and-white) seems so much like the work of Cinema Studies majors; and the trio, who do double duty as filmmakers and actors, move so convincingly between self-consciousness and professionalism that it is possible to view "the project" as a real experience and not a course assignment.

This is especially true near the end, when Heather, who once used her camcorder on others, now turns it on herself, delivering (supposedly) her apologies to the parents of Josh, who has disappeared, in case she herself should never return home. With only Mike left, the two enter an abandoned house that is gutted and devoid of life—or so it seems. As Heather and Mike race through the shell of the house, the camera appears to go haywire, zigzagging its way up and down the stairs to the point of inducing dizziness in the spectator. When the film is over, and the students seem to have disappeared in the hollows of the ghostly house, we are left wondering whether we have seen a student project, whose creators vanished in the Maryland woods, or a fiction film parading as a project that purports to use documentary techniques (interviews, on-camera and voice-over narration, unscripted conversations). That *Blair Witch* was perceived as a movie attests to the filmmakers' ability to seduce audiences into accepting an amateurish film with some brilliant moments (Heather's confession into the camcorder, for instance) as a horror movie. That it did horrify many viewers suggests that the real and the invented were blended so successfully that only in retrospect can they be separated.

"History has many cunning passages, contrived corridors," T. S. Eliot wrote. Ever since movies began, filmmakers have been exploring these passages and corridors that epic poets, dramatists, and novelists had discovered earlier. But because the passages are "cunning" and the corridors "contrived," filmmakers, including makers of documentaries, must not fall victim to the belief that their version of the truth is the only one; it is only another one.

No matter how objective a documentary purports to be, the footage must still be edited. And it is in the editing that objectivity breaks down, as the filmmaker begins making his or her selections—deleting some shots, arranging others in a particular order for reasons of contrast, dramatic effectiveness, or ideology. The more passionate a documentary filmmaker is about his or her subject, the less likelihood there is of a thoroughly impartial film.

The artist is a liar in the sense of favoring the ideal over the real, the eternal over the temporal, illusion over reality. Hence, Plato would banish poets (or creative artists in general) from the ideal state because they lie, depicting life as it should be rather than as it is in order to present a *version* of the real that is superior to mundane reality.

Every artist worthy of the name presents truth cloaked in illusion. No medium offers the unvarnished truth. Life is what we live; what we experience in a work of art is life on a higher or, at least, a different level. In *Book of Shadows: Blair Witch 2* (2000), the main character declares, "Film lies; video tells the truth." The line is true only in terms of the plot in which video plays a pivotal role. Taken out of context, it is as fallacious as Plato's theory that art is inferior to philosophy because it derives from an inferior part of the soul. Video can lie as effectively (or ineffectually) as any medium. If the end result is art, the lie has been transformed into a truth.

MISE-EN-SCÈNE

We have been treating films as texts—works to be analyzed and interpreted. A movie is a text, and it is similar to any other text, including a textbook used in a course. *Text* comes from the Latin *textus* (to weave). A text weaves the material together in an orderly and coherent fashion. A movie is a text that interweaves sound in any or all of its aspects (noise, music, speech) and image (everything from the printed word to physical action, movement, gaze, and gesture) for the purpose of telling a story. There is a particular term for this kind of blending: the French phrase *mise-en-scène*.

You may have been told in an English class never to use a foreign word or phrase when an English one would suffice. This was one of the cardinal rules in Strunk and White's classic, *The Elements of Style*: "Some writers, however, from sheer exuberance or a desire to show off, sprinkle their work liberally with foreign expressions, with no regard for the reader's comfort. It is a bad habit. Write in English."

The rule is a good one, although it is frequently violated by film scholars, who rely so heavily on jargon—using words like *fabula* (Latin), *diegesis* (Greek), and *syuzhet* (Russian) in discussing "plot"—that they do more than make the reader uncomfortable: they lose the reader altogether. Some terms, however, have become so much a part of our critical vocabulary that, though they derive from other languages, they crystallize a complex idea in a single word or phrase that, if properly understood, allows the discussion to proceed without further explanation. For example, literary critics often refer to *mythos*, the Greek word for, among other things, "plot." They do not mean "myth" in the sense of "story"; they mean recurring themes or narrative patterns that make up what we call plots. Similarly, film critics use *mise-en-scène*, a French phrase derived from the theater and meaning the various elements (script, direction, music, costumes, makeup, lighting, movement, and so forth) that make up the production.

In film, *mise-en-scène* has a similar meaning: the "staging" of a movie, giving it the same attention to detail (set decoration, lighting, costumes, hairstyles, sound, line readings, movement, camera angles, and so forth) that is lavished on a theatrical production, so that the filmmaker, like the stage director, can realize his or her vision of the material. Like opera, film is a hybrid art. Opera is an art form that draws on other arts: theater, painting, music, and, depending on the opera, dance, and mime.

Film can draw on all of these, too; film, however, is also an outgrowth of another art (and one that took a while to be recognized as such): photography. Film is often called a collaborative art, in the sense of requiring the talents of a vast number of specialists, all of whom are generally acknowledged in the end credits. It is also an art in which one person, the director, is expected to integrate all of these contributions into a totality. In the next few chapters, we will be anatomizing film—viewing it piecemeal. It is not too early to start thinking in terms of the whole, however. In a sense, you already know many of the elements that make up what is called a "movie." Let us analyze those that make up the opening of *Shakespeare in Love* (1998): print, sound (dialogue, music, noise), camera movement, setting, costumes, and performance.

Even before the action begins, a printed title, "London—Summer 1593," appears on the screen in white lettering on a black background. Another title follows in the same monochrome: "In the glory days of the Elizabethan theatre two playhouses were fighting it out for writers and audiences." Then, without our noticing it, black and white changes to color, and soothing music is heard—not period music, as one might expect in a movie deliberately advertising itself as set in Tudor England but, rather, music that transcends time, evoking neither present nor past.

Against a blue sky, a third title materializes: "North of the city was the Curtain Theatre, home to England's most famous actor, Richard Burbage." As the camera slowly descends from the sky, the thatched roof of what turns out to be a typical Elizabethan theater comes into view, along with more text: "Across the river was the competition, built by Philip Henslowe, a businessman with a cash flow problem." The competition is the Rose. Although *Shakespeare in Love* has yet to appear on the screen, audiences have been given enough of an introduction to prepare them for the film proper.

The camera is now inside the Rose, gradually revealing a theater with three galleries and an apron stage. Even if we did not know that Henslowe's theater has been reconstructed with painstaking accuracy, the detail suggests that this is so, and a brief look at the diagram of an Elizabethan playhouse confirms it. The thatched roof covered only the galleries, leaving the groundlings, who paid a penny for what today would be called standing room, exposed to the elements. Thus, the theater has a dirt floor, on which we see the tattered poster of a play that was produced there.

A scream is heard as the camera zooms over to a curtained area behind which a man is being tortured. The victim is Henslowe, whose name has already been made known to us—an important figure in the history of the English stage. The ensuing dialogue makes it clear that Henslowe is being tortured because he has been unable to pay his debts for reasons that soon become apparent. The opening dialogue is typical of what is heard throughout the film. The language is not exactly Elizabethan, although Shakespeare's own language is spoken at times, notably during a performance of *Romeo and Juliet*. Still, the dialogue has an authentic ring because the actors look and speak as if they were in London in 1593. Once Henslowe tells his creditor that he has a new play by Shakespeare, the music returns, as if to assure us that all will be well.

Finally, the film proper begins after the names of the production companies (Miramax, Universal, and Bedford Falls) come on. Someone with ink-stained hands and ink-encrusted nails is practicing his signature. From the various spellings (Will Shagsbeard, W. Shakspur), we conclude that it is Shakespeare. Then, in the same script, the movie's title appears on the screen.

The setting now changes to a marketplace where vendors ply their wares and buyers can purchase anything from eggs to cloth. Henslowe makes his way through the teeming crowd to Shakespeare's untidy room. Shakespeare's first words could not be more authentic: "Doubt thou the stars are fire, doubt that the sun doth move." Even though the audience may not know the lines from *Hamlet* (II, 2), they sound as if they were written by Shakespeare, and that is what matters.

Shakespeare owes Henslowe a play, but the playwright is suffering

Shakespeare (Joseph Fiennes) and his muse, the fictional Viola (Gwyneth Paltrow) in the multiple-Oscar-winning *Shakespeare in Love* (1998). *(Courtesy MOMA/FSA)*

from writer's block for lack of inspiration and needs to consult his therapist, a combination pharmacist-alchemist-astrologer. On the way to his "weekly session," Shakespeare hears a Puritan preacher fulminating against two of London's best-known playhouses, the Curtain and the Rose, and calling for "a plague on both their houses." Shakespeare takes note of the phrase, "a plague on both their houses," filing it away in his memory. Anyone who is familiar with *Romeo and Juliet* would appreciate the allusion.

The film abounds in such allusions, as one might expect from the script's coauthor, Tom Stoppard, one of Britain's best-known playwrights, who came to prominence with his drama (later made into a film) *Rosencrantz and Guildenstern Are Dead*, which, like *Shakespeare in Love*, can be understood on two levels: as a play about two men caught up in a scheme they do not understand; and as a play about two minor characters from *Hamlet*, who have been given a play of their own. Those who know *Hamlet* can appreciate Stoppard's play on both levels; those who do not will understand it only on the first level. Even so, they will not feel cheated, as they would in the case of a work requiring such specialized knowledge that anyone lacking it would feel frustrated and perhaps even angry with the author for being so obscure. *Shakespeare in Love* can also be enjoyed on two levels; if it proved to be such a popular film that it won seven Academy Awards, including best picture, screenplay, and actress (Gwyneth Paltrow), it was partly because all the allusions were so successfully worked into the dialogue that they seemed natural even to moviegoers who knew little or nothing about Shakespeare. For them, the film was a bittersweet romance between Shakespeare (Joseph Fiennes) and the fictitious Lady Viola (Paltrow). Anyone who has read Shakespeare's *Twelfth Night* or seen the 1997 movie version might remember that Viola is also the name of one of the main characters from that comedy. They would also get the point of Queen Elizabeth's request, at the end of the film, that Shakespeare write a comedy to celebrate Twelfth Night—the twelfth night after Christmas, which was always a time of great festivity.

Shakespeare in Love is not the kind of film in which the camera calls attention to itself. The scene between Shakespeare and the therapist begins with the playwright lying on a couch. Slowly, the camera begins circling the couch, executing a 180-degree turn that ends with Shakespeare's being face-to-face with the therapist, who, true to his profession, is taking notes. Although the therapist could have been introduced differently (by being seen as Shakespeare enters his cluttered room, for example), the method that director John Madden has chosen suggests that the camera is an active participant in the narrative, not a passive recorder of the action.

Within the first ten minutes of the film, we have been introduced to a cross section of Tudor society. The merchants wear aprons and caps; the gentlemen, doublets and ruffs (uncomfortable-looking circular collars). At the queen's palace at Whitehall, where Shakespeare's *Two Gentlemen of Verona* is to be performed, we see the nobles, splendidly dressed—but none more so than Queen Elizabeth (Judi Dench, who won an Oscar for best supporting actress), whose richly embroidered gown is so massive that she looks imprisoned in it. Elizabeth's costume, which is so elaborate that it restricts her mobility, suggests both rigidity and rank, implying that rank has made her rigid and inflexible. The lords and ladies look more comfortably dressed; Viola's gown, in particular, has fluidity and grace. If the Whitehall audience is dressed more fashionably than the theatergoers whom we saw in the galleries of the Rose, the reason is that *Two Gentlemen of Verona* is not being performed at a theater but in a banqueting hall for the queen and her guests. Elizabeth, although she was a fine scholar and a linguist, loved low comedy and enjoyed nibbling on sweets during the performance. She was so taken with a bit of comic relief involving a dog that she laughed raucously and threw the animal a sweet.

Suddenly, we are aware that the sound has been muted, as often happens in movies when a character sees someone who is so captivating that the character becomes oblivious to everyone else. Shakespeare has just caught sight of Viola—a typical case of love entering through the eyes, which is a recurring theme in Elizabethan poetry and is borne out in *Romeo and Juliet*. The camera cooperates in the mood by changing focus, reducing the rest of the characters to a blur so that Viola stands out as the object of Shakespeare's attention.

However authentic a film may look, audiences will never be convinced unless the actors fit the parts. *Shakespeare in Love* is perfectly cast, from the leads to the supporting and minor roles. Shakespeare (Fiennes) behaves like a romantic hero, in love with the idea of love, like Romeo or Orsino in *Twelfth Night*. This Shakespeare is closer to the author of the sonnets and romantic comedies (for example, *As You Like It* and *Twelfth Night*) than he is to the tragedies. The characterization of Henslowe (Geoffrey Rush) rings true: the historical Henslowe was a wheeler-dealer who had been everything from a lumber merchant and farmer to a tavern owner and realtor. Elizabeth (Dench) is properly regal, imprisoned in a gown that makes her look like an overdressed mechanical doll. Yet her response to the routine with the dog is delightfully real, suggesting that there may be a human being under all that finery. Although Viola (Paltrow) has just appeared, she turns out to be an incurable romantic, like Shakespeare. In the opening scenes, print, setting, costumes, dialogue, color, sound, camera movement, and performance mesh seamlessly. The mise-en-scène has been anatomized, enabling us to appreciate the various ways in which film elements work. The same elements that make up the opening of *Shakespeare in Love* keep reconstituting themselves throughout the film. Thus, to understand *mise-en-scène*, one must apply this brief analysis to the entire film, studying the way everything locks into place, like the pieces of a picture puzzle, to form a whole—"the whole consort dancing together," to quote T. S. Eliot in the last of his *Four Quartets*.

NOTES

[1]Stephen Galloway, "When Worlds Collide," *Hollywood Reporter*, Independent Producers & Distributors edition, August 2000: 9.

[2]John Howard Lawson, *Film: The Creative Process* (New York: Hill & Wang, 1967), 292.

[3]James Naremore, *Filmguide to Psycho* (Bloomington: Indiana University Press, 1977).

CHAPTER

Graphics and Sound

A movie's running time and the speed at which the action progresses are among the many decisions that are made before or after production. Who has made these decisions is not the point; often we do not know who was responsible for a particular image or line of dialogue. Some directors—Woody Allen and Robert Altman, for example—allow actors to improvise certain scenes. Several writers worked on the *Casablanca* (1942) screenplay, but the final line, "Louis, I think this is the beginning of a beautiful friendship," never appeared in any of the drafts. It was the inspiration of the producer, Hal Wallis, who also decided that the film (originally called *Everybody Comes to Rick's*) would be entitled *Casablanca*.

Although Victor Fleming is credited as the director of *Gone with the Wind* (1939), Sam Wood and George Cukor also worked on the film. But none of these three directors were responsible for the impressive burning-of-Atlanta sequence; that was the work of the film's art director, William Cameron Menzies. Thus, in writing about film, we use the general term *filmmaker* because it is often difficult to know who was responsible for what effect.

GRAPHICS

Logos

Although we may never know exactly how all the decisions involved in producing a film were made, we do know that a film is intended to begin and end with a certain image. In American films, the first image to appear on the screen is generally the studio's or the distributor's logo.

A logo is an example of **graphics,** the combination of print and design. It is also a studio's trademark. Although the studios are not what they were during Hollywood's golden age of the 1930s and 1940s, the logos of such studios as MGM, Warner Bros., Columbia, Paramount, Twentieth Century-Fox, and Universal have either remained the same or have been slightly modified. Universal's globe still spins in the sky, but it is no longer encircled by an airplane as it was in the early 1930s; nor is it made of Plexiglas, as it was from 1936 to 1946. Columbia's Lady with a Torch is intact, except that the torch shines more brightly and the lady is slimmer. In *Transparent Things*, Vladimir Nabokov claimed that contained within each word is its own history; if this is so, we might also say that encapsulated within each logo is the studio's history. In the 1930s and 1940s, moviegoers knew the difference between the studios. When they heard MGM's lion roar its greeting, they could expect a well-produced film with an outstanding cast; at that time, MGM was Hollywood's biggest studio, boasting of "more stars than are in the heavens." When an audience saw the Republic eagle, they knew they would be seeing a B-movie; Republic was known for programmers (for example, Gene Autry and Roy Rogers westerns)—movies that filled out the second half of a double bill. Students of film should be able to distinguish between the studios whether they are studying films of the past or attending those of the present.

While it is true that filmmakers have no control over the logo, they often try to integrate it with the film so that it is not merely a trademark. Steven Spielberg's *Indiana Jones and the Temple of Doom* (1985) opens with Paramount's snowcapped mountain, which appears concurrently with the Indiana Jones theme on the soundtrack. The combination of logo (Paramount's mountain) and music (the familiar Indiana Jones theme) says that what follows is both a Paramount picture and an Indiana Jones movie.

Some filmmakers even start the action with the logo. In *That's Life!*

Universal's globe. Universal is now a subsidiary of MCA (Music Corporation of America), a diversified entertainment and leisure company. *(Copyright by Universal Pictures, a Division of Universal City Studios, Inc. Courtesy MCA Publishing Rights, a Division of MCA, Inc.)*

A 1940s version of the Columbia logo, which is only slightly different today. *(Courtesy Sony Pictures Entertainment and MOMA/FSA)*

(1985), the Columbia logo appears simultaneously with background conversation that continues throughout the credits. We do not know whose voices we are hearing; they seem to belong to surgeons performing an operation (they are indeed surgeons, as we discover when the credits are over). The surgeons have just performed a biopsy, the results of which will not be made known until the end of the movie. Since *That's Life!* was a Columbia picture, it had to open with the Columbia logo. However, director Blake Edwards made an imposition work to his advantage: he synchronized the opening action with the appearance of the logo. In effect, Edwards wanted the audience seated at the very moment the movie began. Writer-director Nora Ephron apparently felt the same way about her film *You've Got Mail* (1998). The Warner Bros. logo is accompanied by the clicking sound of computer keys. Then the title appears, each letter popping up on the screen as it would on somebody's laptop. What better way to start a movie about two people corresponding anonymously through e-mail?

In the Universal release *Waterworld* (1995), one of the most expensive pictures ever made ($175 million), the logo is directly related to the film's setting: the earth sometime in the future, when it is completely covered with water. The first image to appear is the blue Universal globe in a sky of much darker blue. Gradually the globe begins to fall from the sky, filling the screen with an expanse of blue that resembles an ocean. Next comes the title, *Waterworld*; there are no further credits until the end of the movie.

Has the moviegoer missed anything by arriving just as *Waterworld* appears on the screen? Nothing in terms of plot, but certainly something in terms of a filmmaker's desire to establish a mood by using the studio's logo as more than a trademark.

Main Titles, Credits (and Precredits), Sequences, and End Credits

The main reason for being seated when the movie begins is that it is impossible to know exactly how it will begin. Take, for example, the **main title**—the film's title plus the opening credits (although in some cases it is

Cry of the City (Robert Siodmak, 1948) opens with the Twentieth Century-Fox logo. *(Courtesy Margaret Herrick Library of the Academy of Motion Picture Arts and Sciences)*

After the logo, the main title begins with the movie's name, often against an appropriate background. *(Courtesy MOMA/FSA)*

simply the film's title). If you miss the main title when it consists only of the film's name, cast, key personnel, producer, and director, you will not have missed any of the plot. But you will have missed a certain part of the film—a part that is often imaginatively executed. Main titles can be quite creative and even witty. In Preston Sturges's *The Lady Eve* (1941), in which a female cardsharp pursues a timid herpetologist, the main title appears as a snake slithering across the screen; in Billy Wilder's *The Seven Year Itch* (1955), the main title—designed by Saul Bass, who is renowned for his main titles—consists of credits popping out of a jack-in-the-box. *Psycho's* main title was also designed by Saul Bass; here, the credits intersect, coming onto the screen horizontally and vertically as the actors' first and last names split apart. The main title prepares the viewer for a movie about a split personality, as well as one in which slashing and cutting figure prominently.

The main title of Hitchcock's *Vertigo* (1958), created by John Whitney and Saul Bass, is one of the most evocative in all film. First, a woman's eye looks out at us from a reddish haze. The camera then moves down to her mouth and back to her eyes. The title, *Vertigo*, seems to emanate from one of her eyes. Next, reddish and blue-green spirals spin out of the eye, until, by the end of the main title, the spirals have disappeared, and superimposed above the eye are the words "Directed by Alfred Hitchcock." The *Vertigo* main title was not simply flashy artwork; it was integral to a film in which a man becomes obsessed with a woman who resembles his lost love. The relationship literally spirals out of control, resulting in tragedy.

A main title can also be educational. *The Front* (1975), which deals with one of the most shameful periods in American history (the McCarthy-inspired witch-hunt as it affected television in the early 1950s), begins with a 1950s montage of film clips of the Korean War, Marilyn Monroe's wedding to Joe DiMaggio, President Eisenhower and his wife, Mamie, entertaining at the White House, and Ethel and Julius Rosenberg (whose execution as Soviet spies is still a controversial subject) being led away by the police—all to the musical accompaniment of "Young at Heart" as sung by Frank Sinatra.

Although its basic function is that of a program or a playbill, the main title can establish the mood of the film, especially when it is artistically executed and appropriately orchestrated (as it is in *Psycho*, where the credits are accompanied by Bernard Herrmann's tense musical score). Missing a main title like *Psycho's* or that of Bernardo Bertolucci's *The Last Emperor* (1987), whose credits unfold against exquisite artwork to evocative music, is like arriving at a performance of Wagner's opera *Die Meistersinger* after the prelude, which is a major piece of music in its own right. And to miss the main title of Martin Scorsese's *The Age of Innocence* (1993), designed by Saul and Elaine Bass and consisting of roses opening to the sun, is to miss a title that is both elegant and prefigurative. Here, the main title not only implies a privileged existence but also anticipates the way flowers are used both as decorations and as expressions of love.

Sometimes a film dispenses with graphic design, starting immediately with a **credits sequence,** in which the credits are integrated with the main action. *The Four Seasons* (1981) opens with a credits sequence in which one couple picks up two other couples in their car. The credits come on during the sequence. By the time the sequence is over, and the last credit has appeared, we have been introduced to three couples whose trips together constitute the plot.

A good deal of information is imparted during the credits sequence of *Nurse Betty* (2000). At first we see a man and a woman in a romantic mood; then, as the credits continue, we realize that we are watching a television soap, *A Reason to Love,* which Betty (Renée Zellweger) is also watching at the diner where she works as a waitress. Rather than miss anything on the screen, Betty has become proficient at refilling coffee cups with her back to the customers, two of whom are African American—one much younger than the other. When the credits end, we have learned that Betty has such a skewed sense of reality that she cannot distinguish between the leading character of the soap, Dr. David Ravell, and the actor (Greg Kinnear) who plays him; that the soap has a hospital setting; and that the younger of the two African Americans (Chris Rock) is quick-tempered and potentially dangerous, while the older man (Morgan Freeman) is mild-mannered, or so it seems. Miss the credits sequence, and it will take a while to acclimate yourself to the plot. Furthermore, when the two men at the counter reappear in an extremely grizzly sequence involving the scalping of Betty's drug-dealing husband, you will wonder who the men are and why they seem to know who Betty is.

Sometimes a credits sequence involves an image or an object that takes on greater meaning in the course of the film. As the *Forrest Gump* (1994) credits start to roll, a feather floats through the air, eventually resting on Forrest's (Tom Hanks) left shoe. Forrest retrieves the feather and places it in a children's book that he has been reading. Anyone who was not present during the sequence will not appreciate the ending, in which Forrest reopens the book and the feather is released, returning to the sky from which it originally fell. The feather symbolizes the interconnection of chance and destiny, which is one of the film's themes. When the feather first fell, Forrest could not have known that he would become a national figure, much less meet American presidents. Then, he was simply drifting, much like the feather.

Sometimes a film opens cold with a **precredits sequence**—a sort of prologue preceding the credits. In this kind of sequence, the title does not appear until after the sequence is over. If such a technique seems like a gimmick, remember that film is an art form, but it is also a business. And just as businesses experiment with various ways of attracting customers, so does Hollywood. One way to get an audience's attention is to vary the logo/main title/film proper format and offer the unexpected.

Exactly who was the first to alter the format is unknown, but film historians tend to credit Lewis Milestone, who directed the movie version of John Steinbeck's *Of Mice and Men* (1939). The film opens with neither logo nor title but with two men in flight, followed by a posse. The men manage to hop a freight train and scramble into an open boxcar, joining others riding the rails in search of work during the Great Depression. Someone pulls the door shut; then verses from Robert Burns's poem "To a Mouse," which inspired the title, appear, as if they had been inscribed on the door. The key phrase, "Of Mice and Men," is highlighted, thus becoming the title. The remaining credits follow.

A filmmaker might choose a precredits sequence to keep the audience guessing about the identity of the characters or the nature of some pivotal event that is later dramatized. After the Twentieth Century-Fox logo, *Phone Call from a Stranger* (1951) begins with a man rushing out of his home in the rain and entering a waiting cab. "Airport, hurry!" he instructs the driver. Then the credits come on. The man becomes one of the main characters, and the plot hinges on a flight during a rainstorm. *Picnic* (1955) begins with the studio logo (Columbia's Lady with the Torch). However, the title does not come on the screen until we see a man jump off a freight car. He seems to be a drifter; it is only after he washes himself off in a nearby reservoir that the title comes on the screen. The man, Hal (William Holden), becomes a pivotal character, who, in the course of a day, changes the lives of everyone with whom he comes into contact. In *Hustle*'s (1975) precredits sequence, a body is washed up on a beach; we expect to learn the corpse's identity—and eventually do.

Another reason for choosing a precredits sequence is to capture the viewer's attention with the hope of sustaining it for the film's duration. Thus some filmmakers deliberately attempt to draw the viewer into the action at the outset. After the Columbia logo, *Postcards from the Edge* (1994) begins without title or credits. The setting seems to be a Latin American country; a female tourist is stopped at customs, then brought to a police station, where she is brutalized. The viewer is shocked at this treatment but then discovers that the tourist is an actress and her beating is merely a scene in a movie being shot. Once the sequence ends, the title appears, and *Postcards from the Edge*—which dramatizes the difficult relationship between the actress in the precredits sequence and her famous mother—starts. To miss a credits or precredits sequence, then, is not merely to miss part of the film; it is to miss part of the text.

If important information is lost by arriving after the film has formally begun, significant elements may also be lost by leaving before it has formally ended. It is true that **end credits** have become longer than they were in the 1930–1950 period, when they consisted only of the cast of characters. Now the end credits acknowledge everyone from the star's fitness trainer to the caterers. While comics joke about end credits being longer than the movie and mock such job titles as **"gaffer"** and **"best boy,"** the end credits show the complexity of contemporary filmmaking and prove conclusively that film is a collaborative art in which the gaffer (chief electrician) and best boy (the gaffer's first assistant) are among the collaborators.[1]

Since the end credits are prepared by the studio's legal department and must follow a specific format, they do not figure among the filmmaker's decisions. Filmmakers, however, have learned to use the end credits to the movie's advantage so that they are not just the cue to exit the theater. End credits can also function in the following ways:

As epilogue. In *Sweet Liberty* (1986), which depicts the filming of a book about the American Revolution, the end credits are interspersed with scenes from the movie's premiere. Until the very end, the author, a university professor (Alan Alda), is appalled at what is being done to his book. During the end credits, he is interviewed by a reporter who congratulates him on writing history as it should be written. At that moment, a disclaimer appears on the screen to the effect that any similarity between the film and American history is purely coincidental. Anyone who leaves during the end credits misses the point: in the movies, historical truth may have to be sacrificed for the sake of entertainment.

As an informational or educational source. The Front is a highly accurate portrayal of blacklisting in the 1950s. The end credits not only list the actors, the director, and the writer but also identify those who themselves had been blacklisted—the actors Herschel Bernardi, Zero Mostel, and Lloyd Gough; the screenwriter Walter Bernstein; and the director Martin Ritt.

The end credits of *Married to the Mob* (1988) are interspersed with outtakes (shots that were deleted from the film) that make audiences aware of how much they did *not* see. Similarly, the outtakes of *Rumble in the Bronx* (1996) show martial arts actor Jackie Chan sustaining bodily injuries while making the film, thus alerting audiences to the risks actors face when they perform their own stunts. Since *Chaplin* (1992) is based on fact, the end credits consist of shots of the main actors, along with a brief account of what happened to the historical figures they portrayed.

As a musical postlude. The end credits of Woody Allen's *Radio Days* (1987), which is set in 1941, are orchestrated with the music of the 1940s, thereby allowing a nostalgic mood to linger. During the end credits of Martin Scorsese's *GoodFellas* (1989), the popular song "My Way" is heard, suggesting that the narrator, who from childhood has aspired to be a gangster, has no regrets about his profession. Anyone who exited during the end credits of *French Kiss* (1995) missed the chance to hear Kevin Kline sing in French; another lost opportunity (for those who automatically get up when the end credits start) comes during the *Postcards from the Edge* end credits, when Meryl Streep, who is known primarily as a dramatic actress, delivers a completely uninhibited rendition of "I'm Checkin' Out."

As postcredits epilogue. Priscilla, Queen of the Desert (1994), which recounts the adventures of three drag queens touring the Australian outback, has not only end credits worth staying for but an additional scene as well. The end credits roll as one of the performers lip-synchs "Save the Best for Last." When the credits are over, a short scene comes on that does not add to the narrative but is a delightful touch in its own way. Early in the film, the trio launch a kite made of pink crepe paper into the sky. In what can only be called a postcredits epilogue, the kite lands somewhere in Japan, piquing the curiosity of the locals who discover it.

The end credits are similar to a curtain call, except that in a theater the cast—not the crew—takes the bows; in a movie, everybody does. A serious theatergoer would never leave during a curtain call, and a serious moviegoer should not leave during the film equivalent of that. Students who develop this habit will not automatically rise from their seats when they think the film is about to end. Some people do this after Tom Joad (Henry Fonda) in John Ford's *The Grapes of Wrath* (1940) vows to fight for a better world, yet that is only the penultimate scene. By comparison, the final scene is anticlimactic, but it is the one that the producer, Darryl F. Zanuck, wanted. Likewise, Orson Welles's *Citizen Kane* (1941) does not conclude with "The End." Since Welles came from the stage, it is only fitting that his first film should end with a curtain call. The cast was relatively unknown, so Welles identified the important members by name as well as by repeating a shot in which each person appeared. Peter Bogdanovich did the same at the end of *The Last Picture Show* (1971), and for the same reason: the unfamiliarity of the cast.

One might argue that the curtain calls in *Kane* and *Picture Show* are extraneous to the plot. That may be true, but they are not extraneous to the films in which they appear. The process of making a film entails many decisions. A filmmaker may choose to begin with a main title that consists of nothing but the most basic form of graphics: words on a plain background. A director may decide to open with an elaborate main title, a main title that foreshadows the action or includes part of it, or no title at all. A main title like *Psycho*'s is part of the narrative, since it affects the way we see what follows. No matter how a film begins, it should be seen as it was intended to be seen—in its entirety.

Opening Titles and End Titles

There are titles other than main titles. A **title** is simply printed matter that appears in a film. Often, after the main title, there is an **opening title** that can function as:

A time-place designation ("Shanghai, 1935," the opening title of *Indiana Jones and the Temple of Doom*; "Phoenix, Arizona. Friday, December the Eleventh. Two Forty-Three, P.M.," *Psycho*'s quite specific opening title).

A confirmation of the film's authenticity ("This film is based on a true story" [*GoodFellas*]).

A preface explaining an event with which the audience might be unfamiliar. Although World War II moviegoers knew the history of the conflict, later generations might not. Thus, in Steven Spielberg's *Empire of the Sun* (1987), the opening title explains the significance of December 7, 1941, and, more important, what Japanese aggression meant to British subjects living in Shanghai.

An epigraph (literary excerpt) or a **quotation.** George Santayana's "Those who do not remember the past are doomed to relive it" is the epigraph to *Lacombe, Lucien* (1974), which shows how a French boy's apathy has made him a pawn of the Nazis. Perhaps the most memorable opening title is *King Kong*'s (1933): "And the Beast looked upon the face of Beauty and lo! his hand was stayed from killing and from that day forward he was as one dead.—An Old Arabian Proverb." The title invites us to look at the movie in terms of the proverb and regard *King Kong* as a version of Beauty and the Beast.

A disclaimer. Hennessy (1975), which dramatizes an attempt to blow up the Houses of Parliament on Guy Fawkes Day, incorporates newsreel footage of the royal family. The opening title is quite explicit: "This motion picture incorporates extracts from a news film of the Queen at a State Opening of Parliament which, when photographed, was not intended for use in a fictional context." Similarly, the opening title of Martin Scorsese's *The Last Temptation of Christ* (1988) makes it clear that the film is based on a novel and is not a historical account of the life of Christ.

An opening title can be stationary, as in *Empire of the Sun;* it can also roll up or down the screen, in which case it is known as a **roll-up title** or a **crawl.** Roll-up titles were common in the serials of the 1930s and 1940s. To evoke that era, the Star Wars trilogy—*Star Wars* (1977), *The Empire Strikes Back* (1980), and *The Return of the Jedi* (1983)—feature elaborate roll-up titles, in which print moves up the screen.

Just as an opening title can serve as a preface or a prologue, an **end title** can function as an epilogue. An end title is particularly useful as a means of informing the audience of the fate of the characters, especially if extending the action would prove anticlimactic, destroy the mood the ending was supposed to create, or (from a more pragmatic standpoint) send the film over budget.

At the end of Hitchcock's *The Wrong Man* (1957), which is based on a true incident, a musician's wife becomes mentally unbalanced after her husband is falsely accused of theft and imprisoned. The end title informs us that she was eventually cured and is living in Florida. The title is a bald statement of fact and nothing more; when it appears on the screen, it has the effect of a case stamped "Closed." Had Hitchcock shown the wife basking in the Florida sun, he would have shattered the film's somber mood, gratifying only those who want the storm clouds turned inside out so they can see the silver lining. The title he chose, however, provides neither a happy ending nor a triumph for the wrong man, even though he is now free.

Dog Day Afternoon (1975) is a film about a Vietnam vet (Al Pacino) with two children who holds up a Brooklyn bank to finance a transsexual operation for his second wife—a man he married in a wedding ceremony complete with celebrant and bridesmaids. The film ends on a Kennedy Airport runway, a few feet from the jumbo jet the vet has ordered to fly him to Algeria. Then three titles appear on the screen without any fanfare, as if they were being typed by someone concerned only with the accuracy of the transcription, not with its implications: the vet is serving a twenty-year prison sentence; his first wife is on welfare; and his second wife has become a woman and is living in New York. Similarly, in *GoodFellas* an end title tells the audience that the narrator, Henry Hill (Ray Liotta), and his wife have separated and the other mafiosi depicted in the film have either died or been paroled.

In Samuel Fuller's *Shock Corridor* (1963), the opening and end titles are identical: "Whom the gods wish to destroy, they first make mad." The double-duty quotation is appropriate for a movie about an ambitious reporter who feigns madness in order to solve a murder and ends up going mad himself.

The end title of Martin Scorsese's *Kundun* (1997), a solidly researched film about the fourteenth Dalai Lama, is particularly moving: "The Dalai Lama has not yet returned to Tibet. He hopes one day to make the journey." *Kundun* ends in 1959 with the Dalai Lama, unable to accept a Tibet under Chinese Communist control, going into exile in India.

The opening and end titles of the Chinese film, Wong Kar-wai's *In the Mood for Love* (2000) complement each other. The opening title reads: "It is a restless moment. Hong Kong. 1962." The restless are not only the characters (a man and a woman who discover that their spouses are having an affair with each other) but also the director, who wants both to evoke and to transcend the Hollywood model for movies of this kind. Wong Kar-wai would like us to think of the movies of the 1950–1960 period (for example, *September Affair* [1950], *Love Is a Many-Splendored Thing* [1955], *A Summer Place* [1959], *Strangers When We Meet* [1960]), in which adultery was transformed into grand passion through exotic settings, lush photography, and romantic music so that affairs seemed like trysts and cheating was a glamorous pastime rather than a betrayal. However, the end title makes it clear that 2000 is not 1962; Hong Kong is not Hollywood; and Wong Kar-wai is more than familiar with American movies but also has a style that is his own: "That era has passed. Nothing that belongs to it exists anymore."

Intertitles

The silent film made great use of **intertitles,** printed material that appeared on the screen periodically during the course of the movie. The intertitle was one of the ways in which the silent-film maker supplemented the narrative or clarified the action; it is also a reminder of film's early dependence on the printed word. D. W. Griffith used intertitles for a variety of purposes, not just to reproduce dialogue and identify characters. He used them (1) to attest to the accuracy of a particular setting (e.g., the intertitle—"An historical facsimile of Ford's Theater as on that night, exact

An intertitle from *The Birth of a Nation* (D. W. Griffith [1915]). Note the underscoring for emphasis and the DG trademark as a sign of authorship. *(Courtesy MOMA/FSA and Epoch Producing Corp.)*

in size and detail with recorded incidents, after Nicolay and Hay in *Lincoln, a History*"—introduces the assassination-of-Lincoln sequence in *The Birth of a Nation*); (2) to comment on the action or play on the audience's emotions (e.g., the intertitle "Dying, she gives her last little smile to a world that has been so unkind" accompanies the heroine's death in *Broken Blossoms* [1919]); (3) to define terms with which the audience may be unfamiliar (e.g., *Pharisee* and *Sanhedrin* in *Intolerance* [1916]); and (4) to reveal a character's thoughts (e.g., the intertitle "The Inspiration" appears after Ben Cameron sees some white children frighten black children with a sheet in *The Birth of a Nation;* the "inspiration" is the use of bedsheets to make the Klansmen's robes for the cross-burning vigilantes). Griffith treated intertitles as images, integrating them with the film so they would be part of the narrative.

A Woman of Affairs (1928) shows how silent-film makers used punctuation, especially the dash, to suggest how the lines would have been spoken:

> My nerves have gone to pieces—I'm going out—somewhere—I didn't mean to come here—I started driving—Why should a man—happy as David was—take his own life? David died—for decency.

Intertitles did not die with the advent of sound. Martin Scorsese used them in *Raging Bull* (1981) and *GoodFellas*, both of which are based on fact, to achieve a sense of authenticity. Each sequence in *Raging Bull*, which is told in flashback, is introduced by an intertitle (e.g., "New York, 1964"; "The Bronx, 1941"; "La Motta vs. Robinson, 1943"). Scorsese does the same in *GoodFellas* (e.g., "Brooklyn, 1953"; "June 11, 1970"; "Idlewild Airport, August 1963").

Woody Allen may well have chosen to use intertitles in *Hannah and Her Sisters* (1986) because, in addition to being an actor, a director, and a screenwriter, he is also a playwright and a short-story writer. Allen's stories are often vignettes, and *Hannah and Her Sisters* is a series of vignettes about three sisters. Thus, Allen segments the film, introducing each vignette with an intertitle that can be (1) a line of dialogue repeated in the segment (the opening intertitle, "God, she's beautiful!," is also the first line of dialogue, spoken offscreen); (2) a character introduction ("The Hypochondriac" introduces the Woody Allen character); (3) a vignette title ("The Abyss" is the intertitle of the episode in which Allen thinks he has a brain tumor); and (4) a quotation ("The only absolute knowledge attained by man is that knowledge is impossible"—Tolstoy). By using intertitles in so many different ways, Allen allies himself not only with the venerable tradition of the intertitle but also with the written word.

Since Philip Kaufman was both the screenwriter and the director of *The Unbearable Lightness of Being* (1988), he clearly intended the titles to serve a purpose. The film opens like a fairy tale. The first intertitle, "In Prague in 1968 there lived a young doctor named Tomas," is followed by a scene showing Tomas in a less than fairy-tale situation: making love to a nurse. The second intertitle, "But the woman who understood him best was Sabina," is followed by another lovemaking scene, this time between Tomas and Sabina. After the third intertitle, "Tomas was sent to a spa town to perform an operation," the film turns serious, as one might expect of a film about the Soviet-backed invasion of the former Czechoslovakia in 1968. The intertitles, with their storybook connotations, run counter to the erotic scenes that succeed them. Once the intertitles end, the eroticism continues, but within a historical, not a storybook, context.

Subtitles

The **subtitle** shares one of the main functions of the intertitle: the transmission of dialogue. Although subtitles—in which the translation of dialogue appears at the bottom of the screen—are common in international films shown in the United States, they are also used in American films in which there are scenes that require the characters to speak in a language other than English. For such scenes, filmmakers now prefer to have the actors use the characters' native tongue rather than to simulate an accent that suggests their nationality—which was the case until about 1970. *Tora! Tora! Tora!* (1970) is unusual among films about World War II because it was apparently the first Hollywood production in which the Japanese spoke their own language, with subtitles providing the translation. Since then, it has become standard to use subtitles whenever a foreign language is spoken—e.g., Russian (*Red Dawn* [1985]), Sicilian (*The Godfather Part II* [1974]), French (*The Last of the Mohicans* [1992]), Sioux (*Dances with Wolves* [1990]). When a hearing-impaired character used sign language in

Four Weddings and a Funeral (1994), the translation was given in subtitles. In context, the translation is quite funny, since the character is expressing sentiments about someone who, if he understood sign language, would not be amused.

Other Uses of the Printed Word

Printed matter in a film is a visual; as such, it can make a valuable contribution to the narrative. The entire plot of *Citizen Kane* revolves around an attempt to discover the meaning of Charles Foster Kane's dying word, "Rosebud!" Until the end, no one—neither the characters nor the audience—knows what "Rosebud" means. The characters never find out, but the audience eventually does. After Kane's funeral, workmen begin clearing out his cluttered basement, throwing what they consider to be junk into a blazing furnace. One of them tosses in a sled, which, as it burns, allows us to see that it bears a name: Rosebud. The film's resolution is a word, but one that must be seen—a word that symbolizes Kane's lost childhood.

Another example of the symbolic use of print occurs in *Casablanca* when Rick (Humphrey Bogart), standing in the rain, reads a letter from Ilsa (Ingrid Bergman) informing him that she cannot leave with him for Marseille. As Rick reads the letter, the rain falls on it, causing the ink to run, tearlike, down the page. The running ink provides the tears that the stoic Rick cannot show; it also signals the end of an affair that has faded like the words of the letter. In both films, print has been dramatically embellished—by flames in *Citizen Kane* and by rain in *Casablanca*.

Naturally, print does not always operate so symbolically. Generally, print is a visual shorthand that enables the filmmaker to identify locales and impart important information without having to resort to awkward exposition. Thus signposts, street signs, newspapers, and plaques are used to pinpoint setting. Since much of *The Grapes of Wrath* consists of a drive from Oklahoma to California along Highway 66, signs along the way tell the audience which state the Joads are in. A San Francisco newspaper seen at the opening of Hitchcock's *The Birds* (1963) immediately identifies the setting.

It is possible to formulate a general rule about the best use of print in film: print should be used as a means of supplying information that either cannot be imparted in any other way or that will reduce the amount of exposition. Sometimes the script calls for print. In *Dark Victory* (1939), Judith Traherne (Bette Davis) learns that she is terminally ill when she comes across her medical file and sees the words "PROGNOSIS NEGATIVE." In a similar film, *An Act of Murder* (1948), a woman learns from a letter her physician has written to her husband that she is dying. When Bob

The ironic juxtaposition of print and image in *Taxi Driver* (1976), in which Travis Bickle (Robert De Niro) may be ready for the unexpected but is not exactly sane. *(Courtesy Sony Pictures Entertainment and MOMA/FSA)*

Woodward (Robert Redford) realizes that Carl Bernstein's (Dustin Hoffman) apartment is bugged in *All the President's Men* (1976), he turns up the stereo and types: "Deep Throat says our lives may be in danger. SURVEILLANCE. BUGGING."

Since computers are now part of our everyday life, the computer screen has also become an important narrative tool, capable of advancing the plot in the same way the typewriter once did. The computer that the villain in *Ghost* (1990) uses to transfer funds becomes the means of revealing his identity; *The Net* (1995) revolves around an attempt to use computer technology to alter a character's identity.

Film, then, uses print in a variety of ways (signs, plaques, posters, headlines, ticker tape, letters, notices, invitations, telegrams, notes, typewritten or computer-generated texts, and so on). Thus, print can perform an important narrative function; as visual shorthand, it minimizes the need for expository dialogue.

SOUND

Seeing a narrative film without sound would be an abomination. Even the silent films (which were silent only in the sense that there was no spoken dialogue) had some kind of sound effects as well as musical accompaniment. *Nickelodeon* illustrates the importance of sound in the silent film by showing the world premiere of *The Birth of a Nation*, in which men fire cap pistols backstage to simulate the gunfire in the battle scenes.

Gunfire, a staple in westerns, war films, and crime movies, is one of many sound effects used in films. Under the heading of sound effects come all the sounds heard in a film except dialogue, music, and offscreen narration. Noise is an important sound effect in a film, and it can be a legitimate, even powerful, device. Jacques Tourneur's *Cat People* (1942) would not be the horror classic it is if noise was absent in two crucial scenes. As Alice (Jane Randolph) walks home at night, she hears the ominous sound of footsteps. Just when we think that whatever is following her will catch up with her, we hear the sound of brakes; a bus has pulled up alongside Alice, and she quickly boards it. Later, as she is swimming in an indoor pool, she hears growling sounds, as if a ferocious beast were nearby.

The noise in *Cat People* is atmospheric; it is intended to heighten the suspense. In many films, however, noise is essential to the plot. A scene from Hitchcock's *Marnie* (1964), for example, demands noise—a noise that the audience and Marnie must hear but that another character in the scene cannot hear. After taking money from her employer's safe, Marnie (Tippi Hedren) stealthily leaves the office. In the adjacent area, a cleaning woman is washing the floors. In order not to be heard, Marnie removes her shoes, placing them in the pockets of her jacket. One of her shoes falls to the floor. Anyone in the vicinity would have heard the sound, yet the cleaning woman does not look up from her work. As we wonder whether Marnie will be discovered, the janitor calls to the cleaning woman in an unnaturally loud voice, making it clear that she is hard of hearing.

Ordinarily, the sound of rain beating against a window would be audible, but in *And Now Tomorrow* (1944) it is not. When Emily Blair (Loretta Young) wakes one morning, she sees the windowpanes streaked with rain but does not hear the rainfall. The audience discovers that Emily has lost her hearing at the same moment that she does: when the rain silently beats upon the window.

There are times when sound is expected, and instead there is silence. At the end of Neil LaBute's *In the Company of Men* (1997), two misogynistic executives, who have had unsuccessful relationships with women, decide to take their revenge on the female sex by tricking a hearing-impaired woman into thinking that they are interested in her. When one of the men realizes the injustice he has committed, he returns to beg forgiveness. As he pleads, no sound comes from his lips. Another director might have wanted the man's words to be heard, but LaBute decided otherwise. By indicating that the woman cannot hear him, LaBute also makes it clear that, to her, he no longer exists. In *The Godfather Part III* (1990), when Michael's (Al Pacino) daughter is killed on the steps of the opera house, Michael opens his mouth to scream, but no sound is heard. The shock was so intense that it rendered him speechless.

Actual and Commentative Sound

As a form of sound, noise can emanate from a source that is either on- or off-screen. We do not have to see the source of the noise; we only have to know that there is a source. We never see the foghorns in *Long Day's Journey into Night* (1962), but we hear them, and we know they are coming from nearby ships. In Joseph L. Mankiewicz's *A Letter to Three Wives* (1949), everything in the Finney kitchen shakes when the train passes by. We never see the train, but we hear it and witness the results of the vibrations it causes.

Sound, then, can be **actual** (or natural), in the sense of coming from a real source that we may or may not see. It can also be **commentative,** in that it may come from a source outside the physical setting of the action. Perhaps the most familiar type of commentative sound is background music, the recurring motifs or signature themes that can identify a character (Lara's theme in *Dr. Zhivago* [1965]), a place (the Tara theme in *Gone with the Wind* [1939]), a physical state (the blindness theme in *Dark Victory*), or an obsession (the power theme in *Citizen Kane*). In *Dark Victory*, when Judith Traherne discovers that she will experience a short period of blindness prior to death, the blindness theme is heard on the soundtrack. Judith cannot hear the music because it is not coming from a source within the action, but the audience hears it and, having heard it before in various forms, recognizes it as a sign of Judith's fate.

Synchronization and Asynchronization

Another way of looking at sound is from the perspective of synchronization and asynchronization. In synchronization, sound and image are properly matched; the sound comes from within the image or from an identifiable source. Synchronization is not just limited to a literal correlation of sound and image. In many films, characters may be in transit (e.g., in a car or a plane), and the audience will see the car on the freeway or the plane in the air but not see the characters. Yet we hear their conversation. In postproduction, the dialogue has been added and synchronized with the image.

Asynchronization in *M* (1931). When Mrs. Beckmann calls, "Elsie!," the response is not verbal but visual: a place setting never to be used again. *(Courtesy MOMA/FSA and Janus Films)*

There are, however, more sophisticated forms of synchronization. For example, a nonhuman sound may be combined with the image of a person. In *Cat People*, Irena (Simone Simon) tactfully tells her husband on their wedding night that she is not ready to consummate their marriage. As they retire to separate rooms, Irena, who is a descendant of a Serbian cat cult and periodically reverts to panther form, falls to her knees, assuming an animal posture. At that moment, the roar of a panther is heard. The audience knows the source of the sound: the Central Park Zoo, which Irena frequents. However, within the new context of an unconsummated wedding night, the combination of a sound coming from an identifiable source and the image of the crouching Irena adds another dimension to the narrative: her repressed sexuality is given voice. In *The Godfather* (1972), just before Michael kills the drug dealer Sollozzo and the crooked police captain McCluskey in a Bronx restaurant, a screeching sound is heard. We have no idea where it came from, but obviously it is outside. Given the restaurant's location (the Bronx) and the time of the action (the late 1940s), it would have to be coming from the nearby elevated subway, the now defunct Third Avenue El. The sound is appropriate for another reason: it reflects Michael's vengeful frame of mind, which is quite the opposite of his expressionless face.

While sound and image have been synchronized in each of these instances, we know the sound source and see the image before us; it now seems as if the image were making the sound. The combination of growling panther + crouching woman suggests that within Irena there is something waiting to be unleashed; avenger + screeching brakes, that an apathetic face masks Michael's pent-up anger and that it erupts in violence.

Synchronization, then, can be quite imaginative. It can be particularly effective when a character remembers the past. The voice of the person who's remembering can be combined with the image of what is remembered, or the face of the person remembering can be combined with the sound that is remembered. In *A Streetcar Named Desire* (1951), Blanche DuBois (Vivien Leigh) periodically recalls the music that was played on the night that her husband committed suicide. At the end of *Forever Amber* (1947), Amber (Linda Darnell) watches her son go off with his father, never to see either of them again. Earlier, the child's father—Amber's former lover—had said, "May God have mercy on both of us for our sins." In the final scene, Amber, standing at the window, recalls his words—her image synchronized with the sound of his voice.

In synchronization, sound and image are related contextually, spatially, and temporally. In **asynchronization,** sound and image are related symbolically, metaphorically, or ironically. With the latter, the image the viewer expects to see after hearing a particular sound turns out to be something quite different. Asynchronization allows filmmakers to contrast sound and image, substitute a sound for an image, or juxtapose sounds and images that would not normally occur at the same time.

In Fritz Lang's *M* (1931), Mrs. Beckmann is waiting anxiously for her daughter Elsie to return from school. She leans out of the window, calling, "Elsie! Elsie!" On the screen we do not see Elsie but, rather, a series of images: an empty stairwell, an empty attic, Elsie's place at the dinner table, her ball on the grass, and, finally, a balloon that is momentarily caught in some telephone wires and then floats away.

The asynchronization is remarkably subtle. Ironically, Mrs. Beckmann's call is heard, but she is answered only by images that denote absence and emptiness. Elsie will never return. Like the balloon that was caught in the wires and then blown skyward by the wind, she was enticed by a child molester and led away to her death.

Overlap

What might seem to be asynchronization could be **overlapping sound**—sound or dialogue that either carries over from one scene to the next or anticipates the new scene by starting at the end of the previous one. Thus, overlapping sound is really synchronous, since it emanates from a known source. Bridging scenes through sound was rare in the 1930–1950 period, mainly because such a device would have struck audiences as illogical. If *The Age of Innocence* had been released in 1943 instead of in 1993, there would never have been the scene in which Newland Archer (Daniel Day Lewis) stands in front of a flower shop and, before he even enters, a voice says, "Oh, Mr. Archer. Good evening." The florist would have extended the greeting *after* Archer had entered. Today, however, overlapping sound has become so commonplace that it is just a cue for a scene change. It is, then, a transition (a "sound bridge"), the aural equivalent of a **dissolve.**

Still, there are instances in which the scenes being bridged are connected in ways that develop the narrative instead of merely linking segments of it together. In Spike Lee's *Malcolm X* (1992), as Malcolm walks along a street thronged with prostitutes, we hear the words "What has happened to our women?" Is this what Malcolm is thinking? The next scene clarifies the situation: the question is part of a sermon that is about to end. The incident in the first scene inspired the subject matter of the sermon in the second, with the question becoming the link between them.

In *Three Days of the Condor* (1975), a CIA official in Washington is asking questions about an agent, who at that moment is hiding out in a Brooklyn Heights apartment. The official's voice carries into the next scene, which takes place in the apartment. The overlapping voice gives us the unsettling impression that the CIA is present everywhere, including Brooklyn Heights.

At the end of *Medium Cool* (1969), set in Chicago during the 1968 Democratic convention, the director, Haskell Wexler, allows the audience to hear about an event before it happens. As a TV cameraperson and an Appalachian schoolteacher are driving away from a bloody confrontation between the police and Vietnam War protesters, a newscaster's voice describes their death in a car crash before it is actually shown. Like the film, the untimely newscast is disturbing; it is not just a matter of overlap but of omniscience. It is as if the "cool medium," as media critic Marshall McLuhan called television, knew our destiny and could therefore compose our obituary before we died.

Filmmakers seeking alternatives to the sound bridge might consider what Robert Zemeckis did in *Forrest Gump*. On a summer night, as Forrest and Jenny (Robin Wright) are sitting together in Alabama, fireworks light up the sky. This is not a fireworks display in an Alabama town, however, but in Liberty Park in Jersey City, New Jersey; and the occasion is the American bicentennial, as we learn from the next scene, a live telecast of the event. Even though these are the Liberty Park fireworks, the transition is not jarring; such a display on July 4 was as common in Alabama as it was anywhere in the country, including Liberty Park.

Voice-Over Narration

Voice-over, off-camera narration or commentary, has been a standard feature of film since the beginning of the sound era and is now so common in film and television that we scarcely notice it. We have become accustomed to the television voices of unseen individuals promoting products, reading labels, or attesting to the miraculous results of a headache remedy. In airports and train stations, we continually hear voices announcing arrivals and departures. We seldom inquire about the source or identity of the voice because we are usually interested only in the information the voice is conveying. Because disembodied voices are everywhere, we tend to give little thought to voice-over narration in film. It is another case of accepting the familiar uncritically.

Voice-over is also one of the most frequently abused techniques in film. A gifted filmmaker like Woody Allen uses voice-over intelligently; in *Radio Days*, Allen makes voice-over integral to the film, which is a reminiscence by a narrator whose younger self appears as a character. Unfortunately, voice-over can also be a convenience for writers who cannot think of any other way to impart information. Voice-over is understandable in a memory film like *Radio Days*, but there are other movies that are not reminiscences in which the technique is used without consistency or logic. In John Ford's *When Willie Comes Marching Home* (1950), the main character's voice keeps intruding even though there is no reason for him to tell his own story.

Historically, when the movies learned to talk, filmmakers seized upon voice-over as a narrative device and attempted to use it as they had used titles. As often happens, the quest for novelty led to eccentricity, and soon voice-over narration was being entrusted to everyone—and everything. *The First Time* (1952), narrated by an unborn baby, dramatizes the disruptions that come with the birth of a first child. A variation on the same device occurs in *Look Who's Talking* (1989), which is told from the point of view of a newborn baby (with Bruce Willis providing the voice-over). The film had a certain charm, unlike the 1990 and 1993 sequels, which had little audience appeal, suggesting that once may have been enough.

Since voice-over has become so widespread, its appropriateness deserves assessment. Is it a convention, like a soliloquy in a play? Does it function as an expository prologue? Or is it an emergency cord that a filmmaker pulls when he or she is unable to think of another way to convey information? There is no manual a filmmaker can consult to determine whether to use voice-over or titles, or whether to use neither and work the exposition into the dialogue. Sometimes voice-over needs some kind of aural reinforcement: a few sounds, some chords, a musical theme. Sometimes the necessary information can be incorporated into the dialogue, so that neither voice-over nor titles are necessary.

The best filmmakers know intuitively when to use voice-over and when to use some kind of title. They also know that in some instances a combination is required. The 1935 adaptation of Charles Dickens's *A Tale of Two Cities*, directed by Jack Conway, is a good example of the sensible use of print and voice-over. The novel includes two of the most famous lines in English literature: the opening line ("It was the best of times, it was the worst of times") and the closing line ("It is a far, far better thing that I do, than I have ever done; it is a far, far better rest that I go to than I have ever known"). The opening appears as a title without voice-over. This is fitting because these are the words of Dickens, not one of his characters; thus, the text alone is sufficient. At the end, however, voice-over is necessary. The last words of the film, like those of the novel, are the thoughts of Sydney Carton, the main character; they are not Dickens's reflections. Since these are Carton's thoughts, the audience must hear them. Since Carton does not verbalize his thoughts, the audience hears them through voice-over.

The dominant forms of voice-over are the narrating "I" and the voice of God.

The Narrating "I"

The narrating "I" tells the story, or a portion of the story, that we see on the screen. There can be one "I" or several. Some films are narrated by one character (*Murder, My Sweet* [1944]); others by multiple narrators (*Citizen Kane; Sorry, Wrong Number* [1948]). Since anyone can tell a story in the movies, even a corpse has the opportunity in Billy Wilder's *Sunset Boulevard* (1950). Narration by a dead person would pose severe problems of credibility in a work of fiction unless it was a tale of the preternatural; yet the narration works in *Sunset Boulevard*, which, for all its realism, is similar to many other films about old Hollywood that resembles tales of the unearthly. In the film, Norma Desmond (Gloria Swanson), a former silent-screen star half crazed by memories of a past that will never return, believes she can make a comeback in a movie about Salome. She hires an out-of-work screenwriter, Joe Gillis (William Holden), to help her with the script in which she plans to star. When Gillis decides to leave her, Norma kills him. *Sunset Boulevard* begins with Gillis's body floating in a pool; Gillis's voice then proceeds to tell the story of his fatal association with Norma Desmond. The narration is ironically fitting: a corpse talking about the living dead.

On the other hand, the voice-over prologue of *American Beauty* (1999) is the main character's startling admission that he will be dead by the end of the film—and knows it: "My name is Lester Burnham. This is my neighborhood. This is my street. This is my life. I'm forty-two years old. In less than a year, I'll be dead." Lester (Kevin Spacey) was right, and his voice returns at the end. Now at peace, he recalls his favorite childhood memories, realizing how little we appreciate the inexhaustible sources of beauty that exist in the world. "You have no idea what I'm talking about, I'm sure," Lester adds. "But don't worry. You will someday." Even in death, Lester has not lost his sardonic sense of humor.

Billy Wilder's *Double Indemnity* (1944) is considered a classic of "I"

Walter Neff (Fred MacMurray) as the narrating "I" in *Double Indemnity* (1944), one of the finest examples of first-person narration in film. *(Copyright Paramount Pictures. Courtesy MCA Publishing Rights, a Division of MCA, Inc.)*

narration. It opens with Walter Neff (Fred MacMurray) entering a Los Angeles office building shortly before dawn. Neff describes himself as having "no visible scars"—none, that is, that can be seen *now*. Actually, he has just been shot by his lover, whom he then killed. While Neff still has the strength, he recites his whole story into a dictaphone. The film then becomes a flashback in the form of a testimony that is being recorded and dramatized at the same time.

In "I" narration, if there is only one narrator the narrator's voice will recur periodically throughout the course of the film. Narration by one character is a more difficult method, since the narration must unify the film, bridging the scenes as the action shifts from present to past. Neff's narration in *Double Indemnity* succeeds because the flashbacks frequently end with a cue line, a line that triggers the next bit of dialogue so that the action can return to the present without an awkward transition. When Neff and Phyllis Dietrichson (Barbara Stanwyck) are in a supermarket plotting her husband's murder, Phyllis says, "Remember, we're in it together." "Yes, I remember," Neff answers into the dictaphone.

Sometimes the "I" tells his or her story in the hope of learning from it. Robert Bresson's *Une Femme Douce* (1969) opens with a suicide. Someone rushes to the veranda, a chair is overturned, a white shawl flutters through the air, and a woman's body falls to the pavement. A man, later revealed to be the woman's husband, begins to speak of her. Bresson keeps returning to her body, which now lies on a bed, to remind us that her husband is narrating the film. The approach is psychologically valid, for the husband is not so much recalling his wife as trying to understand why she committed suicide. At the end, he knows no more than he did at the beginning.

If the voice of the "I" is flat and dispassionate, the narration will have a distancing effect, which may be desirable in a film in which the characters are not empathetic. "I" narration works well in *Badlands* (1973), whose characters are far from endearing. The heroine is a fifteen-year-old with cornflower eyes that look as if they have lost their physical and moral center; the hero, her boyfriend, can shoot a man in the back and then talk to him as if nothing had happened. Holly (Sissy Spacek), the heroine, narrates *Badlands* in a voice as flat as the western plains that she and Kit (Martin Sheen) traverse. She is presumably telling the story to us, but it sounds as if she might be writing it for a pulp magazine. Some of the narration is grimly amusing, particularly when Holly tries to turn a phrase and instead produces a cliché ("Little did I realize that what began in the backways and alleys of this little town would end in the badlands of Montana"), or when she tries to be poetic and succeeds only in being trite ("When the leaves rustled overhead, it was as if the spirits were whispering about all the little things that were bothering them"). Her boyfriend's inclinations cause Holly to remark, "Suddenly I was thrown into a state of shock: Kit was the most trigger-happy person I ever met." The line is delivered so apathetically that audiences laugh, perhaps without realizing the implications of their laughter. At any rate, Holly's monotone prevents us from sympathizing with her and Kit.

The Voice of God

Between 1945 and the early 1950s, the **semidocumentary** was a popular type of film. While a documentary is nonfiction, a semidocumentary is fiction based on fact (e.g., *The House on 92nd Street* [1945]; *Boomerang* [1947]). In the semidocumentary the credits often appear in a "typewriter" typeface to give the movie a "case history" look. An authoritative voice delivers the prologue, reminding the audience that the film sprang from today's headlines or from the FBI's files and that it was shot on location. Since the voice belongs to no character, it is completely disembodied. As a result, it can weave in and out of the action, commenting, reflecting, even questioning. In the semidocumentary the disembodied voice (or **voice-of-**

God technique, as it is sometimes called) has two advantages: it can impart a feeling of objectivity, which is required by a film of this kind, and it can insinuate itself into the characters, noting their moods and emotional states. The voice in *The Naked City* (1948) speaks directly to the characters as if it were an alter ego, a confidant, and a conscience combined. "How are your feet holding out, Alan?" it asks, or, "Lieutenant Muldoon, what's your hurry?" It even speaks to the audience: "Ever try to catch a murderer?" Since the voice had the first word, it is fitting that it should have the last: "There are eight million stories in the naked city. This has been one of them."

The disembodied voice is not restricted to the semidocumentary. Stanley Kubrick used it ingeniously in his 1975 adaptation of Thackeray's novel *Barry Lyndon*. Both the novel and the film have a narrator; however, in the film the narrator is not Lyndon—as it was in the novel—but a voice behind the scenes, very much like the one in *The Naked City* but wittier and more urbane. It is actually the voice of the British actor Michael Hordern, which, like the traditional voice of God, is omniscient. The voice tells us about something before it happens, or informs us of the outcome of an event without dramatizing it for us. When Lyndon is about to die, the voice even reads his obituary. The voice can speak with authority at this moment because it has been speaking with authority since the film began.

Other Kinds of Voice-Over

Voice-over is often used in movies that are not narrated by one of the characters but that, for purpose of plot, require a character's voice to be heard. Such voices are variously labeled the epistolary voice, the subjective voice, the repetitive voice, and the voice from the machine.

The Epistolary Voice

Advancing the plot through letters is a device common to both fiction and film. The epistolary novel has a long tradition that reaches back to Samuel Richardson's *Pamela* and *Clarissa*, which were written in the mid-eighteenth century. In film, the letter is a familiar means of setting the plot in motion (William Wyler's *The Letter* [1940]; *A Letter to Three Wives*) or of bridging the years (*Sea of Grass* [1947]). When an exchange of letters is used to mark the passage of time, voice-over is sufficient. In François Truffaut's *The Story of Adele H.* (1975), the **epistolary voice** is put to a variety of uses. We hear Adele's voice as she writes to Lieutenant Pinson, whom she has pursued to Halifax in an attempt to regain his affection. When she writes to her father (later discovered to be Victor Hugo), we hear his reply. In addition to Adele's correspondence, we also hear her

This scene from *Barry Lyndon* (1975) between Barry (Ryan O'Neal) and his son (David Morley) was introduced by the off-camera narrator, who said: "Barry had his faults, but no man could say of him that he was not a good and tender father. He loved his son passionately, perhaps with a blind partiality. He denied him nothing." *(Courtesy Warner Bros., Inc.)*

diary entries. When Pinson reads the love notes Adele has concealed in his pockets, her voice discloses their contents to us. After following Pinson to Barbados, she collapses in the street. A native woman brings Adele to her home. After learning that she is Victor Hugo's daughter, the woman writes a letter to the novelist, informing him of his daughter's pitiful condition.

In an era of film censorship, the epistolary voice was one way of having a character repent by voice-over confession. Robert Anderson's play *Tea and Sympathy* was considered unfilmable in the 1950s because of its subject matter: Tom Lee, a prep-school student thought to be homosexual because of his fondness for music and poetry, is initiated sexually by Laura Reynolds, the headmaster's wife. The play is best remembered for the final scene, in which Laura comes to Tom's room and slowly begins to unbutton her blouse. Pressing his hand against her breast, she makes one request: "Years from now, when you talk about this, and you will, be kind." When MGM decided to film the play in 1956, the Johnston Office* felt that any woman who would offer her body to an adolescent should die. After much wrangling, the director, Vincente Minnelli, decided to make the plot a flashback occasioned by a class reunion at which Tom discovers a letter Laura had written to him. As Tom reads the letter, Laura's repentant voice is heard, urging him to forget what they have done (which is "wrong") and go out into the world and write edifying novels.

What we have been discussing are films in which the letter is a plot device whose contents must be heard. There are few films that are totally epistolary; that is, in which the entire film is a dramatization of a letter or a series of letters. In *A Walk in the Sun* (1945) and *Platoon* (1986), the narrator is writing letters to his sister and grandmother, respectively; however,

---

*The Motion Picture Producers and Distributors of America, Hollywood's self-censorship organization, was called the Johnston Office when it was headed by Eric Johnston from 1945 to 1963; previously it had been called the Hays Office and the Breen Office.

it does not follow that each film is a dramatization of the letter the character is writing.

If a film is totally epistolary (and such films are rare), it really is an example of the narrating "I," since the epistolary voice is used only to tell the contents of a letter. Max Ophüls's *Letter from an Unknown Woman* (1948), which revolves entirely around a letter Lisa (Joan Fontaine) has written to her former lover as she lay dying, is totally epistolary. Because the letter is such a personal document, we see only its powerful beginning ("By the time you read this letter I may be dead") and its unfinished ending. Otherwise we hear Lisa's voice and experience the visualization of her words. Yet the letter that is being dramatized is also being read by Lisa's lover, who never even bothered to learn her name. Thus, the audience and the lover learn about Lisa at the same time.

The Subjective Voice

Movies abound with examples of the inner voice that literally speaks its mind, the subjective voice, because the audience requires access to the character's thoughts. Pip in *Great Expectations* (1947) wonders how Joe Gargery, the blacksmith, will greet him when he returns home dressed as a gentleman. In *The Accused* (1948), we hear what a psychology professor, who has killed a student in self-defense, is thinking when she realizes the consequences of her act. During her flight from Phoenix in *Psycho*, Marion Crane imagines what her employer will say on Monday morning when she fails to report for work.

A more complex form of the subjective voice appears in the stream-of-consciousness film. Although **stream of consciousness** has been applied to everything from inarticulate rambling to incoherent prose, it is really the unbroken flow of thoughts, memories, and associations in the waking mind. *Hiroshima, Mon Amour* (1959), a stream-of-consciousness film, opens with a man and a woman making love. At first their skin looks charred, like that of the Hiroshima victims; then it becomes dewy, as though cleansed by the act of love. She is a French actress, and he is a Japanese architect she meets in Hiroshima while making a film. As their bodies move toward fulfillment, we hear their voices—his denying that she knows the significance of Hiroshima, hers insisting that she does. But these are not their actual voices; they sound distant, anesthetized. We are hearing the rhythms of poetry, not prose. It is each character's interior that we hear, an interior expressing itself in the language of memory, which is made up of both words and images. When the architect's voice says, "You know nothing of Hiroshima," her consciousness replies with pictures of the artifacts she has seen at the museum and with newsreel footage of the bombing of Hiroshima. When the woman says, "Who are you?," instead of a verbal reply we see a street in Hiroshima. The man is Hiroshima, the only name she will ever associate with him.

The Repetitive Voice

A character, often the hero or the heroine, tosses restlessly in bed while someone's voice reverberates in his or her unconscious, repeating key dialogue from an earlier scene (in case the audience missed its significance). This kind of repetition, called the repetitive voice, occurs in Hitchcock's *Rebecca* (1940) when some comments made about Rebecca give Joan Fontaine's character a sleepless night. The same technique appears in *Cat People* when Irena keeps hearing the voice of her psychiatrist as Halloween cats prowl across the screen.

The repetitive voice has become so familiar that it runs the risk of becoming a cliché. Yet at times some kind of recapitulation is necessary, and the filmmaker must decide whether the repetition should be aural or visual. If the character's words are important, then it is necessary to hear only what he or she has said. At the end of *Gone with the Wind*, Scarlett recalls the words her father had spoken earlier about the value of land and the importance of Tara. Hearing his words is sufficient. On the other hand, in *Murder on the Orient Express* (1974), the repetition is visual. Since the film is a whodunit, crucial shots are repeated: guilt is often a question not of what one says but of how one reacts, so the passengers' reactions, not just their words, are recalled for us visually.

The Voice from the Machine

Some filmmakers regard voice-over as the modern equivalent of the deus ex machina (god from the machine) of Greek theater. In certain Greek tragedies, particularly those of Euripides, a god would descend from a crane to resolve the action and bring the play to a conclusion. Some movies feature a "voice from the machine"; it belongs to none of the characters and materializes near the end to tie up any loose plot threads or offer some commentary on the action. The voice from the machine is not the voice of God, which is consistent throughout the film; the voice from the machine is heard only at the end. At the end of *The Lady and the Monster* (1944), a voice intrudes to remind us that Patrick Cory (Richard Arlen) has been sent to prison for his role in an experiment to keep a dead man's brain alive. The voice also reminds us that this is to be a film with a happy ending, and that Cory will emerge from jail to find his beloved waiting for him. Since no voice has been heard up to this point, we wonder whose it is. It must belong to a supernatural power that knows more about the script than the screenwriter does.

Despite its title, Jacques Tourneur's *I Walked with a Zombie* (1943) is a superior horror film. Initially, the movie is narrated by the "I" of the title—a Canadian nurse who has come to the West Indies to tend to a woman who turns out to be a zombie. At the end, the zombie is killed by her brother-in-law, who then commits suicide. Suddenly, a male voice asks God to pardon the unholy couple. The switch from the nurse's voice to the voice from beyond imparts a moralistic tone to a film that has otherwise remained aloof from moral issues. Perhaps the coda was a sop to the Legion of Decency, which frowned on suicide. (The Legion of Decency was a Catholic organization that rated films along moral lines from 1934 through the mid-1960s.) Still, it vitiates the artistry of an unusually intelligent B-movie.

Voice-over, then, is not just faceless sound; it is a narrative device that can serve different purposes. It can be personal (the narrating "I") or impersonal (the voice of God); it can reveal the contents of a letter or the contents of the unconscious; it can refresh a character's memory or our own. Because of its versatility, voice-over is often abused; although it is now a well-established narrative tool, it should not be taken for granted and viewed as an emergency cord that filmmakers pull when they run out of inspiration.

NOTE

[1]For a readable guide to all the individuals involved in the making of a movie, see Eric Taub, *Gaffers, Grips and Best Boys* (New York: St. Martin's Press, 1987).

CHAPTER

Film, Space, and Image

3

As we know from Chapter 1, film can manipulate time. But it can also manipulate space. The subject can be near or far, partial or full, stationary or moving. How we see the image, and how much of it we see, are the result of the filmmaker's choice of shot.

TYPES OF SHOTS

A **shot** is simply what is recorded by a single operation of the camera. Shots can be defined in terms of distance. Does the camera appear to be close to the subject? If so, the shot is a **close-up (CU)**—in terms of human anatomy, a shot of the head, for example. Perhaps it is a head-and-shoulders shot, in which case it is a **close shot (CS).** If the shot is a specific part of the body—an eye, a mouth—it is an **extreme close-up (ECU).** A shot of the complete human figure, with some of the background visible, is a **long shot (LS)** or a **full shot (FS).** If the camera is so far away that the result is a broad, panoramic view, it is an **extreme long shot (ELS).** A shot that is neither a close shot nor a long shot but something in between is a **medium shot (MS),** showing, for example, the subject head to waist or waist to knees.

Perhaps the shot defines an area—a room, say, with all its appointments; such a shot is an **establishing shot (ES),** a type of long shot that is often broken down into its components. *Establishing shot* can also mean a shot that identifies the setting (e.g., the Golden Gate Bridge in San Francisco; the Eiffel Tower in Paris) so that the viewer knows where the action is taking place.

Shots can also be defined by what they contain. A **two-shot** includes two characters; a **three-shot** includes three characters. **Shot/reverse shot** is the principle of alternating shots of characters in a conversation so that first one character, then the other is seen.

CLOSE-UPS AND LONG SHOTS

Director Jean-Luc Godard was fond of saying that the close-up was invented for tragedy, the long shot for comedy. This is something of an oversimplification, since long shots and extreme long shots are staples of the western. But at least Godard was suggesting that filmmakers have reasons for choosing one shot over another depending on the kind of movie they are making or the type of scene they are shooting. A close-up can reveal a particular emotion for which, under the circumstances, a long shot would have been inappropriate. When Lucy (Lillian Gish) is denounced by her father in *Broken Blossoms*, D. W. Griffith uses a close-up to express her fear.

The close-up is also a means of emphasis. Hitchcock found it ideal for objects like a suspicious glass of milk (*Suspicion* [1941]), an envelope dropped by a Nazi agent (*Saboteur* [1942]), a wine bottle filled with uranium ore (*Notorious* [1946]), and a necklace that indicates that the wearer is not who she pretends to be (*Vertigo*). These objects are so crucial to the plot that Hitchcock was unwilling to assume they would be noticed unless their presence was emphasized.

Hitchcock also used the extreme close-up for reasons having to do with genre. *Psycho* is a horror film; audiences expect the proverbial chill up the spine, and Hitchcock does not fail them. The extreme close-ups of Marion Crane's screaming mouth and staring eye in the shower sequence stay in the memory. Extreme close-ups of the eye are, in fact, standard in horror films, especially if it is the eye of the killer spying on a prospective victim through a peephole, as is the case in *Psycho* and *The Spiral Staircase* (1946).

The extreme close-up is not just an embellishment; like any shot, it can have a direct bearing on the plot. The words "Prognosis Negative," which confirm Judith Traherne's terminal condition in *Dark Victory*, must be visible, and that can be done only in extreme close-up. If a scar identifies a murderer, as it does in *A Stranger Knocks* (1963), the scar needs to be photographed in ECU.

The ECU should be used with discretion; it is such an extreme form of emphasis that a preponderance of such shots is like the speech pattern of someone who gives equal emphasis to every word, including *a* and *the*.

While the close-up is useful to point up the intense emotion of tragedy, the long shot—despite Godard's assertion—can be ideal for tragedy as well, since it makes death less painful to watch. The death of Santiago (Arthur Kennedy) in Edgar G. Ulmer's *The Naked Dawn* (1955) is photographed in long shot. Santiago is on horseback when the bullet strikes him; we see neither stunned eyes nor spurting blood. The shot has a formalized beauty about it that is reminiscent of a painting like Brueghel's *Fall of Icarus*, in which the death of Icarus is made part of the setting.

Western filmmakers favor long shots and extreme long shots because these shots make the subject part of the environment in addition to conveying the vastness and awesomeness of nature. In George Stevens's *Shane* (1953), a deer laps water from a stream with snow-fringed mountains in the background. A man bids farewell to a woman who merges with the landscape as he rides off in John Ford's *My Darling Clementine* (1946). Many of Ford's long shots have an intensely pictorial quality. In *Clementine*, we see a stretch of sky brooding over the dusty main street of Tombstone, a bar thronged by men—sometimes in silhouette, sometimes illuminated by the kerosene lamps that hang overhead—and Monument Valley with its cliffs and mesas rising skyward from a flat plain and dwarfing all who pass beneath them.

HIGH-ANGLE AND LOW-ANGLE SHOTS

Shots are also defined by the position of the camera in relation to the subject. When Lillian (Jane Fonda) looks out of her hotel window in *Julia* (1977), what she sees on the street below is rendered as a **high-angle shot.** In a high-angle shot, the camera is positioned above (sometimes "high above") the subject. This is occasionally referred to as a **God's eye shot,** a type favored by Hitchcock to suggest an unseen presence looking down

Orson Welles prepares for a low-angle shot, below floor level, in *Citizen Kane* (1941). *(Courtesy MOMA/FSA and RKO)*

on the subject. If the camera shoots up at the subject from below, it is a **low-angle shot.**

A low-angle shot makes the subject loom larger than it actually is. Such a shot can suggest dominance or power, as it does in *Citizen Kane* when Kane's guardian hovers over him as he presents the young Kane with a sled. Conversely, a high-angle shot makes the subject seem smaller than it is. When a member of the French underground interrogates the title character in *When Willie Comes Marching Home*, the high angle from which Willie is photographed suggests the feeling of helplessness that the intense cross-examination produces.

The high-angle shot of the president pacing the floor in D. W. Griffith's *Abraham Lincoln* (1930) reminds us that the burdens of the office dwarf even the great. In *All the President's Men*, as reporters Bob Woodward and Carl Bernstein are sorting out library slips, the camera watches them from above; indeed, they seem to grow smaller as they realize the enormity of their task. The scene ends with the camera peering down at the reading room of the Library of Congress, which looks like a magnified snowflake.

Sometimes the script requires a high- or low-angle shot for reasons that have nothing to do with symbolism or imagery. In *Julia*, the shot following Lillian at the window had to be a high-angle shot; an eye-level shot would have made no sense. If a man is waiting at the foot of a staircase for a woman to descend, as Gabriel (Donal McCann) waits for Gretta (Anjelica Huston) near the end of John Huston's *The Dead* (1987), the woman must be photographed in a low-angle shot to match the man's angle of vision.

In *The Blue Dahlia* (1946), Mrs. Harwood (Veronica Lake) is on the mezzanine of a hotel when she phones down to Johnny Morrison (Alan Ladd) at the registration desk in the lobby; the camera has to shoot down at Morrison in order to match the angle from which Mrs. Harwood sees him. The context of the action determines the nature of the shot.

The same holds true of other types of shots; the screenplay and its interpretation by the filmmaker dictate the nature of the shots.

SUBJECTIVE CAMERA

An **objective shot** represents what the camera sees; a subjective shot (sometimes referred to as a *subjective camera*) represents what the character sees. As the Joads drive into a Hooverville in *The Grapes of Wrath*, the residents are looking straight ahead as they step aside for the truck. At whom are they staring? one might ask. They are looking at the Joads, whom we cannot see. Thus, they are looking at us: we have been put behind the wheel in order to see poverty and squalor through the Joads' eyes. When, through voice-over, Henry Hill in *GoodFellas* recalls the time he entered a Mafia restaurant, director Martin Scorsese used **subjective camera.** Instead of showing Hill personally making a round of the tables, the diners looked directly into the lens as if they were acknowledging Hill's presence. Subjective camera implied that Hill, though unseen, is still a force to be reckoned with.

Sometimes in a film we experience sheer motion without a corresponding image. In Hitchcock's *Marnie*, for example, Mark (Sean Connery) is seated at his desk when Marnie enters the room. Mark looks straight into the camera, acknowledging Marnie's presence. We do not see her, however; we only experience some sense of movement toward the desk. For a moment we have become Marnie, but we cease to be Marnie when she comes into view.

Robert Redford and Dustin Hoffman prepare for the Library of Congress scene in *All the President's Men* (1976). The camera is set for a high shot. *(Courtesy Warner Bros., Inc.)*

Because subjective camera offers a one-sided take on reality, it should never dominate a film as it did in *Lady in the Lake* (1946)—the textbook case of how not to make the audience a participant in the action. The main character in the film, Philip Marlowe (Robert Montgomery), is never seen except in a mirror. As a result, there are scenes in which the other characters, supposedly looking at him, stare straight into the camera, which represents Marlowe and, by extension, us. When a woman kisses Marlowe, she has to purse her lips into the lens, which makes it seem as though she were kissing us. To light Marlowe's cigarette, she thrusts the lighter into the lens as if she were about to ignite the viewer. When Marlowe is socked in the jaw, it seems that the camera (and, therefore, the viewer) is the one getting punched.

Subjective camera should be restricted to specific scenes or sequences, as is the case in *Dark Passage* (1947), in which the plot requires subjective shots. Unjustly convicted of his wife's murder, Vincent Parry (Humphrey Bogart) escapes from San Quentin to track down the real killer. He cannot solve the murder looking as he does because his picture is in every newspaper, so he chooses to undergo plastic surgery. Director

A low-angle shot of Gretta (Anjelica Huston) descending the stairs in *The Dead* (1987). *(Frame enlargement courtesy Vestron Pictures)*

Delmer Daves, who also wrote the screenplay, had two options. He could use another actor in the early scene and, after the operation, introduce Bogart, or he could use a combination of subjective camera and Bogart's voice for the first thirty minutes and then drop subjective camera after Bogart finally appears. Daves was pretty much forced to do the latter: in 1947, Humphrey Bogart was too big a star to make his initial appearance thirty minutes into the picture.

Parry escapes by concealing himself in a barrel that has been loaded onto a prison truck. The camera is totally subjective, jostling us as Parry maneuvers the barrel from the truck and making us reel with dizziness as it rolls down a hill. When the barrel comes to rest, we peer out of it cautiously but get no more than a tunnel-like view of the outside. Parry is now a presence. When he hitches a ride, the driver speaks to the presence, who answers but is still unseen. When the driver recognizes him, the presence knocks him unconscious. Later, the presence scans the highway and climbs into Irene Jansen's (Lauren Bacall) waiting car.

When the presence showers, a hand adjusts the shower head and a jet of water sprays the camera lens. Camera movements express the pres-

A low-angle shot from *Suddenly, Last Summer* (1959), showing Violet Venable (Katharine Hepburn) ascending in her private elevator. *(Courtesy Margaret Herrick Library of the Academy of Motion Picture Arts and Sciences)*

ence's emotional state. When the presence is wary, the camera darts in the same direction as his apprehensive eyes. A telephone rings, and the camera swings around the way a tense person does at an unexpected sound. Gradually, Daves begins to switch from subjective to objective camera, from Parry as a presence to Parry as a character. The transition begins in a cab at night, so Bogart's face is kept in shadow. The sympathetic cab-driver recommends plastic surgery and refers Parry to a reliable doctor. After the operation, Bogart's voice returns to his body, and the camera ceases to be subjective.

Related to subjective camera is the **point-of-view (POV)** shot. A POV shot represents the point of view of the character, or what the character sees. A famous shot of this kind occurs at the end of Hitchcock's *Spellbound* (1945) when Dr. Murchison (Leo G. Carroll) is unmasked as the murderer of the former director of a mental institution. Murchison aims a gun at his accuser and then turns it around to fire at himself. The close-up of the gun with which Murchison commits suicide is a POV shot, representing the way he saw the gun when he turned it on himself.

Philip Marlowe's (Robert Montgomery) reflection in *Lady in the Lake* (1946), the subjective camera film in which Marlowe is visible only when a mirror catches his image. *(Courtesy WCFTR)*

SHOTS AS PARTS OF A WHOLE

It is easy to become enamored of particular shots, especially those that are strikingly photographed. The close-up of the burning crucifix in *Amadeus* (1986) is a powerful moment in the film. It would still have an impact, though perhaps not the same kind, if one saw a still or a frame enlargement of it without having seen the film. It is the context that makes the shot not only powerful but chilling: Salieri, realizing Mozart's superiority, is so angry with God for giving him a rival that he destroys a symbol of his faith. The clock without hands that the main character sees in his dream in Ingmar Bergman's *Wild Strawberries* (1957) is a shot that would still have an effect if it was taken out of context. Shown a still or a frame enlargement of the clock and asked what it means, one might say something like "time has stopped" or even "death"—a good answer, and not that different from what it means in the film. But in *Wild Strawberries* the clock without hands is one of the film's many death symbols; it therefore

Tight framing in *Detour* (1946). The camera tracks in for a close-up of Roberts (Tom Neal), who looks imprisoned within the frame. *(Frame enlargement courtesy John Belton)*

takes on its deepest meaning within the context of the film, which is a death odyssey.

At the end of *Radio Days*, a father holds his son lovingly on his lap. Anyone who saw a still of that scene without knowing anything about the film would assume that the character was a caring father. Yet throughout the movie it is obvious that the father is not especially affectionate toward his son. The reason the boy is on his father's lap is that he is getting a spanking. As he is being spanked, a report comes over the radio that a child who had fallen into a well has died. Suddenly the father's attitude changes, and instead of punishing his son he caresses him. The death of someone else's child has made the father feel warmer toward his own.

While every film text requires illustrations, stills and frame enlargements are like the shadows in Plato's allegory of the cave: reflections of the real that fall short of the real. A film is a moving picture, not a series of still photographs. Similarly, shots are like excerpts; just as some excerpts communicate more information than others, so, too, do some shots. The excerpt is part of the work, just as the shot is part of the total film in which its meaning resides.

FRAMING THE SHOT

The concept of **framing** is easily understood by anyone who has either studied painting or has actually painted. Framing is the act, and sometimes the art, of composing a shot, reflecting decisions similar to those painters make about how their canvas will ultimately look. The filmmaker's canvas is the frame, the strip of celluloid on which the image is captured. Like a painter, the filmmaker must arrange the details of the frame in terms of the visual or dramatic points being made, or the ideas being expressed. Although there are no ironclad rules of framing, certain principles are widely followed.

The shadows cast by the Cossacks create ominous diagonals on the steps in *Potemkin* (1925). *(Courtesy MOMA/FSA and Janus Films)*

The juxtaposition of strong verticals (the soldiers' legs) and stable horizontals (steps) with broken lines (sprawled bodies and hands raised in supplication) suggest the dominance of the Cossacks and the helplessness of the people in *Potemkin*. *(Courtesy MOMA/FSA and Janus Films)*

Tight framing gives a feeling of oppression. In **tight framing,** the subject appears to be confined within the horizontal and vertical borders of the frame, so that there is not even a hint of offscreen space. To create an atmosphere of fatalism, Edgar G. Ulmer chose tight framing for several shots of Roberts (Tom Neal) in *Detour* (1946). When Roberts's face is trapped within the frame, destiny seems to be closing in on him.

The frame should be slightly asymmetrical. Whatever is to be emphasized should occupy a position of prominence, but not in the center of the frame. If the image were dead center, a sense of depth would be lost because the subject would seem to be stamped on the frame. If a disorienting or unusual effect is sought, the extremity of the frame might be used. For example, in *Detour,* when Roberts discovers that Vera (Ann Savage) has accidentally strangled herself with a telephone cord, her body is seen right of frame, the head hanging above the bed.

Vertical and horizontal compositions denote solidarity; diagonals and oblique compositions denote tension. In *Potemkin,* the masts of the ships, the raised arms of the sailors, and the waving arms of the people suggest a sol-

CANTED SHOTS

A canted shot of Orson Welles as Harry Lime in *The Third Man* (1949). *(Courtesy MOMA/FSA)*

idarity that is destroyed when the Cossacks appear at the top of the Odessa Steps. Their shadows falling on the steps create a diagonal that breaks the unity. A **canted shot** (also known as a Dutch-angle shot) results in an oblique composition in which the frame looks lopsided. Edgar G. Ulmer uses canted shots in *Bluebeard* (1944) to emphasize the mental state of the mad puppeteer; the canted shots in *The Third Man* (1949) imply a world in which things are askew. In the violent argument between the title character and her mother in *Carrie* (1976), the frame looks as if it will tip over.

When an IRA hostage speaks wistfully of his "special friendship" with a hairdresser in *The Crying Game* (1992), director Neil Jordan chooses a canted shot, which should cause us to wonder why the frame is tipped. Is Jordan suggesting that the relationship is not entirely conventional? Eventually we discover that this is the case: the hairdresser is a transvestite.

DECEPTIVE AND DEBARRING VERTICALS

Griselle (K. T. Stevens) in *Address Unknown* (1944) is framed between two trees, expecting to be saved from the mob that is pursuing her. Here the verticals are a support, but only a temporary one. *(Courtesy Sony Pictures Entertainment)*

Griselle before the gate leading to the home of a family friend who will not receive her *(Address Unknown). (Courtesy Sony Pictures Entertainment)*

Sometimes vertical framing is intentionally ironic. In *Address Unknown* (1944), Griselle (K. T. Stevens) flees from a mob that has discovered she is Jewish. She hopes to find refuge in the home of a family friend. Framed by trees, she looks hopefully into the distance where the friend lives. Ordinarily such a composition, with its strong verticals, would imply hope. However, Griselle is a Jew in Nazi Germany, and the man she assumes is a friend has become a Nazi.

Vertical bars across the face, on the other hand, have another connotation: mystery, imprisonment, exclusion. When Carmen (Rita Hayworth) appears behind a beaded curtain in *The Loves of Carmen* (1948), the verticals give her face an exotic yet dangerous look. When Griselle, in *Address Unknown*, finally arrives at the friend's house and stands before the gate, the composition recalls the earlier one in which she was framed by trees. Here, however, the gate is a barrier, and even though she reaches it she does not gain access to the house. The use of verticals in this different composition, as bars across the face, suggests exclusion: prevented from entering, Griselle is killed by the Gestapo.

Geometrical compositions can be symbolic as well as visually interesting. In Jungian psychology, the circle is a symbol of wholeness, suggesting unity and commonality. Such is the case in *Sahara* (1943) when Sergeant Joe Gunn (Humphrey Bogart) passes a cup of water around to his thirsty men, who stand in a circle. If a composition involves three characters, triangular arrangements can make a statement about their relationship, as is the case in François Truffaut's *Jules and Jim* (1961), in which two men share the affections of the same woman.

Iconography—*conscious pictorialism, in which a scene is intended to evoke a famous painting, or a character is meant to represent a famous person from another era—should be as unobtrusive as possible.* If the filmmaker is imitating a painting or a sculpture, the composition should look natural even though it is a replica of, or an homage to, a favorite work of art. The beggars' banquet in Luis Buñuel's *Viridiana* (1961) is an obvious parody of Leonardo da Vinci's *The Last Supper*, made even more so by the use of the "Hallelujah Chorus" as background music. A less blatant parody of *The Last Supper* occurs in Robert Altman's *M*A*S*H* (1970) when the medics stage a literal last supper for the dentist who plans to commit suicide because he thinks he is impotent. Christ imagery, crucifixion, and Way of the Cross motifs tend to call attention to themselves; the bloodied Terry Malloy (Marlon Brando) staggering along the dock at the end of *On the Waterfront* (1954) supposedly suggests Christ painfully making his way along the Via Dolorosa. A more subtle Way of the Cross appears in Capra's *Meet John Doe* (1941) when the title character wends his lonely way through a crowd that reviles him.

TRIANGULAR COMPOSITIONS IN *JULES AND JIM* (1961) SHOWING CATHERINE (JEANNE MOREAU), JULES (OSCAR WERNER), AND JIM (HENRI SERRE), WHO BECOME A *MÉNAGE À TROIS*.

The *ménage* running. *(Courtesy MOMA/FSA and Janus Films)*

The *ménage* shot from below. *(Courtesy MOMA/FSA and Janus Films)*

The angle at which the subject is viewed is determined by two factors: narrative logic and symbolic implications. As we have seen, if a character is looking out of a hotel window onto the street below, the shot that follows must be a high-angle one. Similarly, if a character is on the ground looking up at someone, the person at whom the character is looking must be photographed at a low angle, with the camera shooting upward. Since subjects photographed from a high angle look small and those photographed from a low angle look large, high-angle shots can imply inferiority, defeat, or oppression; low-angle shots, power, dominance, superiority. Susan Alexander Kane is often photographed at a high angle in *Citizen Kane*, because she is dominated by her husband, who is often photographed from a low angle.

The focus within the frame depends on how much or how little is to be seen. If the filmmaker decides that in a particular shot, foreground, middle ground, and background should be equally visible, the shot will have a **deep focus.** In *Citizen Kane*, Orson Welles used deep focus for several reasons: to convey a greater sense of depth, to minimize the need to cut from one shot to another, and to bring out meanings that might otherwise not be apparent. The classic deep-focus shot in *Kane* shows Mary Kane mak-

A different triangular composition from *Citizen Kane* (1941), showing Kane (center) flanked by Thatcher (left) and Bernstein (right) as he is about to relinquish control of his enterprises after the crash of 1929. The position of Kane at the apex of the triangle makes him both the focus of attention and an object of defeat, since he is dwarfed by the more prominent figures of Thatcher and Bernstein. *(Courtesy MOMA/FSA)*

ing arrangements with a banker who is to raise her son as a gentleman because she and her husband cannot. The position of the mother (foreground), banker and father (middle ground), and son (background, seen through the window blissfully playing in the snow) says infinitely more about the way young Kane's life is being signed away without his knowledge than would be the case if the action had been broken down into four separate shots: mother, father, banker, son.

Sometimes **shallow focus** is preferred—for example, when the background should not be as distinct as the foreground because it would detract from the foreground. At other times, the background must remain indistinct until the time for it to be clear. In such a case, the filmmaker will pull focus: first, the background will be a blur and the foreground sharp; then the background will be sharp and the foreground blurry. This technique, known as **rack focus,** is used in *Time After Time* (1976). Someone is behind the heroine, but the person's face is a blur. Then the face comes into focus, and we realize that it is Jack the Ripper's. Likewise, in *Sea of Love* (1989), there is a particularly tense scene in which a murder suspect (Ellen Barkin) suddenly comes into view behind a policeman (Al Pacino), as if a vague presence had taken on recognizable form.

ICONOGRAPHIC FRAMING

The Last Supper parody in
Viridiana (1961). *(Courtesy
MOMA/FSA and Janus Films)*

Another *Last Supper* parody in
M*A*S*H (1970). *(Courtesy
Margaret Herrick Library of the
Academy of Motion Picture Arts
and Sciences)*

Focus may be deliberately erratic, with the image going in and out of focus, as might happen if a character is hallucinating, disoriented, or drunk. In *Detour*, when Roberts realizes that Vera has accidentally strangled herself, objects go in and out of focus as he looks around the room in a state of shock.

*If the frame is to be **masked**—that is, if its shape is to be altered—the same considerations that govern other framing techniques apply: narrative logic and symbolic value.* If a character is peering through a pair of binoculars, a telescope, a microscope, or a keyhole, the next shot should assume the appropriate configuration. There are times in *The Truman Show* (1998) when we seem to be looking through a camera lens. Actually, we are, since Truman Burbank's (Jim Carrey) life is being televised, although he has yet to realize it.

If a character is positioned in a doorway, the result is a frame-within-a-frame, or double framing; within the film frame is another frame—the frame created by the doorway. Double framing may reveal something about the character so framed. John Ford often uses the frame-within-the-frame, especially in *The Searchers* (1956). When Ethan (John Wayne), who will always be a loner and a searcher, returns with Debbie, the object of his search, he remains in the doorway while the others go inside the house.

Because doorways and archways resemble the proscenium arch of a theater, they have a dramatic effect. In John Ford's *The Quiet Man* (1952),

Mary Kate (Maureen O'Hara) is framed in the doorway as Sean (John Wayne) pulls her toward him. In William Wyler's *The Little Foxes* (1941), the Hubbards do their plotting in the archway of the drawing room, thus seeming like the stage villains they were in Lillian Hellman's play.

*The **long take**—a shot that lasts more than a minute—can also be framed.* Recall the definition of a shot: a single run of the camera. The camera can accommodate ten minutes' worth of film, although few filmmakers would allow it to run for that length. (Hitchcock did so in *Rope* [1948], an eighty-minute film consisting of eight takes, each running approximately ten minutes. *Rope*, however, was an experiment—and not an especially successful one.) The average shot lasts between ten and twenty seconds, but many shots are often longer, and even a three-minute shot can be framed.

The most famous long take in American film is the credits sequence in Orson Welles's *Touch of Evil* (1958), which lasts almost three minutes. Someone puts a time bomb in the trunk of a car. Two people get into the car and proceed down the street of a Mexican border town, past Mr. and Mrs. Vargas (Charlton Heston and Janet Leigh). The Vargases reach the customs booth before the couple do. In their conversation with the customs officer, we learn that Mrs. Vargas is American and Mr. Vargas, soon revealed to be Mexican, is a narcotics agent. Then the car with the couple pulls up to the booth. The driver, Mr. Linnekar, is known to the customs officer. The woman with him, who admits that she is not an American citizen, complains about a "ticking noise," but the customs officer does not take her seriously. The Vargases, who behave like newlyweds, are more interested in each other than in the occupants of the car. The car crosses the border, continues a short distance, and then explodes into flames. Within less than three minutes of uninterrupted camera movement, we have had the credits, been introduced to two of the main characters, discovered that the drug trade will be an important element of the plot, learned that Mrs. Vargas is American while her husband is Mexican, witnessed a car bombing that will have to be explained, and entered a world where the unpredictable and the incalculable are the norm. Welles chose to make the credits sequence of *Touch of Evil* a long take and framed it accordingly, creating an atmosphere of restlessness with a camera that is continually moving.

In *GoodFellas* there is a long take that lasts well over a minute. It begins with Henry Hill and Karen entering the Copacabana through the kitchen; as they do, the camera follows them, proceeding through a labyrinth of corridors and past stoves, ovens, and sinks—up a flight of stairs and into the foyer, where, despite a reservations line, the couple are immediately escorted to a table to which a waiter brings their specially prepared meal. But the shot does not end there; Scorsese pans right to left—to the next table, where a party is seated that obviously knows Henry; and then diagonally to the bandstand, where the comedian Henny Youngman is set to perform. The beauty of Scorsese's long take is its ability to capture the unbroken rhythm of an action through camera work of incredible fluidity.

Shots can be framed graphically in terms of lines (horizontals, verticals, diagonals); they can be framed geometrically or iconographically; in deep or shallow focus; from a high or a low angle; in a frame that has been masked or doubled. A shot can last a second or run ten minutes. Guided by a script that requires a scene to be filmed in a particular way and by aesthetic considerations that will enhance the script and enrich the narrative, the filmmaker makes his or her decisions. These decisions, however, should not be accepted on faith; rather, the viewer should ask if the decisions were the right ones.

THE MOVING SHOT

Movement in film can be deceptive. In the *Touch of Evil* long take, the camera was literally moving. However, when the camera rotates horizontally on a fixed axis (**pan shot**) or vertically (**tilt shot**), it is not, strictly speaking, moving. The camera head—but not the camera itself, which is probably on a tripod—is moving. For **mobile camera** shots, the camera is on a moving vehicle such as a dolly, a truck, or a crane, or on specially built tracks. The mobile camera has the advantage of being able to add to the narrative by opening up more space, thereby augmenting what is seen. The pan and the tilt can add to our knowledge, too.

Pan shots generally move left to right in imitation of the reading eye, but they can also go from right to left. In *The Thin Man* (1934), it does both in the same shot. As Nora Charles (Myrna Loy) opens a door on the right, the camera pans right to left, from the doorway to the interior, where her husband is comforting a weeping girl. When the husband catches sight of his wife, the camera pans left to right, back to Nora in the doorway, as if it, too, were embarrassed at what it has discovered. Through panning, a filmmaker can have the camera comment on a situation, thus making it almost a character. As David Locke (Jack Nicholson) in Michelangelo Antonioni's *The Passenger* (1975) cries aloud in desperation because his Land Rover is stalled in the sand, the camera answers by panning the indifferent desert. Martin Scorsese uses slow, almost languid pans of the characters' living rooms in *The Age of Innocence*—the slow panning suggesting lives of leisure. A **swish pan** (unusually rapid panning that produces a momentary blur) can suggest a sudden change or a transformation. In Rouben Mamoulian's *Dr. Jekyll and Mr. Hyde* (1932), there is a swish pan immediately after Dr. Jekyll drinks the potion and becomes Mr. Hyde.

When the camera pivots vertically, the result is a tilt shot (sometimes called a vertical pan; hence the expression pan up/down). Tilting also mimics eye movement: in this case the eye's tendency to move up the face of a building to take in its height, or down a column of names. In *Jane Eyre* (1944), the camera tilts down from a plaque that reads "Lowood Institution" to the figure of the sleeping Jane Eyre, who is being carried into it. In *Citizen Kane*, the camera tilts up to the entrance gate of Kane's estate, Xanadu, past the No Trespassing sign, reminding us that the warning applies to everyone but itself. At the end of the film, the camera tilts down the gate to the No Trespassing sign as it returns to its starting point.

Like the pan, the tilt shot can be a silent spectator, commenting visually on a situation. As the vampire is about to sink her teeth into a victim's neck in *Dracula's Daughter* (1936), the camera begins tilting up the wall, leaving the rest to the viewer's imagination. A tilt shot can even suggest the actual or potential fate of a character. When Phillip Vandamm (James Mason) in Hitchcock's *North by Northwest* (1959) discovers that his mistress is an American agent, he decides to kill her aboard a plane. "This matter is something that is best disposed of at a great height—over water," he remarks. At the mention of height, the camera tilts up—to nothing but empty space.

As the camera pans or tilts, it guides the eye horizontally or vertically, determining both the direction and the object of the audience's vision. Tilt-pan and pan-tilt combinations are also possible, to direct the viewer's or the character's gaze across one surface and up or down another. In *The Passenger*, the camera is in the process of tracing the curve of a surface wire up the wall of a hotel room when a sudden knock at the door interrupts its ascent, causing it to backtrack over to the door to see who is there.

A combination of panning and tilting occurs in the notorious flashback in Hitchcock's *Stage Fright* (1950), which is later revealed to have been a total lie. Jonathan Cooper (Richard Todd) is explaining to his bewildered girlfriend how Charlotte Inwood (Marlene Dietrich) begged him to go to her flat and bring her a new dress; it seems the one she was wearing is stained with her husband's blood. As Cooper enters the flat, the camera pans across the room to Mr. Inwood's body and then tilts up a closet door. At first the camera's tilting up a clothes closet seems odd, but it is part of Hitchcock's plan to make Cooper's story believable. Thus, Hitchcock has the camera guide Cooper to the closet, from which he removes the dress, as if Cooper did not know where the closet was. If Cooper had headed straight for the closet, the audience would sense that he was more familiar with Charlotte's flat than he should be and would therefore not accept his story.

As we have seen, in panning and tilting the camera itself does not move. Strictly speaking, then, a pan or a tilt is not a moving shot, since the camera merely rotates on a tripod. In a **moving shot,** the camera moves with, toward, alongside, or away from its subjects. There are several kinds

Preparing for a crane shot in *Cover Girl* (1944), with the camera in a mechanical arm. *(Courtesy MOMA/FSA)*

of moving shots, depending on the way in which the camera moves. If it moves on tracks, what you have is a **tracking shot;** if it is mounted on a dolly, a **dolly shot;** if it moves up and down, in and out of a scene on a crane, you have a **crane shot,** which is easily identified by its ascending or descending motion, although a crane can move laterally as well.

Some writers use the terms *dolly shot* and *tracking shot* interchangeably; the camera dollies in (tracks in) when it moves toward the subject and dollies out (tracks out) when it moves away from the subject. Other writers simply call any shot in which the camera is moving on a vehicle (a truck, a dolly, a bicycle) a tracking shot, which is identified by the direction of the camera: forward tracking shot, vertical tracking shot, diagonal tracking shot.

Tracking shots have distinct advantages over other shots because they can encompass a greater area and supply more detail; thus, they can sustain a mood for a longer period of time. While the pan and the tilt can act as a silent commentator, the track can be a character's alter ego or unseen companion. Max Ophüls was a master of the moving shot. In his films, the camera seems to waltz and glide; it can rush up the stairs with the breathless lovers or accompany them on a stroll, occasionally slipping behind a fountain so as not to be conspicuous. In *Letter from an Unknown Woman*, Ophüls makes the camera almost human. As a provincial band ruins Wagner's "Song to the Evening Star," the camera, unable to stand the tinny sound, rises up fastidiously and leaves the square. In the same film, the camera accompanies the operagoers up the grand staircase as if it were escorting them.

The moving camera can physically draw viewers into the action, and it can even lure them into a character's consciousness, as it does in the film version of Eugene O'Neill's *Long Day's Journey into Night* (1962). The crane shot that ends the film is one of the great feats of moviemaking; in it Lumet manages to incorporate almost all of Mary Tyrone's great monologue. Mary (Katharine Hepburn) is in her parlor with her husband and their two sons. She recalls how a nun had dissuaded her from entering the convent because she claimed to have visions of Our Lady of Lourdes. If regression could be visualized, it would consist of gradual diminution. Almost as soon as Mary begins her monologue, the camera starts pulling back from her; then it rises up as her thoughts leave this world. As Mary grows smaller, so do her husband and sons. As the monologue draws to a close, Mary appears in close-up as she speaks the final lines: "That was in the winter of senior year. Then in the spring something happened to me. Yes, I remember. I fell in love with James Tyrone and was so happy for a time." Mary's close-up is followed by close-ups of the other Tyrones; then there is one last close-up of Mary's face, now strangely peaceful.

Many filmmakers today favor the **Steadicam** for moving shots because it reduces the need for complex camera setups. The principle is simple: the camera is attached to a body harness worn by the cameraperson, enabling him or her to achieve the fluidity of a mobile camera without the jerkiness that usually results from a handheld camera.

ZOOMS AND FREEZES

Likewise, many filmmakers prefer the **zoom**—a lens of variable **focal length** (the distance from the center of the lens to the point where the image is in focus) to the moving shot because it is both economical and timesaving. Technically, the zoom is not a moving shot because the camera does not move; rather, an adjustable lens gives the impression of its moving close to, or far away from, the subject (hence the terms **zoom in/zoom out**). There are occasions when a zoom is useful: to single out someone in a crowd, to pinpoint the criminal's hiding place in the woods, to capture a facial expression without the person's being aware of the camera's presence. Zooming also flattens the image, creating an unreal

The most famous freeze frame in film: the final shot in *The 400 Blows* (1959). *(Courtesy MOMA/FSA and Janus Films)*

sense of depth and generally resulting in the loss of detail. However, some filmmakers may prefer such a two-dimensional effect. Stanley Kubrick clearly did in *Barry Lyndon,* in which he deliberately zoomed out of close-ups to reveal scenes that resembled paintings—a technique in keeping with his purpose of portraying the eighteenth century as if it were a museum exhibit.

The opposite of the zoom, which represents deceptive motion, is the freeze, which is a form of stopped motion. In a **freeze frame,** all movement suddenly halts, and the image "freezes" as it turns into a still photograph. The most famous freeze occurs at the end of François Truffaut's *The 400 Blows* (1959). Antoine Doinel (Jean-Pierre Léaud) escapes from a reformatory and heads toward the ocean. When he reaches the water's edge, he walks into the shallows; then he turns and faces the shore. At that instant Truffaut freezes the frame, trapping Antoine between the reformatory and the ocean, between the past and the present. The freeze implies immobility, helplessness, or indecision.

The zoom and the freeze are similar in that they can call attention to details more dramatically than other devices do. Because of their strong underscoring power, they are as easily misused as italics are by inexperienced writers. Since many contemporary films end with a freeze frame, which then becomes the background for the end credits, examples of intelligent use of the freeze frame are hard to come by. A great filmmaker will freeze for a reason; a mediocre one will freeze for effect. The freeze at the end of *Women in Love* (1970), the film version of D. H. Lawrence's novel, is perfectly motivated. The novel comes to no real resolution. The film duplicates the unresolved ending by repeating Lawrence's dialogue, which leads to a natural freeze. When Birkin (Alan Bates) tells Ursula (Jennie Linden) that he wants an "eternal" relationship with another man, Ursula, who cannot conceive of such a relationship, says, "You can't have it, because it's false, impossible." Birkin replies, "I don't believe that," and with these words the novel ends. The same dialogue appears in the film, but when Birkin says, "I don't believe that," Ursula's face freezes into utter bafflement. His words have left her speechless, and what conveys speechlessness better than a freeze?

COMBINING SHOTS: THE SEQUENCE

In film, shots combine to form sequences, or what we generally think of as scenes. Note that some writers prefer to distinguish between a scene and a sequence. A scene, they would say, is a unit of action that takes place in the same location and is made up of one shot (e.g., a long take) or many shots. A **sequence** is a group of shots forming a self-contained segment of the film that is, by and large, intelligible in itself.

From the above definitions, *scene* and *sequence* appear to be virtually synonymous, and for all practical purposes they are. The chief difference is that there can be scenes within a sequence, but not sequences within scenes. In the key sequence in *Notorious*, there are several scenes. The sequence begins in the bedroom with Alicia's removing the key to the wine cellar from Alex's key chain (scene 1); next, she gives the key to Devlin downstairs (scene 2); finally, Devlin and Alicia go down to the wine cellar (scene 3).

There are several kinds of sequences, two of which have already been discussed: credits and precredits sequences (Chapter 2). Someone who has not seen Sam Peckinpah's *The Wild Bunch* (1969) and is shown only the credits sequence would still be able to make some sense of it. What appears to be a detachment of cavalry troops rides into a small town. Some children are feeding a pair of scorpions to a horde of ants. The soldiers ride past the children and proceed up the main street toward the payroll office. On the rooftops of the buildings flanking the street is a band of armed men crouching behind the parapets. The soldiers dismount at the payroll office, enter it, flash their .45s, and pistol-whip the employees. By the time all the credits have appeared, a drama in miniature has unfolded in the form of a sequence. The peaceful tenor of the town has been established and threatened. We now know that the troops are bandits; the rooftop crowd, bounty hunters in the employ of the railroad; the townspeople and children, unsuspecting victims of the crossfire that will certainly erupt.

Sequences can also be identified as *linear, associative,* and *montage.* Note that these types of sequences are not mutually exclusive. Credits and precredits sequences can be linear (with a beginning, a middle, and an end); they can also be a montage of various shots (like the New York montage that accompanies the credits of Woody Allen's *Manhattan,* 1979). Similarly, an associative sequence can be linear (although a linear sequence is not associative). When a sequence is designated as associative, it means that the links between beginning, middle, and end are not so much narrative as visual.

The Linear Sequence

In a linear sequence, one action links up with another, creating a miniature drama with a beginning, a middle, and an end. Let us return to the key sequence in *Notorious.* The beginning of the sequence initiates the action: Alicia removes the key. The middle adds to the action: Alicia slips the key to her coworker, Harry Devlin, during the party; they proceed to the wine cellar, where they discover that one of the bottles contains uranium ore; meanwhile, the champagne supply dwindles, and Alicia's husband and the wine steward go down to the cellar. The end follows and completes the action: the husband discovers his wife with Devlin. In a linear sequence, then, the connections between the incidents are like links in a chain.

After *The Age of Innocence* main title, with its rose motif, the action begins with a shot of a basket of daisies—another instance of the role flowers play in the film. A hand plucks one of the daisies; it is the hand of the soprano-singing Marguerite in a performance of Gounod's *Faust.* The setting, then, is an opera house. Everyone is elegantly attired, as is indicated by shots of bejeweled hands and necks. And the audience is less interested in the opera than in who is sitting next to whom, as the camera imitates the way gossipmongers might use their opera glasses. Newland Archer (Daniel Day Lewis) is seated in a box, wearing a white rose in his lapel. In another box are three women, two of whom will play important roles in his life: his fiancée, May (Winona Ryder), and the Countess Olenska (Michelle Pfeiffer), whose colorful past has made her an object of speculation and, among the self-righteous, scorn. Although Newland insists that his engagement be announced at the ball following the performance, he chooses to sit behind the countess. Indifferent to the opera, they recall their childhood together. *Faust*, which will be heard again, was not an arbitrary choice on Scorsese's part. In the opera, Faust gives up his soul to possess Marguerite. In the film, Archer sells his soul, one might say, to respectability by choosing to marry the conventional May rather than the unconventional countess, whom he really loves. Although the opening sequence lasts only a few minutes, it establishes the setting (New York in the 1870s) and introduces the characters (New York society), three of whom (Archer, May, and the countess) become the principal ones. The beginning introduces us to a privileged world; the middle, to a world where appearances alone count; and the end, to a world where a man who cannot wait to announce his engagement to an innocent young woman chooses to sit next to a woman whose innocence is questionable.

In some linear sequences, however, a few links may be missing; in such cases, the sequence is elliptical. A linear sequence is designated as elliptical when certain details have been omitted because viewers are expected to make the connections for themselves. The "Wedding of Angharad" sequence in John Ford's *How Green Was My Valley* (1941) comprises three episodes that appear, on the surface, to be loosely related: "The Courting of Angharad," "The Visit to Gruffydd," and "The Wedding." In the first episode, Evans, a mine owner's son, comes to court Angharad (Maureen O'Hara) after his pompous father has made the initial arrangements. Since Angharad appears to have a mind of her own, there is little likelihood that Evans will win her despite his wealth. Thus, we do not take the courting seriously. In the second episode, Angharad calls on Mr. Gruffydd (Walter Pidgeon), the minister, whom she really loves. There is something disturbing about this episode—it hints at love never to be consummated. Angharad speaks of her affection for the minister to discover if he feels the same toward her. But his only concern is his low salary, which makes marriage impossible. In the third episode, Angharad steps wraithlike into a carriage, her bridal veil billowing in the breeze.

The three episodes become linked by the impressions they create in the audience's mind. Initially, there seems to be no connection between the courting and Angharad's visit to Gruffydd, but the link becomes clear with the final episode: money, which means nothing to Angharad but means a great deal to the minister. In choosing Evans, she chose what Gruffydd considered the prerequisite for marriage. The folly of her choice is a mirthless wedding where the wind makes sport of her veil as if it were a kite. The tragedy of her choice is mirrored in the minister's face as he watches the wedding party drive away.

Harry Devlin (Cary Grant) on the verge of forgetting the champagne in *Notorious*
(1946). Hitchcock ends the scene with a close-up of the bottle, the object that unifies
the entire sequence. *(Courtesy ABC Picture Holdings, Inc.)*

The Associative Sequence

In an associative sequence, the scenes are linked together by an object or
a series of objects. In another sequence in *Notorious*, Alicia, who has fallen
in love with Devlin, plans an intimate dinner for the two of them. As Devlin leaves for headquarters, Alicia asks him to pick up some wine. In the
next scene, Devlin enters his supervisor's office with a bottle of champagne, which he leaves on the desk. When he discovers that Alicia's assignment requires her to seduce Sebastian, he is so disturbed that he
forgets the champagne. Scene 2 ends with a close-up of the bottle. In the
third scene, Devlin is back in Alicia's apartment, where the dinner is
burned and there is not even any wine to salvage the evening. He looks
around for the champagne. "I guess I left it somewhere," he mutters.
These three episodes coalesce into a sequence that might be entitled "The
Ruined Dinner," whose three scenes might be called "The Bottle Sug-

gested," "The Bottle Purchased," and "The Bottle Forgotten." The bottle is an object that unifies the sequence: the close-up of the bottle in scene 2 links scenes 1 and 3, bringing them into dramatic focus. *associative item or thought*

A similar sequence occurs in Hitchcock's *Rebecca*. Maxim de Winter's new bride lives in the shadow of her husband's first wife, Rebecca, whose presence is everywhere. In a sequence that might be called "The Ubiquitous Rebecca," we first see a shot of Rebecca's room, which has been closed since her death and guarded by her dog; then a napkin with Rebecca's initials; finally, Maxim de Winter (Laurence Olivier) and his young bride (Joan Fontaine) at opposite ends of a long table. What separates them is not just distance but the spirit of Rebecca, who is present even in the napkins on the table. Hitchcock has fashioned a sequence out of three different shots, each dominated by an object associated with the late Rebecca de Winter: a bedroom door, an embroidered napkin, and a dining-room table.

In the sequence that ends another Hitchcock film, *North by Northwest*, Eve Kendall (Eva Marie Saint) is holding on to the hand of Roger Thornhill (Cary Grant) to keep from sliding off Mt. Rushmore. Thornhill encourages her to "hang in there" and, as an added incentive, proposes marriage. In one of the smoothest transitions in film, the hand to which Eve was just clinging is now helping her climb to the upper berth of a compartment on the *Twentieth Century Limited*. Without the audience's suspecting it, the scene changed from Mt. Rushmore to the train compartment. Thornhill's hand was the unifying image; it rescued Eve from death and saved her for marriage.

The Montage Sequence

Montage is a word that has many meanings. When it is used to describe a sequence, *montage* can be defined as a series of shots arranged in a particular order for a particular purpose. In a montage sequence, the shots are arranged so that they follow each other in rapid succession, telescoping an event or several events of some duration into a couple of seconds of screen time. *A New Life* (1988) contains a dating montage that shows a newly divorced woman trying to resume a form of socializing that she has not engaged in for twenty-five years. Another kind of montage, called **American montage** because it was so prominent in American films of the 1930s and 1940s, works from the same principle: time is collapsed as shots blend together, wipe each other away, or are superimposed on each other. A typical American montage might consist of calendar pages blowing away as one month yields to another, then one year to another, while over the blowing pages are superimposed headlines giving the main events that took place during that time period. Finally, the montage ends, and the action resumes.

Just as an associative sequence can also be linear, a montage sequence can have features of both the linear and the associative sequence. A montage sequence compressing a decade into ten seconds could be linear in its chronological arrangement. The World War II montage was common in films of the 1940s. First, one would see a headline announcing the Japanese attack on Pearl Harbor, then subsequent headlines would enumerate key battles, and the last headline would proclaim the Japanese surrender.

A montage can also be unified by images. For example, the tour-of-Washington montage in Capra's *Mr. Smith Goes to Washington* (1939) combines shots of the Capitol, the White House, the Washington Monument, the Lincoln Memorial, and excerpts from Lincoln's Second Inaugural Address and the Gettysburg Address, all of which are associated with the spirit of American democracy.

FROM SHOT TO SHOT

Cuts

Cut is one of the most commonly used terms in film. It can be a verb a director shouts to terminate a shot ("Cut!") or a noun meaning a strip of film or a joint between two separate shots. It can also be a version of a movie in its various stages (**rough cut, director's cut, final cut**). In the context of this chapter, a cut is the joining of two separate shots so that the first is instantaneously replaced by the second, showing something the preceding shot did not. There are five basic kinds of cuts: straight, contrast, cross (parallel), jump, form, and match.

In a **straight cut,** one image instantaneously replaces another. Straight cuts are the most common kind of cuts: shot B replaces shot A. In *The Lady Eve* (1941), Preston Sturges cuts from Charlie Pike (Henry Fonda) sitting at a table in a ship's dining room (shot A) to a group of women staring in his direction (shot B). In a **contrast cut,** the images replacing each other are dissimilar in nature; for example, the cut from the manacled feet of slaves to the galloping hooves of horses in *Slaves* (1969) contrasts the enslaved and the free.

The **crosscut,** or **parallel cut,** presents two actions that occur simultaneously. In *Saboteur,* an attempt to sabotage a battleship at a christening in the Brooklyn Navy Yard is crosscut with the ceremony itself. In *Moonstruck* (1987), a mother is having dinner with a university professor, while her daughter is at the Metropolitan Opera with her lover. *King and Country* (1964) includes two actions that are crosscut: the mock trial of a rat the soldiers are staging in the rain, and the actual trial of a deserter that is being conducted in the barracks. Thus, the plight of the soldier is equated with the plight of the rat. Both the soldier and the rat are victims—the former of a dubious military code and the latter of the soldiers' cruelty, which stems from boredom.

The Godfather ends with a baptism and a series of killings. Michael Corleone's nephew is about to be baptized, and Michael will, literally, be his godfather. However, Michael's brother-in-law, Carlo, the child's father, has betrayed Michael's brother, Sonny, causing his death. In Michael's world, which is that of the Mafia, the law of retribution applies to family members as well as outsiders: Carlo must pay, along with others who have violated the code of honor. In one of the most chilling examples of cross-cutting in film, at the same time that Michael is witnessing the baptism of his nephew, who will also be called Michael, and renouncing Satan and his pomps, as the ceremony requires the godfather to do, the assassinations he has ordered are taking place, resulting in the deaths of various enemies, including Carlo.

A break in continuity that leaves a gap in the action constitutes a **jump cut.** In *Darling* (1965), a shot of a couple about twenty yards from the entrance to a building is followed by a shot of them going through the door to the interior of the building. Obviously, not everything has to be shown in a particular scene or sequence, but excessive jump-cutting can give a film the continuity of a comic strip. On the other hand, when a knowledgeable director jump-cuts, there is probably a reason. In Jean-Luc Godard's *Breathless* (1959), the main character shoots a police officer in Marseille, runs across a field, and emerges in Paris. Godard is too talented a filmmaker to break continuity without a reason. *Breathless* is the kind of movie that calls attention to itself as a movie. It is dedicated to Monogram Pictures, which produced low-budget films during the 1930s and 1940s, and re-creates the style of the low-budget American film in which a character can move from one location to the other without being seen in transit.

A **form cut** is a cut from one object to another that is similarly shaped. In *Detour*, there is a cut from a record in a jukebox to a drumhead—one circular object replaces another. Similar in principle to the form cut is the **match cut,** in which one shot "matches" the other, following it so smoothly that there seems to be no break in continuity as far as time and space are concerned, although there often is. However, if the match is designed to bring us into a different time frame, it should be done so naturally that we barely notice it. For example, in *Indiana Jones and the Last Crusade*, Steven Spielberg uses a match cut to bring Indiana from youth to adulthood. In the first shot, Indiana the boy (River Phoenix) bows his head to receive the famous hat; as the head lifts in the second shot, it is Indiana the man (Harrison Ford) who is wearing the hat. Probably the most famous match in film is the one in Stanley Kubrick's *2001: A Space Odyssey* (1968), when an ape hurls a bone into the air in one shot and a space shuttle appears in the next. The match condenses the history of evolution into two images.

Transitions

In a cut there is no bridge between shots; one shot simply replaces another. Just as writers use transitional phrases ("however," "moreover," "in fact") to bridge ideas, filmmakers use **transitions** to bridge scenes. And just as one can spot transitional phrases, one can also spot transitional devices in film because they are more noticeable than cuts. The following are the chief transitional devices used in film.

The Fade

The **fade-out** is the simplest kind of transition: the light decreases, and the screen goes dark. The opposite is the **fade-in,** where the light increases as the picture gradually appears on the screen. (The term *fade* generally refers to a fade-out.) Most fade-outs are no more profound than a blank screen, but some can bring an action to an artful close, much the way a gifted orator rounds out a sentence. A good illustration is the first fade-out in William Wyler's *Mrs. Miniver* (1942). The first sequence covers a day in the lives of the Minivers. Both husband and wife feel guilty for having purchased something the other might find frivolous: Kay (Greer Garson) has bought a new hat, and Clem (Walter Pidgeon) a new car. At the close of the day, the camera pans the bedroom, pausing at the hat smartly perched on the bedpost. The scene fades out with the hat in silhouette. Fading out on the hat brings the sequence full circle: it began with Kay's buying the hat and ends with the hat's being displayed. We smile at the fade because it provides the same pleasure of recognition we receive when a speech begins and ends with the same image. But we also smile at its wisdom, for it represents one of those little domestic triumphs that seem more meaningful at the end of the day than at the beginning.

In the theater, the curtain sometimes descends between the scenes of an act to mark the passage of time. In film, a fade can function in the same way. The first fade in *Notorious* occurs at a particularly dramatic moment. There is an unidentified guest at Alicia's party, sitting with his back to the camera. Curiously, he remains after everyone else leaves. Hitchcock fades out on the back of the man and fades in on his face, which is none other than Cary Grant's. Hitchcock interrupts the party with a fade to indicate a lapse of time; but the fade is also a clever way of introducing the male lead by linking two scenes in which he appears—one ending with his back to the camera, the other beginning with his face coming into view. The fade

Harry Devlin as the uninvited guest at Alicia's (Ingrid Bergman) party in *Notorious*. Hitchcock will fade out on the back of Grant's head and fade in on his face. *(Courtesy ABC Picture Holdings, Inc.)*

produces a more natural rhythm than would be the case if Hitchcock had cut from the back of Grant's head to a close-up of his face.

A fade can also be commentary. In *Mr. Skeffington* (1944), the aging Fanny Skeffington (Bette Davis) reassembles her former suitors, who are now either married or going bald. The scene fades out as the men enter the dining room and fades in on a gentleman's hat and gloves. A cut would spoil the mood, which is one of genteel hypocrisy. The hat and gloves belong to Edward (Jerome Cowan), an impoverished suitor who has returned to court Fanny. The fade-out allows us to see a connection between the two scenes. In the first, Fanny has invited her suitors to dinner to reassure herself that she is still beautiful. However, Edward is not interested in her beauty, which is nonexistent, but only in her money, which is also nonexistent although he does not know it. One charade fades out and another fades in. A cut would have been too abrupt, and it would also not have conveyed the idea of one farce rising out of another.

fade → end

The Dissolve

A fade denotes demarcation—it indicates the end of a narrative sequence. A **dissolve** denotes continuity by the gradual replacement of one shot by another. This kind of transition, in which the outgoing and incoming shots

dissolve → continuity

merge, serves a variety of functions. Sometimes a dissolve simply has the force of "in the meantime" or "later." In *North by Northwest*, Hitchcock dissolves a shot of Roger Thornhill bribing his mother to get a key from the desk clerk at a hotel to a shot of the two of them walking down the corridor toward the room Thornhill was so anxious to enter.

A dissolve can also mean "no sooner said than done." The Mother Superior in *The Song of Bernadette* (1943) no sooner asks to see Bernadette than the shot dissolves into Bernadette's room. In Max Ophüls's *Caught* (1948), a shot of a woman gazing at a picture of a model in a mink coat dissolves into a shot of the woman, who has become a model herself, wearing a mink.

When is a dissolve a transition, and when is it more than a transition? This is like asking when is a word simply a conventional sign and when is it a symbol. Water can simply be a liquid, or it can be a sign of birth, rebirth, or fertility. It depends on the context: in T. S. Eliot's poems, water is never just water. It is the same with a dissolve. What a dissolve means—if, in fact, it means anything—is determined by the context. The dissolve in *North by Northwest* was just a way of getting two characters from the hotel lobby to one of the floors.

When two images blend in such a way that their union constitutes a symbolic equation, however, the result is a metaphorical dissolve. This is a visual form of **synecdoche** (or **metonymy,** to which synecdoche is very similar), a species of metaphor in which the part is substituted for the whole (roofs for houses, sails for ships) or a sign replaces the thing signified (green = Go, crown = royalty). We often use this figure of speech without knowing it: "Give us this day our daily bread" (bread = food); "All hands on deck" (hands = crew); "He addressed his comments to the chair" (chair = chairperson).

In *The Two Mrs. Carrolls* (1947), Geoffrey Carroll (Humphrey Bogart) is a wife poisoner. Early in the film, Sally (Barbara Stanwyck) discovers a letter he dropped, addressed to his wife. Because Sally is in love with Geoffrey, she questions him about his marriage. He replies that he is getting a divorce. The letter dissolves into a neatly wrapped package of poison Geoffrey has just purchased from a pharmacist. The merging of the two images, the letter and the package, results in the equation: Mrs. Carroll + package = death. Dissolving an envelope bearing a woman's name into the means that will make her only a name is an ingenious touch.

The dissolves in George Stevens's film have an effect similar to the homogenization of cream and milk. In *Shane*, when Starrett (Van Heflin) and Shane (Alan Ladd) succeed in uprooting a stubborn tree trunk, Stevens slowly merges their triumphant faces into the landscape, making the men one with nature. Later, when Starrett watches a homesteader's property go up in flames, Stevens dissolves his vengeful face into the burning house.

The resulting equation—man + nature = natural man; face + burning house = consuming rage—do not advance the plot; their purpose, rather, is to illustrate one of the film's main themes: the pioneer's oneness with nature, which enables him to become a part of everything he sees or does.

A dissolve can sometimes have the effect of **dramatic foreshadowing** if the filmmaker prepares the audience for subsequent events by hinting at their outcome earlier. In *King and Country*, a skull mired in mud dissolves into the face of a soldier playing a harmonica. The dissolve prefigures the fate of the soldier, who later dies in the mud, his voice silenced by a pistol shot in the mouth.

Just as dissolves foreshadow, so, too, can they recapitulate. At the end of *The Last Picture Show*, Sonny (Timothy Bottoms) returns to the house of Ruth Popper (Cloris Leachman), the coach's wife, with whom he has been having an affair. The movie house has closed its doors forever; Sam the Lion and Billy are dead; Duane is on his way to Korea. All that remain are Ruth and the dreary Texas town where the tumbleweed rolls down the main street. As Sonny and Ruth look at each other, their eyes forge the only bond that can unite them—loneliness. At that moment, Sonny and Ruth dissolve into the town and the vast Texas flatlands. There is no difference between a young man without prospects, a middle-aged woman without hope, and a town without a future. Their destinies have become one.

At the end of *Colorado Territory* (1949), Raoul Walsh's western remake of his earlier success, *High Sierra* (1941), the hands of Wes (Joel McCrea) and Colorado (Virginia Mayo), touching in death, dissolve into a shot of a ringing bell. The dissolve does not so much connect two images as two events that the lovers' hands and the bell represent. Earlier in the film, Wes had hidden some stolen money in an abandoned church. After the deaths of Wes and Colorado, a priest discovers the money and uses it to restore the church bell, telling the villagers it was the gift of two lovers who passed by.

The Form Dissolve

A filmmaker can merge two images with the same shape or contours through a **form dissolve.** Often, a form dissolve is merely easy on the eyes. For example, in *Jane Eyre* the figure of a ballerina on top of a music box dissolves into a little girl dressed in the same costume. A form dissolve can also be directly related to the plot. In Hitchcock's *The Wrong Man*, a jazz musician is falsely accused of committing a holdup. As the musician (Henry Fonda) prays in front of a picture of Jesus Christ, the scene gradually changes to that of a man walking down a dark street. Then the man's head merges with the musician's, which in turn becomes hollow enough to accommodate the other's face. The man whose head fits into the musician's is the real criminal. The dissolve shows how easy it is to mistake the innocent for the guilty; it is just a matter of superimposing one face upon another.

The Wipe

Some television news programs change news items by means of a line traveling vertically across the screen. That traveling line is a **wipe,** and in the 1930s and the 1940s this device was the most stylish of the transitions. Since the screen is rectangular, the wipe can move vertically, horizontally, or diagonally; it can create a theatrical effect by rising or falling like a drop curtain, as it does in a scene in *The Thin Man,* where it moves from the bottom of the screen to the top, revealing a stage full of dancers.

Sometimes wipes complement each other: one shot ends with a wipe that travels from left to right; the next with a wipe that moves across the screen from right to left. The best example of complementary wipes can be found in the opening of *The Petty Girl* (1950).

More fluid than a cut and faster than a dissolve, the wipe is ideal for presenting a series of events in quick succession. Wipes are often used in the opening sequences of Frank Capra's Columbia films of the 1930s, notably in the opening sequences of *It Happened One Night* (1934), *Mr. Deeds Goes to Town* (1936), and *Mr. Smith Goes to Washington.* In the handwriting sequence in *Mr. Smith Goes to Washington,* for example, one expert after another testifies to the authenticity of Jeff Smith's signature. After each expert speaks, Capra simply wipes him off the screen, thereby showing the inanity of the investigation.

Rouben Mamoulian's excellent use of the wipe is apparent in *Dr. Jekyll and Mr. Hyde.* After Jekyll (Fredric March) becomes Hyde, he goes off into the night, deserting Muriel Carew (Rose Hobart), his fiancée, who expects him at her dinner party. A wipe opens like a fan, dividing the screen diagonally: on the left is the departing Jekyll; on the right, the party in progress. When Jekyll leaves the Carew estate, Mamoulian wipes him out of the frame, which expands to disclose the dinner guests and the worried Muriel. At that point, the frame divides diagonally again: on the right is Ivy (Miriam Hopkins), the woman Hyde will kill, sipping champagne; on the left is Muriel, the woman Jekyll yearns to marry. The wipe acts as a parallel cut, informing us that while Muriel was at her party, Ivy was at home. But the split screen also represents the protagonist's ideal woman, who is similarly halved. It is only fitting that for a double man (Jekyll/Hyde) there should be a double woman (Ivy/Muriel).

When Muriel's father, furious at Jekyll's absence, cries, "Muriel, you will have nothing more to do with that man," a wipe begins to move him from the left of the screen to the center, revealing the man himself. However, it is not Jekyll but Hyde whom we see. The wipe is an ironic commentary on the father's outburst; clearly, he did not mean that Muriel should have nothing to do with Hyde (whom he cannot know) but with Jekyll. At this point, however, Jekyll is Hyde.

Some writers compare the wipe to a windshield wiper. Hitchcock uses it as such in *Rebecca*, when the second Mrs. de Winter sees Manderley for the first time through the windshield as the wipers clear away the rain. He repeats the technique in *Psycho:* as Marion drives in the rain, the sign for the Bates Motel materializes on her windshield. In each film, the wipe introduces a new phase of the character's life by bringing the future before her eyes. In Mrs. de Winter's case, it was the house where she learned the truth about Rebecca, her husband's first wife; in Marion's, it was the motel where she met her death.

The Iris

Mt. Rushmore, as seen through a telescope in *North by Northwest*, appears inside a circle in the middle of the darkened screen. This is a **masking shot,** or, to be more accurate, an **iris shot,** in which everything is blacked out except what is to be seen telescopically. The frame can also be altered to simulate other shapes (e.g., the view from a keyhole, a crack in a door, binoculars, a submarine periscope), depending upon the form in which the director wants the audience to see the image.

In addition to the iris shot, there is what is known as irising in and irising out. **Irising in** consists of opening up the darkened frame with a circle of light that keeps expanding until the picture fills the frame. **Irising out** is the opposite; it is as if darkness were seeping into the frame from all sides, forcing the diminishing picture into some part of the frame until it becomes a speck and disappears.

A director can dolly in or out of a scene or, today, zoom in or out of one; but there is nothing quite like an iris to open the frame. In *The Birth of a Nation*, Griffith used the iris breathtakingly in Sherman's march to the sea. The frame opens from the upper-left-hand corner to reveal a mother and her children on a hill; at first we do not know why they are huddled in fear, but as the frame opens we see Sherman's soldiers in the valley below. In *Intolerance*, Griffith gradually disclosed the splendor of Babylon by expanding the frame, starting at the lower-right-hand corner.

The iris is especially effective in death scenes. Lucy of *Broken Blossoms* and the Mountain Girl of *Intolerance* both die in iris. Irising out can suggest death because of the way in which darkness creeps into the frame, reducing the size of the image to a pinpoint and then annihilating it. Orson Welles chose the iris to symbolize both the death of Wilbur Minafer and the end of the horse-and-buggy era in *The Magnificent Ambersons* (1942). A

A frame enlargement of an iris shot from *The Birth of a Nation.* In an iris shot, the image appears within a circle on an otherwise dark screen. *(Courtesy MOMA/FSA and Epoch Producing Corp.)*

horseless carriage moves in long shot across the snow. The passengers sing merrily, but their song is in sharp contrast to the landscape, which is dominated by a dead tree with wiry branches. As the motor buggy moves out of the frame, Welles starts irising out until it disappears in the darkness that floods the screen. Welles irises out into a fade. One would have expected him to iris out of one scene and into another, but the shot that follows the fade is of a black wreath on the door of the Amberson house. The iris and the fade imply finality in different ways—the iris gradually and poetically; the fade, irrevocably.

The flashbacks in George Stevens's *Penny Serenade* (1941) are also unified by irising. Julie (Irene Dunne) recalls incidents from her marriage by playing old records of songs that had meaning for her and her husband. Each flashback begins with a close-up of the center of the record, which then opens up, irislike, to reveal the scene.

Because of their fondness for the movies of the past, both François Truffaut and Jean-Luc Godard used the iris more readily than did many of their peers. Truffaut irises out repeatedly in *The Wild Child* (1970) to make the scenes resemble the stages of a scientific experiment conducted as dispassionately as possible. In *Breathless*, Godard uses the iris for sheer nostalgia. In one scene, he irises out on Michel gazing idolatrously at a poster of Humphrey Bogart in his last film. One is tempted to say that Godard is irising out on the old Hollywood—except that irising is still being practiced, although not as regularly as it was in Griffith's day or during the 1930s and the 1940s. However, we do find irising on certain television programs and in movies where techniques of the past function as period touches. When George Roy Hill irises out on the two con men at the close of *The Sting* (1973), it gives the ending a deliberately old-fashioned look. Similarly, the irising in Peter Bogdanovich's *Nickelodeon* lends an air of authenticity to the film, which is set in the early days of the movie industry.

Contemporary filmmakers such as Steven Spielberg, Francis Ford Coppola, Woody Allen, and Martin Scorsese, who have immersed themselves in the films of the past, understandably draw on techniques of the past; these filmmakers use wipes, irises, and fades because they respect the place those techniques have occupied in film history and know how effective such devices can be. Brian De Palma chose a fade as a sign of demarcation at the beginning of *Dressed to Kill* (1980) when he fades to white after Kate's sexual fantasy. Steven Spielberg fades to black in *Empire of the Sun* to indicate that the first part of the action is over. In Francis Ford Coppola's *Peggy Sue Got Married* (1986), a wipe takes Peggy Sue (Kathleen Turner) from high school, where she is talking with a male student, to her bedroom, where she is talking with her girlfriends. Two iris shots appear in Scorsese's *The Age of Innocence*—one of May's unusual engagement ring, an emerald in a diamond setting; the other of Newland and the countess at the opera, either to suggest intimacy by placing them within a circle of privacy or to imply that they may have come within the range of some gossip's opera glasses. Wipes and irises abound in the Star Wars trilogy, which evokes the old movie serials in which wipes and irises were common. Here they have the double function of evoking nostalgia and promoting the narrative. Alan Alda ends *Sweet Liberty* with a variation on the iris-out; the image does not narrow into a circle but into a rectangle that grows progressively smaller until it disappears. *The Golden Bowl* (2001), an adaptation of Henry James's novel, also ends with an iris shot—but for a specific reason. The film, set at the turn of the twentieth century, concludes with a newsreel showing the return of an American millionaire and his English wife (Nick Nolte and Uma Thurman) to the United States. Since early newsreels often closed by irising out on an image, director James Ivory did likewise to provide an air of authenticity as well as to suggest that the couple's reputation as patrons of the arts has made them newsworthy. As more film disciples go on to become filmmakers, their work will reflect what they have learned and what they have seen.

ASSEMBLING THE SHOTS

When Alfred Hitchcock said that a film must be edited, he meant that the shots that make up the movie must be assembled and arranged in such a way that the action proceeds in a logical and coherent manner. **Editing** involves selecting and arranging the shots based on the following considerations: their place within the narrative, their contribution to the mood of a particular scene or to the film as a whole, their enhancement of the film's rhythm, their elucidation of the film's deeper meaning, and their fulfillment of the filmmaker's purpose.

The most common form of editing in the narrative film is **continuity editing**, which entails assembling shots so that they follow each other smoothly and without interruption, as opposed to the piecemeal way in which a movie is filmed. Although movies are shot out of sequence (with location filming usually done before soundstage filming, and scenes involving actors with other commitments shot when the actors are available), filmgoers do not care which scenes were shot first or that the climax in the Grand Canyon was shot on the second day of shooting because the weather happened to be ideal. Continuity editing preserves the illusion of an ongoing narrative.

Eisenstein's Theory of Montage

While montage is sometimes used as a synonym for editing (e.g., montage and American montage sequences), it had deeper implications for the great Russian filmmaker Sergei Eisenstein, who believed that shots should not so much connect as collide, and that the viewer should be affected by their collision. Thus, montage calls attention to itself, unlike continuity editing, which is supposed to be unobtrusive. If a man postures like a peacock, cut from the man to the peacock; if he is figuratively a horse's ass, pair him with a real one. If the purpose of a scene is to show people being killed like animals, cut from workers being massacred to an ox being slaughtered. If one wishes to state visually that all wars waged in the name of God are immoral, arrange a series of shots starting with a baroque Christ and ending with an idol, thereby making militarism a form of regression. This is the kind of montage that Eisenstein practiced.

Eisensteinian montage is based on contrast and conflict, which can exist both within the film as a whole and within a particular shot or scene. In the Odessa Steps massacre in Eisenstein's *Potemkin*, a body lies diagonally across the steps; the Cossacks cast shadows that fall menacingly at oblique angles to the steps; the steps form three contrasting planes, with the Cossacks at the top firing at a woman on a landing behind which lies a trail of bodies.

Eisenstein discovered how ideas could arise from the contrast and conflict of images. Without creating an actual series of cause and effect, he opened *Potemkin* with a shot of breaking waves and followed this image of turbulence with shots of men sleeping in hammocks that formed a shroudlike tangle, mess tables swinging back and forth, meat crawling with maggots—each image jarring us, disquieting us, but ultimately preparing us for the sailors' revolt.

Eisenstein's influence was enormous, but not always beneficial. Instead of producing an artistic effect, the collision of images sometimes produced only pretentiousness. There is an embarrassing scene in Mamoulian's otherwise impressive *Dr. Jekyll and Mr. Hyde* when Jekyll, exulting over his impending marriage to Muriel, shouts, "If music be the food of love, play on!," as he sits down at the organ and pounds away. Five shots appear in rapid succession, commenting on his rapture: a lighted candelabra, an illuminated art object, a smiling statue, the butler's beaming countenance, and a blazing hearth. Jekyll's rapture is evident from the way he plays the organ; the accompanying montage is superfluous.

To Eisenstein, montage meant the visual conflict of images. On the Continent, it means editing: selecting and arranging the shots that will form the scenes and sequences of a film. In England, the same process is called editing, or cutting, but with a slight difference: "editing" means the step-by-step assembling of the shots in the cutting room, while "montage" refers to the process considered as a whole. A further complication is that during the 1930s and 1940s American films employed what has become known as American montage, which, as we have already seen, is a convenient way of collapsing time. In a typical American montage scene, newspapers would spin across the screen announcing a murder trial as one headline obliterates the other. The face of the judge would dissolve into the defendant's; during the trial, one shot would wipe away another. Superimposed over the defendant's face would be that of his anguished wife and, over hers, the face of the real murderer, who is hiding out in a sleazy room above a bar. Although this form of montage, in which time is telescoped through a blend of dissolves, wipes, and superimposures, is not in vogue today, in its time it was highly effective and was regarded as sufficiently important to warrant screen credit for the montage editor. Slavko Vorkapich was especially adept at montage (*Mr. Deeds Goes to Town, Mr. Smith Goes to Washington*); Don Siegel began in montage at Warner Bros. before going on to become a well-known director (*Invasion of the Body Snatchers* [1956]; *Dirty Harry* [1971]; *Escape from Alcatraz* [1979], and so on).

Continuity Editing

While montage may seem to be intellectually more exciting than continuity editing, it would be a mistake to dismiss continuity editing as merely the sequential arrangement of shots. Continuity editing is based on other editing principles that affect a film's rhythm, time, space, tone, and theme.

Rhythm

No great film is rhythmically uniform. Some shots remain on the screen longer than others; some sequences move more rapidly than others. One sequence may be uncommonly slow, while another may be unusually fast. The best filmmakers vary speed, movement, and pace, knowing that long strips of film produce a slower rhythm, short strips a more rapid rhythm. The process itself is not the issue here; the effects are, as one can see in the first two sequences of *Citizen Kane*, "The Death of Kane" and "News on the March."

Citizen Kane begins with the camera ascending the gate of Xanadu, defying the No Trespassing sign. A series of dreamlike dissolves culminates in a shot of a lighted window that suddenly goes dark. A mouth utters "Rosebud!" through a veil of falling snow, and a glass paperweight with a snow-covered house inside it smashes without making a sound. A nurse enters a room and folds a dead man's arms across his chest. The mood of the first part of "The Death of Kane" is slow and languid. As the camera draws closer to the window, the rhythm accelerates. Snow falls to the sound of crystal-pure music, evoking Kane's Colorado boyhood. The paperweight breaks, and the nurse enters. Then the rhythm decelerates, and the mood becomes solemn as she places Kane's arms on his chest.

Without warning, a voice bellows, "News on the march!," as a newsreel of Kane's life unfolds. In the second scene the pace is frenetic; fifty years of a man's life are compressed into a few minutes. The pace builds inexorably until the "News on the March" is over and the camera sputters out, as if in exhaustion.

Frame enlargement of the glass paperweight that falls from Kane's hand. The lighted window of Kane's bedroom goes dark. Suddenly snow begins to fall; it is the artificial snow in the glass paperweight that falls from Kane's hand as he utters his last word, "Rosebud!" *(Courtesy MOMA/FSA)*

Time

Parallel cutting makes it possible for two concurrent actions to be depicted on the screen without one being completed before the other begins—the filmmaker simply cuts back and forth between them. Most novelists would never narrate two simultaneous episodes by completing the first before going on to the second; the novelist would bring the first to a certain point and, leaving the reader in suspense, proceed to the second. The novelist would then gradually add to each episode until the episodes are resolved either separately or jointly. D. W. Griffith understood this principle when he made *The Lonely Villa* (1909), in which he cut back and forth between a mother and her daughters being terrorized by thieves who have broken into their home, and the father en route to rescue them. The action is resolved by the last-minute rescue.

Space

Film's ability to alter our perception of space is well known. A filmmaker can combine a shot of a tractor trailer that has jackknifed on the New England Thruway with a shot of a girl who has just gotten off the Cyclone at Coney Island, looking appropriately dazed. The combination could lead

As the nurse enters Kane's room, her image is refracted through a piece of the shattered paperweight. *(Courtesy MOMA/FSA)*

one to conclude that the girl witnessed the jackknifing, even though one event occurred outside Boston and the other took place in Brooklyn.

D. W. Griffith's *Intolerance* is a four-plot film about injustice as seen in four different periods: the early twentieth century, the age of Cyrus the Great (sixth century B.C.), the time of Christ, and the St. Bartholomew's Day massacre of the Huguenots in 1572. Although the film depicts events in four different parts of the world, everything converges at the climax. By alternating between shots of Christ on his way to Calvary, the Mountain Girl on her chariot to warn Cyrus, a modern-day race against the clock to save the life of an innocent man, and Prosper the Huguenot rushing through the streets of sixteenth-century Paris to rescue his beloved, Griffith makes it seem that everything is occurring not only at the same time but also in the same general area. The parallel cutting has affected our sense of time and space, as well as reflecting the film's theme: the existence of intolerance at all times and in all places.

Tone

Just as tempo should vary in a film, so too should tone, which is primarily light, shade, and color. Again, *Citizen Kane* is an excellent example. The first sequence, "The Death of Kane," is dark and eerie. The second sequence, "News on the March," is the exact opposite; it is a newsreel, and looks as grainy as any newsreel ever made.

Theme

A filmmaker might deepen a film's theme by juxtaposing contrasting shots. As we have seen, there is a cut in *Slaves* from the manacled feet of slaves to the galloping hooves of horses. Whether the horses are in the same vicinity as the slaves is irrelevant; the point of the cut is the contrast between the enslaved and the free. In *A Doll's House* (1973), there is a cut from Nora's upper-middle-class home to Krogstad's hovel; seeing how Krogstad lives makes it easier to understand his blackmailing Nora.

The Role of the Editor

Since it is a common fallacy that films are made in the editing room, students often have difficulty distinguishing between the editor's role and the filmmaker's. We have seen that editing involves selecting and arranging the shots in a particular order. But who does the arranging, the editor or the filmmaker?

Let us use an analogy from student life. After you have written an essay or a term paper, you submit it to your instructor. Before submitting it, you have edited it: removed superfluous words, substituted the right words for the wrong ones, corrected spelling and grammar. Still, your essay may not be perfect; you have been too close to it to catch all the mistakes. Since your instructor did not write it, he or she can be more objective. You may have sentences, or even paragraphs, that should be transposed. What you thought was an introduction might work better if you made it your conclusion. Perhaps you did not prune the paper of all its excesses; your instructor will note that. A good instructor can take what you have submitted and, by making the proper corrections and suggestions, show you how it can be improved. Your instructor did not write the paper, yet he or she has done something for it that you have not done: your instructor has made it better.

An editor performs a similar task: he or she takes what has been shot and improves upon it. The ideal film editor is the director's alter ego, carrying out what the director would do if he or she had the time to be all things to the film. Thus, an editor may select the shots or decide which portion of a shot should be used. An editor can give an action scene its distinctive rhythm by alternating tempo and varying directional movement. If a sequence needs greater momentum, an editor can cut it in such a way that it acquires this feature. If a scene is especially violent, an editor can cut it so rapidly that the movie will receive a PG-13 instead of an R rating. If shot A shows the pursuers moving left to right, shot B must show the pursued fleeing left to right; otherwise, it would look as if they collided. If a character exits shot A from the left, the character must enter shot B from the right.

Because all films require some form of editing, the importance of editors has often been exaggerated, and their role sometimes equated with that of directors. Lee Bobker compares editors with painters, working in isolation to create the movie's pace, mood, and rhythm. Yet, despite

Bobker's respect for the editor's function, he is forced to admit that it is a subservient one: "The editor should always enjoy a wide creative latitude, but he should never fall prey to the illusion that he is creating a new film from scratch. His primary purpose is to bring to completion an artistic work already in progress."[1]

In the first edition of *The Technique of Film Editing*, Karel Reisz dubbed the editor "the interpreter of the small details rather than the prime creator of the continuity."[2] For the second edition, Professor Thorold Dickinson provided an introduction to the second part of the book in which he stated that "the modern editor is the executant for the film-maker and no longer his equal on any self-respecting film."[3]

Most good editors would agree. The best answer to the question "What is film editing?" was given by the British editor Anthony Gibbs: "Film editing is putting into dramatic form the basic filmed material given to the editor by the director."[4] However, just as there are average, good, and great directors, there are average, good, and great editors. Gibbs would call a good editor someone who can achieve "the total interpretation of the director's and the writer's intentions," and a great editor someone who is capable of "taking their intentions even farther, showing them a dimension to their project which even they may not have imagined to be there."[5]

True greatness is rare in any profession; thus, great editors are probably at a premium. It is not unlikely that an editor capable of bringing to the surface what the filmmaker did not even know was there would go on to become a director. The motto of Edward Dmytryk, who began his career as an editor and then went on to direct some fifty films between 1935 and 1975, is relevant: "Substance first—then form."[6] The filmmaker must provide the substance if the editor is to provide the form.

COLORING THE IMAGE

The Black-and-White Film

Film theorist Rudolph Arnheim has argued that color is accidental to film and that audiences can accept the absence of color in black-and-white movies. The history of film proves that a movie photographed in black and white can render all of the important plot details without loss of verisimilitude. Just as sound films cannot be considered superior to silent films simply because the dialogue can be heard, color films cannot be considered superior to black-and-white because all the colors can be seen. Nor are black-and-white films that include references to color less effective because the color cannot be seen; the color can be imagined. In William Wyler's *Jezebel* (1938), a black-and-white film, Julie (Bette Davis) arrives at

The creative use of black and white in *The Merry Widow* (1934). *(Courtesy MOMA/FSA)*

a ball in a red dress that she has been forbidden to wear. The dress photographs as nonwhite, and white was the color Julie was expected to wear. Julie's act of rebellion is as effective today, when color films are the norm, as it was in 1938, when color films were the exception.

One should always remember that it is only since the late 1960s that color has been the norm. Yet, even when black and white was the norm, filmmakers could work within the parameters of monochrome and achieve something akin to color. In *Twelve O'Clock High* (1949), Gregory Peck plays an Air Force general whose inflexibility results in a nervous breakdown. He tolerates no deviation from the rules—he might even be described as someone who thinks in "black and white." When the general breaks down, the blackness of his hair and his leather jacket and the stark whiteness of his face set against a translucent gray background imply that the gray area in human affairs that lies between the extremes of black and white was something the general had relegated to the background. It was his inability to perceive shades of difference that led to his breakdown.

In Ernst Lubitsch's *The Merry Widow* (1934), the black-and-white photography produces a color scheme that even the most advanced form of color technology would find hard to rival. Since the film is based on a Viennese operetta, everything looks as if it came from a confectionary. It is impossible not to think of chocolate, icing, and whipped cream when watching the film: the widow's mansion looks like a tiered wedding cake; her boudoir is like a pastry shell; the walls of her boudoir are creamy and incandescent. When the widow wears a black negligee, the dramatic contrast of her attire and the appointments of her boudoir satisfy whatever craving for color a viewer might have.

In the 1930s and 1940s, Paramount's films were renowned for their "white look," which was partly the creation of art director Hans Dreier, who helped to forge the studio's visual style. Middle-class bedrooms gave off a glow, telephones were opalescent, and walls and staircases gleamed like burnished ivory. Paramount seemed to revel in whiteness, from satin sheets to that indisputable touch of class, the white telephone. The suite in the luxury hotel that we see in Mitchell Leisen's *Easy Living* (1937) is a typical example of Paramount's white look. The suite is so luminous that it looks as if it had been decorated by a silversmith.

Although *Citizen Kane* was photographed in black and white, it is rich in color symbolism. Throughout the film, white is an ambivalent symbol. It suggests innocence as well as the loss of innocence; it is the color of the real snow that Kane knew as a boy in Colorado and the color of the artificial snow in the glass paperweight he keeps as a memento of that happy time. White is also a symbol of freedom; when Susan leaves Kane, a white cockatoo screeches and flies away. But white also evokes sterility and death. Xanadu, Kane's palatial home, is adorned with useless statues and white marble; the nurse who enters Kane's room at the moment of his death wears a white uniform. The symbolic values of white can be rendered so artfully by black and white that color is not missed.

The Color Film

Although color has become the preferred format since the late 1960s, some directors will choose to work in black and white occasionally. This is their prerogative, their artistic choice. Color may be more natural to us than monochrome, yet it can also be argued that the black-and-white image is closer to reality because it has not been prettified or given the embellishments that color can provide. One would never want to see anything done to Walker Evans's stark photographs of the Great Depression. To add color to them would be to mock the disparity between the haves and the have-nots, making images of privation look like some ancient fresco.

Thus, realism has nothing to do with color. In fact, in *The Wizard of Oz* (1939), color is used to represent the world of the imagination (an imagined as distinct from a real world). To illustrate the disparity between the real and the imagined, the Kansas scenes (reality) were photographed in sepia and the Oz scenes (fantasy) in color. Thus, to say that a color film is more "realistic" than one in black and white is to give color a power it does not possess: namely, the power to determine how lifelike an image is. Oliver Stone's *Natural Born Killers* (1994), one of the most violent movies ever made, alternates between color and black and white. Stone deliberately disorients audiences accustomed to color by forcing them to see two different worlds: in one, blood is red; in the other, it is black. To a generation that grew up with color television and color film, violence in monochrome may seem too remote to be real. The sight of blood-splattered walls in black and white has a distancing effect: dark splotches on a white surface are not blood; in fact, they look like something created by a young artist infatuated with abstract expressionism. To a generation that grew up with black-and-white photography and film, violence in color may seem painterly, with red being just another color on the artist's palette. Regardless, blood has been spilled; whether it is blood drained of color or blood oozing red is irrelevant. Realism and color are not synonymous.

That certain contemporary directors chose to film in black and white when they could have worked in color is further evidence that realism and color are not synonymous. Realism is basically truth portrayed in the medium chosen by the artist. But artistic truth is fidelity to a vision of reality, not necessarily to "the real" in the sense of what exists whether or not we think about it. A dreary Texas town still has color, no matter how drab it seems. However, a filmmaker might think that drabness would be better rendered in black and white than in color. If such a filmmaker decides to use monochrome, as Peter Bogdanovich did in *The Last Picture Show*, the question is not whether he should have used color but whether he achieved what he wanted by using black and white. Set in the early 1950s, *The Last Picture Show* depicts life in a small Texas town, where the only escape from a boring existence is the local movie theater. Since Bogdanovich wanted not only to capture the look of a dying town but also to give the town and the film a 1950s look, he decided on black and white.

When Steven Spielberg decided to make the film version of Thomas Keneally's *Schindler's List* (1993), he was at a point in his career where he could make it in whatever way he chose. Spielberg chose black and white for virtually the entire film, believing that no movie about the Holocaust, the darkest event in twentieth-century history, could be made in any other way. Still, there is color at the beginning as the Sabbath candles are lit. The color, however, is short-lived; one of the candles melts, leaving darkness where there once was light. On two other occasions—each involving a young girl in a reddish coat—there is a trace of color in an otherwise black-and-white shot. The girl, Genia, is hardly even a character, but Spielberg uses her as a symbol of the six million Holocaust victims, some of whom are not even known by name. The first time we see Genia, the color of her coat stands out against the stark monochrome. Spielberg seems to be calling attention to the ambivalent nature of red, which suggests both blood, the animating source, and death, the extinction of that source. When we first see Genia, she is alive; later, her body, identified only by the color of her coat, is seen on top of a pile of corpses. Full color returns with the epilogue in the Jerusalem cemetery where Oskar Schindler is buried, as we see some of the Jews whom Schindler succeeded in saving.

Alfred Hitchcock's first color film was *Rope* (1948), in which two young men, influenced by Nietzsche's theory of the superman, lure a former classmate to their swank apartment where they strangle him, believing that superior beings such as themselves are not bound by moral laws. For this kind of movie, most directors in 1948 would have chosen black and white, which would have been warranted by the plot. Black and white would also have been cheaper. Hitchcock, however, chose color; as we have seen, he also chose to shoot the film in eight approximately ten-minute-long takes. The credits appear against a shot of a quiet New York street. The only hint that there is something amiss is the bold red lettering of the title, "Rope," which seems to have been splashed onto the screen. The combination of the title and the upscale neighborhood highlights the distinction between the subject matter (murder for thrills) and the setting (an elegantly furnished apartment with a superb view).

From 1948 to 1960, Hitchcock alternated between color and black and white. *Under Capricorn* (1949) was in color, while *Stage Fright* (1950), *Strangers on a Train* (1951), and *I Confess* (1953) were not. *Dial M for Murder* (1954), *Rear Window* (1954), *The Trouble with Harry* (1955), *To Catch a Thief* (1955), and the remake of *The Man Who Knew Too Much* (1956) were all in color, but *The Wrong Man* (1957) was not. *Vertigo* (1958) and *North by Northwest* (1959) were in color, but not *Psycho* (1960). The reasons were both personal and pragmatic. Hitchcock obviously thought that color would do more justice to Grace Kelly (who costarred in three of his films, *Dial M for Murder, Rear Window,* and *To Catch a Thief*) than black and white, although, ironically, Kelly received an Academy Award for her performance in a black-and-white film, *The Country Girl* (1954). *The Wrong Man* was based on the true story of a musician who was mistaken for a thief and wrongly incarcerated. Hitchcock planned the film as a grim semidocumentary with the kind of detachment ordinarily found in black-and-white newsreels. Although Hitchcock was still under contract to Paramount when he decided to make *Psycho*, the studio had no faith in the project; Hitchcock was forced to shoot the movie at Universal, where his television series, *Alfred Hitchcock Presents*, was filmed. If, visually, *Psycho* recalls Hitchcock's television series, it is because he used the crew from the show.

Vertigo represents Hitchcock's most creative use of color. In the film, Scottie (James Stewart), a retired police detective, is hired by Gavin Elster, a former college acquaintance, to trail Elster's wife, Madeleine, who is supposedly possessed by the spirit of her great-grandmother Carlotta Valdes. The plot is incredibly complicated: the Madeleine Scottie is following is not Elster's wife but an impostor Elster has hired to establish an alibi after he does away with his real wife. Scottie becomes obsessed with the bogus Madeleine (Kim Novak), whose colors are red and green. Madeleine is mesmerized by a portrait of Carlotta wearing a red stone necklace. Crucial scenes occur in the redwood forest. Even earlier, the main title is a study in red: a woman's eye peers out of a red frame as spirals emanate from the iris. When Scottie sees Madeleine, it is in a San Francisco restaurant with striking red wallpaper; she is wearing a black gown with a green stole. She also drives a green Jaguar. Hitchcock is again exploiting the ambivalence of color: red, with its evocations of fire, excitement, danger, passion, experience (the Red Knight) as opposed to innocence, and even death (the Red Death); green, which symbolizes life, fertility, growth, hope, and particularly rebirth. Elster's Madeleine does indeed die, but Scottie's Madeleine does not. She appears to have been reborn in the person of a young woman by the name of Judy (also played by Novak), whom Scottie encounters on a street in San Francisco. Thinking that she would be free to lead her own life after participating in Elster's masquerade (and never believing she would ever see Scottie again), Judy, the bogus Madeleine, finds herself as attracted to Scottie as he is to her.

Madeleine may have died, but her colors haven't. When Scottie first sees Judy, she is wearing a green dress. Judy lives at a hotel, where at night a neon sign gives off a greenish glow. Gradually, Scottie makes Judy over until she looks as much like Madeleine as possible. Scottie learns the truth only when Judy puts on the red stone necklace, which apparently Elster had given her when she was pretending to be Madeleine. Significantly, the moment of truth occurs in the redwood forest, the scene of *Vertigo*'s tragic climax.

Color, then, can be simply part of the way a movie is made or it can be used creatively by filmmakers like Hitchcock, who think creatively. Although the heroine of Hitchcock's *Marnie* has suppressed all memory of a murder she committed as a child, the guilt persists in the form of an intense aversion to red. Instinctively, she removes red gladioli from a vase and replaces them with white mums. A drop of red ink on her white blouse sends her rushing to the washroom; the red polka dots on a jockey's uniform petrify her. Not until the end of the film do we learn that Marnie's aversion to red is the result of her having struck a sailor with a poker to protect her prostitute mother from possible harm.

The title character in Federico Fellini's *Juliet of the Spirits* (1965) is a

Vertigo's (1958) tragic climax in the bell tower after Scottie (James Stewart) discovers that Judy (Kim Novak) is not what she seems to be. *(Courtesy MOMA/FSA)*

wife whose fantasies are dominated by erotic reds. When we first see Juliet, she is trying on a red wig; then she sets the table with red candles. When she visits a clairvoyant, she wears a red scarf. Yet red is not her color; it is the color of the women of her fantasies. At the end of the film, Juliet reverts to white, the color that typifies the kind of person she is.

In *Carrie* (1976), the title character is a high-school senior with telekinetic powers. Her mother is a religious fanatic, and both have reddish hair. When Carrie menstruates for the first time, she thinks she is bleeding to death. Her naïveté makes her an object of derision to her classmates, who humiliate her publicly at the senior prom by dropping a bucket of pig's blood on her. The blood reddens Carrie's pink dress, and Carrie literally sees red. Her revenge, as one might suspect, is appropriately bloody.

Red also predominates in Nicholas Ray's *Rebel Without a Cause* (1956), the film that gave James Dean his first starring role. Despite the title, the three main characters—Jim (Dean), Judy (Natalie Wood), and Plato (Sal Mineo)—who bond together have a reason to rebel: parental indifference. In Jim's case, it was a weak father and a domineering mother; in Judy's, an affectionless father; in Plato's, the absence of a father, which caused him to seek a surrogate in Jim. Red has always been the rebel's color; *Jezebel*'s Julie Marsden was certainly rebelling against convention when she insisted on wearing red to the ball. In *Rebel Without a Cause*, the credits are in red; when Judy is first seen, she is wearing a red coat and bright-red lipstick. Despite his meekness and emotional instability, Plato even tries to play the rebel by wearing red socks. Jim dons a red windbreaker during the "chickie run," a dangerous coming-of-age ritual in which teenage males prove their manhood by driving their cars to the edge of a bluff. When Plato is killed, Jim uses the windbreaker as a shroud, placing it on his friend to suggest that at least Plato died a rebel.

Another film that used red, but in a radically different way, is *American Beauty* (1999), which features one of the most dysfunctional families ever to appear on the screen: Lester Burnham (Kevin Spacey), a husband and father, who, in addition to masturbating in bed with his wife and in the shower, fantasizes about his daughter's friend Angela (Mena Suvari), whom he would like to seduce; Lester's wife, Carolyn (Annette Benning), who tries to hide the rot within her household by planting American Beauty roses in her picture-book yard; and their daughter, Jane (Thora Birch), who is so repelled by her father that she would like to see him killed. Then there is the family next door: a homophobic retired Marine colonel; his wife, whose anguish is so intense that she barely speaks; and their voyeuristic son, who deals drugs and delights in videotaping the Burnhams, especially Jane. Red imagery begins with the title in red lettering against a background that looks like a home movie. The alternation between traditional cinematography and home video occurs sporadically, suggesting two different views of reality, each of which is created by a different medium (celluloid as opposed to videotape).

As in *Vertigo*, red is ambivalent in *American Beauty*, in which it symbolizes vitality, passion, and death. When Lester sees Angela at a basketball game, he envisions her unzipping her cheerleader's uniform, as rose petals pour out of it. Later, he imagines Angela lounging in a tub of rose petals, waiting for him to bathe her. The bloodletting at the end comes as no surprise; Jane's wish that her father be killed and Lester's voice-over prologue announcing that he would be dead within the year prepare us for the climax, which occurs in the Burnham kitchen. A vase filled with red roses is on the counter. Lester is seated at the kitchen table, as a gun appears against his head. A shot is fired, and blood spills across the table and onto the floor.

American Beauty represents a deliberate choice of color to complement the narrative: a wife can make American Beauty roses bloom gloriously in her yard by using eggshells and Miracle-Gro, but she cannot work a similar miracle inside the house. The film also juxtaposes two ways of looking at reality: through the lens of a motion picture camera and that of a videotape recorder. There is a crucial scene in the film when Ricky (Wes Bentley), the colonel's son, who is infatuated with Jane, shows her what he considers to be the most beautiful sight he has ever filmed: a white bag

Lester's (Kevin Spacey) fantasy of Angela (Mena Suvari) in her rose petal bath in *American Beauty* (1999). *(Courtesy MOMA/FSA)*

blown across a gravelly pavement strewn with dead leaves and then against a red brick wall, rising and falling in the wind. To Ricky, the combination of the bag, the wind, and the leaves resulted in art, causing him to exclaim, "Sometimes there's so much beauty in the world I feel like I can't take it." What Ricky has recorded is random beauty; without the bag, the setting, or the wind, there would have been no picture, and therefore no beauty. What has happened is that, without willing it, Ricky was in the right place at the right time, with the right elements in place to provide him with the image. It was different when the director, Sam Mendes, and his production designer, Naomi Shohan, made artistic choices as to how red would be used in the film. Ricky couldn't change the color of the wall; a filmmaker, however, can change anything because he or she controls the entire palette. But truly creative filmmakers use color for more than mere embellishment; they use it to direct the eye to what the script is saying verbally but cannot say visually; they use color to suggest, characterize, and forge symbolic connections. Yet they can use black and white for the same purposes. An astute filmgoer will know when color is decorative or functional, and when monochrome is perfunctory or motivated.

Colorization

Colorization is the use of a computer-aided process to apply color to black-and-white movies. Colorization requires the film to be analyzed shot by shot and scene by scene so that the colorization is consistent. The colors of the opening frames must be determined first by consulting sketches, memos, and set designs if they are available. Once the colors for the opening frames are selected, a computer applies the same colors throughout, varying the hues in terms of the lighting pattern in the original. Still, there is no guarantee that a color sketch provided for a black-and-white film would be valid if the studio had decided to shoot the film in color. Thus, the claim that a colorized version of a black-and-white film would have proved satisfactory if the filmmaker had the opportunity to shoot it in color is false.

The foes of colorization—and there have been many, including James Stewart, Burt Lancaster, Woody Allen, Frank Capra, and Martin Ritt—contend that colorization vitiates the principle of creative choice, which is essential to art. When a studio chose to film a movie in black and white rather than in color, that choice entailed several factors, the chief one being, no doubt, the cost. During Hollywood's golden age, there was no aesthetic policy that dictated what kinds of movies should be made in black and white as opposed to color. One cannot say, for example, that color is more suited to westerns than black and white, since some of John Ford's classic westerns were photographed in black and white: *Stagecoach* (1939), *My Darling Clementine* (1946), *Fort Apache* (1948), *Wagonmaster* (1950), *The Man Who Shot Liberty Valance* (1962). Nor was color considered mandatory for musicals; the great musicals of the 1930s, notably those starring Fred Astaire and Ginger Rogers, were black and white. Color was expensive and was not lavished on every film, only on those the studio deemed important enough to warrant it or on those that needed color to realize fully their dramatic potential. *Gone with the Wind* was intended to be in color; another film set in the South and released the previous year, *Jezebel*, was not.

When the decision is made to shoot a film in color, everything—costumes, lighting, makeup, settings—is planned and executed in terms of that choice. That choice, however, was to shoot the film in a color process such as Technicolor, Trucolor, Warnercolor, and so on. Colorization is not a color process; it is a computer-aided process that, in the absence of any guiding intelligence, allows a computer to make the choices that should be the prerogative of the filmmaker.

LIGHTING THE IMAGE

The classic Hollywood film is an example of **three-point lighting**—key, fill, and back lights used in combination to light the subject. These are not the only lights; still, three-point lighting is a standard lighting scheme that, if understood properly, explains how lighting can affect one's perception of a character or a setting.

The **key light**, the principal source of illumination, leaves shadows if it is used alone. For this reason, another light is necessary to fill in the areas the key light has left unlit and to soften the shadows it has cast: the **fill light**, an auxiliary light that is softer and less intense, placed opposite the

High-key lighting in *Meet Me in St. Louis* (1944). *(Courtesy MOMA/FSA)*

key light on the other side of the camera. But even a combination of key and fill light is not sufficient if a sense of depth is desired. Hence, a **back light,** placed above and behind the subject, is required. The back light alone would merely produce a silhouette. But in combination with the key and fill lights, the back light separates the subject from its environment, thereby creating a feeling of depth.

In terms of effect, lighting can be categorized as high-key and low-key. A low-contrast ratio of key and fill light will result in an image of al-

Anatomy of Film

Low-key lighting in *Crossfire* (1947). *(Courtesy WCFTR)*

most uniform brightness, or what is called **high-key lighting,** the kind used in musicals, comedies, and for scenes of tranquillity and peace. Conversely, a **high-contrast** ratio of key and fill light will result in low-key lighting and create a shadowy effect and a nighttime aura, often with intensely white faces against an onyx-black background. Directors of horror films, melodramas, and film noir (a type of melodrama where passions run high in urban settings that are grimy and often fogbound and where streets are dark, mean, and continually rain-slick) prefer low-key lighting for its shadows and its strong contrast of light and darkness.

In addition to these two general categories of lighting, there are five other types, distinguished by the angle from which the light source illuminates the subject: front, back, top, side, and bottom. Front lighting has a softening effect that makes whatever we are viewing seem more attractive than it actually is. Front lighting of the face creates an ageless look, but it also robs the face of character. **Back lighting,** as we have seen, adds depth and brings out subtleties of design and pattern. When a character is backlit, as Esther (Barbra Streisand) is when she sings "Evergreen" at the end of *A Star Is Born* (1976), a halo-like aura is produced that gives an

Film, Space, and Image

Back lighting in *Sunset Boulevard* (1950). The back light is coming from a projector during the screening of a silent film starring Norma Desmond (Gloria Swanson), who, in the middle of it, stands up and with arm raised vows to return to the screen. *(Courtesy WCFTR. Copyright © 1949, Paramount Pictures Corporations. All rights reserved.)*

ethereal quality. Similarly, **top lighting** creates an atmosphere of youthfulness or spirituality, as is the case in *The Song of Bernadette*, where it emphasizes Bernadette's saintliness. **Side lighting** leaves the subject half in light, half in shadow; thus, it can denote a split personality, a morally ambiguous character, or a femme fatale. Greta Garbo and Marlene Dietrich were often photographed in this fashion. **Bottom lighting** gives the subject a sinister air; it was the kind of lighting D. W. Griffith employed in *Dream Street* (1921) to bring out the villainy of Sway Wan.

In a black-and-white film, the interplay of light and darkness can produce visual symbolism. Throughout *Citizen Kane*, Thompson, the reporter trying to decipher the meaning of Kane's dying word ("Rosebud!") is always seen in shadow. He is literally in the dark, and remains in that state throughout the film. Just as darkness can denote ignorance, so light can intimate knowledge. When Thompson enters the Thatcher Memorial

Library to read the memoirs of Kane's guardian, shafts of light illuminate the mausoleum-like room. Perhaps the memoirs will explain the meaning of "Rosebud." But the light is deceptive, and Thompson leaves the library as much in the dark as ever.

Thompson is not the only character who suffers from ignorance. Although Thompson is ignorant of the meaning of "Rosebud," Kane is ignorant of himself. When Kane delivers his Declaration of Principles, promising to be a "fighting and tireless champion" of the people, his face is in darkness. Kane does not know that he will never live up to his declaration, and the lighting states as much.

Lighting is also used effectively in Preston Sturges's *Sullivan's Travels* (1941). In that film, some black parishioners invite the white prisoners of a local chain gang to their church to watch a movie. When we see the prisoners making their way to the church, they are in darkness; for a moment, they look like black men. The lighting establishes a bond between the black congregation and the prisoners; it also reinforces the film's theme that moviegoing is a form of brotherhood that erases all distinctions, including racial ones. Movies are the great leveler; in the dark, everyone is equal.

SPECIAL EFFECTS/VISUAL EFFECTS (SFX, VFX)

Morphing—a computer-graphics effect that allows the filmmaker to change one shape into another (a circle into a square, a person into an animal)—might seem to challenge our perception of reality. So does another form of synthetic image reproduction, in which, for example, a fictional character is shown in conversation with a historical figure whose image has been obtained from a film archive or some other outside source. The result, **virtual reality,** is, like any innovation, a novelty when first seen. It worked well in *Forrest Gump*, in which Forrest is shown interacting with Presidents Kennedy, Johnson, and Nixon, and John Lennon of the Beatles. The reason is that Forrest, who gave every indication of being a loser, eventually triumphs by going from obscurity to fame, which is a familiar version of the American dream. However, the danger is that once audiences catch on to the device, they will dismiss it as a gimmick, one that gives the filmmaker a power that the pre–digital age directors never had. The extent to which morphing and synthetic image reproduction can engage an audience depends upon how intelligently it is handled. Far more realistic is the digital placement of an actor in a disaster scene. First, the actor is photographed at the site; then the disaster is photographed; finally, the actor is situated digitally in the scene. Despite the perennial interest in special effects, they can only be a means to an end; if the end is to falsify reality, mock history, or compensate for a mediocre script that is devoid of human emotions, special effects are the equivalent of trick photography: gimmickry, not art.

Special effects have been such an integral part of moviemaking that they no longer even seem special. **Visual effects** is now the more common term. We can go back to the time of Georges Méliès, who delighted audiences by showing characters vanish in a puff of smoke or by having one object (or person) turn into another. Méliès used such effects for their ability to astound and amaze, as well as for their storytelling potential; the effects in *A Trip to the Moon* are actually part of the plot. Even though we know how Méliès achieved his effects, we still marvel at the result. The transformations were accomplished through **stop-motion photography,** in which one frame at a time is exposed, allowing adjustments to be made between frames and producing the illusion that one object has turned into another or has disappeared.

The best filmmakers knew that visual effects were part of the narrative. When Rouben Mamoulian decided that in his production of *Dr. Jekyll and Mr. Hyde* Henry Jekyll would turn into Mr. Hyde on-screen, the transformation was accomplished by dissolving a series of shots of Fredric March (Jekyll) in various stages of makeup. Jekyll's decision to take the transforming potion occurs immediately after he has encountered the prostitute Ivy (Miriam Hopkins). Mamoulian slowly dissolves a shot of Ivy's bare leg dangling over a shot of Jekyll and his friend walking along a dark London street. Knowing that he could never enjoy Ivy's favors as the respectable Dr. Jekyll, he prepares the potion that turns him into Mr. Hyde. Although the transformation may look like special effects, it was based on Mamoulian's decision to combine the arousal of Jekyll's passions with the only way they can be satisfied: by Jekyll's becoming his other self. Mamoulian also decided to accompany the transformation with a montage of images swirling across the screen, suggesting what was going through Jekyll's mind while the potion was taking effect.

Unless effects, whether they are called special or visual, are integrated with the narrative, they are the equivalent of spectacle. In the *Poetics*, Aristotle considered spectacle (any theatrical effect appealing more to the eye than to the mind) to be the least important element of drama. Today, anyone interested in learning how certain effects are achieved in a film can (1) log on to the film's Web site; (2) query a movie critic such as Roger Ebert, who answers questions in his syndicated column; (3) watch for documentaries on cable television, such as *Cinema Secrets* on American Movie Classics (AMC); or (4) read *American Cinematographer* and the *ICG Magazine*, the publication of the International Cinematographers

Guild. However, even though you may have discovered "how they did it," you still may know nothing about it. All you know is the technology that produced the effects; the next step is to determine whether the effects have been designed to dazzle the viewer perhaps because the film has little else to offer; or whether they function as narrative strategies that advance the plot and give it momentum.

Audiences seeing *King Kong* upon its release in 1933 marveled at how lifelike Kong was, even though they knew he wasn't real. That there were six eighteen-inch models of Kong, along with a twenty-foot model with a crane-operated arm, was unknown at the time; nor did moviegoers realize that the (then daring) scene of Kong pulling off pieces of Ann's (Fay Wray) tattered dress and sniffing them was miniature rear projection, in which a scaled set is placed in front of a screen on which live action is projected. According to *King Kong*'s codirector, Merrian C. Cooper, "a movie was first taken of [Wray] alone while invisible wires pulled off her clothes. Then the miniature Kong was placed on a set built on a waist-high platform . . . on which miniature trees, ferns and plaster of Paris rocks had been arranged. Back of this the movie of Fay Wray was projected and Kong's movements made to correspond with it."[7] The scene does not call attention to itself the way so many contemporary effects scenes do because it is integral to Kong's humanization as he makes the transition from beast to lover and finally protector. Clearly, Kong is perplexed by the strange creature he holds in his hand; he is also mildly aroused by her. If generations of moviegoers have thought of Kong as human, even to the point of weeping at his death, it is because Cooper and special effects genius Willis O'Brien used film technology to further the plot, not to amaze the audience.

Digital technology, however, has made it possible for filmmakers to achieve effects that would have been impossible in the 1930s. When Universal decided to make *The Invisible Man* (1933), based on H. G. Wells's novel of the same name, it was relatively simple to simulate invisibility. Wires held up objects, making it seem as if they were suspended in midair; an actor wearing black tights and a black headpiece was photographed against a black background. If the actor wore a suit over his tights, the result was a suit without a body. Of course, it was more complicated to get the suit to move around. That called for an **optical printer,** a camera-projector arrangement that "rephotographs" previously exposed images, making it possible to mask off a particular part of the frame and print in the special effects (e.g., the moving clothes).

Computers have totally changed the creation of special effects. Compare *The Invisible Man* with a recent film on the same theme, *The Hollow Man* (2000), in which Kevin Bacon disappears piecemeal; or, rather, his

Kong with Fay Wray in one hand as he dispenses with a pterodactyl with the other in *King Kong* (1933), a marvel of special effects. *(Courtesy MOMA/FSA)*

digital equivalent does. No optical printer could have achieved such a transmogrification. What we are witnessing, however, is the triumph of technology, not great moviemaking. It is hard to imagine *The Hollow Man's* ever achieving the classic status of *The Invisible Man.*

There will always be effects-driven movies. *The Matrix* (1999), for example, which imagines a computer-controlled world, could never have been made without them, nor could *X-Men* (2000), based on Marvel Comics characters. Although we may marvel at the visual effects in *X-Men,* they were integral to the plot. Audiences do not turn out for a movie about mutants whose powers are narrated but never shown. Similarly, there was no way the storm in *The Perfect Storm* (2000)—in which, among other awesome sights, a helicopter falls into the water, and a boat turns over and then upright—could have been created except digitally. Audiences expecting a "perfect storm" were not disappointed, even though the human factor may have been submerged in the process. When visual effects become the prime reason for seeing a movie, they make it difficult for audiences to care about the characters or the plot, since both have become the servants of technology. It is like fireworks on July 4, which, if they are impressive enough, can rob the day of its historical significance; or a play that is so elaborately produced that all one remembers are the sets and costumes.

Certainly there have been times when digital effects were able not only to cut down on production costs but also to save the production. When Oliver Reed died during the shooting of *Gladiator* (2000), his image was digitized into the scenes for which his character was needed so the film could be completed. Visual effects tend to call attention to themselves, regardless of the form they take. However, when effects advance the plot, moving it along like dialogue, we notice them, but within the context of the film. Thus, the storm that lashes the island at the climax of John Ford's *The Hurricane* (1937), leaving devastation in its wake, is presented not just as a force of nature but as a force of nature affecting human beings, some of whom take refuge in a church (which, tragically, cannot sustain the impact of the storm), while others are spared so that they can go on to better lives. Even today, *The Hurricane* is a moving experience, because Ford subordinated the visual effects to the story he wanted to tell, making them only one part of the mise-en-scène.

Whether **digital cinema** (film that is computer-readable) is the wave of the future is hard to say. Its advocates, who sound like the apostles for a paperless world, argue that films shot digitally and projected digitally have greater visual clarity and superior sound. Independent filmmakers are particularly eager for a digital future, since it would make the entire process quicker and cheaper. Editing would become simpler. Footage could be accessed easily; transitions such as wipes and dissolves could be added or deleted without affecting the original footage. However, it is impossible to imagine technology improving the quality of film art, which is quite different from the quality of the image or the sound. As T. S. Eliot wrote in "Tradition and the Individual Talent": "Art never improves, but . . . the material of art is never quite the same." One cannot say, for example, that *Citizen Kane* is a greater film than *The Birth of a Nation*, only that Orson Welles had more technology at his disposal than did D. W. Griffith. Yet each produced a masterpiece, working with the available technology. Whether in a hundred years digital cinema can boast of a treasury of classics equal to that of celluloid is problematic. Still, one must not be closed-minded about change. Innovation is preferable to stagnation.

NOTES

[1] Lee R. Bobker, with Louise Marinis, *Making Movies: From Script to Screen* (New York: Harcourt Brace Jovanovich, 1973), 209.

[2] Karel Reisz and Gavin Miller, *The Technique of Film Editing*, 2nd ed. (New York: Focal Press, 1968), 84.

[3] Ibid., 277.

[4]"Film Editors Forum," *Film Comment* 13 (March–April 1977): 24.

[5]Ibid.

[6]Edward Dmytryk, *On Film Editing: An Introduction to the Art of Film Construction* (Boston: Focal Press, 1984), 145.

[7]As quoted in John Bronson, *Movie Magic: The Story of Special Effects in the Cinema* (New York: New American Library, 1976), 159.

CHAPTER

Film Genres

4

S o far we have been talking about techniques, using examples from such films as *My Darling Clementine, Detour,* and *Carrie.* While these films illustrate certain principles of moviemaking, they also illustrate certain types of films. Each of these films represents a particular genre: *Clementine,* the western; *Detour,* film noir; and *Carrie,* the horror film.

When English professors speak of a **genre,** they mean a literary form with certain conventions and patterns that, through repetition, have become so familiar that readers expect similar elements in works of the same type. In Periclean Athens and Elizabethan England, the two great ages of tragedy, audiences attending a performance of *Oedipus the King* or *Hamlet* were not witnessing a wholly new dramatic form. The protagonist embarking on a quest that will result in his or her undoing was already a familiar one. Equally well established was the tragic progression from ignorance to self-knowledge and from prosperity to catastrophe.

The conventions of tragedy (protagonist with a tragic flaw, fatal mistake, reversal of fortune, and the like) appear in all tragedies; they do not, however, always appear in the same way. The Elizabethan tragic heroes, for example, exercise free will to a greater degree than did their Greek counterparts. Modern tragedy, on the other hand, seems to be deterministic, with characters such as Blanche DuBois of Tennessee Williams's *A Streetcar Named Desire* and Willy Loman of Arthur Miller's *Death of a Salesman* destroyed by forces over which they have no control. Yet *Death of a Salesman* is as much a tragedy as *Oedipus* or *Hamlet*, even though it may not be written in verse and the protagonist may not be of royal descent. The same basic elements that make *Hamlet* a tragedy also make *Salesman* one.

There are also tragedies that blur into melodrama, which also features flawed characters who make tragic mistakes. But in melodrama the characters represent the extremes of good and evil, chance seems more important than causality, and the action turns violent or grotesque for theatrical or shock effect. Like most distinctions, the tragedy-melodrama one is theoretical. Some of the greatest tragedies contain melodramatic elements. Shakespeare avoids stereotypical characters in *Macbeth*, but he was not averse to including such melodramatic touches as witches, apparitions, the onstage murder of a child, a sleepwalking scene, and an ending that calls for Macbeth's head to be displayed on a pole. In Orson Welles's 1948 movie version of *Macbeth*, the melodramatic scenes are intensified by the darkly lit interiors, windswept heaths, and eerie incantations of the witches, and Lady Macbeth's suicide leap from a cliff. *Macbeth* is undeniably a tragedy, but it has its moments of sensationalism, as does Sophocles' *Oedipus the King*, with the messenger's graphic description of Oedipus's self-blinding. If genres can intermingle in literature, why should film be any different?

Genres are not monolithic. Although tragedy is clearly a genre, there are various kinds of tragedy: Greek, Elizabethan, French neoclassical, historical, modern. As we have seen, there are also tragedies that veer off into melodrama. And there are various kinds of comedy: slapstick, bedroom farce, romantic comedy, drawing-room comedy, and Chekhovian comedy (which blends pathos and humor in a unique way). Similarly, mystery fiction can be subdivided into crime fiction, detective fiction (soft-boiled and hard-boiled), gothic fiction, espionage fiction, and the police procedural.

It is not easy, therefore, to pigeonhole a work of literature. While a long work of prose fiction can be classified as a novel, the crucial question is what kind of novel. Film genres are equally complex. Although some literary genres reappear in film, not all do. Comedy is itself a genre in literature, but not film, where genres tend to be more specific. Not every kind of comedy has succeeded on the screen. While a book can be written about drawing-room comedy and comedy of manners in the theater, one would be hard-pressed to produce one about the film equivalents. On the other hand, screwball comedy, which is not a type of theater, is a well-established film genre. Film genres—compared with, say, literary genres—are unique. Literary genres represent a hierarchy created by critics, while film genres represent the studios' response to the marketplace. By the sixteenth century, a hierarchy of literary forms had been established, beginning with the lowly pastoral and culminating in the lofty epic. While this particular hierarchy no longer exists, the mentality behind it does. There are still literary scholars who rank poetry above fiction and drama below it; there are others who would relegate the essay to the category of expository or informal prose and deny it literary status. In film, there is no hierarchy of genres; there are only types of movies that succeed and types that do not. (Traditionally, for example, sports films do not succeed, while horror films do.) Furthermore, genres that succeed in one era may not succeed in another unless they can adapt to the changing times. The woman's film was popular in the 1930s, and especially in the 1940s, when women constituted the majority of the moviegoing public. The woman's film still exists, as we shall see, but it is not what it was when stars like Bette Davis and Joan Crawford reigned supreme.

Finally, while the best examples of a film genre may be pure (e.g., *Stagecoach* is pure western, *Bringing Up Baby* [1938] is pure screwball, *Meet Me in St. Louis* [1944] is pure musical), there are also films that cross genres. Genre mixing occurs for various reasons, one being commercial: If whodunits, westerns, and comedies are successful, why not a western whodunit (Raoul Walsh's *Pursued* [1947]) or a comedy whodunit (Woody Allen's *Manhattan Murder Mystery* [1993])? A comic western like *Blazing Saddles* (1974) or *Wild Wild West* (1999)? A comic horror film like *Young Frankenstein* (1974)? The end of the world is no laughing matter, but director Stanley Kubrick must have thought it could be when he made *Dr. Strangelove, or: How I Learned to Stop Worrying and Love the Bomb* (1964). Mitchell Leisen's *Easy Living* (1937) is a screwball comedy that is implicitly critical of those who enjoyed "easy living" during the Great Depression and thus takes on overtones of the social-consciousness film. Some musicals end unhappily—for example, *Tonight and Every Night* (1944), *A Star Is Born* (the 1954 and 1975 versions), and Martin Scorsese's *New York, New York* (1977).

The point is not to come up with a definitive classification of a particular movie; categorizing a movie is not like categorizing a biological species. Nominally, *Pursued* is a western and *Dr. Strangelove* is science fiction. Genre-blending gives each a distinctive quality, so that one ends up saying, "Yes, *Pursued* is a western, but it also reminds me of a detective story"; "Yes, *Dr. Strangelove* is science fiction, but it's scary and hilarious at the same time"; and "Yes, *Blazing Saddles* is a western, but in the traditional western nobody passes gas—at least not on the screen." Rather, the point is to see how various kinds of movies have survived over the years by repeating, varying, or altering their conventions.

THE MUSICAL

The musical is a good genre with which to begin because its plot conventions are relatively simple. It is axiomatic that, in a musical, emotions are expressed, and the plot is advanced, through song and dance. Although this may seem self-evident, there are still moviegoers who look down on the musical because of its unreality. Historically, there has been some justification for this view: the lack of integration of song and action in many musicals results in a film in which the plot is constantly being interrupted for a production number. For example, in *Lady Be Good* (1941), there is no motivation for Eleanor Powell's tap dance except that Powell was a superb tap dancer whose role in the movie was minor but whose fans expected her to dance—which she did in a showstopping number.

Ideally, Eleanor Powell's tap dance should have been a natural outgrowth of the action, not a diversion. However, the seamless blending of song and narrative is rare in film musicals. Indeed, the early movie musicals were not integrated in the sense of constituting such an inseparable union of script and song that the musical sequences could not be rearranged without seriously altering the plot. In the musicals of the 1930s, the plots were thin; what is memorable about such musicals are the chic dancing of Fred Astaire and Ginger Rogers, and the production numbers in which the chorus formed intricate geometric patterns. We may have vivid memories of Astaire and Rogers dancing the carioca in *Flying Down to Rio* (1933), but few of us can reconstruct the plot.

Whether the first integrated musical was *On the Town* (1949) or *Singin' in the Rain* (1952) is a matter of debate. *On the Town* was based on a Broadway musical that was itself superbly integrated with music by Leonard Bernstein and a book by Betty Comden and Adolph Green. *Singin' in the Rain*, which was neither a Broadway show nor a play set to music, is something of a rarity: an original screenplay (also by Comden and Green) with songs that flow out of the action. Although the film is remembered for the title song, danced in the rain by Gene Kelly, the sequence is related to the plot: the boy is so in love with the girl that he dances for joy despite the elements.

If we remember that genres are not simple, we can better appreciate the diversity of the movie musical, which can assume various forms:

The revue. Although the stage revue was a popular form from the 1920s
through the mid-1950s, its amorphous nature (sketches interspersed

with song and dance) did not lend itself to film, where audiences require some kind of plot. When the Broadway revue *New Faces of 1952* was filmed, a wisp of a plot was added, but not enough to conceal the fact that the film was a photographed stage show. Some movie musicals (e.g., *Star Spangled Rhythm* [1942]; Vincente Minnelli's *Ziegfeld Follies* [1946]) were disguised revues that offered a number of stars an opportunity to do their specialty within a loosely plotted format.

The operetta. Most movie operettas have been adaptations of stage operettas (e.g., *Naughty Marietta* [1935]; *Bittersweet* [1940]; *The Student Prince* [1954]; *The Vagabond King* [1956]). Occasionally there is an operetta-like film such as Billy Wilder's *The Emperor Waltz* (1948) with a fairy-tale plot shored up by music, or *The Umbrellas of Cherbourg* (1964), in which everything, including the dialogue, is sung. Operettas, however, are rarely written for the screen.

The comedy with music. One of Paramount's most successful series was the Road movies of the 1940s and early 1950s, featuring Bing Crosby, Bob Hope, and Dorothy Lamour in zany adventures that took them across the world (for example, *Road to Singapore* [1940], *Road to Morocco* [1942], *Road to Utopia* [1945]). Since all three performers could sing, musical numbers were added, most having no relation to the plot, which itself had no relation to reality. Many of the so-called Elvis Presley musicals were really comedies and, in a few cases, dramas with music.

The drama with music. Neither a dramatic musical nor a musical drama, the drama with music is rarer than the comedy with music because it provides a true fusion of music and a serious story. In George Cukor's *A Star Is Born* (1954), a musical version of the 1937 nonmusical film about the price of Hollywood fame, the basic plot remained intact: a fading male star marries a newcomer, whose career skyrockets while his plummets. This remake, with Judy Garland and James Mason, includes some excellent musical numbers, all of which fit neatly into the action. The third version of *A Star Is Born* (1975) also had no choice but to feature music, but of a different sort: rock, because the main characters were now rock stars. A woman's career also eclipses a man's in another drama with music, *New York, New York*, in which the songs (the title song as well as standards of the 1940s) were expertly woven into the plot.

The show-business musical. Sometimes called the backstage musical, this type of film chronicles the joys and heartaches of show business. The backstage musical has five common plot pegs: the overnight sensation, breaking up the act, writing the song, the crucial song, and career versus marriage.

The overnight sensation is the "unknown" who substitutes for the star and achieves instant stardom. The best-known overnight sensation is Peggy Sawyer (Ruby Keeler), the understudy in *42nd Street* (1933), who is told by her director (Warner Baxter): "Sawyer, you're going out a youngster, but you've got to come back a star." She did, and a Hollywood cliché was born. The "Born in a Trunk" sequence in the 1954 *A Star Is Born* is both a parody of, and a touching tribute to, the overnight-sensation movie.

The breakup theme usually gets under way when one member of an act is hired for a Broadway show but the other isn't. In *The Jolson Story* (1946), Steve Martin (William Demarest) stays in vaudeville while his protégé, Al Jolson (Larry Parks), goes on to become a star. A family act breaks up when the children go their separate ways in *There's No Business Like Show Business* (1954); a husband-and-wife team in *The Barkleys of Broadway* (1949), when the wife decides to do serious drama instead of musical comedy; a marriage, in *The Jolson Story*, when a husband prefers an adoring audience to his wife.

Several backstage musicals revolve around pairing the right lyrics with the right melody. This kind of movie assumes that the audience knows the actual lyrics and will therefore be amused by all the difficulties the lyricists are having: the songwriters working out the lyrics to "Lady Be Good" in *Lady Be Good*; the lyricist trying to find the "three little words" for the title song in *Three Little Words* (1950).

Some musicals feature a crucial song heard so often that it becomes inseparable from the plot (e.g., "You'll Never Know" in *Hello Frisco, Hello* [1943]). Sometimes the crucial song is sung either incorrectly or at the wrong tempo until the singer is forced to sing it correctly. In *Coney Island* (1943), Betty Grable ruins "Cuddle Up a Little Closer" with her exaggerated gestures until George Montgomery handcuffs her, thereby forcing her to tone down her delivery and sing the song as a ballad.

The backstage musical often climaxes in a big production number that illustrates another convention of the genre: the production number, which seems to be taking place in a Broadway theater, has been filmed on a Hollywood soundstage because no theater had facilities that were comparable to Hollywood's.

No Broadway theater could ever have accommodated the winding ramp down which Rita Hayworth rushes in *Cover Girl* (1944) or the gigantic platform on which Frank Sinatra sings "Ol' Man River" at the end of *Till the Clouds Roll By* (1946). A movie musical that is an adaptation of a stage musical clearly shows the difference between a soundstage and a theater stage. Vincente Minnelli's movie version of

Lerner and Loewe's *Brigadoon* (1954) was shot entirely on an MGM soundstage. In both the stage and screen versions, the lovers walk through the heather on the hill as they sing the duet "The Heather on the Hill." No stage designer could have created such spectacular heather, nor could there ever have been as much of it on the stage as there is in the movie.

The dance musical. In the theater, a dance musical is one in which the cast functions as a kind of chorus that both sings and dances. *A Chorus Line* and *Cats* are both dance musicals in the sense of lacking real stars and appearing to have been choreographed rather than staged. In film, a dance musical is one in which dance is a means of furthering the action as well as expressing the characters' emotions and psychological states (for example, *The Red Shoes* [1948]). A film featuring only dancing (for example, Gene Kelly's *Invitation to the Dance* [1956]) is a rarity; it will attract ballet lovers but few others. Even *The Red Shoes*, arguably the best film about ballet ever made, has a memorable plot. More common is the song and dance musical, which has a discernible plot, unlike, say, *Cats*, which has none at all.

While every conceivable kind of dance (Charleston, fox-trot, waltz, jitterbug, conga, rumba, hula, and so forth) has been featured in movie musicals, the courting dance is the most familiar. Its effectiveness depends on star chemistry. In the Astaire-Rogers musicals, the chemistry is complementary. Astaire courted an aloof Rogers, who gradually responded as he encircled her, wooing her with every step. Their dancing was the epitome of Art Deco, stylized and sleek. When Astaire danced with Rita Hayworth in *You Were Never Lovelier* (1942) and later with the long-legged Cyd Charisse in *The Band Wagon* (1953) and *Silk Stockings* (1957), the dancing became more erotic, since Astaire had more sensuous partners. When Gene Kelly and Rita Hayworth danced to the music of "Long Ago and Far Away" in *Cover Girl*, their dancing took on elements of yearning, as if each were looking for the dream lover suggested by the lyrics ("I dreamed a dream one day").

The two great exponents of the dance musical, Fred Astaire and Gene Kelly, had diametrically opposed styles. Astaire was cool and aristocratic; he was born for top hat, white tie, and tails. On the other hand, Kelly, who once played ice hockey and taught gymnastics, was more athletic. Yet Kelly could work aspects of ballet into his dancing, which was something Astaire couldn't do. Astaire, for example, could never tap-dance on roller skates as Kelly did so brilliantly in *It's Always Fair Weather* (1955). Although each performer represented a different style, together they epitomized the golden age of the Hollywood musical.

Fred Astaire (in his signature clothes) and Ginger Rogers, the musical film's most popular dancing team, in *Swing Time* (1936), with a score by Jerome Kern. *(Courtesy MOMA/FSA)*

Gene Kelly, who combined athleticism with a ballet dancer's gracefulness, and Rita Hayworth in *Cover Girl* (1944). *(Courtesy Sony Pictures Entertainment and MOMA/FSA)*

Whether or not the traditional musical will return to its glory days is debatable. When the studio system ended in the 1960s, actors were no longer groomed for certain types of films. Judy Garland, Rita Hayworth, and Betty Grable became stars in the 1940s because their respective studios (MGM, Columbia, Twentieth Century-Fox) put them in films that revealed their special talents. The principle was simple: the script is tailored to the star. Since Garland, Hayworth, and Grable could sing and dance, they were cast in musicals that allowed them to do both. Esther Williams was a passable singer but a superb swimmer, whose talents were highlighted in water ballets. Ann Miller's specialty was tap, not the easiest form of dance to work into a plot. But that rarely mattered in an Ann Miller musical. In *On the Town*, Miller, playing an anthropologist, started tapping away in New York's Museum of Natural History—an action that, under ordinary circumstances, would have had her removed from the building.

The present lack of interest in movie musicals is due to the demise of the studio system, under which actors were cultivated for their singing and dancing abilities; Hollywood's failure to replace the great musical stars of the past; and the dearth of original Broadway musicals that can be adapted for the screen. The musical stars of the present are rockers and pop artists, who dominate MTV and VH1 and regularly appear in concert. Even when some of them try to cross over into film (for example, Diana Ross, Bette Midler, Madonna), they fail to make an impact because audiences do not associate them with "the movies." Finally, Broadway, which in the past provided Hollywood with so many memorable musicals, has reverted to totally plotless spectacles (*Cats*), minimally plotless ones (*Phantom of the Opera*), or revivals of shows that have already been made into movies (*The King and I; Guys and Dolls; Cabaret; Annie Get Your Gun; Kiss Me, Kate; Bells Are Ringing; The Music Man;* etc.). When Andrew Lloyd Webber's hit musical *Evita* was turned into a movie in 1996, it flopped despite the presence of Madonna as Eva Perón. Ironically, the movie musicals of the 1930s and 1940s still enjoy great popularity on television, particularly on such cable stations as American Movie Classics (AMC) and Turner Classic Movies (TCM), which suggests that there is more of an audience for Hollywood's golden age of musicals on the small screen than there is for contemporary ones on the big screen.

On the other hand, genres never die; they simply reinvent themselves, emerging in other forms. Currently, the musical of choice is the animated musical, which has an interesting history. The first full-length animated feature, *Snow White and the Seven Dwarfs* (1937), was also a musical that introduced such perennial favorites as "Whistle While You Work" and "Some Day My Prince Will Come." Since then, there have been frequent attempts to create not so much animated musicals as animated films with songs (e.g., *Pinocchio* [1940], with its famous "When You Wish upon a Star") that are integrated with the story. There have also been attempts to combine animation with live action and music, such as *Anchors Aweigh* (1945), *Song of the South* (1946), and *Mary Poppins* (1964). If the animation is realistic enough, audiences will accept it in the same way they accept comic-strip characters as stand-ins for real people; and if the score is at least on a par with the classic Hollywood musical, no one can claim that the musical has died—only that it has undergone a sea change.

The team of Alan Menken (music) and Howard Ashman (lyrics) must be credited with the revival of interest in the animated musical. Their collaboration has resulted in a form that was traditionally considered to be little more than a full-length animated feature with songs. Although Menken and Ashman changed that perception with *The Little Mermaid* (1988), it was really *Beauty and the Beast* (1992), the first animated feature to receive an Academy Award nomination for best picture (it won for best score and best song), that captivated the public in a way that no other film had since *Snow White*. One reason for the film's popularity was its structure. Except for the animation, *Beauty and the Beast* resembles a typical fiction film. It begins, as any contemporary film might, with a precredits sequence: immediately after the Walt Disney Pictures logo, there is a prologue, at the end of which comes the title.

If you miss the prologue, you learn nothing about the background—specifically, why a handsome young prince has been transformed into a beast. The prologue, dramatized with voice-over narration, portrays the prince as a self-absorbed young man who mocks a beggar woman who comes to his castle seeking shelter. When she suddenly metamorphoses into a beauty, the prince relents. But it is too late: a spell has been cast on both the prince and his household. The prince's only hope is a rose that will bloom until he is twenty-one. If he has learned to love before the last petal falls, he and his household will be released from the spell.

How Beauty—or Belle, as she is called—encounters the Beast and aids in his reverse transformation constitutes the main action of the film. There are several reasons that *Beauty and the Beast* is generally considered to be the quintessential animated musical, the most important of which is the credibility of the characters. It is easy to imagine a heroine like Belle, who is not the typical ingenue of operetta but a fearless young woman devoted to her widower father and an avid reader as well. She shares a love of reading with the Beast, which makes her his double. After a series of complications (e.g., the rescue of Belle's father, whom her jealous suitor, Gaston, tries to institutionalize), the spell is broken, and Belle and the (former) Beast pledge their love for each other.

Not only is *Beauty and the Beast* a tightly constructed narrative; it is also an integrated musical. The musical numbers bear directly on the action. For example, the title song is sung by the enchanted teapot, Mrs. Potts (the voice of Angela Lansbury) to her favorite cup, Chip. First, one hears Mrs. Potts's voice on the soundtrack, explaining how two dissimilar people could be attracted to each other—particularly a beautiful woman to a grotesque. The song, motivated by the desire of the maternal Mrs. Potts to explain an important fact of life to Chip, also expressed the film's eternal theme: "Tale as old as time/Song as old as rhyme."

Apart from being a "two-for-the-price-of-one" movie, the animated musical does not require stars, only singers and actors whose voices fit the characters. Audiences would not flock to theaters to see Jody Benson in *The Little Mermaid* (1988) if it were just another fiction film. However, in an animated film, Benson's lack of a "name" was unimportant. She was only lending her voice to an animated mermaid, just as, half a century earlier, Adriana Caselotti lent hers to Snow White. To audiences, what mattered were *Snow White and the Seven Dwarfs* and *The Little Mermaid*, not Caselotti and Benson.

THE WESTERN

The American western is more complex than the overworked and often misleading distinction between the black-hatted villain and the white-clothed hero suggests. In fact, some westerns totally disregard that color code. In *My Darling Clementine*, Doc Holliday (Victor Mature), who is far from evil, dresses in black, but so does the true villain, Old Man Clanton (Walter Brennan). In Fred Zinnemann's *High Noon* (1952), the marshal (Gary Cooper) wears a black hat; so does Ethan (John Wayne) in *The Searchers*.

As James Kitses has demonstrated in his study of the western, *Horizons West*,[1] the western is not so much a matter of good vs. evil as one of wilderness vs. civilization. Within these extremes are three others: the individual vs. the community, nature vs. culture, and West vs. East. The tension between the wilderness and civilization is evident in *Clementine* when the civilizing institutions of the church and the school begin to encroach on the frontier, bringing order and stability into lives that have neither. As the film shows, the frontier is changing: the one-street town of Tombstone sports a barbershop where a haircut is capped by a spray of cologne; a church is being dedicated; an actor gives a reading of Shakespeare; Clementine (Cathy Downs) becomes Tombstone's first teacher.

In the western, opposites continually confront each other: freedom/responsibility, self-concern/commitment, ignorance/education, the desert/the garden. The western hero is a loner, often fiercely independent. If he is to develop as a person, he must assume a sense of responsibility—for example, by marrying or by serving the community as peace officer, educator, or wagon-train leader. Nor can retirement stand in his way if he is needed, as Captain Brittles (John Wayne) is needed in John Ford's *She Wore a Yellow Ribbon* (1949).

Initially, the western hero avoids marriage because it is an institution that curtails freedom. Thus the hero can be comfortable only with a woman who is his alter ego or his complement. If the hero has a criminal past, he may be drawn to a social outcast, as Ringo (John Wayne) is to the prostitute Dallas (Claire Trevor) in *Stagecoach* or as Link (Gary Cooper) is to Billie (Julie London) in Anthony Mann's *Man of the West* (1958). If he is an upright man, like Wyatt Earp (Henry Fonda) in *Clementine*, he will be attracted to a virtuous woman.

The frontier encourages a survival instinct that is so strong it can cause a community to abandon its lawman, as the townspeople do in *High Noon* when they refuse to come to the aid of their marshal. The frontier is also parochial: easterners are regarded with suspicion because they bring with them education and a knowledge of the law. In *The Man Who Shot Liberty Valance*, an eastern lawyer is an object of ridicule; in Anthony Mann's *The Man from Laramie* (1955), a frontier woman dismisses her rival as "a piece of fluff from the East." The East, however, is necessary to the West; it can bring the garden to the desert in the form of irrigation. In *Liberty Valance*, the cactus rose is all that can bloom in the desert until the arrival of irrigation—the result of legislation initiated by an eastern lawyer, who was dismissed as a "dude."

Still, there are those who cannot adapt to the wilderness turned garden: outlaws, uncompromising individualists, romantic idealists. For the unassimilated, there are two choices: flight or a return to the wilderness. In *Stagecoach*, Ringo and Dallas are "saved from the blessings of civilization," as one of the characters observes—they head for Mexico, bringing the individualism of the frontier with them. In *The Searchers*, Ethan spends

John Wayne as the black-hatted but hardly villainous Ethan in *The Searchers* (1956). *(Courtesy MOMA/FSA and Warner Bros., Inc.)*

five years trying to find Debbie, who had been abducted by Indians as a child. When he brings her back at the end, he stands in the doorway momentarily as the others enter the house. He does not enter, because home and community are not meant for him; instead, he returns to the wilderness like the gods of myth, who descend to earth to help humankind and leave when their job is done.

In *Beyond Formula: American Film Genres* (1976), author Stanley Solomon offers a single explanation for the plots, characters, and locales of the western: the landscape, which determines not only setting but also the kind of people who would be attracted to it and the kinds of situations they would encounter there.[2] Because the West is rugged, only the hardy can survive there. But even they need protection from unscrupulous bankers, cattle barons, crooked lawyers, and land speculators. Hence, they need the cavalry, lawmen, crusading newspaper editors, honest lawyers, fearless clergymen—the traditional heroes of the western.

The landscape explains a certain sameness of setting: plains, valleys, mesas, deserts, ranches, trading posts, forts, and towns with a single street that features a combination saloon, gambling house, and brothel and, if civilization has made any incursions, a barbershop and a newspaper office. It also accounts for modes of travel—stagecoach, horseback, wagon train, rail—and helps to explain recurring plot devices and rituals. The western plot often revolves around a quest or a journey: a search for a loved one in *The Searchers*, or for a loved one's killers in *The Bravados* (1957) and *Last Train from Gun Hill* (1956). It can also include a trek across inhospitable terrain: the trip through Apache territory in *Stagecoach*, the cattle drive in Howard Hawks's *Red River* (1948), the Mormons' journey across the mountains in John Ford's *Wagon Master* (1950).

Those embarking on the quest or making the journey are a varied lot, usually a mix of indivualists and traditionalists, the educated and uneducated, moral people and amoral ones, romantics and realists. The passengers in *Stagecoach* are representative: the loner hero with a criminal past, the prostitute, the good woman, the drunken doctor, a southern gambler, a whiskey salesman, an embezzling banker, a kindly lawman, and a driver with a Mexican wife. Other films broadened the list to include homesteaders, cavalry officers, miners, trappers, prospectors, geezers, bullies, and matriarchal and patriarchal figures. As the genre matured, unusual variations on traditional character types were introduced: the sheriff turned bounty hunter in Anthony Mann's *The Tin Star* (1956); bilingual and trilingual Indians (*Fort Apache* [1948] and *She Wore a Yellow Ribbon* [1949]); the white men who marry Indian women in *Broken Arrow* (1950) and *Broken Lance* (1954); and the loner heroine in Nicholas Ray's *Johnny Guitar* (1954).

Despite its realistic nature, the western is also ritualistic. Certain acts are invested with a ceremonial quality, as if they were being performed according to a rite or a liturgy. Such rituals include gunplay, confrontations, dress, returns, departures, and burials. In a western, one does not just reach for a gun and shoot; one draws from the hip, with style. The gun is more than a weapon; it is an extension of one's personality. Sometimes a character removes it slowly from the holster with a cool gracefulness; at other times, the character whips it out and fires it by thumbing or fanning. A character might even fire two guns, standing defiantly with legs apart and holding the guns at different angles. The gun is also an icon—an image that inspires awe—to be held as one might hold a talisman or a sacred object.

In a western, clothes make the character. The virtuous woman is dressed primly and simply, covered up to her neck. The prostitute is usually dressed provocatively, in an off-the-shoulder blouse and ruffled skirt, plumes and feathers, or a low-cut gown with a rhinestone bodice. In symbolic westerns like *Shane* and *The Searchers*, the hero's dress is so striking that it gives him the aura of a medieval knight or an epic warrior. Shane, who materializes like a god descended to earth to aid a homesteader and his family, wears white buckskins that set him apart from the others. Ethan in *The Searchers* makes his first appearance wearing a black neckerchief and a Confederate cloak, and carrying a saber. His rifle is in a fringed buckskin cover that resembles an aegis. His dress, a vestige of his Civil War days, marks him as an anachronism in postbellum Texas, but it also gives him heroic stature.

Ever since the first western, E. S. Porter's *The Great Train Robbery* (1903), the shoot-out has been a dramatic, sometimes an operatic, event. In *The Great Train Robbery*, when one of the outlaws is shot he does a ballet-like twirl, firing his gun as he falls. Sam Peckinpah's westerns continue the tradition of choreographed death, often in slow motion, that adds a macabre quality to the bloody climax. Perhaps the most operatic death occurs in King Vidor's *Duel in the Sun* (1947), in which Pearl and Lewt (Jennifer Jones and Gregory Peck) are firing away at each other when suddenly they realize they are in love; thereupon Pearl crawls up rocks and boulders to die, blood-splattered, in Lewt's arms.

Most shoot-outs, though less bizarre, are still theatrical. Even those that seem to be conventional usually have a theatrical touch: Doc Holliday's handkerchief fluttering in the wind after he has been killed at the O.K. Corral in *Clementine*, McCabe's solitary death in the snow in Robert Altman's *McCabe and Mrs. Miller* (1971). Sometimes the shoot-out takes the form of a long walk: the hero walks down a street that the townspeople

Alan Ladd in his white buckskins in *Shane* (1953). *(Courtesy MOMA/FSA and Paramount Pictures)*

have cleared or deserted to confront the villain or the villain's gang, as in *High Noon*. A variation on the shoot-out is the climax of *Red River*, when Tom Dunson (John Wayne) strides down a street intending to challenge his surrogate son, Matt (Montgomery Clift), only to discover that Matt has too much respect for him to retaliate.

Homecomings, departures, and burials in the western are also acts of ritual. The homecoming is often a *nostos*, a return in the epic sense (for example, Odysseus's return in *The Odyssey*). When Ethan returns from the Civil War at the beginning of *The Searchers*, it is as a hero; he walks toward his brother's house as if he were in a one-person processional, with each member of the family looking at him with awe. When Wyatt Earp takes leave of Clementine, and Shane of Marion, each behaves like a knight bidding farewell to his lady. In John Ford's cavalry films, the cavalry does not merely leave the fort; it troops out in the grand manner to the music of "The Girl I Left behind Me" or "She Wore a Yellow Ribbon." Burials are strikingly framed, with the mourners set against the horizon as if they were figures in a painting. Occasionally a touch of pathos is added. In *Shane*, the dead man's dog stretches out a paw to touch his master's casket as it is lowered into the ground; in *She Wore a Yellow Ribbon*, a woman uses part of her red petticoat to make a flag for an officer's burial.

The western, then, is far from a gathering of the good, the bad, and the ugly; it is a complex genre that, in its own way, records the history of America.

Throughout the 1960s, the Vietnam War polarized the nation as no other conflict had. However, except for *The Green Berets* (1968), which glorified America's involvement in Vietnam, filmmakers tended to avoid the war until well after it ended in 1973. Yet the war was not entirely absent from the screen; since the public was not interested in Vietnam War movies (they could see the war on the television news), the western performed a double function: it became a metaphor for an ugly war as well as a mirror of an America that the civil rights movement had made more sensitive to the portrayal of minorities. The two functions were related: Vietnam was perceived as a war that discriminated against minority males who were unable to attend college, thereby qualifying for a deferment, and ended up being drafted.

If the West became less mythic in the 1970s, and the movie western more violent, part of the reason was the documentation of the atrocities American troops had committed in Vietnam. The 1968 My Lai massacre inspired *Soldier Blue* (1970) and *Ulzana's Raid* (1972), which contained some of the most graphic violence seen in a western—but nothing compared with what had happened in Southeast Asia.

By the 1990s, the Vietnam western had run its course, leaving in its wake a demythologized West that could no longer be considered a metaphor for an ideal America. John Ford's mythic West had become too closely associated with John Wayne (still an icon but also a symbol of the gung-ho patriots who supported the war) to inspire filmmakers to imitate it. If the West is a microcosm of anything, it is of America as it was (and perhaps still is), not of an America that could have been. In the absence of myth, there is antimyth and revisionism. The myths are either inverted or the historical events that inspired them are reexamined in an attempt to provide a less fanciful depiction of "what really happened" or "what it was really like." Revisionism, which challenges received interpretations, is hardly new. John Ford had been experimenting with revisionism since the late 1940s with *Fort Apache*, as he gradually altered the way Native Americans had been portrayed on the screen, even to the point of presenting their point of view in *The Searchers* and *Cheyenne Autumn* (1964). Unfortunately, Ford's revisionism (Spanish-speaking Apaches, for one thing, instead of the gibberish that was often used to suggest authenticity) may have been too subtle to register the impact it should have. While other westerns (for example, *Broken Arrow* [1950], *Apache* [1954]) also tried to correct the negative image of Native Americans that Hollywood had fostered, they came at a time when television was usurping the role that movies once played in influencing the public's attitude toward everything from sex to race.

It was in the early 1970s that American filmmakers began looking at the Old West more closely, questioning the way it had been portrayed. The Native American, in the past the perpetrator of violence, was now the victim. *Little Big Man* (1971) challenged the legend of the heroic George Custer and his last stand at Little Big Horn; far from being the romantic figure Errol Flynn played in Raoul Walsh's *They Died with Their Boots On* (1941), the Custer of *Little Big Man* was almost deranged, and the Native Americans were the victims of his madness. The revisionist western was already established when *Dances with Wolves* (1990) appeared; *Dances with Wolves* marked the culmination of two decades of revisionism, which succeeded in reversing the familiar character types of the savage Native American and the civilized white man. The film's popularity also suggests that audiences are now less inclined to think of good and evil in terms of race and ethnicity.

Antimyth is similar to revisionism: the original myth, along with its plots and character types, is either parodied or turned inside out. Two westerns in which Clint Eastwood starred and which he directed are clearly antimythic: *Pale Rider* (1985) and, particularly, *Unforgiven* (1992). Eastwood came to prominence in the spaghetti westerns of Italian director Sergio Leone, who, despite his professed love of the American western, also loved to portray violence as graphically (and, at times, operatically) as the times allowed. Instead of heroes, there were antiheroes.

No longer was the protagonist a man with a violent past (for example, the Ringo Kid, Shane, and Ethan Edwards) that he would like to put behind him; he *was* that past. The protagonist was now the dark side of the hero that was only hinted at in films like *Shane* and *The Searchers*. Leone's anti-heroes were nameless men who appeared out of nowhere, looking like prophets of doom, who kill off their rivals, go off with the gold or ransom money, and clean up the town, leaving a trail of bodies behind them—not just the villain's corpse, as Shane did. *Pale Rider* is, in fact, almost a parody of *Shane*, with gold miners replacing the homesteaders and the Shane figure transformed into the Preacher (Clint Eastwood, playing another nameless character, as he did in the Leone films and in his own *High Plains Drifter* [1973]), who, like the Pale Rider in the Apocalypse, brings death with him.

Because of its ambivalence and its avoidance of obvious parallels with other films, Eastwood's *Unforgiven* is perhaps the finest example of the antimythic western. The traditional character types and themes of the classic western have been inverted, so that instead of a hero, there is a hero-as-villain—the other villains having no redeeming qualities. The hero-villain has at least two: the desire to reform and lead a decent life, and a code of retribution that is the flip side of the code of honor. William Munny (Eastwood), as ex-gunslinger who remains faithful to the memory of his dead wife, wants nothing more than to raise his two children in peace. However, the prospect of a $1,000 reward for killing the men who disfigured a prostitute prompts him to return to his old life. No western, even an antimythic one, ever opened like *Unforgiven*—with a woman's face being slashed. And no western ever used contemporary vulgarisms and obscenities in such profusion, as if the language of R-rated movies had become the language of the Old West.

In the classic western, there were gunfighters who tried to forget their past but whose "eye for an eye" philosophy required them to avenge the coldblooded murder of a friend (*Shane*); and gunfighters goaded into killing by glory-seeking kids who scoff at the idea of a reformed killer (*The Gunfighter* [1950]). There have been bounty hunters before (*The Naked Spur* [1953]) and even bounty hunter-sheriffs (*The Tin Star* [1957]). In the traditional western, the protagonist embarks on some kind of journey (quest, search, cattle drive, rescue operation), often accompanied by an old friend (*Red River*) or saddled with a bipolar opposite (*The Searchers* and *Two Rode Together* [1961]). Sometimes there is a boy or a young man who either learns from the reformed gunfighter (*Shane*) or represents the kind of reckless youth the gunfighter once was (*The Gunfighter*). Finally, there is a sheriff who can be anything from a tough law-enforcement officer (*My Darling Clementine*) to a sympathetic fellow human being who bends the law for those whom society has misjudged (*Stagecoach*). All these types (the

An ex-gunslinger (Clint Eastwood) and his friend (Morgan Freeman) off to collect a reward in *Unforgiven* (1992), one of the finest examples of the antimythic western. *(Courtesy MOMA/FSA)*

ex-gunfighter, the old friend, the callow youth, and the sheriff) appear in *Unforgiven*, but in a completely inverted way.

In the traditional western, the ex-gunfighter might come to the aid of a farmer (*Shane*), but he is not a farmer himself. In *Unforgiven*, Munny is a pig farmer (and an unsuccessful one at that). In the traditional western, the sidekick is white; in the multicultural 1980s and 1990s, the partner's color is irrelevant. Thus there was nothing unusual about Munny's old friend Ned Logan (Morgan Freeman) being an African American with a Native American wife. Munny learns about the reward money from the Sheffield Kid, who, despite his youth, boasts of having killed five men, when the truth is that he is nearly blind and has yet to kill anyone. No sheriff in the traditional western was ever nicknamed Little Billy (Gene Hackman), who uses a goon squad to keep law and order in the town of Big Whiskey. Occasionally the upholder of the law is a villain (the federal judge in *The Man from Colorado* [1948], the marshal in *Pale Rider*), but there has never been a more sadistic one than "Little Billy" Daggett, who derives great pleasure from kicking and flogging lawbreakers, or those he assumes to be such. When Munny becomes Ned's avenger, he does not wear buckskins like Shane but drab brown. Nor is he the avenging angel;

he is the angel of death, who leaves a saloon floor littered with corpses, including the sheriff's, before he heads back to his farm.

Except for a few shots, notably the opening and closing scenes of the Munny homestead at sunset, this is a dark world, epitomized by the color of Eastwood's face, which is not so much tan as brown, with his clothes looking much the same.

By inverting the past, *Unforgiven* brings the Old West into the present, suggesting perhaps that there is not that much difference between them. However, the success of *Unforgiven*, which won Oscars for best picture and best director (Eastwood), did not spark a revival of interest in the western among moviegoers. Subsequent westerns proved far less popular, even though they starred well-known actors (Kevin Costner in *Wyatt Earp* [1994]; Robert Duvall and Gene Hackman in *Geronimo: An American Legend* [1993]; Sharon Stone in *The Quick and the Dead* [1995]). Perhaps the only way the western can regain its pride of place is with iconic actors like Eastwood starring in movies that speak as much to the present as they do to the past, encouraging viewers to rethink their own era as well as the one portrayed in the film.

THE CRIME FILM

Filmmakers have always been intrigued by the gangster and the criminal. The gangster era coincided with the beginning of Hollywood's golden age in the late 1920s, thereby providing screenwriters with fresh plot material. The plots often came straight from the headlines—and with Al Capone, Bonnie Parker and Clyde Barrow, John Dillinger, and "Lucky" Luciano making headlines, there was no dearth of subject matter. Filmmakers weren't the only ones who were attracted to criminals—the public was also. Gangsters were colorful figures amid the bleak Great Depression, doing what moviegoers couldn't do, even if they wished to. Gangsters didn't so much break the law as flaunt it. But they flaunted it in accordance with the American success scenario. They practiced their own form of upward mobility, beginning with holdups and graduating to bank heists. They started as lackeys and ended up as heads of syndicates. As they advanced, they acquired the trappings of success—overcoats, fedoras, and dark or pin-striped suits. But, most of all, gangsters exercised their freedom, the quality Americans prize most dearly. Unrestrained by conventional mores, they gloried in their independence, achieving an emancipation that moviegoers might envy but could never experience because the price was too high.

Thus, the crime film portrays gangsters and criminals with a combination of fascination and compassion, stopping just short of exoneration.

As the Production Code insisted, crime could not pay; but this stricture didn't stop Hollywood from giving gangsters a sinister charisma and making their lives high drama until the last few minutes when it came time for retribution. And, even then, the gangster died in a grand manner, whether in the street or on a sidewalk, the surface of which was always elegantly black, as if specially prepared for those who revealed their dark side.

In addition to being gunned down in the streets (Howard Hawks's *Scarface* [1932]) and on sidewalks (*He Ran All the Way* [1951]), gangsters often met their end on steps and cliffs, symbolizing their fall from power. In Raoul Walsh's *The Roaring Twenties* (1939), Eddie Bartlett (James Cagney) dies on the steps of a church, cradled in the arms of his mistress. When a police officer asks Eddie's identity, his mistress replies, "He used to be a big shot." Roy Earle (Humphrey Bogart) in *High Sierra* (1941) plunges from the top of a cliff. His death is a literal fall from the heights, as opposed to the figurative fall in classical tragedy. Sometimes when a criminal and his beloved die, one body is draped over the other (Robert Siodmak's *Criss Cross* [1949]). Sometimes physical union is impossible; at

Stylized death in the classic crime film as seen in *The Public Enemy* (1931). *(Courtesy WCFTR)*

the end of Arthur Penn's *Bonnie and Clyde* (1967), Bonnie's (Fay Dunaway) body is hanging out of a bullet-ridden car, while Clyde's (Warren Beatty) lies a few feet away on the ground.

Like the western, the crime film has inspired theatrical death scenes. Two of the best occur in James Cagney films. In Michael Curtiz's *Angels with Dirty Faces* (1938), Rocky Sullivan (Cagney) agrees to feign cowardice in an effort to discourage the teenagers who idolize him from turning to a life of crime. Walking cockily to the electric chair, Rocky suddenly turns craven and begs hysterically for his life. In Raoul Walsh's *White Heat* (1949), Cody Jarett (Cagney) dies amid an apocalyptic explosion of chemical tanks, yelling, "Top of the world, Ma!" Cody Jarett made it to the top, only to go up in flames.

The crime film has other features in common with the western. In both, the gun is an icon. Just as the gun in the western can be a reflection of the user's personality, the gun in the crime film can be a projection of the user's neurosis or sexuality. Cody Jarett brandishes a gun as a child would who fancies himself an adult. Jarett's behavior is understandable: he has a relationship with his mother that is so oedipal that he sits on her lap. In *Bonnie and Clyde*, the gun is sexual. For the impotent Clyde, it is a substitute for potency; for Bonnie, it is the equivalent of a sexual thrill.

The crime film unfolds within a world of back rooms, bars, diners, sleek cars, mean streets, sleazy hotel rooms, speakeasies, nightclubs, tenements, gaudy apartments, and mausoleum-like homes. Unlike the western, which allows loners—even if they have been on the wrong side of the law—to find a mate and live happily ever after, the crime film cannot. Usually gangsters find their true love (another criminal or someone like Marie in *High Sierra*), only to die in the loved one's arms.

The classic American crime film depended for its effectiveness on performers who were themselves icons: James Cagney, Humphrey Bogart, Edward G. Robinson, John Garfield. With actors who were able to ignite a human spark in characters that could be otherwise flat or unlikable, the gangster and the criminal become both lower and higher versions of ourselves. They are our dark side, doing what we would never dare, and yet achieving the American dream of success, wealth, and fame. While we are glad we are not they, at the same time we cannot help but envy their daring because, as one film scholar has noted, the gangster is "the archetypal American dreamer whose actions and behavior involve a living out of the dream common to most everyone who exists in the particular configurations and contradictions of American society, a dream in conflict with the society."[3]

Since the contemporary screen is much freer than it was during the 1930s and 1940s, acts of violence are bloodier and more violent than they were in the past. Perhaps no film was criticized for its violence more than

Oliver Stone's *Natural Born Killers* (1994), which opens with a precredits sequence in a truck stop somewhere in the Southwest. Two of the patrons, Mickey and Mallory (Woody Harrelson and Juliette Lewis) look like locals, yet an offensive remark from one of the truckers to Mallory results in a bloodbath. Mickey and Mallory, "natural born killers," always spare one person so that there is an eyewitness who can add to the ongoing saga of Mickey and Mallory.

Oliver Stone is a serious moviemaker, who does not portray violence for its own sake. He is implicitly criticizing the tabloid media for capitalizing on our fascination with violence by giving Mickey and Mallory the kind of coverage deserved by those who improve society, not those who threaten it. A television interview with the couple after they have landed in jail results in a prison riot that leaves the corridors strewn with corpses. The fact that the couple become media figures—as have American gangsters, Mafia figures, criminals, and murder suspects—suggests that the public can't get enough of types they would never want to encounter in real life, but only on the screen. It is therefore not surprising that, of the one hundred films the American Film Institute (AFI) judged the best of those made during the first one hundred years of the American cinema (1896–1996), crime plays a major role in many of them. In the order in which the AFI has ranked them, these films are *The Godfather* (#3), *Psycho* (#18), *Chinatown* (#19), *The Maltese Falcon* (#23), *Bonnie and Clyde* (#27), *The Godfather Part II* (#32), *Double Indemnity* (#38), *Rear Window* (#42), *A Clockwork Orange* (#46), *Taxi Driver* (#47), *Silence of the Lambs* (#65), *The French Connection* (#70), *GoodFellas* (#94), and *Pulp Fiction* (#95). That these films are internationally recognized as well shows that a fascination with violence is not unique to the American cinema.

FILM NOIR

While **film noir** has its roots in hard-boiled detective fiction, it can take the form of either a private-eye story or a crime film without a private eye. Note, however, that neither a private-eye film nor a crime film is necessarily film noir. *Murder, My Sweet* is a private-eye film that is also a classic film noir; *Meet Nero Wolfe* (1936) is just a private-eye movie. *Criss Cross* and Joseph H. Lewis's *Gun Crazy* (1950) are crime films and film noir; *Angels with Dirty Faces* and *The Roaring Twenties* are just crime films.

Film noir is virtually impossible to define, yet its characteristics are among the most recognizable of any genre. Literally, the term means "dark film"—film that is both dark in its look, with the look of nighttime rather than daylight, and dark in the sense of revealing the dark side of humankind and society. In film noir, the interplay of light and dark is ac-

THE NOIR NIGHT (ABOVE) AND THE NOIR CORPSE (PAGE 141) IN *MILDRED PIERCE* (1945). Wally (Jack Carson) and Mildred Pierce (Joan Crawford) on the pier. *(Courtesy WCFTR)*

complished by high-contrast photography and low-key lighting, which create a monolinear world of white and black. Street lamps shed circles of light on glistening black pavements; neon signs illuminate dark skies; blondes wear black gowns decorated with silver stripes; the hoods of dark cars look glazed by the moonlight. Murders are committed in darkness or in shadow, but during the struggle a table lamp is often knocked over, so that when the body is discovered the victim's face is illuminated by the overturned lamp.

The world of film noir is one of paranoia and entrapment, of forces bearing down on the individual that are too overwhelming to resist. Tight framing encloses characters within a universe from which there is no escape. Slow tracking shots create a mood of uncertainty; long backward tracks suggest continuous movement, pursuit, life on the run. Canted shots imply a world gone haywire. That world is often enshrouded in fog. Riverside Drive in New York is seldom fogbound, but when Roberts and

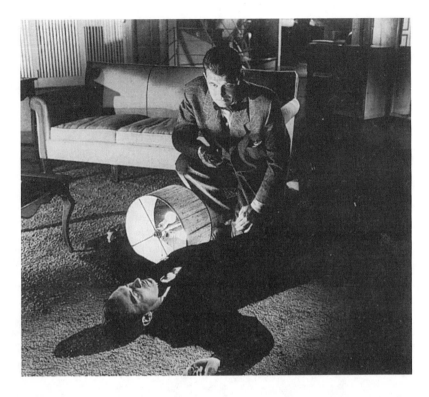

Wally discovering Monty Berrigan's (Zachary Scott) body in *Mildred Pierce* (1945). Note the overturned lamp, a typical noir prop in a typical noir framing. *(Courtesy WCFTR)*

Sue walk down it in *Detour*, they seem to be walking through a fog bank. The fog is not so much real as symbolic of a universe whose workings are impenetrable and whose design, if there is any, can never be known. The stock characters of film noir—private detectives, insurance salesmen, prostitutes, murderous housewives, two-time losers, ex-convicts, or gamblers—are essentially reducible to two: a man and a woman caught up in a chain of circumstances from which only the death of one—or both—can extricate them. When the woman is a femme fatale, the man can either follow her to his—or their—fate or free himself from her snares. In either case the end is violent, sometimes dramatically so. While O'Hara (Orson Welles) does free himself from Elsa Bannister (Rita Hayworth) in Orson Welles's *The Lady from Shanghai* (1948), Elsa dies in a hall of mirrors where she shoots it out with her husband as their images, reflected in the mirrors, shatter with the glass. (Mirrors are a favorite prop of film noir because the characters are often mirror images of each other.) Before he fires at Elsa, Bannister, appropriately, tells her that in killing her, he is killing himself.

Sometimes the climax of a film noir is a Liebestod (love-death). Common to film noir is the theme of *l'amour fatal* (fatal love)—love generated by a combination of passion and infatuation that takes a perverse turn, causing one lover to kill or attempt to kill the other. At the end of *Double Indemnity*, the adulterous lovers plan to kill each other. Phyllis fires at Neff, wounding him; then, suddenly regretting what she has done, she moves toward him. Neff takes her in his arms and embraces her while at the same time firing a bullet into her heart.

Film noir plots are convoluted, reflecting the intricacies of fate. Voice-over narration and **flashbacks** are common; in *The Locket* (1946) there are flashbacks within flashbacks. Chance—in the sense of a character's being in the wrong place at the wrong time—is more significant in film noir than in most other genres. In *Gun Crazy*, a young man, whose fascination with guns landed him in reform school, wanders into a carni-

The hall of mirrors in *The Lady from Shanghai* (1948). *(Courtesy MOMA/FSA and Columbia Pictures)*

val featuring a female sharpshooter; the chance encounter changes both their lives, as they become bank robbers in the tradition of Bonnie and Clyde and end up dying in a foggy swamp. In *Detour*, Roberts (Tom Neal), hitchhiking from New York to Los Angeles, is picked up by a man with a heart condition who dies en route. Thinking the man's death will be misconstrued as murder, Roberts adopts the dead man's identity. He later makes the mistake of picking up a woman who knew the dead man and who therefore knows that he is not the owner of the car. The woman, Vera (Ann Savage), makes Roberts her prisoner and dies in a manner that is bizarre even by film noir standards. Drunk, Vera grabs the phone, rushes into the bedroom, and locks the door behind her. Falling on the bed, she becomes entangled in the telephone cord, which is coiled around her neck. Outside, Roberts pulls at the part of the cord that is under the door, not knowing the rest of it is around Vera's neck. When he finally breaks the door open and bursts into the bedroom, we see the reflection of the prostrate Vera in the mirror. This is Roberts's second brush with fate; he is now a two-time loser.

Unlike the western, whose popularity is intermittent, film noir has never gone out of fashion because its stylistic elements are applicable to a wide range of plots: the whodunit, the man/woman in hiding, the old dark house, the cover-up, the murderous couple, the murderous lover, and so on. The familiar husband/wife/wife's or husband's lover plot admits of several possibilities: wife and lover can plot to kill husband in the tradition of *Double Indemnity* (or *Body Heat* [1981]); the husband's lover can terrorize the husband's household until his wife takes action and kills her (*Fatal Attraction* [1989]); the husband's lover can be killed when she accidentally discovers that the government is using American service personnel as guinea pigs for atomic tests (*Mulholland Falls* [1996]). An interesting variation on the adulterous trio occurs in *The Grifters* (1990), in which the three are a mother, her son, and the son's lover, who is as amoral as his mother.

While purists may argue that true film noir is black and white, the same high contrast can be obtained by creating a color scheme where black and white predominate. It was not unintentional that in *Body Heat* and *The Grifters*, the *femmes noires* (Kathleen Turner and Anjelica Huston) wore white, which looked striking against a dark background.

Although Curtis Hanson's *L.A. Confidential* (1997) deals only with a third of James Ellroy's novel, the film captures the noirish mood of Ellroy's Los Angeles of the 1950s. This "city of angels" is more of a modern Inferno, with its ever-widening circles of sins and sinners in all categories: sleazy police sergeants, racist cops, corrupt politicians, tabloid publishers, blackmailers, pornographers, movie stars who consort with gangsters, and prostitutes who undergo plastic surgery so they can resemble Hollywood sex symbols. All the elements of film noir appear in the movie: the unsuspecting male, the *femme noire* (blonde, as is often the case, but not the predator she often is), the usual assortment of villains, including those in high places, frame-ups and cover-ups, dark streets lit only by neon, cheap motels, a coffee shop that becomes the scene of a homicide, and the climactic shoot-out that leaves its usual share of corpses. Hanson's palette captures every hue Los Angeles noir can offer, ranging from decadently bright to the ominously dark, with the tacky and the garish in between.

THE COMBAT FILM

The appeal of the combat film, or war movie, has always depended upon the particular war, the public's attitude toward it, and the way the war is portrayed. The War of Independence may have given birth to the United States of America, but one would never know it from the unenthusiastic reception to *Revolution* (1985) and *The Patriot* (2000), even though the films starred Al Pacino and Mel Gibson, respectively. The musical *1776*, which dramatized the events leading up to the signing of the Declaration of Independence, was a huge hit on Broadway in the late 1960s; the 1972 movie version, which could not conceal its stage origins, turns up on television on or about July 4 but is hardly anyone's idea of a real movie musical. The Revolution and the Declaration of Independence are matters Americans appear to take for granted.

The same holds true of the Civil War—at least as far as movies are concerned. The Civil War seems to attract audiences only when it is treated as an epic: Civil War = epic = *The Birth of a Nation* and *Gone with the Wind*, both of which run over three hours without addressing the "peculiar institution" that led to the conflict: slavery. Instead, each film seems to lament a way of life that has "gone with the wind." While contemporary filmmakers have dealt with slavery (Steven Spielberg in *Amistad* [1998], Jonathan Demme in *Beloved* [1999]), neither movie registered the impact it should have, perhaps because those interested in the subject felt they learned enough from *Roots* (1977), one of the most popular shows in television history, or from Ken Burns's classic Public Television Series, *The Civil War* (1990).

World War I, which produced some of the greatest antiwar poetry ever written, also occasioned two of the finest American antiwar movies ever made, Lewis Milestone's *All Quiet on the Western Front* (1930) and Stanley Kubrick's *Paths of Glory* (1957). But perhaps because "the war to end all war" proved to be such a disastrous experience for the Americans who fought in it (as well as becoming the prelude to a far worse conflict), World War I has never been an attractive proposition for moviemakers; it

Robert Taylor firing away at the enemy in *Bataan* (1943), a typical World War II combat film. *(Private collection)*

is difficult to muster much enthusiasm for a conflict that left so many maimed, disfigured, and embittered.

It was quite different during World War II, the great age of the American combat film. No sooner had a significant event occurred than there was a movie about it: the London blitz (*Mrs. Miniver* [1942], *Journey for Margaret* [1943]); the December 7, 1941, attack on Pearl Harbor (*Remember Pearl Harbor* [1942]); the battles of Wake Island (*Wake Island* [1942]), Guadalcanal (*Guadalcanal Diary* [1943]), Bataan (*Bataan, So Proudly We Hail* [both 1943]); Corregidor (*So Proudly We Hail, Corregidor* [1943]); the fall of France (*Arise, My Love* [1940]) and Norway (*Edge of Darkness* [1943]) to the Nazis; the Allied bombing of Monte Cassino (*The Story of GI Joe* [1945]), and so forth. Even after the war ended in 1945, filmmakers continued to mine its potential, and with good reason: World War II had been declared the "good war," not because it was good (no war can claim to be that) but because it represented a concerted effort to defeat the forces of fascism, which, had they prevailed, would have led to worldwide genocide.

The best World War II films did not rely on combat scenes (whether staged at the studio or inserted from newsreels) to attract audiences. Screenwriters had to devise a plot, centered around a battle, that would deal with emotions and relationships that made the film more of a movie than a history lesson. Thus they drew upon such themes as male bonding, the loss of a spouse or another family member, the importance of faith in time of crisis, heroism in the face of death, the last-ditch stand against the enemy, two men in love with the same woman, the fate of women in war, cowardice vs. courage, a raw recruit's coming of age, and so forth.

Like the musical and the western, the combat film has had a spotty history. While it thrived in the 1940s and, occasionally, during the next two decades, everything depended upon the war in question. The Korean

Women in war: *Cry Havoc* (1943), an unusual World War II film with an all-female cast. *(Private collection)*

War (1950–1953), or "Police Action" as it was called, resulted in some harrowing films—for example, Sam Fuller's *The Steel Helmet* and *Fixed Bayonets* (both 1951), which were unappreciated in their time because Korea was not a "good" war. Vietnam, a far more unpopular war (and difficult to date, in terms of America's involvement), was not something American audiences wanted to confront until well after it had ended in 1973, since it was a war that the United States clearly lost. Then, such films as *Platoon* (1986), *Full Metal Jacket* (1987), and *Casualties of War* (1989)—the last being the best of the lot—emphasized the horrors of the Vietnam War, which could have been the horrors of any war. Had it not been for the Southeast Asia setting, *Casualties of War* could have taken place wherever men, denied their "rest and relaxation," decide to abduct a woman to satisfy their needs, as if they were owed sexual gratification for serving their country. *The Deer Hunter* (1978) and *Apocalypse Now* (1979), even though they dealt with Vietnam, told audiences little about the war or the reasons for America's involvement in it from the early 1960s through 1973. Rather, these films emphasized such universal themes as friendships and relationships altered and even shattered by war (*The Deer Hunter*) and the mental deterioration caused by the war (*Apocalypse Now*). At the end of *Apocalypse Now*, whether or not we know the source was Joseph Conrad's *The Heart of Darkness*, we might still find ourselves echoing Kurz's dying words from Conrad's novel: "The horror! The horror!"

The phenomenal success of Steven Spielberg's *Saving Private Ryan* (1998) proves that the combat film can still attract audiences. The opening sequence, the Normandy invasion of June 6, 1944, is presented in such harrowing detail—with limbs being blown off and entrails spilling forth (hence the R rating)—that previous re-creations of D-Day seem like dress rehearsals. However, once the landing is over, *Saving Private Ryan* takes on the features of a 1940s World War II movie, complete with such familiar characters as the bereaved mother (here, one who has lost three of her four sons in action), the surviving son who becomes the object of a rescue operation, the compassionate captain eager to locate Private Ryan so that he can return to his family and his teaching job, the treacherous Nazi, the nostalgia addict, and the intellectual who comes of age by killing one of the enemy.

While the Normandy invasion formed the prologue of *Saving Private Ryan*, the attack on Pearl Harbor became the centerpiece of *Pearl Harbor* (2001). Yet the movie itself is little more than another variation on the "two men in love with the same woman" plot (in this case, two pilots with a nurse), a staple of the World War II film—for example, *Thunder Birds* (1942), *Aerial Gunner* (1943), *Crash Dive* (1943), *Bombardier* (1943), and the best of the lot, John Ford's *They Were Expendable* (1945). The World War II movie provides the template; any screenwriter interested in the subject has only to impose that template on the story he or she wants to tell.

THE SCREWBALL COMEDY

Like tragedy, comedy has its own conventions: mistaken identity, lovers' quarrels and reconciliations, marital mixups, the deflation of the pompous, trickery, deception, and masquerade. It also has its own gallery of stock characters (irate fathers, errant husbands, clever servants, fops, foundlings, and amorous wives) all of whom speak in maxims, non sequiturs, puns, double entendres, and malapropisms—the traditional sources of verbal humor.

Although film comedy draws on the same sources of humor as stage comedy, it has a genre that is peculiar to itself: **screwball comedy.** While screwball comedy may have overtones of drawing-room comedy or romantic comedy because of its witty and sophisticated dialogue, it also contains elements of farce and slapstick that are alien to the comedy of the

Clark Gable as a reporter and Claudette Colbert as a runaway heiress in *It Happened One Night* (1934). *(Courtesy Sony Pictures Entertainment and MOMA/FSA)*

drawing room: a food riot in an automat (*Easy Living*), a leopard on the loose (Howard Hawks's *Bringing Up Baby*), destruction of property for comic effect (the shooting spree that leaves a club car in shambles in Preston Sturges's *The Palm Beach Story* [1942]).

Like film noir, screwball is better described than defined. One or both of the leading characters is a screwball—an oddball whose unconventional nature is responsible for the equally unconventional situations in which the characters find themselves. In *It Happened One Night*, an heiress rebels against her father, ends up hitchhiking with a reporter, masquerading as his wife, and finally discarding the masquerade for marriage. In *Easy Living*, a young working woman is riding on the top deck of a double-decker bus at the very moment an irate husband hurls his wife's sable coat from the roof of their apartment house. The coat lands on the young woman, who is then mistaken for the husband's mistress and ensconced in a luxury hotel. She later falls in love with a worker at an automat who turns out to be the son of the man who threw the coat off the roof. A socialite and a paleontologist become involved with a leopard that responds to the song "I Can't Give You Anything but Love, Baby" in *Bringing Up Baby*. In *The Awful Truth* (1937), a couple in the process of divorcing vie for custody of their dog and then try to sabotage each other's prospects for re-marriage.

The hero in screwball is usually a professional: a reporter in *It Happened One Night* and *Nothing Sacred* (1937); an editor in Howard Hawks's *His Girl Friday* (1940); a herpetologist in *The Lady Eve* (1941); a film director in *Sullivan's Travels*; a professor in Howard Hawks's *Ball of Fire* (1941). The heroine can be a socialite, as in *It Happened One Night*, *Bringing Up Baby*, and *My Man Godfrey* (1936); a Cinderella figure (*Easy Living*); a reporter (*His Girl Friday*), or a gold digger (Mitchell Leisen's *Midnight* [1939], *The Palm Beach Story* [1942]). Rarely are hero and heroine from the same social class. Sometimes the heroine is from the higher class (*It Hap-*

Cinderella (Jean Arthur) in the automat in the classic screwball comedy *Easy Living* (1937). *(Copyright by Paramount Pictures. Courtesy MCA Publishing Rights, a Division of MCA, Inc.)*

pened One Night, My Man Godfrey); at other times the hero is (*The Lady Eve, Easy Living*). In any event, class barriers never stand in the way of a happy ending.

One distinguishing feature of screwball comedy is dialogue that is sharp, fast, and witty. One character picks up on what another says to put the other down and score a point. In *Sullivan's Travels*, Sullivan (Joel McCrea) is trying to convince a studio executive of the importance of making social-consciousness films. When he is told that one such film failed in Pittsburgh, he scoffs, "What do they know in Pittsburgh?" "They know what they like," the executive replies. "If they knew what they liked, they wouldn't live in Pittsburgh" is Sullivan's capping retort. Later, he makes the same appeal to an unemployed actor, extolling a somber movie called *Hold Back Tomorrow*. "You take a picture like *Hold Back Tomorrow*," he begins. "You hold it," she replies dryly.

Screwball comedy delights in non sequiturs. In an attempt to fend off

Susan's (Katharine Hepburn) advances in *Bringing Up Baby*, Henry (Cary Grant) informs her that he is engaged to be married. Susan replies with screwball logic: "Then she [his fiancée] won't mind waiting. If I was engaged to be married to you, I wouldn't mind waiting. I'd wait forever."

Double entendre, too, is common in screwball. Since the Production Code frowned on suggestiveness in dialogue and situations, writers encoded the dialogue with double meanings, expecting that at least some members of the audience would choose the right meaning; most did. In *The Palm Beach Story*, a millionaire tells the fortune-hunting heroine that he admires women who can cook. "You should taste my popovers," she says playfully. "I'd love to," he replies. Somewhat more subtle but also more suggestive is a character's slip of the tongue about a boys' magazine in *Easy Living*; instead of calling it by its correct name, *The Boy's Constant Companion*, the character keeps calling it *The Boy's Constant Reminder*.

Like film noir, screwball comedy will never become extinct. Audiences are always ready for a "meet cute." In *Only You* (1994), a high-school teacher (Marisa Tomei), who is convinced that her soul mate's name is Damon Bradley, expects to find him in Italy, where, instead, she finds her true love, a shoe salesman (Robert Downey Jr.). *French Kiss* (1995) reverses the classic screwball situation, in which the bride-to-be bolts from the altar because she cannot say "I do." (The paradigm is *It Happened One Night*, with such spinoffs as *It Had to Be You* [1947] and *The Runaway Bride* [1999].) In *French Kiss*, the prospective bridegroom (Timothy Hutton) phones his fiancée (Meg Ryan) from Paris to inform her that he has found someone else. En route to Paris to reclaim him, Ryan finds herself seated next to a Frenchman (Kevin Kline), who happens to be a thief. In screwball, a profession, no matter how shady it might be, has never been known to stand in the way of romance.

One of the best contemporary screwball comedies is *While You Were Sleeping* (1994), in which a subway employee (Sandra Bullock) comes to the aid of a handsome passenger (Peter Gallagher) when he is mugged on the platform. When the passenger becomes comatose, his family assumes that the employee is his fiancée. The subway employee is not meant to marry the passenger, although she does become part of the family. In screwball there is only one constant—true love, which rarely occurs at first sight; everything else is a variable.

As long as there are performers like Tom Hanks, Richard Gere, Meg Ryan, Sandra Bullock, and Julia Roberts, who have the right combination of breeziness and style, and can handle battle-of-the-sexes dialogue without becoming shrill, screwball will thrive. The best screwball is really romantic comedy with irrepressibly wacky but articulate men and women instead of gawky adolescents. But, like adolescents, they have the same need for love, except that, as adults (and professionals), they cannot show it as openly. That one of 1999's most successful films was *The Runaway Bride*, a title inspired by the title of Elizabeth Kendall's critical study of the same name about the romantic comedies of the 1930s, is a tribute to screwball's abiding appeal.

OTHER KINDS OF FILM COMEDY

Farce. While screwball comedy is indigenous to film, farce is not. Farce is sometimes referred to as low comedy, an unfortunate term for a venerable art form that over the centuries has brought pleasure to countless audiences. Farce abounds in improbable situations: men dress up as women and join an all-female band (*Some Like It Hot* [1959]); a prime minister makes his entrance by sliding down a fire pole (Groucho Marx in *Duck Soup* [1993]); a college president appears at a faculty meeting shaving (Groucho in *Horse Feathers* [1932]). However, in farce the pace is so brisk, and the laughter so incessant, that no one bothers to question what kind of college would hire a wisecracking comic as president.

Some of the greatest comedies written for the stage contain farcical elements. The Greek playwrights, for example, did not think farce was beneath them. Aristophanes' *Lysistrata*, in which the women of Athens resolve to abstain from sex until war is outlawed, has some outrageously funny scenes. Men enter, visibly excited (the costumes included a phallus as well as padding for the stomach and buttocks); one of the women pretends she is pregnant by placing a helmet under her dress. Aristophanes' comedies contain farcical situations, but the plays themselves are not pure farce, since they deal with serious issues (war, education, politics, utopianism, the state of the theater).

Farce was even more natural to the Romans. Roman comedy evolved out of farcical skits with such stock characters as the foolish father, the amorous son, the swindler, the glutton, the cheating wife, and the cuckolded husband. These early farces, which were often quite bawdy, gave birth to comedy, which never abandoned its origins. The Roman playwright Plautus wrote several farces, including the *Menaechmi* (the basis of Shakespeare's *Comedy of Errors*), about long-lost twins with the same name; and *Casina*, in which a male slave disguises himself as a woman to prevent the heroine from being married to someone she does not love, only to end up married to one of her suitors. Naturally, everything is resolved happily. The movie version of the Broadway musical *A Funny Thing Happened on the Way to the Forum* (1966), an interweaving of Plautus's stock characters and plot devices set to music by Stephen Sondheim, comes close to illustrating the nature of classical farce.

Mistaken identity, disguise, and deception are staples of farce. Cross-dressing is almost as old as the theater itself. As we have already seen, Plautus used it in *Casina*, which was written somewhere around 200 B.C. However, the play that immediately comes to mind is *Charley's Aunt*, which was filmed three times (1925, 1930, 1941) and became the basis of the 1948 Broadway musical *Where's Charley?* (also made into a movie in 1952). The comic potential of drag has never been exhausted, as is evidenced by the highly successful *Tootsie* (1982) and *Mrs. Doubtfire* (1993). Nor is the cross-dresser always a male. Women try to pass as men in Shakespeare's *Twelfth Night* and *As You Like It*. However, in Shakespeare's time women's roles were played by men. Thus the Elizabethans who attended performances of *Twelfth Night* and *As You Like It* saw male actors playing women impersonating men. Perhaps no other film has gone so far as Blake Edwards's *Victor/Victoria* (1982) in terms of gender-bending. Here, Victoria (Julie Andrews) disguises herself as a man (Victor), who is then hired as a female impersonator. Thus, a woman pretends to be a man impersonating a woman. That Victoria succeeds in making herself desirable to both sexes proves that, without human folly, comedy could not exist.

The same holds true of *Some Like It Hot*, in which two musicians (Jack Lemmon and Tony Curtis), who have witnessed a gangland slaying, go into hiding by masquerading as women. Lemmon is so convincing that he attracts a millionaire who proposes marriage. But the masquerade has also affected Lemmon, who begins thinking as a woman and seriously considers the proposal. Cross-dressing is also at the heart of *Tootsie*, in which an actor (Dustin Hoffman), unable to get decent roles as a male, disguises himself as a woman and becomes a soap opera queen. *Tootsie* is unusual in that it begins with a farcical situation (the consequences of cross-dressing, some of which are hilarious) and then turns serious as the cross-dresser realizes the indignities that women often experience at the hands of men. Like any device, cross-dressing can be treated lightly or seriously. After *Boys Don't Cry* (1999), in which a young woman's attempt to pass as a male results in tragedy, the subject can no longer be considered the preserve of comedy. Everything depends on the writer's approach to the subject and the filmmaker's vision of the script. The abandoning of a child can result in a classic tragedy like Sophocles' *Oedipus the King* or a classic comedy like Oscar Wilde's *The Importance of Being Earnest*.

Musicians in drag (Tony Curtis, left, on saxophone; Jack Lemmon on bass fiddle) in *Some Like It Hot* (1959). *(Courtesy the Margaret Herrick Library of the Academy of Motion Picture Arts and Sciences)*

Sight gags. However well crafted a film farce may be, there are moments when the absurd and the incongruous take over. On such occasions, logic is thrown to the winds, and the only question is not how such scenes fit into the plot (they often don't) but how well they do what they are supposed to do—namely, provoke laughter. The Marx Brothers film *A Night in Casablanca* (1946) opens with Harpo (the silent brother) propping himself against a wall next to a building. A suspicious police officer comes along and asks, sarcastically, if he is trying to hold up the building. Harpo nods yes. The officer tells him to move on, and, as he does, the building collapses. In an earlier Marx Brothers film, *A Night at the Opera* (1935), people start piling into the stateroom of an ocean liner, despite the fact that there is room for only one occupant. The scene reaches the height of absurdity when an engineer, his assistant, a manicurist, a cleaning woman, and stewards arrive, as if there were no limit to the number of people the room could hold. A similar scene occurs in *Some Like It Hot* in the upper berth of a sleeping car.

Farce can—and does—involve elements of slapstick, a name that derives from the paddle that comic actors once used to hit one another. The impact caused such a loud noise that it automatically got a laugh, even if what was happening onstage wasn't especially funny.

Sight gags, however, are one thing; structure, another. Naturally, there are sight gags in the best of farces, but the plots are quite intricate. In pure slapstick, any semblance of a plot disappears in an eruption of crude humor, abusiveness, bodily contortions, and generally immature behavior. The result truly deserves to be called low comedy. The Three Stooges shorts are a prime example of pure slapstick; in fact, some of their antics (eye-poking and head-bashing) looked so realistic that, when the shorts were first aired on television, the networks warned children not to imitate what they saw.

It is important to distinguish between films that are pure slapstick and those that are true farce. The former (for example, *Wayne's World* [1992], *Dumb & Dumber* [1994]) appeal to audiences that judge a movie by the number of belly laughs it provides, regardless of how they were achieved; the latter (for example, *A Night at the Opera*, *Some Like It Hot*), to audiences who laugh at humor in context, not just at sight gags and one-liners that could be inserted in any movie and get the same response. Great farceurs like W. C. Fields and the Marx Brothers knew there were no easy laughs, only laughs that must be earned. A comedy with the Marx Brothers or W. C. Fields is not simply a series of sight gags or tired vaudeville routines. Much of the humor is verbal and is intended for viewers who appreciate wit and wordplay.

In the Marx Brothers comedy *A Day at the Races* (1937), Groucho, the best known of the brothers, performs a number for which he will always be remembered, "Lydia the Tattooed Lady," in which he extols Lydia's illustrated body, noting that "when her robe is unfurled/She will show you the world." Groucho was never tasteless, only suggestive. He relied on puns and metaphors rather than on bluntness. In *Monkey Business* (1931), after commiserating with Thelma Todd about all the "dirty breaks" she has received, Groucho then puns "breaks," claiming that he will "clean and tighten [her] brakes," which will require her to stay in the garage all night. In *My Little Chickadee* (1940), Fields, as con man Cuthbert J. Twillie, refers to Mae West's "hot house cognomen" because her character's name is Flowerbelle. *My Little Chickadee* also contains an interesting variation on the bed trick, an old comic device in which one bed partner is substituted for another. In Shakespeare's *Measure for Measure*, Angelo, thinking he will be spending the night with Isabella, really spends it with Mariana, who has taken Isabella's place. In *My Little Chickadee*, Flowerbelle substitutes a goat for herself. Twillie does not realize that he is snuggling up to an animal, even though the odor is not particularly enticing, until the goat bolts out of the bed.

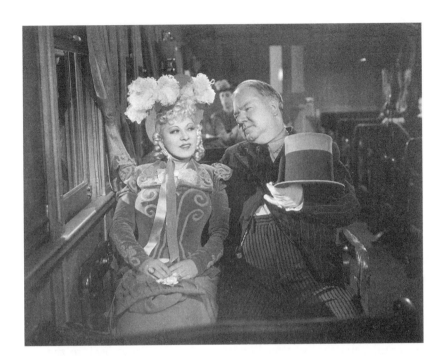

Two comic icons, W. C. Fields and Mae West, in *My Little Chickadee* (1940). *(Courtesy MOMA/FSA)*

Gross-out. Farce is a true genre, but gross-out comedy (for example, *There's Something about Mary* [1998]; *American Pie* [1999]; *Me, Myself and Irene* [2000]; *Scary Movie* [2000]) is, if anything, a subgenre, rather like a second-level heading in an outline. Gross-out began with *National Lampoon's Animal House* (1978) and *Porky's* (1981), which seem wholesome compared with the above. *Animal House* portrayed campus fraternities as breeding places of bad manners and boorish behavior, and *Porky's* (along with its two sequels) suggested that there were high-school males who could end up like the fraternity brothers in *Animal House*. These movies, however, were more vulgar than offensive. But as the 1990s came to an end, America was rocked by the news of President William Jefferson Clinton's liaison with a White House intern, which was reported in more detail than any affair had ever been before.

 Not coincidentally, gross-out became more audacious on the principle that anyone, and anything, is good for a laugh. It is not even a question of taste, since gross-out filmmakers admit they have none; they aim for easy laughs, which, if they resonate widely enough, will be heard at box offices throughout the world. In gross-out, nothing is sacred: dogs, cows, hamsters, minorities, senior citizens, the disabled. In classic farce, if a scene is to culminate in a burst of laughter, the audience must be prepared for it—perhaps by a scene or a series of scenes leading up to it. The goat incident in *My Little Chickadee* makes sense because, earlier, Flowerbelle had tricked Twillie into a "marriage" that he is anxious to consummate but she is not. Hence, the goat substitute. In gross-out, the buildup is unnecessary, since what matters is the laugh. How the laugh is achieved is irrelevant. In gross-out, what is funny is not a man's finding himself in bed with a goat but a man's getting his genitals caught in the zipper of his fly (*There's Something About Mary*). Some may defend gross-out on the grounds that it observes the "offend and mend" rule of comedy: shatter taboos, shock the prudish, and transcend the boundaries of good taste—but at the end turn kind-hearted, so that what appeared to be grossness will seem like good dirty fun. Until gross-out joins the canon of comedy, there is still more to explore in the crazy-quilt world of the Marx Brothers and W. C. Fields.

Satire. Like practically every literary genre, satire goes back to the ancients, who thought of it as a way of poking fun at human folly. The subjects of classical satire ranged from hypocrites, upstarts, and social climbers to untalented writers, gluttons, and overdeveloped athletes—in short, those lacking in self-knowledge. Literary satire has a long and venerable tradition, with outstanding examples in verse (the *Satires* of Horace and Juvenal, Pope's *Dunciad*), prose (Erasmus's *Praise of Folly*), prose fiction (Swift's *Gulliver's Travels*, Waugh's *The Loved One*), and theater (the satires on the movie industry, *Beggar on Horseback*, by Marc Connelly and George S. Kaufman, and David Mamet's *Speed-the-Plow*).

Just as there is pure farce, there is also pure satire. *Wag the Dog* (1998) is pure satire, centering around an attempt to divert attention from a presidential scandal by staging a war with Albania, even if it means using fake newsreel footage to fool the public. The ideal audience for *Wag the Dog* was one familiar with the President Clinton–Monica Lewinsky affair, not to mention conditions in the former Yugoslavia, where Albanians were victims of ethnic cleansing. However, future audiences, to whom the Clinton-Lewinsky affair is a memory, and Albania is the name of a country in eastern Europe, will still be able to understand how fabrication can become fact when the right combination of a president, a producer, and a staff conspire to create history.

Montgomery Clift about to remove an arrow from Joanne Dru's shoulder in *Red River* (1948), "the last picture show" in *The Last Picture Show* (1971). *(Private collection)*

Most movie satire is not as topical or as outrageous as *Wag the Dog* or *The Player* (1992), the latter being such a jaundiced view of Hollywood that it should cause the fainthearted to think twice before entering the business. Generally speaking, Hollywood has been willing to kid itself, but in moderation. For example, *Singin' in the Rain* pokes fun at silent stars with atrocious voices who had to face the advent of sound; *The Big Picture* (1989) makes it abundantly clear that a major in Film Studies is no preparation for the world of corporate Hollywood; and *The Freshman* (1990) mocks the esoteric jargon that academics use in their film classes.

Whether film satire will grow into a genre with as many classics to its name as screwball comedy or the musical remains to be seen. The most that can be said is that human folly has always found a place on the screen, where it was sometimes treated gently, sometimes scathingly. To its credit, the movie industry has never exempted itself from the company of fools who labor for our enjoyment and edification.

THE REFLEXIVE FILM

Reflexive literature calls attention to itself as literature: a reader, for example, may sense that the novel he or she is reading is really about the art of the novel or the act of writing a novel, and not just a work of prose fiction. Literary critics use the term **intertextuality** to describe texts that draw on other texts—mentioning them by name, alluding to them, commenting on them, or imitating them. Authors who draw on the works of others hope their readers are familiar with their sources; or, if readers are not, that at least they understand that what they are reading is more than the mere telling of a story. Iris Murdoch's novel *Under the Net* is a deliberate reply to Jean-Paul Sartre's *Nausea*, which deals with, among other matters, the subject of language—finding the right words to describe experiences so intensely personal that they almost defy expression. At the end of *Nausea*, the narrator, Roquentin, wonders if the way to express the inexpressible is through fiction. *Under the Net* deals with the same subject, but in the traditional novel form. While *Under the Net* can be understood without recourse to *Nausea* or Sartre's brand of existentialism, anyone who is familiar with both will appreciate Murdoch's subtle criticism of existential fiction, which, she feels, sacrifices the personal to the philosophical.

Intertextuality is not limited to literature. In discussing films, we generally use the term **reflexivity,** although the idea is the same. The root meaning of *reflect* is "turn back"; the reflexive film "turns back" on itself, calling attention to itself as film with the hope that it will be perceived as more than a movie. There are varying degrees of reflexivity:

Films that suggest something about the nature of film. Woody Allen's *The Purple Rose of Cairo* (1985) explores the consequences of mistaking the illusion of the screen for the reality of life. During a movie, which also has the same title, a character steps off the screen and into the audience, leaving the other characters stranded in mid-plot. The other characters then become autonomous, refusing to continue with the plot until he returns. The character's adventures in the real world point up the difference between life and art: one cannot live art, only life.

Films that refer to specific films. These are sometimes called "movie movies," because they depend for their effectiveness upon an audience's knowledge of film. It is true that one can enjoy *The Last Picture Show* for its plot alone; however, anyone who is knowledgeable about film will have a deeper appreciation of Bogdanovich's movie. "The last picture show" of the title is *Red River*, which serves two purposes: it allows the movie theater to close with a bang rather than a whimper—with an epic western and not, as was the case in the original novel, with a minor one, *The Kid from Texas* (1950). *Red River* is also a metaphor for the film itself. In *Red River*, the John Wayne character befriends a fatherless boy (Montgomery Clift), with whom he develops a close relationship. In *The Last Picture Show*, Sam the Lion (Ben Johnson) befriends two boys who might as well be fatherless. With its references to *Red River*, *The Last Picture Show* establishes itself as a film that, at least on one level, is about America's film heritage, reflecting not only the way generations of Americans behaved but also the way generations of filmmakers portrayed America.

Likewise, Steven Spielberg's *Raiders of the Lost Ark* (1981) presumes some knowledge of the old movie serials, especially *Nyoka and the Lost Tablets of Hippocrates* (1942), which, along with the anti-Nazi films of the 1940s, inspired *Raiders*. It also helps to know that Nora Ephron's *You've Got Mail* (1998) is a remake of *The Shop Around the Corner* (1940). Those who are familiar with the original will appreciate the name of the children's bookstore in *You've Got Mail:* The Shop Around the Corner. Ephron's *Sleepless in Seattle* (1993) not only alludes to an earlier film, *An Affair to Remember* (1957), but also uses one of that film's main plot points, a meeting planned on the observation deck of the Empire State Building.

Lars Von Trier's *Dancer in the Dark* (1999) contains a scene in which Selma (the Icelandic pop singer Björk) and Kathy (Catherine Deneuve) are sitting in a theater watching the Warner Bros. musical *42nd Street* (1933). Since the time is the 1960s, and the place is a small town in the state of Washington, such a choice seems idiosyncratic, to say the least, although one could argue that it was "revival night" at the local cinema. Selma, who is suffering from a congenital eye disease that will lead to blindness, is unable to perform in a community theater production of *The Sound of Music*. Regardless, she needs the "sound" of music—the melody, rhythm, and, above all, the liberating effect. Nowhere is that freedom more evident than in the movie musical, where characters break into song and dance even on crowded streets. As a respite from the tedium of her factory job, Selma imagines herself and the other employees dancing to the rhythms produced by the machines. There are several such musical sequences in the film. Those moments when life turns into a movie musical may seem bizarre; however, they are not so much an affectionate tribute to the old movie musicals as evidence of their influence on the lives of ordinary people—the same people for whom such musicals were intended.

The title of Pedro Almodóvar's *All About My Mother* (1999) suggests Joseph L. Mankiewicz's *All About Eve*. In fact, Almodóvar's film opens with Manuela (Cecilia Roth), a single parent, and her son, an aspiring writer and movie buff, watching a Spanish-dubbed version of *All About Eve* on television in their Madrid apartment. The film has reached the point at which Margo Channing (Bette Davis) is inveighing against the "coyotes," the fans who pursue her for her autograph. To celebrate her son's birthday, Manuela takes him to a local production of Tennessee Williams's *A Streetcar Named Desire*, which also functions as an intertext. Eager to get the autograph of the actress who plays Blanche DuBois, the boy pounds on the window of her taxi, only to be ignored. Rushing after the cab, he is hit by a car and dies. Unable to forget what happened, Manuela leaves for Barcelona, where she discovers that the actress whose autograph her son wanted is appearing in another production of *Streetcar*. In *All About Eve*, the aspiring actress Eve Harrington ingratiates herself with Margo, eventually becoming her understudy and even going on for her. Similarly, Manuela "pulls an Eve Harrington"; after becoming the actress's personal assistant, she finds an opportunity to play the role of Blanche's sister, Stella, by taking unfair advantage of a cast member who has a drug problem. Manuela, however, is far less manipulative than Eve. Her reason for becoming part of the *Streetcar* company is that the play provides the only link she has with her dead son.

All About My Mother also draws on a familiar plot device from the movies of the 1930s and 1940s: one woman's adopting another's child for reasons often having to do with illegitimacy (*The Old Maid* [1939], *The Great Lie* [1941], *The Corn Is Green* [1945], *To Each His Own* [1946], and so forth). By befriending a young woman who is dying of AIDS, Manuela becomes the foster mother of her son, Estéban (which also happens to have been the name of her own son), thus bringing the narrative full circle: what began with loss ends with gain. *All About My Mother* is a film that works on many levels, one of which is the intertextual. It is also an outstanding example of the woman's film, a genre that will be discussed shortly. In the world depicted in *All About My Mother*, movies and plays are more important than men.

Films that evoke other films. This category differs from the previous one the way an echo differs from a sound. There are some films that have clearly been influenced by other films and reveal their debt through visual quotations—not necessarily by incorporating actual shots from the film, as was the case with the *Red River* excerpts in *The Last*

Picture Show. The much admired assembly-line sequence in Chaplin's *Modern Times* (1936), in which mechanization comes in for some sharp satire, was not original; it was derived from an earlier French film, René Clair's *À Nous la Liberté* (1931). Hitchcock's *Saboteur* inspired the climax of *The House on Carroll Street* (1988)—not atop the Statue of Liberty, as Hitchcock had done, but at another American landmark, Grand Central Station. The result, however, was the same: the villain plunges to his death from a high place.

When Martin Scorsese decided to remake *Cape Fear* (1991), he knew that he would be inviting comparison with the 1962 original, in which Robert Mitchum played Max, an ex-convict who terrorizes the family of the judge who convicted him. Since one of Scorsese's favorite actors, Robert De Niro, would be playing Max, Scorsese incorporated elements of another Mitchum characterization, Harry Powell, the murderous preacher Mitchum played in *The Night of the Hunter* (1955), and had De Niro play Max as a sadist who is also a Bible-spouting religious fanatic. Thus, Scorsese fashioned a character that brings to mind two of Mitchum's best-known roles; still, Scorsese's Max is neither Mitchum's Max nor Mitchum's Powell but merely evokes them.

Under this category comes the *hommage* (French for "tribute"), a film that literally "pays homage" to another filmmaker or genre, either in whole or in part. Rarely is an entire film an hommage, in the sense of replicating the original the way Gus Van Sant's 1998 remake of Hitchcock's *Psycho* did. Generally, the acknowledgment is in the form of a shot or a sequence that recalls another film. For example, Spielberg was a great admirer of Hitchcock. *Close Encounters of the Third Kind* acknowledges the climactic scene in *North by Northwest* when Cary Grant is trying to prevent Eva Marie Saint from sliding off Mt. Rushmore. In the Spielberg film, however, it is Melinda Dillon who does the same for Richard Dreyfuss in the Devil's Tower sequence. *Young Frankenstein* and *Dead Men Don't Wear Plaid* (1982) are, respectively, more than just spoofs of horror and film noir. They are rooted in a fondness for these genres that results in a special kind of parody: parody that is "rooted in affection," to use the phrase of the author William Golding.

The credits of Joel Coen's *O Brother, Where Art Thou?* (2000) claim the film is based on Homer's *Odyssey* (George Clooney's character is named Everett Ulysses McGill, and John Goodman plays a Cylopian figure with one eye). However, its real inspiration is Preston Sturges's *Sullivan's Travels*, in which a Hollywood director, John L. Sullivan, known for his comedies, wants to "go serious" and make a social-consciousness movie based on a fictitious proletarian novel, *O Brother, Where Art Thou?* Refusing to listen to studio executives and even his own butler, Sullivan embarks on an odyssey to learn deprivation firsthand and eventually ends up in a chain gang because he has failed to heed his butler's warning that attempts by the "morbid rich" to learn about poverty can be "extremely dangerous." Coen's film, which recounts the odyssey of three fugitives from a chain gang, is an hommage to Sturges's film as well as an attempt to imbue screwball comedy with a sense of humanity, as Sturges had done in *Sullivan's Travels.*

Films about the filmmaking process, including a behind-the-scenes look at the movie world and those who work in it. Nickelodeon is historically accurate in its portrayal of silent-film making; *Sweet Liberty* and Vincente Minnelli's *Two Weeks in Another Town* (1962) are valid depictions of contemporary on-location filming. *Shadow of the Vampire* (2000) is a reconstruction of the making of Murnau's horror classic, *Nosferatu* (1922). Although *The Perils of Pauline* (1947) is loosely based on the life of silent serial queen Pearl White, the movie is quite accurate in sticking to the chaotic conditions under which silent films were often made.

"What price Hollywood" films, which demythologize the industry by stripping away the glamour and exposing the grim reality beneath the painted surface. All three versions of *A Star Is Born*, even though the third is about the rock scene, show the extent to which stars are replaced in the pantheon. *Sunset Boulevard* dramatizes a silent star's descent into madness because she cannot adjust to a Hollywood that is not the one she remembers. Vincente Minnelli's *The Bad and the Beautiful* (1952) and Robert Altman's *The Player* (1992) reveal the awesome power that movie executives have over writers; *The Player,* a darkly satiric look at corporate Hollywood, goes so far as to have an executive kill a writer.

There is always the danger that a reflexive film will become so obscure in its allusions and quotations that it will appeal only to film buffs. No one enjoys being trapped in a conversation that's so specialized only experts can participate in it. The films mentioned in this section can be appreciated by anyone, regardless of his or her knowledge of movies or lack of it. On the other hand, a film like Godard's *Detective* (1985), which expects the viewer to be familiar with all of the incongruities of the private-eye movie that Godard renders even more incongruous, is a parody of reflexivity; by its elitism, it alienates moviegoers who can accept the incongruous but not the incomprehensible.

THE WOMAN'S FILM

While woman's film is an accepted term in film criticism as well as a legitimate film genre, man's film is neither. The woman's film became a genre for two main reasons: Hollywood's early attempts to woo female audiences and the emergence of female stars whose personalities elevated them to the level of icons. Female audiences were always special to the industry, either because it was assumed that women had more time for moviegoing than men or that women were more inclined to be movie fans than men. Whatever the reasoning, in the early days of film some nickelodeon owners attempted to attract middle-class women to their theaters by offering them free admission for prenoon shows. Others, less generous, allowed women in for half price.

Theater owners used a different tactic in the 1930s and 1940s: they sponsored "dish nights." Once or twice a week, a free piece of dishware was included in the ticket price and, in the course of time, a complete set of dishes could be acquired. Because women made up such an important—and, during World War II, major—segment of the audience, Hollywood responded by giving them their own genre, with such stars as Bette Davis, Joan Crawford, and Barbara Stanwyck—actresses who became so inseparable from their personae that one often speaks of a "Bette Davis movie" or a "Joan Crawford movie."

Bette Davis and Joan Crawford could not play subservient women. They played women who were the equal and, at times, the superior of men. In Michael Curtiz's *Mildred Pierce* (1945), Mildred (Joan Crawford) goes from being a housewife to owning a restaurant chain; in *The Corn Is Green* (1945), Miss Moffat (Bette Davis) establishes a school for Welsh coal miners and sends her prize student to Oxford.

In a woman's film, the plot revolves around the woman, and her only limitations are those imposed by her mortality. Yet, even when faced with death, the woman dies nobly. In *Dark Victory*, Judith Traherne (Bette Davis), dying of a brain tumor, not only manages to conceal her imminent death from her husband; she also chooses to die alone. In *No Sad Songs for Me* (1950), a wife faces terminal illness with a spirit of resignation that puts her husband to shame.

The woman's film of the 1930s and 1940s promoted self-sacrifice. When a daughter decides to marry above her class, her mother disappears from her life but reappears to watch the wedding ceremony through the window (King Vidor's *Stella Dallas* [1937]). Women struggled to provide a better life for their children (*Mildred Pierce*) or were willing to raise a friend's illegitimate child (*The Great Lie* [1941]). Forced to give up an ille-

Bette Davis as Judith Traherne and George Brent as Dr. Steele in *Dark Victory* (1939), a major woman's film. *(Courtesy Movie Star News)*

gitimate child of their own (*The Old Maid* [1939]), they must stand by, watching the child address someone else as "mother."

While women suffered nobly in many films of the 1930s and 1940s, they were also depicted as being able to succeed in male-dominated professions. The woman's film of the period portrayed women in a variety of occupations: lawyers, copywriters, reporters, actors, surgeons, nurses. By the 1960s, there was nothing unusual about a successful woman lawyer or entrepreneur. Terminal illnesses had become standard television fare and were no longer special. The cancer victim had become the cancer patient, and resignation to the inevitable was no longer the noble gesture it was in *Dark Victory* but, rather, the final stage of a process that begins with denial and ends with acceptance.

The portrayal of women on the screen has changed through the years. In the classic woman's film, women did not so much have friends as confidantes, who were either supportive sisters or wisecracking sidekicks. Genuine friendship between women was rare on the screen; women who seemed to be friends were actually rivals (*Old Acquaintance* [1943]). It was not until *Julia* (1977) that American audiences saw a true friendship between women depicted on the screen. The title character (Vanessa Redgrave) and her friend Lily (Jane Fonda, playing Lillian Hellman) are not at odds with each other; they complement each other. Thus, the politically committed Julia inspires the apolitical Lily to take a stand against the spread of fascism that is soon to bring about World War II.

When Barbara Stanwyck played a young widow in *My Reputation* (1946) who refused to wear black as a sign of mourning, she scandalized her friends. In Martin Scorsese's *Alice Doesn't Live Here Anymore* (1975), Ellen Burstyn plays a widow who would no more wear black than she would mourn in silence. Instead, she takes her son on the road in an attempt to resume her singing career but eventually has to work in a diner. The point is that each of these women, although they belong to different eras, exercised the same kind of independence; one defied her mother and refused to have her dresses dyed black (*My Reputation*); the other defied convention and took off with her son in search of work (*Alice*). Thus, it is not entirely correct to say that contemporary films portray women more realistically than did those of the past—unless realism is measured by explicit language, nudity, and overt sexuality. On the other hand, had the Production Code not inhibited filmmakers, the dialogue of the films of the 1940s and 1950s would have been far less subtle, and the portrayal of sexuality more direct.

It is important to remember that the women depicted on the screen during Hollywood's golden age were often strong-willed, but various factors (the Production Code, audience expectations, a general suspicion of—if not bias against—women who succeed in a male-dominated profession) necessitated either a last-minute conversion to marriage, always regarded as more satisfying than a career, or some sign of imperfection on the woman's part.

Rosalind Russell was known for her career women, who were always elegantly dressed, witty, and the equal of any male. Yet, in movie after movie, she ended up preferring marriage to a career. In *Tell It to the Judge* (1949), Russell played the title character, who is in every way the intellectual superior of her ex-husband. However, the script called for Russell not only to take him back but also to utter the incredible line "A woman's place is in the home." To her credit, Russell tossed the line off as if she didn't believe it—and hoped the audience agreed with her.

MGM's *Woman of the Year* (1942), the first pairing of Spencer Tracy and Katharine Hepburn, was to end with Tess Harding (Hepburn) telling her husband, Sam Craig (Tracy), that she wishes to be known as Tess Harding Craig, not as Mrs. Sam Craig. This should have posed no problem, except that MGM thought audiences would leave thinking that Tess had scored a victory over Sam. Instead, a scene was added in which Tess tried to make breakfast for Sam and proved to be totally incompetent in the kitchen. Her inability to brew coffee was apparently a cardinal sin, despite her awesome intelligence and fluency in various languages.

MGM insisted on some sign of Tess's vulnerability; unfortunately, the kitchen scene—which Hepburn has admitted she hated—marred what might have been a truly feminist film. Still, there were films in the 1930s

Rosalind Russell, the quintessential career woman of the 1940s, in *A Woman of Distinction* (1950). *(Courtesy Sony Pictures Entertainment)*

and 1940s in which women defied convention but paid the price for it, which was often death. *Back Street* (both the 1932 and the 1941 versions) portrayed a woman who accepted her role as mistress, even sailing to Europe with her married lover (but always boarding the ship after he and his family had done so). However, the prevailing mentality—that the wages of sin is death—meant that both husband and mistress died at the end.

In 1968, an event occurred that affected all of the genres, but especially the woman's film: the movie ratings. The changeover really began in the 1950s, when filmmakers, motivated by the need to offer audiences something other than what was available on television, started challenging the Production Code. Thus, language and subject matter that were once forbidden ("You go to hell!" shouted by Marlon Brando at a Roman Catholic priest in *On the Waterfront;* virginity as an object of humor in *The Moon Is Blue* [1953]; heroin addiction in *The Man with the Golden Arm* [1955]) found their way to the screen. By the early 1960s, another taboo subject, homosexuality, was clearly implied—though not depicted—in *Suddenly, Last Summer* (1959) and *The Children's Hour* (1962). As a result, the Production Code proved to be obsolete and was replaced by a rating system, which originally consisted of G (general audiences), M (mature audiences), R (restricted to viewers over sixteen, unless accompanied by parent or guardian), and X (under sixteen not admitted). As film content became more explicit, the designations changed, eventually becoming G,

PG (parental guidance), PG-13 (parental guidance for children under thirteen), R (restricted to anyone under seventeen unless accompanied by an adult), and the rare NC-17 (no children, only seventeen and older).

These changes, combined with the attack on female stereotypes mounted by women's groups, allowed filmmakers to explore a theme in the woman's film that had been treated superficially in the past: female bonding. The traditional woman's film never denied the possibility of close relationships between women; however, the notion of women bonding like the title characters played by Paul Newman and Robert Redford in *Butch Cassidy and the Sundance Kid* (1969) was unthinkable in the 1935–1960 period. Women could be friends or rivals. If two women were friends, at least one of them would marry (*These Three* [1936]); if they were rivals, they would resolve their differences, realizing that they might have to spend the rest of their lives together (*Old Acquaintance*). But in *Julia*, Lily and Julia are the closest of friends but not rivals; they differ only in the degree of their social commitment. Prior to the ratings, if there was the slightest chance of a woman's having a relationship with another man after her husband left her, she would never forgo it to open an art gallery; but that is exactly what happens in *An Unmarried Woman* (1978). In 1946, the year after World War II ended and Hollywood turned its attention to the problems of returning veterans, no studio would have considered a film about a married woman who falls in love with a paraplegic veteran. But Vietnam was not World War II, and a situation that was unthinkable in 1946 worked some thirty years later in *Coming Home* (1978).

Although the woman's film has undergone many changes since a woman was expected to give up her career for marriage or her lover to preserve the integrity of the family name (always the man's family), it is not entirely accurate to say that women are no longer depicted as victims; rather, women are at least allowed to retaliate against their victimizers. In *Thelma and Louise* (1991), a female-bonding film in which the women become fugitives from justice, Louise (Susan Sarandon) comes upon her friend Thelma (Geena Davis) as she is about to be raped. Louise might have spared the rapist's life if he were repentant, but when he becomes verbally abusive she shoots him in the face. Thelma and Louise thus become women on the run. Pursued by the police, they take a suicidal drive over the Grand Canyon; the car heads into space, the frame freezes, and Thelma and Louise move out of time into eternity (or, at least, myth). The ending recalls *Butch Cassidy and the Sundance Kid*, in which the pair, outnumbered and about to be killed, also freeze into a composition that is slowly drained of color until it becomes monochrome. If men can bond, turn outlaw, and freeze into myth, why not women?

At present, there seem to be two kinds of woman's films: the terminal illness and the woman-as-free-spirit kind. Although women have been dying from cancer on the screen since *Dark Victory*, men had been spared that particular death until *My Life* (1993), which showed that a man (Michael Keaton in a brilliant but, unfortunately, unheralded performance) could succumb to the disease as well. Still, *My Life* did not usher in a spate of male terminal-illness movies. That is still the domain of the woman's film, particularly now that the "disease of the month" movie has run its course on television, and cancer has become just another plot peg.

In *Terms of Endearment* (1984), the cancer victim is a young mother (Debra Winger); in *Stepmom* and *One True Thing* (both 1998), the mothers are older (Susan Sarandon and Meryl Streep, respectively), but the subject matter is the same. Then there is the freewheeling mother personified by Shirley MacLaine in *Postcards from the Edge*—the postmodern Auntie Mame, who upstages her daughter (Meryl Streep) whenever she can; and the madcap mother—the kind that would think nothing of taking off for Los Angeles with her daughter to make her into a movie star, even if it means leaving family and friends behind (Susan Sarandon in *Anywhere but Here* [1999]). Winger, Sarandon, and Streep are gifted actresses, but cancer victims and flighty mothers are only two of the many kinds of women the screen has to offer. Even during the patriarchal studio system, there was a greater range of roles.

The chief obstacle to the woman's film is presently the dearth of decent scripts for middle-aged women. The woman's film will never die out, but it will never regain the popularity it once had until producers and screenwriters realize there can be as much drama in a movie about a middle-aged woman as there is in a movie about a younger one; that cancer is neither a woman's disease nor the only cause of death for female characters of a certain age; and that there are many more kinds of mothers than those who hog the spotlight from their children and subordinate their children's interests to their own. Above all, writers attempting to create an "Auntie Mame" mom should remember that Auntie Mame, as played definitively by Rosalind Russell in the 1958 movie of that name, was never a mother.

THE HORROR FILM

The classic horror film involves a metamorphosis: an individual is transformed into an animal (panther, ape), insect (fly), semihuman (werewolf), antihuman (somnambule, ghoul, zombie, vampire), antiself (Dr. Jekyll), shrunken self (homunculus); or, as in the Frankenstein tradition, a synthetic creation is turned into a living creature. The inanimate can also be an object of transformation: a house can change from a habitation for humans to a habitation for ghosts (*The Uninvited* [1944]); it can even acquire an evil personality that affects those who live there (*Burnt Offerings* [1976]; *The Haunting* [1963, remade in 1999], *The Amityville Horror* [1979]). The same principle applies to the hotel in Stanley Kubrick's *The Shining* (1980).

The ghost story is transformation in reverse, with the ghosts taking on human qualities. The ghosts may be benign or vengeful; both types are featured in *The Uninvited*. If they are not at rest, they work through the living until they are vindicated (e.g., the mother's ghost in *Lady in White* [1988], which cannot be reunited with her daughter in the hereafter until the daughter's murderer is apprehended). The ghost story is a perennial favorite with moviegoers; not coincidentally, one of 1999's most successful films was *The Sixth Sense*, a highly intelligent example of the genre that, like most such films, has a plot twist that many moviegoers took as a surprise ending, although it had been anticipated from the beginning when a psychiatrist (Bruce Willis) is shot by his ex-patient. The film purports to be about the psychiatrist's attempt to help a nine-year-old boy (Haley Joel Osment), who can actually see ghosts, adjust to his special sense, although it has an otherworldly aspect as well that is best appreciated at the end.

The prototypical horror film is *The Cabinet of Dr. Caligari* (1919), whose visual style, pruned of exaggerations, became a standard for the genre. Visually, *Caligari* is expressionistic; its asymmetrical and bizarre settings suggest a world out of joint, a world not so much of our dreams as our nightmares. Chimneys look as if they will topple over, windows are shaped like diamonds, walls seem on the verge of caving in. The American horror film uses a less extreme form of expressionism; the high-contrast photography of the German-made *Caligari*, in which there are no grays but only black and white, was not entirely discarded by American filmmakers but made less pronounced through low-key lighting that allowed for the interplay of light and shadow.

Caligari also features two plot devices that have become conventions of the horror film: the team of the mad doctor and his subhuman accomplice (whose most familiar successors were Dr. Frankenstein and his hunchback assistant in James Whale's *Frankenstein* [1931]); and the creature's desire for a mate. In *Caligari*, the doctor's accomplice may be a somnambule, but he is not impervious to the heroine's charms; nor are the Wolf Man and Dracula unaffected by the presence of beautiful women. Embalming does not stop the mummy from searching for his beloved Princess Ananka, even if she happens to be in the United States (*The Mummy's Curse* [1946]). A synthetic creature like Frankenstein's monster needs a bride: when his bride rejects him (James Whale's *Bride of Frankenstein* [1935]), he retaliates by destroying the laboratory in which he was created. The monster's attraction to women is easily explained; the creature is the personification of the id, or the libido, which is virtually all that

THE MONSTER AND THE GIRL

Caesare the somnambule and Jane in *The Cabinet of Dr. Caligari* (1919). *(Courtesy MOMA/FSA)*

is left after the transformation. The creature's libido may even be more active because it is no longer under the control of reason.

The basic types of horror films—ghost, creature, dual-personality, and mad scientist—had been established in the 1930s and 1940s along with the conventions of low-key lighting, shadowy surfaces, dissolve transformations, cellar laboratories with overflowing test tubes, fogbound woods, and Gothic mansions. While the musical and the western were photographed in either monochrome or color, the horror film was shot almost exclusively in black and white. In the 1950s, the use of color began with *House of Wax* (1953) and *Phantom of the Rue Morgue* (1954), but it was the British-made *Curse of Frankenstein* (1957), the first of Hammer Films' horror series, that set the trend toward the color horror film.

Although color and horror are not incompatible, as Roman Polanski's *Rosemary's Baby* (1968) and *Carrie* prove, color cannot capture the shadowy world of the unconscious as well as black and white, which is also more conducive to horror by suggestion. Color is suited to gore, the hallmark of the latest kind of horror film: the slasher film. Like every addition to a genre, the slasher film is not without precedent; its parent is *Psycho*, a genuine horror film with a subtle transformation. The oedipal Norman Bates becomes so closely identified with his mother that he assumes her personality, even to the extent of dressing in her clothes and murdering in her name. Significantly, Norman does not die at the end of *Psycho*; and as the years passed and *Psycho* became a classic, the need for sequels arose— *Psycho II* (1983), then *Psycho III* (1986). As long as there is an audience for horror, there will be a *Psycho* of some sort, although it is hard to imagine any of them surpassing or even equaling Hitchcock's.

The *Psycho* sequels illustrate a time-honored tradition in horror: the monster ceases to exist when the series or the cycle does. Even though it seems obvious that, at the end of *Frankenstein*, the monster dies in the fire that destroys the mill, he is discovered in the cellar at the beginning of *Bride of Frankenstein*. And even though the monster clearly perishes again in the inferno at the end of *Bride of Frankenstein*, he is resurrected for *Son of Frankenstein* (1939) four years later and paired with the Wolf Man in *Frankenstein Meets the Wolf Man* (1943) four years after he was revived by Frankenstein's son.

The same principle applies in the slasher film, the most popular being *Friday the 13th* (1980), although it is hardly the most inventive. Far more original is *Halloween* (1978), which introduced a plot device that *Friday the 13th* and similar films (e.g., *Prom Night* [1980]; *Terror Train* [1979]) imitated: a prologue depicting an earlier murder that bears heavily on the plot. *Halloween* led to three sequels (1981, 1983, 1988), but the public was

Larry Talbot (Lon Chaney, Jr.), whose transformation does not diminish his interest in the heroine in *The Wolf Man* (1941). *(Copyright by Universal Pictures, a Division of Universal City Studios, Inc. Courtesy MCA Publishing Rights, a Division of MCA, Inc.)*

more taken with *Friday the 13th*, which, within eight years after its release, had spawned seven films.

Like other horror cycles, the *Friday the 13th* spinoffs work from the premise of the undying monster. In *Friday the 13th*, two teenage camp counselors are killed because they were making love when they should have been rescuing the drowning Jason. The killer is Jason's mother, who is also killed at the end. The sequels feature Jason himself, who emerges from the mud to continue his mother's work.

In addition to the obligatory prologue, the slasher film practices its own form of voyeurism: subjective camera. The camera is often stationed outside a window, representing the point of view of someone looking in; it tilts up to a bedroom, as if someone were spying. The slasher film also uses off-center compositions and framing that exclude the killer, leaving only the victim in the frame. While the slasher film may be a lesser form of horror, its use of subjective camera is a feature worth noting.

The slasher film, however, does not have a monopoly on subjective camera, a technique that has been used in movies as dissimilar as *The Grapes of Wrath* and *Marnie*. Whether or not the slasher film can be considered a genre or merely a subgenre of horror, as the doomsday film is a subgenre of science fiction, is problematic. Those who favor genre status argue that director Wes Craven (*Nightmare on Elm Street*) in his *Scream* trilogy—*Scream* (1995), *Scream 2* (1997), and *Scream 3* (2000)—codified the conventions of the slasher film, thereby suggesting that it constitutes a genre of its own. Just as film noir and the musical have certain features that distinguish them as genres, so does the slasher film: voyeuristic camera, terrorized teens, the psychopathic phone caller, quick cuts punctuated by ominous sounds, sex as a prelude to death, eerie music with an echolike quality, the sudden appearances of a character at a window or doorway, the "everybody's a suspect" philosophy, a murder that occurred prior to the main action, the climactic blood bath, the dead mother whose sins are visited upon her children, and the undying monster figure in the form of the killer(s), who, even after they have apparently expired, get up on their feet for one last charge.

What distinguishes the Craven trilogy from slasher films like *Prom Night* (1980), which occasioned four sequels, and *Halloween* (1978), which gave rise to seven, is its self-consciousness: not only do the films reflect Craven's knowledge of the slasher conventions, but the characters' knowledge of them as well. The teens in *Scream* appear to have seen every horror movie ever made. There are references to such films as *Nightmare on Elm Street*, *The Exorcist*, *Psycho*, *Silence of the Lambs*, and *Prom Night*, to mention only a few. The first victim (Drew Barrymore) is terrorized by a phone stalker who interrogates her by asking, among other questions, the identity of the killer in *Friday the 13th*. *Frankenstein* is on the screen in the local video store; in the knife-wielding finale, *Halloween* is on television. The teenage lovers, Billy Loomis and Sidney Prescott (Skeet Ulrich and Neve Campbell), characterize their relationship in terms of movie ratings (R, PG-13); later Loomis tells Sidney that life's "one great big movie, but you can't pick your genre." Loomis's knowledge, it turns out, is not restricted to movies; he knows a great deal about Sidney's mother, who was brutally raped and murdered a year earlier. But, as horror buff Randy Meeks (Jamie Kennedy) notes, in slasher films everyone's a suspect, and "sex is death"—particularly R-rated sex.

Just as *Scream* is conscious of being a slasher film, in which the characters are living out a slasher scenario (and in some cases know it), *Scream 3* is conscious of being the last installment of a trilogy. In *Scream 2*, the events depicted in *Scream* become the basis of a best-seller, "The Woodsboro Murders"; the book is made into a movie called "Stab," which becomes so popular that it spawns a trilogy of its own. *Scream 3* is about the making of "Stab 3," which, like *Scream 3*, is the last of a trilogy. By the end of *Scream 3* we realize that we have seen what would have been "Stab 3," if such a movie had ever been made. One of the *Scream 3* characters even states the three requirements of the finale: firing at the killer's heart is ineffective, since his bullet-riddled body will continue to lurch forward (hint: try another way or aim elsewhere); anybody can die, including those we would prefer to live; and finally, "the past will come back to bite you in the ass."

Although Craven's trilogy makes a good case for treating the slasher film as a genre, his films remain isolated examples of a form that has yet to show the range and depth of the horror film.

THE SCIENCE-FICTION FILM

"There is no clearly recognized border between SF [science fiction] and such genres as fantasy and horror," a science-fiction expert notes.[4] Such a statement is not surprising, since, as we have seen, genres often overlap or share conventions. While the western and the crime film portray both sides of the law, the designations are different: bandits in one, criminals in the other; sheriffs in one, police officers in the other. Moreover, what one critic would call horror, another might term science fiction. In *Science Fiction in the Cinema*, John Baxter considers *The Birds* to be science fiction even though it is neither futuristic nor a fantasy. *The Birds* does, however, deal with an invasion—not of Martians but of killer birds. The invasion motif suggests science fiction; the transformation motif (benign creatures turning malevolent), horror. Another anomaly is *Frequency* (2000), a variation of the time-warp film, with elements of the supernatural thriller and the "three-hankie movie"; in other words, a tearjerker (but the extremely rare male tearjerker) set in two time periods, 1969 and 1999. In 1969, a firefighter (Dennis Quaid) perishes in a fire; in 1999, his son (James Caviezel), while playing around with his father's ham radio set, discovers that he can communicate with his father, thus altering destiny by saving his father from perishing in the fire and his mother from becoming the victim of a serial killer so that his parents can enjoy a tranquil middle age.

The Birds and Frequency are hard to classify, although the latter is clearly a fantasy unfolding in the twilight zone and can therefore be termed science fiction. Utopian, fantasy, and doomsday films, as well as those about space travel and warring planets, are never mistaken for anything other than science fiction.

Nonhumans, often extraterrestrials, play a major role in science fiction; they are also a diverse lot and even differ in their attitude toward humans. While some extraterrestrials seek the destruction of the planet (War of the Worlds [1953]), not all are treacherous. Some have come to warn humankind of the dangers of nuclear testing (The Day the Earth Stood Still [1951]); others, to enlighten humans about the nature of aliens in the hope of bridging the gap between "us" and "them" (Close Encounters of the Third Kind); still others have come to use Earth's resources for their own purposes (This Island Earth [1955]). The aliens in It Came from Outer Space (1953) mean no harm; they merely wish to repair their spaceship.

The creatures themselves represent various life-forms: plant life (The Thing [1951]); aquatic life (the Gill-Man in The Creature from the Black Lagoon [1954] and Revenge of the Creature [1955]); a protoplasmic mass (The Blob [1958]); birds (The Giant Claw [1957]); and insects such as spiders (Tarantula [1955]), grasshoppers (Beginning of the End [1957]), and ants (Them! [1954]).

In Seeing Is Believing, Peter Biskind argues that just as the western is bipolar (wilderness vs. civilization, West vs. East, and the like), so, too, is science fiction, with its political extremes of right and left.[5] In conservative science fiction, science, the federal government, and the military appear as forces for good: science succeeds in destroying the alien (It Came from Beneath the Sea [1955]; The Thing [1951]). Liberal science fiction either depicts science, the federal government, and the military as ineffectual or criticizes their methods. In I Married a Monster from Outer Space (1958), salvation comes not from the government but from a dog. In conservative science fiction, aliens have no redeeming features. In liberal science fiction, they are portrayed sympathetically. In The Seven Year Itch, The Girl (Marilyn Monroe) remarks on how moved she was by The Creature from the Black Lagoon. In Close Encounters of the Third Kind, the government, learning that an alien spacecraft will be arriving in the vicinity of Devil's Tower in Wyoming, concocts an elaborate scam to evacuate the area, thereby causing enormous hardships to the residents. It is the Machiavellian principle of

Science fiction as mythology in *Return of the Jedi* (1983): the confrontation of Good and Evil, Luke Skywalker (Mark Hamill) and Darth Vader (David Prowse). *(Courtesy Lucasfilms, Ltd.)*

the end justifying the means: find out what the aliens are up to, even if it means deceiving the public. The possibility that the aliens are coming in peace is never even considered.

Both *Pleasantville* and *X-Men* (both 2000) are blatantly liberal. In the former, the brother and sister plan to watch a marathon rerun of an old sit-com, "Pleasantville," on television, only to find themselves transported to Pleasantville's black-and-white world, where they discover a community in which color is a sign of individuality and is therefore suspect. Eventually, as the brother and sister introduce more emancipated ways of thinking, those who embrace the new philosophy find color entering not only their lives but also themselves, as their faces become suffused with it. Naturally, there are those who feel that color is subversive, but eventually the liberal spirit wins out, and the brother and sister return to their own time frame, leaving Pleasantville a more "colorful" place. The mutants in *X-Men*, gifted men and women who by their very nature are "different," find their civil rights threatened by an ultraconservative, racist senator. The battle lines are drawn, with the evil Magneto (Ian McKellen) willing to resort to violence to block the legislation, and the benign Xavier (Patrick Stewart) preferring nonviolent resistance, which does not preclude a display of the mutants' powers. The senator is forced to relent, and Xavier's philosophy, which reflects that of Dr. Martin Luther King, Jr., prevails.

Since creatures abound in both horror and science fiction, how are they to be distinguished from each other? The most basic way is to determine the roles of science (including technology), time (past/present/future), and experimentation (individual, local, global) in the film.

Science. While neither horror nor science fiction mirrors the real world, science fiction tries to convince us that it does by dealing in specifics. Horror tends to be more general. In *Bride of Frankenstein*, we never know how Dr. Pretorious shrinks humans to the size of miniatures. In *Dr. Cyclops* (1940), on the other hand, we know that the physicist creates his homunculi by subjecting humans to atomic radiation. Because science is the film's point of departure, *Dr. Cyclops* is viewed as science fiction.

Time. The horror film, like the gothic novel, tends to be set in remote times. Even when a horror film is set in the present, it recalls cults (the cat cult in *Cat People*) and practices (devil worship in *Rosemary's Baby*) that go back centuries. Science fiction, on the other hand, can either reflect the present or evoke the future. The futuristic film is easily recognized; the future portrayed in such films is usually unsettling (*Things to Come* [1936]), if not nightmarish (Fritz Lang's *Metropolis* [1926]). The time travel film is a special case; one can easily argue that unless science is actually involved (e.g., the construction of a time machine in *The Time Machine* [1960]), fantasy is the more accurate term. Yet time travel is not limited to the future. In some films, the traveler journeys backward in time. In *Berkeley Square* (1933), Peter Standish (Leslie Howard) is transported to his favorite era, the eighteenth century. Standish had an easy time of it: he just stepped into a painting. Time travel is not always that simple, nor is it always voluntary. The brother and sister in *Pleasantville* expected to watch "Pleasantville" reruns until they were magically drawn into the set, and into the sitcom, becoming not only part of "Pleasantville" the series but also the town in which it takes place, and in which they are exposed to values that are totally different from their own.

Science fiction's approach to the present can be quite subtle. In the 1950s, science-fiction movies capitalized on two of America's major fears: flying saucers and the atomic bomb. The possibility of extraterrestrial life resulted in one of the era's best science-fiction movies, Don Siegel's *Invasion of the Body Snatchers* (1956), in which aliens descend upon a California town and take possession of the inhabitants by an ingenious method of transformation: pods are placed under their beds, absorbing the inhabitants' personalities and leaving them as parodies of human beings. The film's implications were far-reaching: aliens threatened the race with a unique form of extinction—the extinction of the human personality. The threat to civilization posed by the atomic bomb triggered a host of science-fiction movies that imagined the results of atomic detonations: mutants in the form of giant ants, creatures dislodged from the ocean depths, humans turned into steel.

In the 1950s, a villain that was a computer would have made sense to only a few. By 1968, the name of HAL, the dispassionate computer of Stanley Kubrick's *2001: A Space Odyssey*, had entered the movie vocabulary, joining such unforgettable names as *Casablanca*'s Rick Blaine and *Gone with the Wind*'s Rhett Butler.

In the 1970s, the science-fiction movie took an interesting turn. The threat of the atomic bomb had mushroomed into the fear of nuclear destruction. Since, as T. S. Eliot observed, "humankind cannot bear very much reality," George Lucas in *Star Wars* (1977) amalgamated science fiction, which was never a pure genre to begin with, not with horror but with adventure. The result was not mindless escapism but a return to myth in its earliest stage: fairy tale or dream narrative with stock characters rather than individuals—heroes, princesses, villains, half-humans, nonhumans, animal-like humans, and humanlike animals—that we have met many times before in our dreams. In the Star Wars trilogy, the characters include the pure-hearted Luke Skywalker, the virginal Princess Leia, the evil Darth Vader, the 900-year-old Yoda, the patriarchal Obi-Wan Kenobi, Chewbacca the Wookie, the treacherous Jabba the Hut, the porcine Gamorrean guards, the reptilian Admiral Ackbar, and a lovable pair of robots, C-3PO and R2-D2.

Equally important are the contributions of Steven Spielberg to the genre. While Lucas added adventure and an uncritical form of myth to science fiction, Spielberg humanized the genre. *Close Encounters of the Third Kind* portrays real people—a man, a woman, and a child—whose response to aliens reflects the film's philosophy. The child and the childlike characters in the film do not fear the aliens. Spielberg is advocating tearing down the wall that divides one group from another, one race from another, and humans from extraterrestrials. The aliens bring love; thus, one can learn from them. The humans who return to Earth at the end of *Close Encounters* have been changed for the better. Likewise, in Spielberg's *E.T.: The Extra-Terrestrial* (1982), a human—again, a child—learns from an alien.

There are two important facts to remember about genres:

Genres never die. A genre may go out of fashion for a while or reconstitute itself. When it reappears, it may look like a totally new creation, when it is really "old wine in a new bottle." All that has happened is that the film reflects both the conventions of the genre and the mores (language, values, morality, etc.) of its own age. In 1937, the very idea of using strong language in a screwball comedy like *Easy Living* was unthinkable; in 1999, the screwball comedy *Notting Hill* was classified PG-13 for language. Yet each film observed the conventions of screwball, as well as being a product of the times.

Genres can no more be pigeonholed than can human beings. Even though we are all classified in one way or another (race, gender, ethnicity, age, marital status, religion, and so forth), human beings can—and do—transcend the limits of classification. And so do films. Unless it can be determined that a particular film belongs to one, and only one, genre, it is best to say that while a film may typify a particular genre, it contains elements of others. Similarly, we can say that someone is a male with qualities that go beyond those traditionally ascribed to males. Teenage females responded to Leonardo DiCaprio's androgynous appearance and sensitivity in *Titanic* (1997); however, these were the same qualities that alienated many teenage males, who considered DiCaprio's looks unmasculine because their image of masculinity had been conditioned by male athletes and media icons. However, the most interesting actors, male and female, are impossible to categorize in terms as limited as gender. Obviously Meryl Streep is female, and Jack Nicholson is male. Yet each seems to possess his or her own gender (a "Streep," a "Nicholson"). Such actors—and there are many—belong to a particular sex as well as a particular gender—a combination of elements traditionally called "male" and "female" but unique to the one who possesses them. To say that Katharine Hepburn is female is to state the obvious; to say that her performance style is defined not by her sex ("female") but by her gender (a "Hepburn") is to say that it is possible to speak of a "Hepburn movie," a "Hepburn role," or a "Hepburn-like performance."

Genres work the same way. Think of a film genre as a handle that enables you to get a grasp of a particular kind of movie. Once you understand the various genres, you can see how a film belongs more properly to one than to another yet still have features of another—or maybe several others. Ford, for example, manufactures several kinds of cars. Nominally, an Escort is a Ford. Specifically, it is a Ford Escort. Practically, it is just an Escort. *Some Like It Hot* is primarily farce; it also belongs to a subgenre of farce, drag comedy. It can also be considered as screwball, but with music thrown in; and let's not forget romantic comedy, which it is as well. But what is *Some Like It Hot* essentially? A classic farce. Remember that *farce* comes from the Latin word for "stuffing." And a good many elements from other genres can be folded into a farce, as they can into any kind of film.

NOTES

[1]James Kitses, *Horizons West* (Bloomington: Indiana University Press, 1969), 8–27.

[2]Stanley J. Solomon, *Beyond Formula: American Film Genres* (New York: Harcourt Brace Jovanovich, 1976), 12–15.

[3]Jack Shadoian, *Dreams and Dead Ends: The American Gangster/Crime Film* (Cambridge, Mass.: MIT Press, 1977), 2.

[4]William Johnson, "Journey into Science Fiction," in *Focus on the Science Fiction Film*, ed. William Johnson (Englewood Cliffs, N.J.: Prentice-Hall, 1972), 1.

[5]Peter Biskind, *Seeing Is Believing: How Hollywood Taught Us to Stop Worrying and Love the Fifties* (New York: Pantheon Books, 1983), 102–59.

CHAPTER

Film
Subtext

5

H
ow often have you read a story or seen a film that you felt was not entirely what it seemed to be about? Many first-year college students read "The Widow of Ephesus," a tale from Petronius's *Satyricon*, written in the first century A.D. In this frequently anthologized story, a woman is so shattered by her husband's death that she cannot practice the ancient rites of mourning (breast-beating and hair-tearing). Instead, accompanied by her maid, she retires to the underground tomb where the body lies. A soldier, patrolling a crucifixion site nearby to prevent the bodies from being taken down from the crosses, notices her presence, enters the tomb, quotes Virgil, and finally wins her over. When a corpse disappears from one of the crosses, the soldier fears that his negligence will cost him his job. But after three consecutive nights of lovemaking, the widow of Ephesus offers him her husband's body as a fair exchange.

What was just summarized is the story's plot, which consists of a situation (a widow in mourning), a complication (the soldier's appearance), and a resolution (the substitution of the husband's body for a criminal's).

However, a classic tale like "The Widow of Ephesus" cannot be reduced to its story line. In every narrative worth studying, whether it's a work of fiction or a work of film, there is a **subtext,** a complex structure beneath the narrative consisting of the various associations the narrative evokes in us. In other words, there is a surface meaning and a deeper meaning. "The Widow of Ephesus" has a surface wit that cannot mask the underlying cynicism. The surface meaning is that love conquers all; the deeper, or subtextual, meaning is that love conquers lovers, generating such passion in them that they think nothing of sleeping three nights in a row next to a corpse.

Film also has a subtext, or what might be called an infranarrative. Whether we realize it or not, film has a dual nature. There is the film projected *on* the screen and the film projected *from* the screen. The first is the narrative in the traditional sense: a text that is the result of the collaboration between a director, a writer, a cast, and a crew; in other words, what audiences would think of as the "movie" they are about to see.

The situation is analogous to a novel that has just been published; prior to publication it was revised and edited. Now it awaits readers. The text is there, but readers, reviewers, and scholars must find their own way into it. When they do, they will be entering the infranarrative and will experience the text more deeply, finding levels of meaning (symbols, image patterns, references to other works, including the author's) that are there but must be discovered through sensitive reading.

Film infranarrative, or subtext, is the result of the various associations we make during the film, comparable to the symbolic or metaphorical level in literature. In a literature class, a professor may say that Dante's *Inferno* is, *literally*, about a man's descent through the nine circles of hell; *symbolically*, however, the *Inferno* is about a man who's trying to put his life in order by envisioning what awaits him in the hereafter. Another professor may argue that although Robert Frost's "Stopping by Woods on a Snowy Evening" seems like a poem about a man stopping to observe the snow-covered woods, it is actually about a man contemplating death on the longest night of the year.

Naturally, the narrative and infranarrative (or text and subtext) are not two separate entities (there is, after all, only one film). Think of them, rather, as two concentric circles, the infranarrative being *within* the narrative. But, just as English teachers distinguish between form and content, and philosophers between matter and form, we do the same with the two narratives. Beneath Narrative 1 (the plot as the ordered arrangement of the incidents) is Narrative 2 (the associations, conscious and otherwise, that arise from the plot's visualization). The former can be summarized as one would a novel or a play; the latter, however, has no place in a synopsis. Asked for a plot synopsis of *Psycho*, for example, one would never say it is about an Oedipus complex gone haywire, sexual repression, voyeurism, transvestism, schizophrenia, and necrophilia, although these are all part of the film's subtext. But saying that *Psycho* is about such matters implies that certain associations must have been made between what we saw on the movie screen (big or small)—a film about a woman who absconds with a $40,000 bank deposit and ends up in a motel, where she is murdered by a young man who can kill only by dressing as his mother—and what we experienced, consciously or otherwise: a film showing a man so obsessed by the spirit of his dead mother (whom he killed, along with her lover) that he dresses like her and kills women of whom his mother would have disapproved; an indentation in his mother's bed, suggesting that her corpse had occasionally been placed there; and an identification with her that is so deep that, finally, the young man believes he has become his mother. The film may remind us of a famous story about necrophilia, Faulkner's "A Rose for Emily." It might even remind us of certain Greek myths in which sons murder their mothers—e.g., Alcmaeon killing his mother, Eriphyle; Orestes killing his mother, Clytemnestra, and her former lover (now her husband) Aegisthus. Or it might recall a novella like Stevenson's *Dr. Jekyll and Mr. Hyde*, in which the respectable Henry Jekyll is incapable of doing what his evil alter ego, Mr. Hyde, can. By making certain associations between *Psycho*, mythic figures, and literary characters, we have gone beneath the film's surface into its infranarrative.

These associations can be mythic, visual/iconic, intellectual, or musical; they can even exist in some combination. For example, an iconic association (one in which the actor's screen persona is associated with the character, so that the actor *is* the character) can also be mythic in the sense of reminding us of some mythic type or mythological figure; but it is primarily iconic. For example, the character that Barbra Streisand plays in *The Mirror Has Two Faces* (1996)—a plain-looking college professor who transforms herself into a chic and highly attractive woman—might recall the story of the ugly duckling or the crone, who is really a beautiful woman in disguise. But Streisand herself has become such a screen legend, and has capitalized on her metamorphosis from gawky performer on early 1960s television to world-class singer-actor-writer-director-philanthropist, that we are more apt to identify her with the character than with the underlying myth of transformation.

MYTHIC ASSOCIATIONS

The Nature of Myth

To understand how myth becomes part of a film's subtext, we must reconsider the concept of myth. In the popular mind, *myth* is synonymous with *falsehood.* In literary and film criticism, however, it has another meaning altogether. William York Tindall defined myth as "a dreamlike narrative in which the individual's central concerns are united with society, time, and the universe."[1] Erich Fromm called myth "a message from ourselves to ourselves."[2] The film critic Parker Tyler regarded myth as "a free, unharnessed fiction, a basic prototypic pattern capable of many variations and distortions, even though it remains imaginative truth."[3] Lillian Feder's definition is the most detailed: "Myth is a narrative structure of two basic areas of unconscious experience which, of course, are related. First, it expresses instinctual drives and the repressed wishes, fears, and conflicts that they motivate. These appear in the themes of myth. Second, myth also conveys the remnants within the individual consciousness of the early stage of phylogenetic development in which the plots were created. This characteristic is evident mainly in its plots."[4] In other words, myth is a form of racial history—a narrative distillation of the wishes and fears both of ourselves and of the human race.

Common to all four definitions are the following:

1. Myth is a narrative, and as such obeys the rules of narrative (e.g., the beginning-middle-end structure).
2. Myth also operates on an unconscious level, presenting us with characters (questers, the enchanted and the enchanter, ogres, scapegoats, monsters), themes (the homeward journey, the quest, ancestral curses, revenge, patricide, matricide), and settings (caves, wastelands, subterranean rivers, enchanted islands, flat-topped mountains, ominous castles, desolate moors) that we recognize without having experienced them because they tap into our racial memory and recall early stages in the development of humankind, as well as events that occurred during those stages and are now regarded as stories.
3. The themes of myth are universal: the return of the hero, the desire for forbidden knowledge, the quest for identity, the rebellion against tyranny. No single age has a monopoly on such themes. Thus myth transcends time and place and can never be said to be dated.
4. Myths are ultimate truths about life and death, fate and nature, God and humans. For this reason, they can never be false, even though the characters they portray may not have existed. Myths also endure long after the civilizations that produce them have vanished because they crystallize, in narrative form, unchanging patterns of human behavior. There will always be rebels like Antigone and Prometheus, homeward-bound voyagers like Odysseus, vengeance seekers like Medea, those who pursue reason

and favor Apollo over Dionysus, and those who favor emotional release at the expense of reason and prefer Dionysus to Apollo.

Film is receptive to myth for two reasons. First, film and myth can speak the same language—picture language. Long before myths were written down, they were transmitted orally through epics and visually through artwork on walls, vases, bowls, and wine vessels. Thus, from the outset myth was oral and visual; and so was film, for even during the silent period there was always some form of sound, as we have seen. Another reason film and myth are so compatible is that both are intimately associated with dreams. Parker Tyler coined a phrase for film: "the daylight dream." Neither is it coincidental that Hollywood has been dubbed "the dream factory." We dream individually, of course; but we also dream collectively. The stuff of our dreams is the stuff of fairy tales, legends, and romances: quests, evil enchanters, enchanted princes and princesses, talking animals, transformations of humans into beasts and the ugly into the beautiful (and vice versa), apparitions, conversations with the dead, and so forth. Such dream material belongs to the human race, and thus our dreams make us one with humankind. The psychologist Carl Jung compared the dream to a screen on which the history of the race is projected; the same can be said of the movie screen. When mythic figures appear on the screen, they strike a responsive chord because they are familiar: we have encountered them before—if not in actual myths or fairy tales, then in our dreams.

Film has a dream level to which we respond the way we respond to myths: we respond instinctively, never questioning their origins or even their existence. Making a mythic association involves remembering a pattern of experience that is universal. Sometimes we can determine the specific myth: *King Kong* evokes Beauty and the Beast; *The Blue Angel* (1930), in which a respected teacher is destroyed by a seductive singer, recalls myths about such temptresses as Circe, Calypso, and the Lorelei. More often, you will not be able to isolate the specific myth but only a mythic type (the searcher, the exile, the knight-errant, the blessed damsel, the earth mother, the eternal child, the messiah/liberator/savior/deus ex machina) or a mythic theme (the descent to the underworld, the quest for the grail, the journey into the unknown, the homeward journey, the birth of the hero, the life force vs. the force of reason, wilderness vs. civilization, and the like).

The Transformation Myth in *Cat People* (Jacques Tourneur, 1942)

The transformation myth is one of the most common myths, as anyone who has ever read Ovid's *Metamorphoses* knows: Daphne is transformed into a laurel tree, Philomela into a nightingale, Chiron the centaur into the constellation Sagittarius, Niobe into stone, and so on. There are also instances of mythological figures who are capable of changing form (Proteus, the sea nymph Thetis). In *Cat People*, Irena (Simone Simon), the ill-starred descendant of a Serbian cat cult, is doomed to revert to a panther whenever her passions are aroused; the reason could be anything from jealousy to sexual desire—not so much on her part as on the male's.

The script, as might be expected of any early-1940s script, skirts the issue of Irena's frigidity; instead, the assumption is that Irena, who bears the curse of the cat women (her ancestors who rejected Christianity and embraced pagan rituals and black masses), is unable to consummate her marriage because she is afraid of turning into a panther and killing her husband. Rather, she insists on a relationship of friendship; her husband tries to understand but eventually turns to a female coworker, Alice, who recommends a psychiatrist, Dr. Judd. The psychiatrist is so intrigued by Irena that he tries to seduce her, not realizing that a man's touch can release the panther in her. The panther emerges and attacks Judd, who mortally wounds Irena with his sword cane.

The narrative seems to be a Freudian reworking of a transformation myth. But the infranarrative points to something far deeper: a woman who wants a man only as a friend, not as a lover; who cannot bear a man's touch; who, after taking on animal form, pursues Alice, now her rival, through Central Park (unseen, thanks to the ingenious direction of Jacques Tourneur) and later to a health club, where—also unseen—she terrorizes Alice while she is swimming. Discerning audiences now regard *Cat People* as more than just another horror movie: some see elements of lesbianism in the way Irena stalks Alice; others see Irena as a mother goddess to whom men are meant to be subservient; still others view her as a woman who yearns in vain for a healthy relationship with a man, a woman who, when she commits an act of violence (which she does when, as a panther, she at-

Irena (Simone Simon) and her husband in name only (Kent Smith) in *Cat People* (1942). *(Courtesy MOMA/FSA)*

tacks a herd of sheep), must cleanse herself by taking a hot bath. For a movie that was not taken seriously in its time, *Cat People* now enjoys critical acclaim.

The Savior Myth in *Shane* (George Stevens, 1953)

Every critic who has written about *Shane* has sensed a mythic subtext in the film. In *Shane*, there appear to be at least three mythic levels.

Shane as a Christ Figure

Shane begins with the credits, with Alan Ladd as Shane entering on horseback from the left to the "Shane theme," a melody that suggests cantering horses and deer drinking peacefully from a stream against a background of snow-decked mountains. Shane is descending into a valley; he is not moving horizontally across the frame like a gunfighter, although he will later change both speed and direction during his ride of vengeance. For the moment he is moving *downward*—in symbolic terms, he might be said to be lowering himself—as he descends into the lives of the Starretts, a family of homesteaders.

Shane can be seen as a Christ figure. Just as Christ descended from heaven and humbled himself by assuming human nature, so Shane descends into the valley, temporarily putting aside his divinity to serve humanity. Shane's resemblance to Christ has been noted by the critic Donald Richie:

> Shane . . . came from nowhere and he is going nowhere—like the vagrant Jett Rink in *Giant*, like the hitchhiking George Eastman [in Stevens's *A Place in the Sun*], like Jesus Christ. . . . His difference from the romantic hero is that he—like Christ himself—rather than merely feeling that he ought to do something to express his inner values and to affect the world, actually does something about it.[5]

Shane's past is as enigmatic as Christ's. Christ's life before he began his public ministry at thirty is a mystery. And so is Shane's; he simply appears one day, looking like a god in white buckskins. As part of his ritual incarnation, he sheds his divine trappings and dresses in the clothes of mortals—blue denim and dark trousers. But he will not retain that outfit forever. Before he avenges the death of Torrey (Elisha Cook, Jr.), he changes back into his buckskins, becoming a god once more.

Jesus Christ preached meekness: "If someone strike thee on the right cheek, turn to him the other also" (Matt. 5:39). Shane displays his meekness when Chris (Ben Johnson) challenges his manhood after Shane orders a bottle of soda pop for young Joey Starrett. Chris offers Shane a "man's drink" by spilling a jigger of whiskey on his shirt. At that moment, Shane does not retaliate; but later, when he returns to the saloon, he reciprocates by buying Chris a drink and disposing of its contents in the same way. In the ensuing brawl, the abandon with which Shane swings his fists suggests a wrathful god not unlike the Christ who overturned the tables of the moneychangers as he drove them out of the Temple of Jerusalem. Meekness and righteous anger are not incompatible.

Shane's message is for the chosen. It is for the homesteaders, not for the cattle ranchers. Sometimes, as history has proved, the chosen must take up arms. Thus, Shane teaches young Joey how to shoot. When Marion Starrett (Jean Arthur) finds Shane teaching her son how to handle a gun, Shane's explanation is simple: "A gun is as good or bad as the man using it." Joey, who has a male child's notion of manhood (men do not

Shane's farewell to Joey in *Shane*. Shane leaves Joey (Brandon de Wilde) with the command to grow up "strong and straight," as he departs, presumably to aid another family of homesteaders. *(Courtesy Paramount Pictures)*

flinch when turpentine is applied to an open wound, and they settle disagreements with their fists), is given a rare opportunity to see his theory put to the test when he watches Shane kill Wilson (Jack Palance), the gunfighter. Shane leaves Joey with the command to grow up "strong and straight." Now Shane is no longer a man but a god delivering one of his commandments before he disappears from view.

Shane as Apollo-Hercules

One writer has called Shane "the frontier Christ, coming down from a Western Olympus."[6] This description characterizes Shane as part Christ, part Greek deity.

In Greek mythology, Zeus punished Apollo for killing one of his sons by forcing him to spend a year of servitude in the household of Admetus, the king of Thessaly. Admetus respected Apollo's godhead, and in gratitude Apollo allowed him the privilege of living beyond his allotted time, provided he could find someone to die for him. Unable to find a volunteer, Admetus turned to his wife, Alcestis, who agreed. During the funeral, Hercules stopped off at the palace on one of his labors, learned what had happened, wrestled with Death, and restored (or so the legend goes, although Euripides' *Alcestis* is intentionally vague on this point) Alcestis to her husband.

Although Shane's golden hair is a good metaphor for Apollo's radiance, Shane is as much a Hercules as he is an Apollo. His power of endurance is Herculean; in one scene a stubborn tree trunk is uprooted, a task that required Shane's perseverance as well as Starrett's brawn. Two themes are common to both *Shane* and the Greek myth: a god's bondage in a mortal's household in expiation for a crime, and a god's saving a mortal's life. As we have seen, Shane's life is a mystery, yet from the way he draws when little Joey Starrett clicks the trigger of his unloaded rifle, he seems to be an ex-gunslinger. That he humbles himself through voluntary servitude suggests that he is atoning for his past.

Just as Apollo served the family of Admetus, Shane serves the Starretts; just as Hercules restored Alcestis to her husband, Shane restores Starrett to his wife. Instead of allowing Starrett to kill Wilson (and lose his life in the bargain), Shane knocks him unconscious and goes in his place, thus increasing Starrett's life span and saving him for Marion and Joey.

Shane as Knight-Errant

According to André Bazin, the subtext also encourages us to think of Shane as a "knight errant in search of his grail," pursuing the ideals of courtly love in the American West.[7] While it is Starrett whom Shane aids, it is Marion whom he serves. But in the tradition of courtly love the knight not only served the lady but tried to emulate her gentleness and thus acquire some for himself to offset his rough ways. Physically, there is a great resemblance between Shane and Marion. Both have golden hair, blue eyes, and a diminutiveness that suggests a gentle heart, not a natural failing. It is significant that Shane chooses to wear blue, one of the lady's favorite colors. However, the medieval knight was a living paradox; the lady he honored as the embodiment of natural perfection was frequently the unsatisfied married woman he took to his bed.

Here the analogies cease; the closest Shane comes to Marion is to dance the Varsouviana and to shake her hand in a farewell gesture. Yet *Shane* is a magnificently subtle film. When Marion is tucking Joey into bed, we hear his voice from behind the closed door: "Mother, I just love Shane." Good-nights are exchanged; Marion enters her bedroom, and Shane retires to the barn. "Good night, Shane," Joey calls, but there is no answer. A declaration of love has taken place, shared by mother and son, but in different ways. Marion's graceful entrance into the bedroom is neither slinking nor erotic but willowy and feminine. She may be retiring to her husband's bed, but she is clearly thinking of Shane. The mythic hero has many faces. Three of Shane's have been described here.

The War of the Worlds in *The Matrix* (The Wachowski Brothers, 1999)

On the surface, *The Matrix* seems like nothing more than high-tech science fiction with dazzling special effects (for which it received four Oscars); mythically, it illustrates the agon, or clash between the forces of good and evil—between those who would preserve human life as we know it and those who would reduce it to a computer-generated dream world where humans are the equivalents of batteries energized by artificial-intelligence machines within the Matrix, an elaborate computer simulation that understands only virtual reality.

The Matrix, as the name implies, is a model of that world—the equivalent of the evil planet Mongo in *Flash Gordon* (1936); if the Matrix could take on human form, it might look like Darth Vader of *Star Wars* or the characters in Richard Wagner's opera cycle *The Ring of the Nibelungs*, who lust after the ring, knowing that whoever possesses it can wield unlimited power. What makes *The Matrix* different from other good vs. evil movies is the plot twist: the conflict takes place in a world of programmed reality, where a handful of humans, holding on to their humanity, resist becoming slaves of the Matrix. Mythically, *The Matrix* evokes other battles that have been waged in antiworlds, myth's equivalent of virtual reality.

Virtual combat in *The Matrix* (1999). *(Courtesy the Margaret Herrick Library of the Academy of Motion Picture Arts and Sciences)*

The Greeks, for example, believed that before there was human life on earth there was warfare in the heavens: the Titans' rebellion against the tyrannical Uranus (Sky), led by Uranus's son Cronos, who had to castrate his father so that life could continue; the revolt of the Olympians, led by Cronus's son Zeus, against the Titans, resulting in the enlightened rule of the Olympians. Even then, there was rebellion: Prometheus disobeyed Zeus and gave the gift of fire to humankind; Eris (Discord), though a minor deity, was powerful enough to precipitate a war between Greece and Troy by causing three goddesses to vie for a golden apple.

The Book of Revelation speaks of another heavenly battle—one between the angels, led by Michael the archangel, and those headed by Lucifer, who was expelled from heaven and became Satan. According to Dante, Satan inhabits this world, at the bottom of a conical cavity caused by his fall from heaven and known as hell.

The writers of *The Matrix* must have had biblical sources in mind when they were creating the script, which, however complicated, is merely a reworking of old ideas. Morpheus's (Laurence Fishburne) name suggests the Greek god of sleep, who is also the sender of dreams. The name is apt, since in the inverted world of the Matrix reality and illusion are reversed. Morpheus, eager to overthrow the Matrix, contacts a computer hacker (Keanu Reeves), whose real name is Anderson, but who goes by the code name of Neo (Greek for "new"). It is as if Neo had been sent a reality dream: he does not realize he is living in 1999 but in 2199—1999 being nothing but a virtual construct of the Matrix. Morpheus, who is looking for a messiah, suspects that it might be Neo. First, Neo must be brought before the Oracle (Gloria Foster) to determine if he is the One who is destined to destroy the power of the Matrix.

Ritual initiation by a woman is common in myth. In Homer's *Odyssey*, Circe instructs Odysseus in what he must do to visit the abode of the dead. In Virgil's *Aeneid*, the Sibyl does the same for Aeneas before he makes his descent to the underworld. However, the initiator can do only so much for the hero, who then must face the unknown himself. Similarly, in *The Matrix* the Oracle's knowledge is incomplete (which has always been the case with oracles, whose prophecies must be decoded).

Since Neo becomes the savior Morpheus envisioned (at least in the sense of being the restorer of reality), it is tempting to consider him a Christ figure and interpret "Neo" as a reference to the Greek New Testament. Intriguing as the analogy is, it would not be applicable. If Jesus Christ were alive in the twenty-first century, he could not be a computer hacker and at the same time preach "Thou shalt not steal." It is better to stick to myth: Neo is a savior on the order of Prometheus. He is the New Prometheus, bringing the gift of selfhood to a world of computerized conformity.

VISUAL/ICONIC ASSOCIATIONS

Sometimes we make associations on a visual level; for example, some performers have such a strong screen persona (e.g., Katharine Hepburn, John Wayne, Bette Davis, James Dean, Marilyn Monroe, Sean Connery) that we make no distinction between them and the characters they play. Bette Davis wasn't playing Margo Channing in *All About Eve*; she *was* Margo Channing; and John Wayne was always John Wayne. The similarities between Madonna and Eva Perón (both of whom rose from obscurity to fame as they transformed themselves into celebrities) made it impossible to think of *Evita* (1996) as the story of Eva Perón but, rather, as that of Madonna.

Davis and Madonna are icons. In medieval art, an icon is a pictorial representation of a religious subject invested with a spiritual aura that makes it worthy of veneration. An icon of the Virgin Mary, for example, is not just a picture of a woman but of a special woman, the mother of Jesus Christ. An icon therefore has a dual nature: it depicts not just a person but a person who stands out from the ordinary, as indicated by a halo, a nimbus, or a gilded background.

Humphrey Bogart as Screen Icon in
High Sierra (Raoul Walsh, 1941)

Bogart is a true screen icon, inseparable from the cool, unemotional types he played—characters who seemed totally indifferent to the plight of humanity ("I stick my neck out for no man," Rick, perhaps his most famous character, says in *Casablanca*). Yet when Rick's help is needed, as it is by two Bulgarian refugees in the film, he comes to their aid but is embarrassed when they show gratitude. Bogart's screen persona was forged with his first starring role, Roy Earle, in *High Sierra* (1941). Bogart might never have appeared in the film, which made him a star, if George Raft, who was originally slated for the lead, had not refused to be in a movie in which he had to die. Raft, however, could never have suggested the inward drive for freedom that propels Earle to the summit from which he falls. *High Sierra* is a film about existential freedom—that freedom to which a human being is condemned, as Jean-Paul Sartre would say. It is not surprising that Bogart became an existential cult hero. Throughout his career, he projected the image of a man living in the present, striving for freedom, and performing meaningful actions to achieve it—financing an operation for a girl with a club foot (*High Sierra*); relinquishing the woman he loves to her freedom-fighter husband, who can do more for the world than he can (*Casablanca*); leading a detachment through the desert like Moses (*Sahara* [1943]); refusing to allow his love for the woman responsible for his best friend's death to stand in the way of justice (*Dead Reckoning* [1947]); and defending an underprivileged youth (*Knock on Any Door* [1949]) when no other lawyer would.

At the end of *High Sierra*, Earle lies dead at the foot of a mountain; when Marie (Ida Lupino), the woman who stood by him, asks Healy what it means when a man "crashes out," Healy replies that it means he is "free." "Free," Marie says as she walks triumphantly into the frame, knowing that Earle has won his freedom—and his essence—in death. The existential implications of "crash out" would have eluded a mediocre actor like George Raft. Bogart understood them and embodied them in his performance, thus giving the film its existential character. Even Bogart's face was extraordinary and fittingly existential. It was not a neighborhood face, nor was it especially handsome. It was a face that knew the mixed blessings of life; a face that did not slacken with age but grew tauter, the eyes retreating into their sockets until by the end of his career they had settled into omniscience.

Not every actor becomes an icon like Humphrey Bogart; screen icons are, in fact, rare. But that does not rule out other kinds of visual associations. We make visual associations when (1) an actor's physical appearance coincides with our image of the way a historical figure might have looked (e.g., an actor playing a Christ figure and looking the way

Christ is traditionally represented; an actor playing a rebel in a manner consistent with the popular image of the rebel); and (2) an actor's performance style recalls that of another actor, who is not in the film but whose presence is clearly felt. For example, a generation of actors who came of age in the late 1980s and early 1990s (the late River Phoenix, Brad Pitt, Val Kilmer, Jason Patric) recall the brooding intensity of James Dean; although Dean made only three films that were of any importance, young actors still aspire to achieve the same blend of aggressiveness and sensitivity, detachment and warmth, and indifference and compassion that he exhibited in his films. Dean could not be pigeonholed; if he seemed androgynous, it was because he embodied the best qualities of both male and female and revealed them in his portrayals of Cal Trask in *East of Eden*

(1955), Jim Stark in *Rebel without a Cause* (1955), and Jett Rink in *Giant* (1956). When the latest version of Shakespeare's *Romeo and Juliet* (1996) opened, several critics compared Leonardo DiCaprio's (Romeo) acting style with James Dean's—simple, direct, intense without seeming overwrought. Likewise, to see Meg Ryan in such comedies as *French Kiss* and *You've Got Mail*, and Julia Roberts in *The Runaway Bride*, is to see the incarnation of such screwball icons as Jean Arthur, Carole Lombard, and Claudette Colbert.

Al Pacino as Christ Figure in *Serpico* (Sidney Lumet, 1973)

When *Serpico* opened, several critics noted a resemblance between Al Pacino, who interpreted the title role magnificently, and pop-art pictures of Jesus Christ. The critic Vincent Canby also compared Pacino with St. Francis of Assisi. All sensed that there was more to Pacino's Serpico than just great acting; behind his Serpico they saw either a god-man doomed to suffer for his love of humanity or a saint who resisted the attempts of the religious establishment to interfere with his mission.

It was not merely Al Pacino's beard, his mesmeric eyes, or his uncontrollable rage at corruption that caused critics to think of Jesus Christ. Certain details of Serpico's life also recalled similar details in Christ's; thus, the text (Serpico) is coordinated with the subtext (Christ), and both come together in the person of the star (Pacino). Such coinciding of actor and historical figure does not occur in every movie with a police officer hero. The identification of Christ with Serpico (a cop who found his apostolate on the streets and underwent the traditional scapegoat cycle of harassment, betrayal, and desertion) was present in Pacino's performance in a way that it was not in the performances of Stacy Keach in *The New Centurions* (1972), Robert Duvall in *Colors* (1988), and Morgan Freeman in *Seven* (1995), all of which were hero-cop movies.

Jack Nicholson as Free Spirit and Louise Fletcher as Boss Lady in *One Flew over the Cuckoo's Nest* (Miloš Forman, 1975)

The impression made by an actor's performance is based on many factors, including such seemingly irrelevant details as hairstyle and wardrobe. Yet it is through such details that filmmakers realize their intentions; it is also through such details that we see in the characters what directors want us to see.

Al Pacino as Frank Serpico (*Serpico* [1973]), one of the few visually acceptable Christ figures in film. *(Courtesy Paramount Pictures)*

When Miloš Forman was about to direct *One Flew over the Cuckoo's Nest*, he was faced with the task of making a movie out of a cult book of the 1960s. During the last few years of that decade, Ken Kesey's novel seemed a tragically accurate mirror of America. The animosity between Randle P. McMurphy and Big Nurse paralleled similar confrontations between the pacifist and the draft board, the militant Students for a Democratic Society and the police, the student activists and the campus administration.

In 1975, however, the Vietnam War was a painful memory, the draft had been suspended, and campuses were quiet. To make the film meaningful, Forman had to deemphasize all the political overtones the novel had acquired in the 1960s. The film's text emphasized the humanism and comedy of Kesey's novel; the subtext transformed the conflict between McMurphy (Jack Nicholson) and Nurse Ratched (Louise Fletcher) into a battle between man and woman. Forman capitalized on Nicholson's exposed and often vulnerable masculinity, but he also saw more in it than locker-room bravado. There is an impishness about Nicholson; at times he seems to be putting us on, challenging us to make the hackneyed connection between a man's height (Nicholson is not tall) and his ego. Little details about Nicholson's portrayal of McMurphy suggest the imp: the cap pulled down over the ears, the hornlike tuft of hair that gives the impres-

Nurse Ratched (Louise Fletcher) and Randle McMurphy (Jack Nicholson) in *One Flew over the Cuckoo's Nest* (1976). Louise Fletcher's hairstyle is a throwback to the 1940s. *(Courtesy Fantasy Films)*

Sheila Ryan in an authentic 1940s hairdo. *(Courtesy Twentieth Century-Fox)*

sion of a satyr, the eyes that dart from one direction to another, as if they, too, were free spirits.

Although the time of the film is the 1960s, Louise Fletcher's hairstyle came out of another era. Forman had her wear her hair the way women did in "lady executive" movies of the 1940s, which were typified by such movies as Mitchell Leisen's *Take a Letter, Darling* (1942) and *They All Kissed the Bride* (1942). These films, however, were a harmless type of screwball comedy featuring women as executives and men as their subordinates. *Cuckoo's Nest* is hardly screwball comedy, and Nurse Ratched, by her hairstyle and manner, is a savage parody of the female executive of the 1940s.

Barbara Stanwyck as Marlene Dietrich in *Double Indemnity* (Billy Wilder, 1944)

The name of the femme fatale in James Cain's novel *Double Indemnity* is Phyllis Nirdlinger. When Billy Wilder was working on the screenplay for the film version, which he also directed, he changed the character's last name to Dietrichson. He wanted audiences to think not of Marlene Dietrich herself but of Dietrich's persona, the embodiment of the extremes of desire and danger, passion and aloofness, femininity and masculinity. Wilder even had Barbara Stanwyck, whom he cast in the role, wear a blond wig. Stanwyck is alternately seductive and passionless, ruthless and repentant ("I'm rotten to the heart," she admits just before her ex-lover shoots her—after she has shot him). Thus, throughout the film one senses something about Stanwyck that suggests Dietrich; behind Stanwyck's Phyllis lurks Dietrich's persona.

INTELLECTUAL ASSOCIATIONS

When we make a mythic association, we are reminded of universal patterns that are true of all human beings at all times. When we make an iconic or visual association, we perceive a likeness between an actor's persona and the character, or between the actor's performance and another's persona. When we make an intellectual association, we relate the film as a whole—not just one aspect of it—to history, to another medium (literature, opera, and so on), to another film, or even to an earlier version of itself.

When we relate a film to history, it is a matter of seeing how faithfully the film reflects its time period—for example, whether *The Patriot* depicts life in South Carolina as it actually was at the time of the Revolution. A historian might criticize *The Patriot* for implying that everyone in South Carolina had elegant homes, although the only ones who did were the

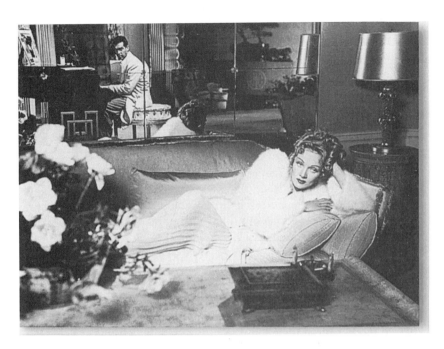

BARBARA STANWYCK AS MARLENE DIETRICH

Fred MacMurray and Marlene Dietrich in *The Lady Is Willing* (1942). *(Courtesy Columbia Pictures)*

Fred MacMurray and Barbara Stanwyck in *Double Indemnity* (1944). Wilder changed the name of Stanwyck's character to Dietrichson and had the actress wear a blond wig to evoke the Dietrich persona. *(Copyright © by Paramount Pictures. Courtesy MCA Publishing Rights, a Division of MCA, Inc.)*

plantation owners. However, squalor is rarely depicted in Hollywood epics, so the cabin-dwellers are unseen, along with the slaves. Accuracy is only one way of relating a film to history. A film can also suggest an era without re-creating that era.

History by Suggestion

Frequently overlooked is history's evocative power, its ability to function as a backdrop for the action without advertising its presence. It is rather like a stage set that subtly captures the mood and theme of the play without competing with the text. *The Day of the Locust* (1975), John Schlesinger's film version of Nathanael West's blatantly anti-Hollywood novel of the same name, seems to be more about the superficiality of Tinseltown than it is about history. Yet the action takes place on the eve of World War II, as we see from the headlines of a newspaper that blows down Hollywood Boulevard on the eve of a movie premiere. The master of ceremonies at the premiere is a Hitler look-alike, and the fans behave like the ones that would turn out for a Nazi rally. They are all oblivious to the world at large, which, in 1939, appeared to be on the verge of destruction; all that matters is catching a glimpse of the stars as they sweep into the theater.

The premiere is portrayed as a sacred ritual that cannot be profaned. When Adore, a child actor, hurls a stone at Homer Simpson (Donald Sutherland), Homer retaliates by stomping him to death. Adore's fame-obsessed mother turned her son into a grotesque by letting his hair grow long and curly like Shirley Temple's. And as if shoulder-length hair weren't enough, she also had it dyed platinum. Because Homer has polluted the holy rite of the Hollywood premiere by killing a male Shirley Temple, the fans turn on him, doing to him what he did to Adore. The film does not equate Homer with Hitler's scapegoats who ended up in death camps. Nor does it equate the frenzied fans with Germans who shouted their support for Hitler at torchlit rallies. *The Day of the Locust* only suggests that their reactions have something in common: destroyers of the dream—whether it is a dream of Hollywood as a Mount Olympus, with gods and goddesses, or the dream of a world inhabited only by Aryans—must be exterminated.

A film, therefore, can be set in a particular era but evoke that era only indirectly. Such a film does not declare itself "historical" in the sense of dramatizing an actual event, as, for example, *Tora! Tora! Tora!* re-created the Japanese attack on Pearl Harbor; or *The Patriot*, the American Revolution. Yet to appreciate a film such as *The Day of the Locust*, one has to know history; unlike the historical film, the background information is not in the dialogue but in the visuals.

A knowledge of history also deepens our appreciation of the screwball comedies of the 1930s, even though such films were intended to take viewers' minds off the Great Depression. The breeziness and happy endings led people to believe that one of the era's most popular songs, "Happy Days Are Here Again," was not all that far-fetched. *It Happened One Night* delighted moviegoers by showing a society woman being put in her place by a middle-class man who didn't even wear an undershirt. Yet the film convinced audiences that the two could live happily ever after, even though they belonged to different social classes.

Easy Living, another classic screwball comedy, was released in 1937—a year in which there were 4,720 strikes in America, the bloodiest being the one against Republic Steel in Chicago, where eighteen people were killed and more than ninety were wounded. However, an America of labor unrest and unemployment, where the average yearly wage was $1,348, was far removed from the America of *Easy Living*, where an irate husband thought nothing of throwing his wife's $58,000 sable coat from the roof of their Fifth Avenue apartment. The movie is best remembered for the automat sequence in which Mary Smith (Jean Arthur), wearing the coat that literally fell on her, is sitting alone, eating a beef pie. Although there are no longer any automats in New York, they were once popular eating places as well as tourist attractions. Automats were coin-operated cafeterias. The selections were inside small windowlike compartments that would spring open when the correct change was deposited in the slot. In *Easy Living*, when a mishap causes all the glass lids to pop up, the customers rush to get the free food. Mary, however, keeps eating, oblivious to the chaos around her. In the context of the film, the sight of people sliding around on a food-spattered floor is uproarious; in the context of Depression America, it is disturbing. When the camera captures the sable-clad Mary eating in the foreground, with the masses fighting in the background, it does more than record a comic free-for-all. By highlighting the extremes of affluence and poverty, the automat sequence defines the Great Depression as a time of fur coats for the fortunate and cloth coats (or no coats) for everyone else.

Film History by Suggestion

Bernardo Bertolucci's *Last Tango in Paris* (1972) is ostensibly about a woman caught between two men, one of whom debases her while the other idealizes her. Bertolucci used this narrative structure to work out a theory of film that he illustrates with references to movies of the past. Thus, when Pauline Kael reviewed *Last Tango*, and alluded to the film's constant "feedback," she meant that much in the film—the performances as well as the imagery—recalled other films.

"Movies are a past we share, and, whether we recognize them or not, the copious associations are at work in the film and we feel them," Kael observed.[8] As we have already seen, the way a movie is cast can create certain associations between the actor and his or her role. In *Last Tango*, Marlon Brando plays Paul, an American in Paris, who meets Jeanne (Maria Schneider) when both of them show up to look at the same apartment; Jean-Pierre Léaud is Tom, the TV director and movie lover who is using Jeanne for a

Cinderella in sable (Jean Arthur) is exposed to the grim realities of the Great Depression in the automat sequence of *Easy Living* (1937). *(Copyright © by Paramount Pictures. Courtesy MCA Publishing Rights, a Division of MCA, Inc.)*

television film. Brando and Léaud are not ordinary actors. Each epitomizes a style of acting and a type of film that revolutionized the cinema. Brando will always be synonymous with the Method, an approach to acting that requires the performer to draw on past experiences, emotions, and memories for a particular role. Brando was the definitive Method actor of the 1950s—brooding, introspective, often inarticulate. Léaud was the discovery of François Truffaut, who cast him as Antoine Doinel, the problem child of *The Four Hundred Blows*. Léaud and Truffaut then went on to make other films: the "Antoine and Colette" episode in *Love at Twenty* (1962), *Stolen Kisses, Bed and Board* (1970), and *Day for Night* (1973). Physically, Léaud even began to resemble the director. Truffaut typified the **New Wave**—that extraordinary burst of creativity that started in France in the late 1950s, when directors like Truffaut and Jean-Luc Godard rejected literary scripts for shooting scripts and improvisation, filmed in the streets rather than in studios, demanded naturalistic acting instead of old-fashioned emoting, and quoted liberally from the movies of the past.

Just as Brando and Léaud represent two different eras of filmmaking, the characters they portray represent two different ways of life. Paul isolates himself in the apartment, where he works out his sexual aggression on Jeanne; Tom roams the streets of Paris, scouting for locations for his movie. Jeanne is trapped not just between two men but between their worlds: Paul's closed world of the apartment and Tom's open world of the city. Yet filmmakers are in the same predicament: Do they remain within the closed world of the studio set (the past) as their predecessors did, or do they venture outside, where an entire city can be their soundstage (the present)?

What Kael calls "feedback" is not limited to the eras Brando and Léaud evoke. Bertolucci used *Last Tango* as a vehicle for his ideas on film

Jean-Pierre Léaud as Antoine
Doinel in *The 400 Blows* (1959),
perhaps the most famous of the
New Wave Films. *(Courtesy Janus
Films)*

Léaud as Tom, the TV director in
Last Tango in Paris (1973), with
Maria Schneider. Even as Tom,
Léaud typified the casual,
naturalistic form of acting that the
New Wave directors encouraged.
(Courtesy United Artists)

in the same way that Paul and Tom were using Jeanne for their respective purposes. Thus Bertolucci invokes movies of the past that have some bearing on his own film. When Jeanne and Tom are on a barge, there is a life preserver with *L'Atalante* inscribed on it. *L'Atalante* is the title of Jean Vigo's classic film (1934), and the barge scene in *Last Tango* pays homage to Vigo's exquisite production, in which a young bride leaves her barge captain-husband to experience the excitement of Paris, only to return to the secure world of the barge at the end. However, Bertolucci is also replying to Vigo's optimism: Vigo's bride can be reunited with her husband, but once Paul and Jeanne leave the apartment no reunion is possible.

Last Tango is like a course in film history. The scene in which Paul looks out on the roofs of Paris before he dies recalls René Clair's *Sous les Toits de Paris* (*Under the Roofs of Paris* [1931]), which the director made when he was thirty, the same age Bertolucci was when he made *Last Tango*. When Jeanne shoots Paul, the scene is a part not only of *Last Tango* but of so many Hollywood movies (for example, *The Letter* [1940], *Double Indemnity*, *Sunset Boulevard*) in which a woman pulls a revolver and pumps her lover full of bullets. *Last Tango* purports to be about male-female relationships, but subtextually it is about the relationship between filmmakers and their art.

With its mix of animation and live action, Robert Zemeckis's *Who Framed Roger Rabbit* (1988), set in 1947, seems to have a double subtext: the animated cartoons of the 1930s and 1940s and the private-eye films of the 1940s. While *Roger Rabbit* has been enjoyed by children who have never seen a private-eye movie and who know cartoons only from television, it speaks most directly to those who have a knowledge of film history. The dancing hippos bring back memories of Walt Disney's *Fantasia* (1940); Roger's sexy wife, Jessica, with her red tresses and low-cut gown, recalls Rita Hayworth in *Gilda* (1946); Eddie Valiant (Bob Hoskins), the private eye hired to trail Jessica, whose infidelity is causing Roger to forget his lines, is a seedier version of the 1940s private detectives Sam Spade and Philip Marlowe.

However, the plot of *Roger Rabbit*—a detective's discovery of a scheme that would, if executed, change the face of Los Angeles—is not to be found in any cartoon or 1940s detective movie, but in one particular film, Roman Polanski's *Chinatown* (1974), the true subtext of *Roger Rabbit*. In *Chinatown*, the private investigator J. J. Gittes (Jack Nicholson) uncovers a shady land deal involving Noah Cross (John Huston), who is buying up property in the San Fernando Valley, where a projected reservoir will turn the area into choice real estate. In *Roger Rabbit*, Eddie Valiant discovers that Judge Doom (Christopher Lloyd) plans to transform Los Angeles from a city that relies on trolley cars for transportation into a city of freeways. To do so, he must destroy Toontown, the enclave in which the cartoon characters live. If he succeeds, he will be destroying a venerable film tradition: the animated cartoon and the characters, like Bugs Bunny, Donald Duck, and Porky Pig, who are part of it.

Judge Doom's plan is thwarted through the combined efforts of Eddie and the Toons. The actual history of Los Angeles and Hollywood, however, has proved otherwise. Thus moviegoers who remember a time when theaters featured a cartoon, two movies, a newsreel, and a chapter of a serial find *Roger Rabbit* bittersweet: the film conjures up a Hollywood of another time and place—to many, perhaps a better time and place.

Remaking the Original:
The Shop Around the Corner (MGM, 1940),
In the Good Old Summertime (MGM, 1949),
You've Got Mail (Warner Bros., 1998)

The Shop Around the Corner was freely adapted from Nikolaus "Miklaus" Laszlo's play *Parfumerie*. Although the play is virtually unknown, it has inspired three films and a Broadway musical. The plot is an unusual variation of the battle of the sexes. Ordinarily, in this kind of movie each tries

James Stewart and Margaret Sullavan as the pen pals in *The Shop Around the Corner* (1940). *(Courtesy MOMA/FSA)*

Judy Garland and Van Johnson as the same in the musical remake, *In the Good Old Summertime* (1949). *(Courtesy MOMA/FSA)*

Tom Hanks and Meg Ryan as yet another pair of anonymous correspondents, this time in cyberspace, in *You've Got Mail* (1998). *(Courtesy MOMA/FSA)*

to beat the other at his or her game, until both realize that the game they have been playing is the game of love. As we have seen, the "battle of the sexes" was a staple of screwball comedy (*It Happened One Night, Twentieth Century, The Awful Truth,* and so forth). However, the usual screwball characters (the runaway bride, the scoop-hungry reporter, the working-class Cinderella, the idle rich who learn how the common folk live) do not appear in *The Shop Around the Corner*, a romantic comedy with an unusual twist: the man and woman are pen pals who communicate anonymously, falling in love through their letters, although in real life they thoroughly dislike each other.

The Shop Around the Corner was directed by the German-born director Ernst Lubitsch, whose genius resulted in a phrase that is still used today: "the Lubitsch touch." The touch that Lubitsch brought to romantic comedy cannot be defined, only described; it is like the touch a master chef brings to a dish that is truly unique, although the ingredients that went into it were common knowledge. Other directors made romantic comedies, but Lubitsch stamped them with his personal signature. When sex was involved, he was slyly discreet, leaving everything to the imagination. Lubitsch knew the difference between a wink and a leer. In *Trouble in Paradise* (1932), one scene ends with the bedroom door closing on two lovers; in the next, each awakens in his or her own room. Lubitsch delighted in posing the "Did they or didn't they?" question. Just when you think they did, the camera implies otherwise. Sex, like life, was a game to be played with wit and discretion. It was passion by suggestion, not depiction.

In *The Shop Around the Corner*, in which sex is virtually nonexistent, the touch consisted in presenting the battle of the sexes as playacting, until the players reach the stage when they can approach each other without having to hide behind a mask—specifically, the mask of anonymity that "lonely hearts" correspondence offers. Most of the action in *The Shop Around the Corner* is set in a gift shop in Budapest, Hungary, where Alfred Kralik, the head clerk (James Stewart), and a new hire, Klara (Margaret Sullavan), take an immediate dislike to each other, not knowing that they have been corresponding. What they have in common is their romantic idealism: they write to each other as "dear friend," expressing their deepest thoughts about love—not as passion but as the shared enjoyment of the pleasure that comes from common interests such as art and literature. Lubitsch, however, is suggesting that the correspondence school of romance is a form of immaturity, allowing writers to reveal themselves at their best and thus avoid the frankness that comes from face-to-face communication.

We wait for the moment when Alfred and Klara will reveal their identities. They plan to meet at a café, where Klara will be at a table with a copy of Tolstoy's *Anna Karenina* and a red carnation. Although Alfred has been fired that day, he keeps the appointment. To his dismay, he discovers that his "dear friend" is none other than Klara; still, he approaches her table. Klara, assuming that "dear friend" might get the wrong impression if another man is sitting with her, treats Alfred so shabbily, even calling him "insignificant," that he leaves without telling her who he is. Since the action is set during the Christmas season, culminating on Christmas Eve, there can only be a happy ending. Alfred and Klara are alone in the shop, getting ready to face Christmas Eve alone. Alfred then recites a passage from one of his letters to Klara, which she immediately recognizes. As the snow falls gently outside the shop, their embrace makes it evident that neither of them will be spending Christmas alone.

Within less than a decade, MGM remade *The Shop Around the Corner* as a musical for Judy Garland and Van Johnson called *In the Good Old Summertime*. It is not surprising that the studio decided to turn the old Laszlo play, which seemed like the perfect text for an operetta, into a musical. Garland and Johnson were still popular stars, although neither was at her or his peak. Garland could still belt out a song, however, and was given several opportunities to do so.

Since Garland's last four MGM musicals (*Meet Me in St. Louis, The Harvey Girls* [1946], *The Pirate* [1948], and *Easter Parade* [1948]) were shot in Technicolor, the studio used the same color process for *Summertime*, resulting in a bigger budget and a more lavish production necessitated by the change of setting: Chicago, in the early years of the twentieth century. While the actors in *Shop* wore contemporary clothes (i.e., those suitable to the late 1930s), the *Summertime* cast had to appear in period costumes.

The time change also required name changes, with Klara and Alfred becoming Veronica (Garland) and Andrew (Johnson). The shop is now a music store. The pen pals meet as Victor is racing out of the post office with his "dear friend" letter, colliding with "dear friend" herself, causing Veronica's hair to come undone, her hat to get crushed, her parasol to collapse, and her skirt to come off. With such an introduction, Veronica can hardly be expected to feel kindly toward Andrew after she joins the sales staff.

There are a few new plot points involving a female violinist and a priceless Stradivarius, but these are superficial, not radical, changes. Since the owner of the music store is now single (and can be paired off with an older employee), there is no wife to seduce, as there was in the original. If there is no seducer, there is no suicide attempt, as there was in *Shop*, when the owner learned that his wife was cheating on him with one of his own employees. The restaurant rendezvous, however, is a replica of the original. A colleague peers through the window, informing Andrew that his "dear friend" is at a table with a red carnation and a book (a copy of Elizabeth Barrett Browning's poetry). When Andrew approaches Veronica's table, she—like Klara—behaves so abominably that he leaves without telling her who he is. The ending also follows the original. Andrew and Veronica are alone in the store on Christmas Eve when Andrew finally decides to reveal his identity by quoting from one of his letters. Since the remake is entitled *In the Good Old Summertime*, there is a dissolve from a

Christmas tree in the store window to a summer scene, with Andrew, Veronica, and their three-year-old daughter, played by Garland's own three-year-old daughter, Liza Minnelli, in her film debut.

Between *In the Good Old Summertime* and the next *Shop Around the Corner* remake, the same plot became the basis of a stage musical, *She Loves Me* (1964), which is extremely close to the original. Although it wasn't a huge hit, *She Loves Me* had a major New York revival in the 1990s. The original cast album is still in print, and Jerry Bock's score is highly regarded by lovers of musical theater. *She Loves Me* made it clear that *The Shop Around the Corner* is perfect operetta material, especially with its old-world setting and Christmastime ambience.

In the 1990s, the movie romance (essentially romantic comedy with serious moments) underwent a renascence, beginning with *Sleepless in Seattle* (1993). Nora Ephron, who coauthored and directed *Sleepless*, was inspired by Leo McCarey's *An Affair to Remember* (1957), in which a man (Cary Grant) and a woman (Deborah Kerr), attracted to each other, plan to meet atop the Empire State Building. Unfortunately, an automobile accident involving the woman prevents their reunion, causing the man to think that she has lost interest in him. Ephron, however, was not remaking *Affair*, which itself was a remake on an earlier film, *Love Story* (1939). But by including specific references to McCarey's film and having *Sleepless in Seattle* climax on the observation deck of the Empire State Building, she established a connection between his film and her own.

Ephron realized that another classic, *The Shop Around the Corner*, could also be given new life; the result was *You've Got Mail*. Ephron adhered to the same story line, updating the method of correspondence (e-mail) and adding a familiar '90s scenario (a neighborhood business threatened by the arrival of a megastore). The cyberspace communicators, Joe Fox III (Tom Hanks) and Kathleen Kennedy (Meg Ryan) are business rivals—and know it. She owns a children's bookstore, the Shop Around the Corner, which is clearly an hommage to the Lubitsch film. His family runs a bookstore chain on the order of Barnes & Noble, which is opening a branch literally around the corner from her shop. To remain true to the spirit of the original, *You've Got Mail* must make use of the following plot devices:

Anonymous correspondence. With e-mail becoming an increasingly popular way of communicating, Joe and Kathleen meet in a cyberspace chat room instead of through the personal columns, although they still address each other as "dear friend." Anonymity is preserved through meaningful code names: hers is shopgirl, which is accurate in view of her store's name; his is Brinkley, his dog's name, and also the means by which he reveals his identity.

An urban ambience. The Shop Around the Corner and *In the Good Old Sum-*

mertime were filmed on MGM soundstages; both had a quaint picture-postcard look. *You've Got Mail*, on the other hand, seems more authentic because most of it was filmed on location, specifically on New York's Upper West Side. What Ephron succeeded in capturing was not just the look of the Upper West Side for those who had never been there but also the lifestyle, rhythm, and ambience of a multiethnic, liberal community where intellectuals and young professionals work and live within walking distance of specialty stores and trendy restaurants. Since Kathleen is an independent bookseller and Joe is part of a conglomerate, they inhabit two different worlds, each of which is shown. Hers is very much like the one in *Shop*, where each worker had his or her distinctive personality (the ladies' man, the delivery boy who yearns to be a clerk, the older employee who's eager to keep his job, and so forth). Similarly, Kathleen's employees include a wistful female college student to whom the store is a refuge from reality; the male, another lost soul who has found solace in children's books; the septuagenarian accountant who may have had an affair with the Spanish dictator General Franco. Joe's milieu is a corporate stereotype: martinis, yachts, gleeful descriptions of the latest rival to go out of business. It is a world devoid of warmth and feeling, signified by the elaborate but impersonal Fox bookstore, with its coffee bar, deep leather chairs for reading, and an uninformed sales staff.

Structure. In *Shop*, neither Alfred nor Klara is romantically involved with anyone else. Ephron, who is familiar with the conventions of 1930s screwball comedy, complicates the action by having Kathleen and Joe involved in relationships that must end if they are to pair off together. Kathleen is living with a self-absorbed, pseudo-liberal journalist; Joe, with a similarly narcissistic book editor. Thus, two couples will have to be reduced to one. In a 1930s comedy, to comply with the Production Code, Kathleen and Joe would have been married to each other; or one (or both) of them would have been engaged to other parties. A broken engagement, even if it ended at the altar with the bride's inability to say "I do," would have been one way of resolving the plot, as was the case in *It Happened One Night* and *Cover Girl*. If Joe and Kathleen were married, they would have to divorce, like the couple in the classic comedy of remarriage, *The Awful Truth*, before making the discovery that they belong together. Not bound by the regulations that earlier screenwriters had to observe, Ephron has the relationships end naturally, as Joe and Kathleen realize the character defects in their respective partners.

The moment of truth. In *Shop*, *Summertime*, and *Mail*, Alfred/Andrew/Joe is the first to learn his correspondent's identity. *Mail* repeats the obligatory rendezvous scene in which Kathleen waits for Joe at a restaurant with a book (here, *Pride and Prejudice*) and a rose. When Joe's colleague looks through the window (as happened in both *Shop* and *Summertime*) and informs Joe that his date is Kathleen, Joe is at first reluctant to enter, but eventually does. And just as Klara's behavior alienated Alfred, and Veronica's Andrew, Kathleen's alienates Joe.

In all the versions it is the male who ends the masquerade. The compassion that Alfred feels for Klara, and Andrew for Veronica, is that of a man for a woman he loves but from whom he has kept the truth. Joe's case is more complex because Ephron's script is more complicated. Kathleen is forced to close her bookstore. While Joe's philosophy has always been "It's not personal, just business," his feeling for Kathleen becomes personal, starting with sympathy and slowly changing to love. Ephron seems to have preferred the ending of *Summertime* to *Shop*, bringing the film to a close when nature is in bloom, not when it is dying. Unlike *Shop*, which ends on Christmas Eve, *Mail* starts at holiday time and ends in early summer. Joe and Kathleen plan to meet in Riverside Park. Kathleen arrives first; then Joe, with his dog. Joe reveals his identity by using his code name when he calls his dog: "Brinkley!" Joe does not quote from one of his letters (which he seems never to have printed); shouting "Brinkley!" is all he has to do.

You've Got Mail, in addition to being a superbly well-acted film, also makes intelligent use of the conventions and plot techniques of the romantic comedies of the 1930s and 1940s.

"I've seen this before," we often say of a particular movie; quite possibly we have. Twentieth Century-Fox constantly remade its musicals: to see *Wabash Avenue* (1950) is to see *Coney Island* (1943). *Three Blind Mice* (1938) was set to music and became *Moon over Miami* (1941), which was remade as *Three Little Girls in Blue* (1946) and later as *How to Marry a Millionaire* (1953). Often time and place were changed, but the basic plot remained the same: Raoul Walsh's *Colorado Territory* (1949) was *High Sierra* in a western setting; *I Died a Thousand Times* (1953) was *High Sierra* again, with Jack Palance in the Humphrey Bogart role. *High Society* (1956) was George Cukor's *The Philadelphia Story* (1940) with a Cole Porter score; *Against All Odds* (1984) was not only a remake of Jacques Tourneur's *Out of the Past* (1947) but also featured one of the stars from the original, Jane Greer. *The Preacher's Wife* (1996) was *The Bishop's Wife* (1947) from an African American perspective. The classic *Detour*, which starred Tom Neal, was remade as a less than classic movie of the same name in 1992; it starred Neal's son, Tom Neal, Jr., and proved that unless filmmakers can enhance, surpass, or at least equal the original—by clarifying ambiguities or bringing out details that were only hinted at initially—they would be advised to stay with less familiar material.

MUSICAL ASSOCIATIONS

Music has two main functions in a film: it either advances or enhances the narrative. When it advances the narrative, it is a plot device and is not subtextual. In Mitchell Leisen's *Lady in the Dark* (1944), a childhood song the heroine tries to remember is the key to her neurosis. Many a Twentieth Century-Fox musical included a tender ballad the heroine was belting out until the hero taught her how to sing it properly (*Coney Island*, *Wabash Avenue*). We have already seen how in many musicals working out the melody or the lyrics to a song was the significant moment in the film. There are also songs that drift in and out of the characters' lives, becoming *their* song and playing at appropriately dramatic moments; the classic example is "As Time Goes By" in *Casablanca*. Some movies have a classical score, usually a ballet or an opera, that catapults an unknown to stardom (*The Red Shoes* [1948]) or notoriety (the synthetic opera *Salammbô* in *Citizen Kane*). Sometimes a piece of music forms the film's climax, achieving an effect that words cannot: "Remember My Forgotten Man" in *Gold Diggers of 1933* (1933), George Gershwin's Concerto in F in *Rhapsody in Blue* (1945), the title ballet in Vincente Minnelli's *An American in Paris* (1951).

Music is even more functional as an element of the subtext when it does not so much advance the narrative as deepen it. Take, for example, a musical phrase that is repeatedly associated with a character, a mood, or a situation. Such a recurring musical phrase is a leitmotif. When a leitmotif identifies a character, it becomes the character's musical signature. Heard in conjunction with the appearance of a character, or the representation of an idea, the leitmotif is inseparable from the individual with whom it is associated or the idea it underscores. It also enjoys a kind of autonomy. A leitmotif can confirm a declaration of love, but it can also recur when the lovers are quarreling or parting, mocking what it had previously celebrated. As part of the character, a leitmotif can remind the audience of what the character is feeling at a particular moment. In Hitchcock's *I Confess* (1952), when Ruth (Anne Baxter) tells her husband she does not love him, we hear the leitmotif that is associated with the man she really loves.

The leitmotif expresses aspects of the character that lie beyond the capacity of language. The nursery tune that opens the 1942 version of *Cat People* is the first indication that the movie is not an ordinary horror film. It is fitting that such a singsong motif should be Irena's signature, for she is emotionally a child.

The leitmotif also concretizes abstract themes. Power is an abstraction, yet Bernard Herrmann, who composed the music for *Citizen Kane*, called one of the leitmotifs of the film "power." As a musical phrase, "power" is no longer abstract because we hear it. The power motif is heard for the first time as the camera ascends the gate of Xanadu, taking us into the pleasure dome and then to Kane's deathbed. But it is a *synesthetic* experience: we see, feel, and hear power. We watch its calculatingly slow rise, feel the isolation it brings, and hear the grim consequences it holds for those who seek it.

There are all kinds of motifs—love motifs, death motifs, and even love-death, or *Liebestod*, motifs. At the end of *Duel in the Sun* (1947), which has one of the lushest scores ever composed, Pearl Chavez (Jennifer Jones) crawls over sunbaked rocks to die in her lover's arms. As their blood mingles, the love motif heard when they first met seems to surge out of some chasm in the great Southwest to become their Liebestod.

For *The Private Life of Sherlock Holmes* (1970), Billy Wilder fashioned a love motif out of a few measures of Miklos Rozsa's Concerto for Violin and Orchestra. It is a bittersweet but dignified theme expressing a yearning that is never to be satisfied—in this case, Holmes's love for Ilse von Hofmannstahl. When Holmes receives the news of Ilse's death, the same theme is heard, no longer an expression of unfulfilled love but of love irretrievably lost.

Music is also capable of forging ethnic and national connections. In the pre–civil rights era, blacks were stereotyped both dramatically and musically. When they appeared on the screen, the original soundtrack often ceased, and a spiritual was heard, presumably because it was more fitting. Even in such a brilliant film as *The Little Foxes*, blacks were given this kind of musical treatment, which not only equated them with their music but also perpetuated the misguided image of southern blacks as passive. Music, whether it wishes to or not, equates, and a moviegoer's earliest associations are equations: "Deep River" = blacks; "The International" = Communists; a few gongs = the mysterious East; "Deutschland über Alles" = Nazi Germany; a tarantella (or "O Sole Mio") = Italy, and so on. Although only the slightest references were made to the title character's being Jewish in *Mr. Skeffington* (1944), a leitmotif that was vaguely based on traditional Jewish melodies left no doubt of it.

During World War II, movie music programmed its audiences to patriotism. People not only saw flag-wavers; they also heard Old Glory hymned on the soundtrack. Planes streamed across the sky to the accompaniment of "Wild Blue Yonder," which also doubled as death music for the marines who went off to be executed by the Japanese at the end of *The Purple Heart* (1944). To evoke American values, Frank Capra frequently incorporated typical American songs like "Red River Valley" and "Buffalo Gals" into his films.

Using classical music that was written centuries ago is a special case, since it is music that was not composed for a specific film. Yet the media have made extensive use of classical music. In the 1930s and 1940s, when radio was a mass medium, listeners were exposed to classical music without being aware of it. Rossini's *William Tell* Overture ushered in *The Lone Ranger*; Sibelius's "Valse Triste" introduced *I Love a Mystery*; Prokofiev's March from *Love for Three Oranges* was the theme of *The FBI in Peace and War*; the second movement of César Franck's Symphony in D Minor heralded the opening of *Quiet, Please*. Thus, associations were created between the radio programs and their introductions, which were the equivalents of musical signatures.

Movies used classical music in the same way. Before many moviegoers even knew what Rachmaninoff's Second Piano Concerto was, they had heard it as background music in *Brief Encounter* (1946). In fact, for people who know the film, the concerto has such indelible associations that it never fails to evoke a dingy railroad station where two married people, on the verge of committing adultery, choose to say goodbye and never meet again.

Thus, the Rachmaninoff Second Piano Concerto took on associations of extramarital love, and was used for that purpose in *September Affair* (1950), where it forms the background for a story of adultery. Like any venerable device, the Rachmaninoff Second ended up being parodied; still, parody attests to its associations. In *The Seven Year Itch*, in which a husband whose wife is away for the summer imagines himself seducing the woman upstairs, Billy Wilder parodies the tradition. In a fantasy sequence, the husband fancies that he's a great pianist, sitting down at the piano and breaking into the concerto to impress his potential conquest.

Since classical music is added to a film rather than being composed for it, it may already have produced certain associations within us; the film may either reinforce those associations or change them, so that thereafter we associate the music only with the movie. Certainly, it is difficult to disassociate the Rachmaninoff Second from *Brief Encounter* and, in a totally different way, from *The Seven Year Itch*. Similarly, anyone who has seen *Shine* (1996), based on the life of the gifted but troubled pianist David Helfgott, will always associate the Rachmaninoff Third, Helfgott's signature concerto, with the film. This type of association should not be surprising, since few *Lone Ranger* fans can separate the *William Tell* Overture from the program.

Wagner's music occupies a peculiar place in the American film. There has always been a connection between Wagner and the Third Reich. Wagner was said to be Hitler's favorite composer; in fact, Hitler identified with Wagner's Siegfried and maintained that to understand National Socialism (Nazism) one first had to understand Wagner. To the Hollywood of the 1940s, then, Wagner was the composer of the Third Reich: it is difficult to recall a movie in which Nazism was not orchestrated with a Wagnerian motif. In *Brute Force* (1947), Munsey (Hume Cronyn), a prison captain, tortures an inmate to the Venusberg music from Wagner's *Tannhäuser*. Munsey performs a kind of ritual before the torture, strutting around with his chest sucked in beneath a skintight undershirt. That the captain is a homoerotic sadist is evident in the film, but Wagner's music, with its historical and erotic associations, characterizes him even further. Music unites his lust for power and his need for sex, neither of which he can achieve except through the degradation of others.

Although *Apocalypse Now* (1979) deals with America's tragic involvement in Vietnam, the film uses Wagner in much the same way it is used in *Brute Force*: as a symbol of sexual energy channeled into militarism. The "Ride of the Valkyries," from *Die Walküre*, orchestrates the parade-of-the-helicopters sequence. Had the same music been used in a World War II movie in which bombs rained down on German cities, American audiences would have applauded; in light of the Vietnam debacle, however, "The Ride of the Valkyries" is accusatory rather than nationalistic. It is as if Coppola were accusing America of emulating Nazi Germany by invoking the spirit of Wagner to justify war.

The use of Wagner's music in *Apocalypse Now* is ironic. Irony is not the easiest of devices to manipulate, however. It can backfire, becoming blatant, as happens in *The Night Porter* (1974) when two inmates in a Nazi concentration camp perform an act of sodomy to the music of Mozart's *The Magic Flute*. What should have been a devastating moment becomes merely appalling. Far more intelligent is Ingmar Bergman's use of Bach in *Through a Glass, Darkly* (1961) when a schizophrenic daughter discovers that her father is using her sickness as material for a novel. The nobility of the music underscores the father's ignoble intentions.

In some films, classical music constitutes the entire subtext. It is not just a question of repeating motifs but of using music—either one work or several works—from beginning to end. What happens to music in Stanley Kubrick's *A Clockwork Orange* (1971) is what has happened to society. The social order gives way as thugs and disenchanted youths, leather boys and loafers become the citizens of the future. There is a corresponding degeneration of music; it becomes estranged from art, perverted, capable of producing effects that its composers never intended.

One of the most innocent songs ever written is "Singin' in the Rain," which brings to mind Gene Kelly sloshing around without missing a tap in the classic 1952 musical of the same name. It is hardly the kind of song we would associate with violence, yet in *A Clockwork Orange* Alex does a soft-shoe to it while brutalizing a writer and his wife.

Rimsky-Korsakov's *Scheherazade* is an exotic piece of music, lush and sensuous, the kind associated with a veiled courtesan on a chaise longue upholstered in leopard skin. Yet this is the music that is heard when Alex imagines himself as a Roman centurion lashing Christ on his way to Cal-

Karin (Harriet Andersson) in *Through a Glass, Darkly* (Ingmar Bergman [1961]) when she discovers that her father is using her schizophrenia for his novel. At that moment, the haunting opening of Bach's Suite no. 2 in D Minor for violoncello is heard. *(Courtesy MOMA/FSA and Janus Films)*

vary. *Scheherazade* is one of the most pleasurable compositions ever written, as Alex would be the first to admit. But the pleasure we receive from it is clearly not his.

Alex is also a lover of Beethoven's Ninth Symphony, with its ringing affirmation of humanity in the last movement. He knows that such sublime music can only be the result of intense suffering. While Alex listens to it, on one occasion masturbating to it, Kubrick cuts to various shots of Christ, because Alex associates Christ with suffering and suffering with music. Therefore the sublimity of the music inspires the hearer to make others suffer. "Preposterous!" we say; or, if this is so, how can the love of music be the mark of a cultivated person? It would be better to raze the concert halls and ban recordings. But in Alex's world, where good and evil have lost their meaning as moral terms, music has no value except the one that is placed on it. In such a society, it makes no difference whether one meditates to Beethoven's music or masturbates to it. Yet Alex is not alone in misusing the classics; his elders have discovered an equally perverted use for the Beethoven Ninth. During his rehabilitation, Alex is forced to watch Nazi films while the last movement of the Ninth is played electronically.

While *A Clockwork Orange* draws on the works of several composers for its musical associations, *Moonstruck* draws on one: Puccini's opera, *La Bohème*. In *La Bohème*, Mimi meets Rodolpho and within minutes they are pouring out their love in a soaring duet. In *Moonstruck*, Loretta (Cher) no sooner meets her fiancé's brother than he whisks her off to bed to the music of *La Bohème*, his favorite opera. Later, he takes her to the Metropolitan Opera House to see it. *Moonstruck* celebrates the passion that brings men and women together, using opera as a point of departure, where the characters experience such powerful emotions that they cannot express them except through song.

Pretty Woman (1990) uses another popular opera, Verdi's *La Traviata*, as a frame of reference. A wealthy entrepreneur (Richard Gere) takes a prostitute (Julia Roberts), with whom he has become involved, to a performance of *La Traviata*. Although she has never seen an opera before, she immediately identifies with the character of Violetta, who belongs to the same profession and also suffers abuse at the hands of men. The film's emotional climax is believable within an operatic context; *Pretty Woman* rewrites the tragic ending of *La Traviata* and allows two people from totally different worlds to (supposedly) live happily ever after.

Close Encounters of the Third Kind illustrates a highly sophisticated use of music. Roy (Richard Dreyfuss), with whom aliens are communicating telepathically, is a mystery to his wife and children. A boy at heart, Roy wants to take his family to see a revival of Disney's *Pinocchio* (1940), in which they profess to have no interest. In a Spielberg film, a movie reference should never be ignored. During the end credits, John Williams's brilliant score segues into "When You Wish upon a Star" from *Pinocchio*, placing *Close Encounters* within a special context. Roy has gotten his wish: he has become a space cadet and will enjoy the experience of interplanetary travel. But more important, like Pinocchio, who wanted to be a real boy rather than a puppet, Roy will remain, spiritually, a child—indifferent to time, which, like a puppeteer, controls human lives. It is significant that the humans, who had been declared missing and return at the end of the film, look the same as they did when the aliens abducted them. Roy will be leaving a world, dominated by time, for one in which time, as we know it, has no meaning.

A film has an outer and an inner world, a text and a subtext or, if you prefer, a narrative and an infranarrative. Beneath the text woven by the filmmaker's creativity and technology is the subtext, with its network of associations and implications that, when understood, broaden our knowledge of the film. Because what lies beneath the surface is usually more intriguing than what lies above it, one may be tempted to proceed to the subtext before the text is understood. However, just as in literature a work's symbolic level cannot be appreciated before its literal level is clear, so, too, in film the narrative must be grasped before it can be transcended. Only then are we free to seek out the associations—mythic, historical, iconic or visual, musical—that provide access to the film's inner world.

NOTES

[1] W. Y. Tindall, *James Joyce* (New York: Grove Press, 1960), 102.

[2] As quoted in W. Y. Tindall, *A Reader's Guide to James Joyce* (New York: Noonday Press, 1959), 129.

[3] Parker Tyler, *Magic and Myth of the Movies* (New York: Simon & Schuster, 1970), xviii.

[4]Lillian Feder, *Ancient Myth in Modern Poetry* (Princeton: Princeton University Press, 1971), 10–11.

[5]Donald Richie, *George Stevens: An American Romantic* (New York: Museum of Modern Art, 1970), 62.

[6]Michael T. Marsden, "Savior in the Saddle: The Sagebrush Testament," in *Focus on the Western*, ed. Jack Nachbar (Englewood Cliffs, N.J.: Prentice-Hall, 1974), 97.

[7]André Bazin, "The Evolution of the Western," in *What Is Cinema?*, vol. 2, trans. Hugh Gray (Berkeley: University of California Press, 1971), 152.

[8]Pauline Kael, "Introduction," *Bernardo Bertolucci's* Last Tango in Paris: *The Screenplay* (New York: Dell, 1973), 17.

The Film Director

I f film is a collaborative art, no single person should get credit for a particular movie. Yet it is standard practice to speak of "John Ford's *Stagecoach*" or "Alfred Hitchcock's *Psycho*," or to suggest that directors enjoy a preeminence that writers do not by placing their names beside their films: *Pollock* (2000) is "A Film by Ed Harris"; *Unbreakable* (2000) is "An M. Night Shyamalian Film." The elevation of the director to the rank of author is an outgrowth of **auteurism,** a theory of filmmaking in which the director is considered the primary creative force behind a film.

When the *New York Times* lists film revivals, the director's name precedes the film's title, just as an author's name precedes the title of his or her book. Certain film critics (e.g., Andrew Sarris, David Denby) still designate films that way; many film historians prefer to place the director's name and release date in parentheses after the film. In the traditional main title, the director's name is the last credit, but it is also the one audiences see before the film begins—a rather subtle way of suggesting what has always been known in the industry: movies are a director's medium. Certainly, movie directors receive a unique form of recognition.

Directors are also accorded retrospectives even though others may have written the scripts of the films for which they are being honored. Then why John Ford's *Stagecoach* and not screenwriter Dudley Nichols's *Stagecoach?* The answer lies in auteurism.

AUTEURISM

The Beginnings of Auteurism

During the German occupation of France in World War II, the French were denied American movies, but after the war was over they began to rediscover the greatness of the American cinema. The movies Americans often took for granted, the French took seriously. André Bazin wrote appreciatively of William Wyler and Orson Welles; Jean-Luc Godard saw more in the B-movies of Monogram Studios than did the American kids who saw them as the second half of double bills at their neighborhood theaters.* The rediscovery of American films by the French led to a reconsideration of the director as artist. What impressed the French was the fact that Hollywood directors could be—and frequently were—handed a screenplay, a cast, and a crew (none of which they had personally selected) and still manage to leave the stamp of their personality on the films.

In 1951 André Bazin and Jacques Doniol-Valcroze began publication of *Cahiers du Cinéma*, a journal that evolved into a critical forum for young film enthusiasts (Jean-Luc Godard, François Truffaut, Eric Rohmer, Claude Chabrol, and others), who expressed themselves in its pages and later went on to become directors. *Cahiers du Cinéma* had the reputation of a maverick; it was often pretentious and erratic in its preference for one director over another. Still, whatever one may think of the journal and the eccentric taste of its writers (e.g., Luc Moullet, who found in such films as Edgar G. Ulmer's *Bluebeard* the theme of humankind's loneliness without God), it moved directors from the background to the foreground, establishing them as creators instead of studio orderlies.

For the first three years of its existence, *Cahiers du Cinéma* had no real editorial policy; in 1954 Truffaut provided it with one in his famous essay "Une certaine tendance du cinéma français," which attacked classic French cinema for preferring literary scripts to shooting scripts, adapta-

---

*Monogram made low-budget movies and "series pictures" (The Bowery Boys, Charlie Chan, Bomba the Jungle Boy, the Cisco Kid). The Monogram product was undistinguished except for an occasional melodrama like *Suspense* (1946) or *The Gangster* (1947).

tions to original screenplays, studio sets to actual locations, and a team of specialists to a single individual. Truffaut argued for "a cinema of auteurs"; and so it was that *auteur*, the French word for "author," entered the critical vocabulary of film.

Cahiers du Cinéma now had a policy: *la politique des auteurs*, "the policy of authors," which has had various interpretations, the most common one being that the journal was partial to certain directors (e.g., Orson Welles, Alfred Hitchcock, Jean Renoir) and indifferent to others (e.g., John Huston, René Clair, René Clément). Another interpretation was that *Cahiers du Cinéma*'s favored directors were infallible and incapable of making bad films. Bazin corrected this misconception in 1957, when he pointed out what should have been obvious: a great director can make a dud, and a mediocre director can occasionally make a classic. Essentially, Bazin endorsed the policy of ranking directors, although he was often disturbed by the indiscriminate taste of some of his writers. Bazin summed up his position in the equation: author + subject = work.

That equation was adopted as the critical principle of Andrew Sarris, through whom auteurism entered America. In his essay "Notes on the *Auteur* Theory in 1962,"[1] Sarris defended the ranking of directors as an extension of a policy that has always prevailed in the arts. We rank Shakespeare over Ben Jonson, Beethoven over Brahms, Mozart's *Don Giovanni* over Beethoven's *Fidelio*. It was inevitable that Sarris would establish a ranking order of his own. In *The American Cinema*, he divided American directors into eleven categories, including the "Pantheon" (Charles Chaplin, John Ford, D. W. Griffith, Howard Hawks, Alfred Hitchcock, Orson Welles); "the Far Side of Paradise" (Robert Aldrich, Frank Capra, Samuel Fuller, Vincente Minnelli); "Expressive Esoterica" (Tay Garnett, Arthur Penn, Edgar G. Ulmer); and "Less Than Meets the Eye" (John Huston, Elia Kazan, William Wyler). Despite the historical importance of *The American Cinema*, it is the kind of book that requires periodic revision. The current critical estimate of Huston and Wyler, for example, suggests that there is more to each of them than met Sarris's eye.

Sarris reduced the auteur theory, which is how la politique des auteurs came to be known in America, to three principles: (1) an auteur is technically competent; (2) an auteur has a personality that manifests itself in recurring stylistic traits that become his or her signature; and (3) an auteur's films exhibit a tension between the auteur's personality and his or her material—that is, there are aspects of an auteur's personality that will seep into the films, aspects that may not be readily discernible but may come out when a number of the auteur's films are studied and analyzed. Thus Hitchcock's ambivalence toward women, especially blondes, is not immediately evident; yet after analyzing such films as *The 39 Steps, Saboteur, Psycho,* and *The Birds,* we see that while blondes held a certain fascination for him, he often subjected them to various forms of degradation—being handcuffed to a man, being slashed to death in a shower, having their faces pecked by attacking birds.

On the basis of Sarris's criteria, it is possible to consider certain directors—admittedly, few—as auteurs or surrogate authors of their films. Film is not the only medium in which auteurism is practiced, however; forms of auteurism exist in all the performing arts. A ballet lover may refer to Nureyev's *Romeo and Juliet* as opposed to another dancer's, emphasizing not Prokofiev's score but its interpreter. A theatergoer who remembers Ralph Fiennes's Hamlet is not remembering Shakespeare's play but its interpretation by a particular actor. Plays are also sometimes thought of in terms of the acting companies that produced them. Thus one theatergoer might ask another, "Did you see the Abbey's *Juno and the Paycock?*," meaning not Sean O'Casey's play but its production by Dublin's Abbey Theatre. Similarly, moviegoers might ask, "Did you ever see Mel Gibson's Hamlet, meaning Gibson's interpretation of Hamlet in Franco Zeffirelli's 1990 film version; or they might ask, "How would you rank Kenneth Branagh's *Hamlet* (1996) in comparison with Laurence Olivier's *Hamlet* (1948)?" These moviegoers are referring to two very different things: they are talking about *Hamlet* as interpreted by two different directors, Kenneth Branagh and Laurence Olivier, both of whom also played the title character in their respective film versions.

A symphony orchestra provides another analogy. If the brass section is mediocre, if the woodwinds fail to come in on time, if the horns sound flat, the conductor shoulders the blame. Critics constantly berate the conductor who "led a sluggish performance of César Franck's Symphony in D Minor" or "who failed to elevate the orchestra to the heights the music demanded." When Leonard Bernstein conducted a Mahler symphony, it was no longer Mahler's symphony but Bernstein's. Bernstein took Mahler's work and attempted to realize the composer's intentions and communicate them to the orchestra. If Bernstein succeeded, he was praised; if he didn't, he was criticized. Similarly, if a director is successful at blending the elements that make up a film into an organic whole that realizes the script's intent, he or she is commended; if not, the director is criticized for being unable to achieve the necessary integration.

However, just as every conductor is not a Leonard Bernstein, every director is not an Alfred Hitchcock. Hitchcock, then, clearly fulfills the criteria of the auteur: when we designate *Psycho* as Hitchcock's *Psycho*, we mean that Hitchcock has been successful at integrating the efforts of the writer, the cast, and the crew into a reflection of his vision of the material.

The Debate over Auteurism

Even though some film scholars agree that there is such a thing as an Alfred Hitchcock film and therefore there are Hitchcockian elements in the films of others, many would argue against establishing auteurism as a general theory of film on the following grounds:

1. The genesis of a film is often too complex to be attributed to a single person. Some films, in fact, are the result of a producer's rather than a director's conception. Victor Fleming is credited as the director of *Gone with the Wind* (although George Cukor and Sam Wood also had a hand in the direction), yet the film was the brainchild of the producer David O. Selznick; if anything, then, it might be called a David O. Selznick film. The disaster films *The Poseidon Adventure* (1972) and *The Towering Inferno* (1975) are associated with the producer, Irwin Allen, not with the directors, Ronald Neame and John Guillermin, respectively. Although Val Lewton never directed a single film, he left his mark on everything he produced at RKO (*Cat People, I Walked with a Zombie, The Curse of the Cat People,* and others). As a result, we think of *Cat People* primarily as a Val Lewton film and only secondarily as Jacques Tourneur's. Michael Bay may have directed *Pearl Harbor,* but the film would never have been made had it not been for producer Jerry Bruckheimer's commitment to the project.

   If there is any similarity between *Poltergeist* (1982) and *E.T.,* it is because Steven Spielberg, who directed *E.T.,* coauthored and produced *Poltergeist* (although he did not direct it). Directed by Tobe Hooper, *Poltergeist* bears the Spielberg signature and is imbued with the same childlike innocence that characterizes *E.T.* If *Batteries Not Included* (1987), in which aliens come to the aid of tenants whom a greedy developer is pressuring into moving, sounds like Spielberg again, it is because the film is a Spielberg production, even though it was directed by Matthew Robbins.

2. Certain films, especially those made when the studios were at their peak (1930–1960), bear the stamp of their studios more than that of any individual and are therefore thought of as "MGM movies" or "Warner Bros. movies." *Singin' in the Rain* is clearly an MGM musical, specifically a musical that came from Arthur Freed's production unit at MGM. If *Singin' in the Rain* is compared with other Arthur Freed productions, such as *Easter Parade, On the Town,* and *An American in Paris,* it is clear that they have something in common: the musical numbers are integrated with the action. While *Singin' in the Rain* was directed by Stanley

Donen and Gene Kelly, film historians consider it an MGM musical or an Arthur Freed production, not a Donen-Kelly film.

3. Films that involve special effects illustrate the limitations of auteurism. When David Denby and Terrence Rafferty reviewed *Who Framed Roger Rabbit* in *New York* and *The New Yorker*, respectively, each referred to "Robert Zemeckis's *Who Framed Roger Rabbit*." Yet Zemeckis was not responsible for the animation; the animation director Richard Williams and his staff were. Furthermore, the film was a cooperative venture between Disney's Touchstone Pictures and Steven Spielberg's Amblin Entertainment. Spielberg is not the kind of producer who remains aloof from a production; in fact, he had certain ideas about how the cartoon figures should look. (For example, he wanted Roger's mouth to resemble Thumper's in *Bambi*.) The answer to the question "Who framed Roger Rabbit?" is easy. The answer to the question "Who made *Who Framed Roger Rabbit*?" is not.

For this reason, not every director can be considered an auteur; actually, comparatively few can. The auteurs are directors whose work is studied in film courses and who have become the subjects of books, articles, and retrospectives. These directors do not necessarily write their own scripts: Woody Allen generally does, but John Ford never did. There have also been directors who worked within the studio system and still made films that were their own. William Wyler made some of his best movies for Samuel Goldwyn, such as *Dead End* (1937) and *Wuthering Heights* (1939). Shortly before Pearl Harbor, Wyler was hired by MGM to direct *Mrs. Miniver*, which dramatized the impact of World War II on a typical British family. In one sense, *Mrs. Miniver* is an MGM film; it was made by a specific studio because the head of that studio, Louis B. Mayer, believed in the "family film." However, Wyler was able to make it a William Wyler film. Wyler always tried to encompass as much as he could in a single shot, thus minimizing cutting. *Mrs. Miniver* is filled with such shots: Kay Miniver sitting on the bed while her husband is off in the dressing room; the Minivers seated at the dinner table while their son is seen talking on the phone in the alcove; Kay standing on the bridge with the station master below her and water behind him.

Directors who are taught, written about, and honored with retrospectives and tributes have two things in common: their films illustrate the collaborative nature of the medium because such directors tend to work regularly with the same—or similar—talent (writer, actors, cinematographer, editor) in a succession of films; they repeat favorite themes in the same or different genres; they allude to their earlier films; and they borrow from the films of others.

COLLABORATION

From a director's standpoint, collaboration can take several forms, the most common of which are as follows:

1. Collaboration between a director and a screenwriter. Sometimes a director will have the same screenwriter for several movies; undoubtedly, those movies will have certain features in common. Joan Harrison worked on the scripts for Hitchcock's *Rebecca, Foreign Correspondent, Suspicion,* and *Saboteur,* in all of which the wrong person was under suspicion. Billy Wilder and Charles Brackett coauthored the scripts for three Mitchell Leisen films: *Midnight; Arise, My Love* (1940); and *Hold Back the Dawn* (1941). All three entail some form of deception.

2. Collaboration between a director and a cinematographer. Historically, the most famous was that between D. W. Griffith and Billy Bitzer. Other creative director-cinematographer collaborations have been between Eric von Stroheim and William Daniels (*Blind Husbands* [1918], *Foolish Wives* [1921], *Greed* [1924], *The Merry Widow* [1925]; Josef von Sternberg and Lee Garmes (*Morocco* [1930], *Dishonored* [1931], *Shanghai Express* [1932]); Ingmar Bergman and Gunnar Fischer (*Smiles of a Summer Night* [1955], *The Seventh Seal* [1957], *Wild Strawberries*).

3. Collaboration between a director and a composer. Examples of this type include John Ford and Alfred Newman (*Arrowsmith* [1931], *The Hurricane* [1937], *The Grapes of Wrath, How Green Was My Valley*); Federico Fellini and Nino Rota (*La Strada* [1954], *La Dolce Vita* [1960], *8½* [1963], *Juliet of the Spirits*); Hitchcock and Bernard Herrmann (*The Wrong Man, Vertigo, Psycho, Marnie*); Spielberg and John Williams (*Jaws, Close Encounters of the Third Kind, Raiders of the Lost Ark, E.T.: The Extra-Terrestrial, Empire of the Sun, Indiana Jones and the Last Crusade, Jurassic Park, Schindler's List, A.I.: Artificial Intelligence* [2001]).

4. Collaboration between a director and an actor(s). Notable here are John Huston and Humphrey Bogart (*The Maltese Falcon* [1941], *Across the Pacific* [1942], *Treasure of the Sierra Madre* [1948], *Key Largo* [1948], *The African Queen* [1951]; von Sternberg and Marlene Dietrich (*The Blue Angel* [1930], *Morocco, Dishonored, Shanghai Express, Blonde Venus* [1932]); George Cukor and Katharine Hepburn (*A Bill of Divorcement* [1932], *Little Women* [1933], *Sylvia Scarlett* [1935], *Holiday* [1938], *The Philadelphia Story* [1940], *Keeper of the Flame* [1943], *Adam's Rib* [1949], *Pat and*

Mike [1952], and the TV movies *Love among the Ruins* [1975] and *The Corn Is Green* [1979]); Truffaut and Jean-Pierre Léaud (*The 400 Blows, Stolen Kisses, Bed and Board, Day for Night*); Bergman and Liv Ullman (*Persona* [1966], *Hour of the Wolf* [1968], *The Shame* [1968], *A Passion of Anna* [1969], *Scenes from a Marriage* [1973], *Face to Face* [1976]); Billy Wilder and Jack Lemmon (*Some Like It Hot* [1959], *The Apartment* [1960], *Irma la Douce* [1963], *The Fortune Cookie* [1966], *Avanti!* [1972], *The Front Page* [1974], *Buddy Buddy* [1981]); John Ford's stock company (Ward Bond, Victor McLaglen, John Wayne, Maureen O'Hara, Ben Johnson); Woody Allen and Mia Farrow (*Broadway Danny Rose* [1984], *The Purple Rose of Cairo* [1985], *Hannah and Her Sisters* [1986], *Radio Days* [1987], *September* [1987], *Another Woman* [1988], *Crimes and Misdemeanors* [1989], *Shadows and Fog* [1992], *Husbands and Wives* [1992]); Martin Scorsese and Robert De Niro (*Mean Streets* [1973]; *Taxi Driver* [1976], *New York, New York* [1977], *Raging Bull* [1980], *The King of Comedy* [1983], *GoodFellas* [1990], *Cape Fear* [1991], *Casino* [1995]).

5. Collaboration between a director and an editor. The collaboration between Woody Allen and Susan E. Morse is noteworthy for its longevity: *Manhattan* (1979), *Stardust Memories* (1980), *A Midsummer Night's Sex Comedy* (1982), *Zelig* (1983), *Broadway Danny Rose, The Purple Rose of Cairo, Hannah and Her Sisters, Radio Days, September, Another Woman, Crimes and Misdemeanors, Shadows and Fog, Husbands and Wives, Manhattan Murder Mystery* (1993), *Bullets over Broadway* (1994), *Mighty Aphrodite* (1995), *Everyone Says I Love You* (1996), *Deconstructing Harry* (1997), *Celebrity* (1998). So is that between Robert Zemeckis and Arthur Schmidt: *Back to the Future* (1985), *Back to the Future Part II* (1989), *Back to the Future Part III* (1990), *Death Becomes Her* (1992), *Forrest Gump* (1994), *Contact* (1997), *What Lies Beneath* (2000), *Cast Away* (2000).

6. Collaboration between a director and a producer. The best examples of this are Wyler and Samuel Goldwyn (*Dead End, Wuthering Heights, The Westerner* [1940], *The Little Foxes* [1941], *The Best Years of Our Lives* [1946]); Jacques Tourneur, Robert Wise, and Mark Robson, who directed the films Val Lewton produced for RKO; William Dieterle and Hal B. Wallis at Paramount (*The Searching Wind* [1946], *The Accused* [1948], *Rope of Sand* [1949], *Paid in Full* [1950], *Dark City* [1950], *Red Mountain* [1951]); Arthur Freed, who had his own musical unit at MGM; and Vincente Minnelli (*Meet Me in St. Louis, Yolanda and the Thief* [1945], *The Pirate* [1948], *An American in Paris* [1951], *The Band Wagon* [1953], *Kismet* [1955], *Gigi* [1958]). Until its dissolution in 2001,

the producer-director team of Jean Doumanian and Woody Allen was one of the most productive in contemporary Hollywood: *Bullets over Broadway, Mighty Aphrodite, Everyone Says I Love You, Deconstructing Harry, Celebrity, Sweet and Lowdown* (1999), and *Small Time Crooks* (2000).

7. Collaboration between a director and a studio. Directors who were identified with particular studios include Frank Capra and Columbia, Ernst Lubitsch and Paramount, Preston Sturges and Paramount, Raoul Walsh and Warner Bros., and Vincente Minnelli and MGM. Paramount was synonymous with sophisticated comedy during the 1930s and 1940s, and it was such directors as Lubitsch, Sturges, and, to a lesser extent, Leisen who gave the studio that reputation. Lubitsch could do more with the closing of a bedroom door than most directors could by keeping it open. In corporate Hollywood, director-studio relationships are short-lived. Until he became a cofounder of DreamWorksSKG in 1994, Steven Spielberg enjoyed a mutually beneficial relationship with Universal, where his production company, Amblin Entertainment, was based. Spielberg's Universal films include *The Sugarland Express* (1974), *Jaws, E.T.: The Extra-Terrestrial, Raiders of the Lost Ark, Jurassic Park, Schindler's List,* and *The Lost World: Jurassic Park* (1997).

VARIETY

A great director need not have a wide repertoire of themes; there is a difference between a varied body of work and a varied number of themes. The same themes can recur within that body of work, repeated or modified to fit a particular type of film. Billy Wilder's films, for example, center around two major themes: deception and its various forms (disguise, fraud, masquerade), and the impact of one social or political order on another (capitalism/communism, rich/poor, youth/age). Even the scripts that he and Charles Brackett wrote before he began directing reflect these themes: the female commissar of Ernst Lubitsch's *Ninotchka* (1939), who comes in contact with capitalism and falls under its spell; the chorus girl of *Midnight*, who impersonates a countess; the female reporter of *Arise, My Love*, who rescues a man from prison by pretending to be his wife; the gigolo of *Hold Back the Dawn*, who feigns love in order to become an American citizen; the college professors of Howard Hawks's *Ball of Fire* (1941), who find themselves learning slang from a stripper.

Then there are the films that Wilder directed himself:

The Major and the Minor (1942): A woman disguises herself as a twelve-year-old in order to purchase a train ticket at half price.

Five Graves to Cairo (1943): A British officer impersonates a lame servant in a desert hotel.

Double Indemnity (1944): An insurance agent tricks a man into signing a policy with a double-indemnity clause; the agent and the client's wife then conspire to kill her husband and collect on the policy; the agent briefly poses as her husband on board a train.

In *The Major and the Minor* (1942), a career woman (Ginger Rogers) disguised herself as a twelve-year-old in order to ride to her home in Iowa for half the fare. *(Courtesy Margaret Herrick Library of the Academy of Motion Picture Arts and Sciences)*

Audrey Hepburn as Sabrina and Humphrey Bogart as Linus in *Sabrina* (1954).
(Courtesy Paramount Pictures and MOMA/FSA)

The Lost Weekend (1945): An alcoholic is continually devising ways to conceal his bottle.

The Emperor Waltz (1948): An Austrian countess meets an American phonograph salesman (a "two social orders" film).

A Foreign Affair (1948): An army captain in postwar Berlin tries to conceal his relationship with a nightclub singer from a visiting congresswoman.

Sunset Boulevard (1950): An aging silent star deludes herself into thinking that she can make a comeback as Salome; her kept man conceals his status from his girlfriend.

The Big Carnival (*Ace in the Hole* [1951]): A reporter deceives the victim of a cave-in into believing he is the victim's friend.

Stalag 17 (1953): An informer infiltrates a POW camp.

Sabrina (1954): A rich young man courts a chauffeur's daughter (a "two orders" film).

The Seven Year Itch (1955): A summer bachelor plays at being Don Juan.

The Spirit of St. Louis (1957): An atypical Wilder film, which depicts Lindbergh's flight across the Atlantic.

Love in the Afternoon (1957): A May-December romance develops between an older man and a young woman whose father is a detective.

Witness for the Prosecution (1957): A woman tricks a noted barrister into thinking she is a cockney.

Some Like It Hot (1959): Two musicians dress up as women; a millionaire (male) falls in love with one of the disguised men.

The Apartment (1960): A woman with a checkered past masquerades as a virgin.

One, Two, Three (1961): An American Coca-Cola executive and a radical East Berliner clash ideologically.

Irma la Douce (1963): To keep a prostitute from sharing her favors with others, her lover resorts to disguise.

Kiss Me, Stupid (1964): A single female bartender impersonates a married woman; a wife allows her songwriter-husband to think his song succeeded on its own merits although it became a hit because she spent the night with a famous pop singer.

The Fortune Cookie (1966): A TV cameraman is persuaded by his brother-in-law to sue for nonexistent injuries.

The Private Life of Sherlock Holmes (1970): Deception is implicit in any treatment of Holmes.

Avanti! (1972): A married man and the daughter of his late father's mistress arrange to have a yearly rendezvous in Italy, repeating the deception their parents (his father, her mother) had practiced until their death.

The Front Page (1974): An editor will do anything to get his star reporter back, even resort to a lie that also happens to be one of the most famous curtain lines in American theater: "The son of a bitch stole my watch."

Fedora (1979): An international movie star who has been facially disfigured passes her daughter off as herself.

Buddy Buddy (1981): To prevent himself from being unmasked, a hit man attempts to save a television censor from suicide.

Variety is achieved more through genre than theme. While deception/disguise is a recurring theme in Wilder's films, it is a theme that manifests itself in farce (*The Major and the Minor, Some Like It Hot, Irma la Douce*); romantic comedy (*Sabrina, Love in the Afternoon, Avanti!*); political comedy (*A Foreign Affair; One, Two, Three*); social comedy (*The Apartment, The Fortune Cookie*); social realism (*The Lost Weekend, The Big Carnival*); espionage and wartime melodrama (*Five Graves to Cairo, Stalag 17*); courtroom melodrama (*Witness for the Prosecution*); gothic melodrama (*Sunset Boulevard*); period pieces (*The Emperor Waltz, The Private Life of Sherlock Holmes*), and film noir (*Double Indemnity*).

The films themselves are derived from several sources: novels (*The*

Lost Weekend, Love in the Afternoon); plays that are either adaptations (*Stalag 17, Sabrina, The Seven Year Itch, Avanti!*) or almost total rewrites, with little of the original left intact (*One, Two, Three; Irma la Douce; Kiss Me, Stupid*); original scripts (*The Emperor Waltz, Sunset Boulevard, The Big Carnival, The Apartment, The Fortune Cookie, The Private Life of Sherlock Holmes*); and other films (*Buddy Buddy*, a reworking of a much better French film known in English as *A Pain in the A—* [1974]).

REPETITION

A great director may repeat favorite themes not only in different kinds of movies but also as motifs within those movies. Thus the deception/disguise theme recurs as various motifs in Wilder's movies:

1. Adultery (*Double Indemnity; The Seven Year Itch; Love in the Afternoon; The Apartment; Kiss Me, Stupid; Avanti!*).
2. Insurance fraud (*Double Indemnity, The Fortune Cookie*).
3. Women physically altering their appearance (*The Major and the Minor, Witness for the Prosecution, Fedora*).
4. Men physically altering their appearance (*Some Like It Hot, Irma la Douce*).
5. A woman deceiving the man she loves (*The Major and the Minor; The Apartment; Kiss Me, Stupid; The Private Life of Sherlock Holmes*).
6. A man deceiving the woman he loves (*The Seven Year Itch, Some Like It Hot, Irma la Douce*).
7. Men deceiving each other (*Five Graves to Cairo, Double Indemnity, The Lost Weekend, The Big Carnival, The Fortune Cookie, Buddy Buddy*).

Similarly, in the "two orders" films the following motifs can be found:

1. Distinctions of class (countess/commoner in *The Emperor Waltz*; common girl/privileged boy in *Sabrina*).
2. Distinctions of age (young woman/older man in *Sabrina, Love in the Afternoon, The Apartment,* and *Avanti!*; young man/older woman in *A Foreign Affair* and *Sunset Boulevard*).
3. Distinctions based on war (allies/enemy in *Five Graves to Cairo* and *Stalag 17*; victor/vanquished in *A Foreign Affair*).
4. Distinctions of ideology (capitalism vs. communism in *One, Two, Three*; freedom vs. fascism in *A Foreign Affair*).

QUOTATIONS

Directors repeat themes, character types, characters' names, or visual motifs. Sometimes repetition is unconscious, but generally it is because directors assume that the audience will interpret the repetition as a sign of continuity—not as a lack of imagination. Thus, in casting John Wayne to play a character called Lt. Col. Kirby Yorke in *Rio Grande*, John Ford might have hoped the audience remembered that two years earlier Wayne played Captain Kirby Yorke in *Fort Apache*.

The opening credits of Ford's *The Man Who Shot Liberty Valance* are on broken crosses intended to evoke the opening credits of *My Darling Clementine*, which appeared on signposts. In the years between *Clementine* (1946) and *Liberty Valance* (1962), Ford's vision of the West had changed from romantic to realistic. The stars of *Liberty Valance*, John Wayne and James Stewart, play roles that would have been more suitable for them twenty years earlier; hence the broken crosses to suggest that time has left its mark on both the director and the stars. In *Empire of the Sun*, when a boy is reunited with his parents amid a vast throng of people, Steven Spielberg repeats a composition from a movie that he made ten years earlier, *Close Encounters of the Third Kind*, in which a man and a woman pushed their way through a crowd to find each other.

Hitchcock often quotes himself, but his quotes are rarely verbatim. Rowley's fall from the cathedral tower in *Foreign Correspondent* prefigures similar falls, but in different contexts, in *Saboteur, Vertigo,* and *North by Northwest*. The airplane wing that becomes a life raft when a plane crashes in the Atlantic in *Foreign Correspondent* yields to the real thing in *Lifeboat* (1944), a totally different kind of film that uses a more conventional form of survival at sea.

In Hitchcock's *Family Plot* (1976) when Blanche (Barbara Harris) and her boyfriend are driving along in a car whose brakes give way, she grabs hold of his necktie, almost strangling him with it. Her action recalls the necktie murders in *Frenzy* (1972). Similarly, when the pair are on a deserted stretch of highway, we almost expect the crop duster from *North by Northwest* to materialize and spray them with bullets. And to avoid detection when he's in a jewel thief's home, the boyfriend takes the same precautions Marnie took in Hitchcock's film of that name: he removes his shoes and tiptoes past the kitchen. In fact, we wait for him to drop a shoe, as Marnie did. These are old tricks, but they appear in new settings.

In *Witness for the Prosecution*, Billy Wilder added a flashback to show how Leonard Vole (Tyrone Power) met his wife, Christine (Marlene Dietrich), in a Hamburg nightclub at the end of World War II. Dietrich had the same profession in Wilder's *A Foreign Affair*. Wilder must have had the

Marlene Dietrich as Erika, a cabaret singer in post–World War II Berlin; and John Lund as her lover, Captain John Pringle, in *A Foreign Affair* (1948). *(Copyright © by Paramount Pictures. Courtesy MCA Publishing Rights, a Division of MCA, Inc.)*

Marlene Dietrich as Christine, who meets her future husband, Leonard Vole (Tyrone Power), in a Hamburg nightclub at the end of World War II in *Witness for the Prosecution* (1957). Wilder added the nightclub scene, which does not appear in the Agatha Christie play, to show how the Voles met. He is clearly repeating a plot device from *A Foreign Affair*—the smoke-filled basement nightclub where Pringle came to hear Erika sing. *(Courtesy MOMA/FSA)*

earlier film in mind when he decided to open up the Agatha Christie play a bit by putting in the flashback. Yet *Witness for the Prosecution* is not *A Foreign Affair*, any more than *Family Plot* is *Frenzy* or *North by Northwest*.

BORROWINGS

Wilder regarded Ernst Lubitsch as the unrivaled master of subtlety. Whenever someone in a Lubitsch film closed a door, drew the curtains, or shut the blinds, one always wondered, "Did they or didn't they?" In *Double Indemnity*, the camera dollies back from Phyllis and Neff as they sit snugly on the sofa in his apartment. "We just sat there," Neff's voice is heard saying. We no more believe him than we believe the Lubitsch heroine who closes the door of her lover's bedroom and in the next shot awakens in her own.

As a rule, great directors are not troubled by the question of originality, because they see themselves as part of a tradition. Although they respect the past, they neither worship it blindly nor lean on it for support; instead, they view it as a legacy on which they can draw. The Odessa Steps massacre in *Potemkin* left its mark on many filmmakers, including Busby Berkeley, who paid it a curious tribute in the "Lullaby of Broadway" sequence in *Gold Diggers of 1935*. Hitchcock did the same in *Foreign Correspondent*, in which an assassination was staged on the steps of an Amsterdam conference hall. Brian De Palma paid homage to the Odessa Steps sequence in *The Untouchables* (1987), which even includes the careening baby carriage. Most directors are flattered when viewers evidence an awareness of a borrowing or a quote; in fact, in some cases viewers are expected to notice the borrowings so they can appreciate the director's integration of past and present.

AN INTERVIEW WITH BILLY WILDER

Billy Wilder is an ideal director for study. He directed his first film in 1942; his last in 1981. He is also a true auteur, inasmuch as he coauthored the scripts of all the films he directed. After *The Big Carnival*, with a few minor exceptions, he produced his own films. Wilder has been the subject of retrospectives, doctoral dissertations, books, articles, and television tributes by the American Film Institute and the Film Society of Lincoln Center. He is a six-time Academy Award winner: twice for direction (*The Lost Weekend, The Apartment*); three times for best screenplay (*The Lost Weekend, Sunset Boulevard,* * *The Apartment*); and once for best picture (*The Apartment*).

D. H. Lawrence once said, "Trust the tale, not the teller." Yet the teller can have much to tell, especially one who writes, directs, and produces his or her own tales. Wilder told much during an interview on June 11, 1976:

> DICK: The critics who like to minimize the director's role will say that all a director did during the Studio Years was carry out the studio's policy. They would not speak of "Billy Wilder's films" but of "Billy Wilder's Paramount

*The Sunset Boulevard Oscar was technically for story and screenplay.

HOMAGE TO THE ODESSA STEPS SEQUENCE

The Odessa Steps massacre in *Potemkin. (Courtesy MOMA/FSA and Janus Films)*

period [1942–1954]." When you were at Paramount, were you conscious of turning out a Paramount product?

WILDER: Never, not even in the early days when I did not have script approval and the right of final cut. If this were true, then Lubitsch's pictures, Sturges's pictures, Mitchell Leisen's pictures, my pictures—in fact, all the pictures made during those interesting days at Paramount—would have been the same. They were not. Once Paramount and I agreed on the subject of the movie, the cast, and the budget, and once they realized I would not have censorship problems (and in those days we had to smuggle things past the censors)—once all of this was settled—I was on my own. I wrote the film the way I wanted to, I cut it the way I wanted to. Of course, I may have to give a little when a picture is sold to television and make a cut here or a cut there. But even when I was beginning and did not have the ultimate control I have now, never for a moment did I think of myself as a foreman on the Paramount lot.

You see, the auteur theory, in emphasizing the director who takes over someone else's script, has little to say about a director like myself, who writes, directs, and produces his own. Although I do not belong to the producers' guild (I do, of course, belong to the screenwriters' and directors'), I think I can evaluate the auteur theory better than most critics. Being the writer, director, and producer of a picture, naturally I am the auteur.

DICK: Then you do not accept the auteur theory?

WILDER: I accept it only up to a point. The auteur theory does not emphasize the script. I deeply believe in the script and in the director's getting

Hitchcock's homage to the Odessa Steps in *Foreign Correspondent* (1940). *(Courtesy MOMA/FSA)*

the maximum out of it. A mediocre director with a great script will still come out on top, but a brilliant director with a poor script will inevitably fail.

DICK: Is it easier to become a director now than it was when you began in the industry?

WILDER: It is much easier now, because television provides you with a training ground. In the past, there was no training ground except shorts and a series like MGM's *Crime Does Not Pay*, where Fred Zinnemann got his chance. Otherwise, unless you worked on Broadway or had important connections, or unless powerful stars requested you, it was extraordinarily difficult to get a break. You might think that by becoming an assistant director you would stand a good chance of becoming a director. Yet the assistant director had the least chance of ever becoming a director. The dialogue coach, the cameraman, the actor, the actor's relatives stood a better chance of becoming directors.

Of course, all that has changed with television. With the enormous demands it makes on one's time, you can learn by being on the set long enough. And with highly trained crews at his disposal, a director can't make a total ass of himself.

Billy Wilder on the set.
(Courtesy Billy Wilder)

Directing is not Chinese glassblowing or the art of making Inca gold stat-
uettes. It can be learned, and it can be learned quickly if you have a flair and
a style for it. It is also an exhausting profession, and one that has a finality
about it. In the theater, you can rewrite a play during its tryout; in my profession you can't say "Let's reshoot the film" if you don't like it. The sets
are down, the actors are in Yugoslavia, and plans have already been made
for the picture's distribution.

DICK: Do you have an image in your mind of what the film will look like
in its final form?

WILDER: Even though you lose yourself in the picture while you're making it, ultimately it is back to what it was when you did the script, which is
proof that the script was good and the choice of material was good. If a film
doesn't work—and often it doesn't—it was because I was telling the wrong
story or an uninteresting story; I was telling a story that didn't have a chance
no matter how brilliantly I might do it. Maybe I chose the right story at the
time, but it turned out to be the wrong time for the picture. If I write an article for a magazine, it will be published a few weeks later. The mood of the
public has not changed, and there is still interest in the subject. But my picture will not see the light of day for two years, when the mood of the public
may be entirely different.

DICK: Are your scripts complete when you begin shooting?

WILDER: They are complete in the sense that I know how the film will end, but I want to see how the first two acts will play before I go on to the third. They are not complete in the sense that every line has been written down. I am always open to suggestions. If a scene does not play well in rehearsal, I will change it. If an actor has a good idea, or even an electrician, I can add it. But you must first have something to add it to.

DICK: Is there any truth to the story that Shirley MacLaine and Jack Lemmon were handed their dialogue for the final scene of *The Apartment* on the last day of shooting?

WILDER: Could be. But we knew very well how it would end: the boy would get what he wanted, give it up, and get the girl. Maybe the actual words were typed the night before. But we did not improvise; I never depend upon improvisation.

DICK: Your films evidence an incredible range—romantic comedy, farce, social drama, film noir, melodrama, biography. Did you aim for such diversity?

WILDER: I know a man who always wears a dark blue suit when he goes out in the evening. It's rather boring, you know. Why not a striped suit once in a while? Sometimes I wonder if I did the wrong thing by experimenting so much. Hitchcock, whom I greatly admire, stayed with one kind of picture. When people go to a Hitchcock movie, they know what to expect. Certain directors develop a style, refine it, and never give it up; they never leave their own neighborhood. I ventured out and tested myself. But whatever kind of film I make, there is always one quality I aim for: a complete simplicity of style, a total lack of pretentiousness; there is not one phony setup in a Billy Wilder picture.

Also, making films is a matter of mood. Now I am in the mood for something a bit serious, so I will do *Fedora*,* which may remind some of *Sunset Boulevard* at least in texture, but it will be quite different.

DICK: It's well known that you write your scripts with a collaborator, but do you ever look upon your editor as a collaborator? I ask because Doane Harrison edited several of your early films.

WILDER: Doane Harrison was an old-time cutter, going back to the time when George Stevens was a cameraman for Hal Roach. He was very close to me when I made *The Major and the Minor*; he taught me a great deal because until then I had spent my life behind the typewriter, not behind the camera.**

DICK: How did you get behind the camera?

WILDER: How I became a director is very interesting. When I was writing scripts with Charles Brackett, we were never allowed on the set when the film was being shot. First of all, directors didn't want writers on the set; and second, we were off writing another picture. I decided to assert myself because I wanted some control over my scripts. So I started to raise hell, and Paramount finally let me direct a picture. Actually, it was no big deal because

Fedora, the first novella in Thomas Tryon's *Crowned Heads* (1976), is about a movie star who does not seem to age.

**Wilder began his career as a reporter in his native Vienna. It was in Berlin in the late 1920s that he turned to screenwriting.

at that time Paramount was turning out fifty pictures a year. They said, "Let Wilder make a picture and then he'll go back to writing." Everyone expected me to make something "fancy-schmancy." Yet I made something commercial. I brought back the most salable hunk of celluloid I could—*The Major and the Minor.*

You see, unless you control your film, you are also at the mercy of actors. It's easy for an actor to argue with a director who is weak or who isn't convinced about the script. I remember Mr. Brackett and I were working on the script for *Hold Back the Dawn*, which Mitchell Leisen was directing. We had written a very fine scene for Charles Boyer, who was playing an immigrant waiting for his visa to come through. Unkempt and unshaven, Boyer waits in a cheap Mexican hotel. Well, to show the kind of hotel it was and to suggest something about the character Boyer was playing, we included a scene where Boyer makes some cynical remarks to a cockroach climbing up the wall. I assumed the scene would be shot as we had written it. A short time later, I ran into Boyer and asked him how he liked the scene with the cockroach. He said, "We cut that scene." I was shocked. "Why was it cut?" I asked. "How can I talk to a cockroach when the cockroach can't answer?" was Boyer's reply. I was so angry I told Brackett, "If that son of a bitch ain't talking to a cockroach, he ain't talking to anybody." We hadn't finished the script yet, so we pared Boyer's remaining scenes down to the bare minimum.

DICK: Is it important for a director to be able to write?

WILDER: It is more important for a director to be able to read. Many directors do not understand the script, and they don't have the nerve to say so. But they go ahead and shoot it, regardless.

DICK: There is a great deal of confusion today about the role of the editor. Did an editor ever change the form of any of your films?

WILDER: No, I learned to shoot with utmost economy, so there is not much an editor can do. I cut the film in the camera. I do not protect myself by shooting the scene eighteen different ways: it exhausts the actors, and the words begin to lose their meaning. I will go over the rushes with the editor and we will discuss them. I may say to him, "I need an additional shot here," but that is the extent of it. The worst that can ever happen is that I must alter my film or add to it.

DICK: Yet some directors rely very heavily on their editors. Dede Allen has become a legend in her own lifetime. Some critics have even said that she bails out Arthur Penn time and time again with her editing.

WILDER: I would not say she "bailed" him out; it was more like the way Maxwell E. Perkins helped Thomas Wolfe reorganize his novels for publication. If an editor bails a director out, it is because he shot crap. Dede Allen fully deserves the billing she gets, because she makes the picture better. It is the same with Verna Fields, who cut *Jaws*. She has the knack of knowing which frames to cut and how fast to cut them.

DICK: You edited *The Front Page* in four days, yet Terrence Malick supposedly spent a year editing *Badlands*.

WILDER: That is because he shot a great deal of film; I don't. I also work with very expensive actors, so I do not have the time. In the case of *Badlands*, you have a crew of very talented beginners who do everything themselves, including moving the camera from place to place. They can go out and shoot where they like; and by the time the sheriff comes around to ask if they have permission, they've gone. I must apply for permission and wait until I get it. If I pick up a chair on the set, I have the unions to contend with. Our approaches are totally different; it's like commedia dell'arte as opposed to the legitimate theater.

DICK: Did you go into producing because you wanted more control over your pictures?

WILDER: Yes, and also because there were so few creative producers. Look at this ad in *The Hollywood Reporter:*

SILVER STREAK

A MARTIN RANSOHOFF–FRANK YABLANS PRODUCTION

AN ARTHUR HILLER FILM

A MILLER–MILKIS–COLIN HIGGINS PICTURE

This is insane. What happens is that somebody buys a property or two people buy it, so their names must appear. If the star becomes involved in the production, then his name appears. The director says it must read "A Bill Friedkin Film" or "Bill Friedkin's Film." Then the schleppers and the hangers-on get into the act. The vanity game is enormous. Even in the theater, it's "a such-and-such production in conjunction with so-and-so." Ultimately, when it's all over, it's Josh Logan's *South Pacific.*

The true producers, like Thalberg, Selznick, and Goldwyn, would add to a picture and enrich it; they were there when you needed them for important decisions. When the picture was finished, they got the maximum exposure for it and arranged for it to be shown in the best theaters.

DICK: Since *Ace in the Hole*, you have produced all of your films except for *The Spirit of St. Louis*, which Leland Hayward produced, and *Witness for the Prosecution*, which Arthur Hornblow, Jr., produced. Was there any reason for your not producing these yourself?

WILDER: Leland Hayward was my agent when I first came to Hollywood, so there was no real problem with his producing my film. Arthur Hornblow produced my very first film, *The Major and the Minor.* He was also a friend of Marlene Dietrich, who wanted the part in *Witness for the Prosecution* and asked me to direct so she would be sure to get it.

DICK: How do you feel about directors like Peter Bogdanovich, who pay homage to the work of other directors?

WILDER: You know what we call Bogdanovich? "The Frank Gorshin of directors." He is so steeped in film history that it is difficult for him to find a style of his own.

DICK: Have you ever paid homage to other directors?

WILDER: If I did, it was unconscious.

DICK: What about Lubitsch? There is a Lubitsch quality about *The Emperor Waltz* and *The Private Life of Sherlock Holmes.*

WILDER: I advise everyone to stay away from Lubitsch; he cannot be imitated. I did not set out to make a Lubitsch film in either case. And incidentally, you picked two of my failures. *Holmes* didn't make a ripple. I even had to cut two episodes out of it.

DICK: It is a film that is gaining in popularity. It was recently revived as part of a Sherlock Holmes Film Festival in New York, and those who had never seen it before were quite taken with it.

WILDER: It was, I think, the lushest of the Holmesiana and truest to the period.

DICK: Most of your films employ some form of disguise or deception. Would you agree?

WILDER: Some, but not all. Not in *Double Indemnity.*

DICK: It does appear in the way Neff gets Dietrichson to sign the insurance policy.

WILDER: Yes, I see what you mean. Well, there is a lot of that in *Fedora*, I assure you.

DICK: You said before that you were not conscious of any Lubitsch influence. Were you aware of the fact that in both *Five Graves to Cairo* and *The Private Life of Sherlock Holmes* you used a parasol as part of the plot and as a symbol of femininity? In *Five Graves*, Bramble places it on Mouche's grave; in *Holmes*, Ilse uses her parasol to send messages as well as to say goodbye to Holmes.

WILDER: No, I was not conscious of *Five Graves to Cairo* when I was making *Holmes.* In *Five Graves to Cairo* the parasol was a sentimental touch; there are no flowers in Tobruk, so he brings her a parasol. In *Holmes* Ilse used it for Morse code. And a parasol is so photographable, you know. There is something exquisite about it, especially when it is opened out against the sun. I am very fond of the proper use of props, and I like to make them part of the script. In *The Apartment* I used a broken compact mirror as the means of identifying Shirley MacLaine as the girl Fred MacMurray had been bringing to Jack Lemmon's apartment.

DICK: Were you influenced by the Book of Genesis when you were writing *Ace in the Hole*? I am thinking of the continual emphasis on serpents, the desert as a kind of Eden that turns into a carnival, the rescue operations that take six days.

WILDER: That is a very interesting theory. You see, personally my mind doesn't go that way. And if it did, I couldn't admit it.

DICK: Several years ago you made this statement: "We're just like the guys in Detroit, putting out cars, no matter what anyone thinks we are." This is rather strange coming from a man who is the subject of retrospectives, books, articles, and Ph.D. dissertations. Do you still believe it?

WILDER: I did not mean what people think. How do you interpret it?

DICK: That directors are assembly-line workers.

WILDER: What I meant was that it takes tremendous artistry to put something into an assembly-line product so it will not have that mass-produced look. If someone is writing a poem or composing a symphony, he is doing it himself and on his own time. In our business we are playing for enormous chips supplied by other people. They give me the chips to gamble with, and I in turn am responsible to them. In this kind of situation it takes more artistry to produce something of value—sometimes to sneak in something of value—than it does when you are given as much money as you want, with no strings attached, and told to go to Salzburg and bring back a two-hour film. If I get behind schedule or exceed my budget, or if I indulge myself, after a couple of such pictures I would be flat on my ass. I would not get a chance to work again. I must do something that is hopefully superior, hopefully innovative, and at the same time it must be profitable. I personally believe that anything worthwhile ultimately finds some kind of audience. If somebody says, "This is the goddamnedest greatest picture ever made but no one went to see it," then it is not the goddamnedest greatest picture ever made.

I assure you, I have as many sleepless nights and as many ulcers as the truest of artists. But I have an added burden. If a painter buys a canvas for a couple of dollars and does not like what he has painted on it, he can throw it away. My canvas costs $4 million; if I don't like it, it can't be thrown in the fire. It's going to be shown, reviewed, maybe even play to empty houses. In the theater the producers can decide to close a show on the road and not bring it to Broadway. I can't. I've always said that the trouble with making pictures is that we can't try out in New Haven. If a picture is bad, it will come back to haunt you on the late-late show. Its stench will endure forever.

AN INTERVIEW WITH ALAN ALDA

In the movie industry, when a writer becomes a director, he or she is said to have "gone hyphenate." To use movie jargon, Alan Alda has gone double hyphenate: while Billy Wilder is a writer-director, Alan Alda is an actor-writer-director. Alda's career began on Broadway, with major roles in *Purlie Victorious* (1961), *The Owl and the Pussycat* (1964), and *The Apple Tree* (1966), which won him a Tony nomination. When Hollywood beckoned, he began the second phase of his career, appearing in such films as *The Paper Lion* (1968), *The Extraordinary Seaman* (1969), and *The Mephisto Waltz* (1971). When the success of the movie *M*A*S*H* led to the television spin-off in 1972, Alda's already varied career took another direction. As Hawkeye Pierce, Alda became one of television's most popular stars, a favorite among college students, and one of America's most sought-after commencement speakers.

What contributed to *M*A*S*H*'s longevity on television was an emphasis on human relationships that was quite different from the absurdist and often cruel humor of the film. The series underwent a transition from sitcom to human comedy, and Alda played a significant role in the change, first by writing some scripts and then by directing them. By the mid-

1970s, Alan Alda was a former Broadway star turned Hollywood actor who was then acting in, writing for, and directing some of the episodes of one of the most popular programs in the history of American television.

By the end of the 1970s, Alda had experience writing for television but had not yet written for the movies. The next stage in an already thriving career was to write his first screenplay, the highly successful *Seduction of Joe Tynan* (1979). Alda didn't direct *Joe Tynan*, however. Thus there was one more height to scale: directing an original screenplay in which he would also appear. He achieved that goal with *The Four Seasons* (1981), which proved to be both a critical and a commercial success. Three other films followed, which he directed and in which he appeared: *Sweet Liberty, A New Life,* and *Betsy's Wedding* (1980).

After the less than successful *Betsy's Wedding*, with which even Alda has admitted he was unhappy, he returned to acting, appearing in both TV movies (*And the Band Played On* [1993]) and theatrical films (for example, *Mad City* [1997], *The Object of My Affection* [1998], and *What Women Want* [2000]). In 1991, Alda returned to the Broadway stage, starring in Neil Simon's *Jake's Women* (filmed for television in 1998 as *Neil Simon's Jake's Women*) and in 1998 in Yasima Reza's *Art*, which proved to be enormously popular.

Although Alda no longer directs, his views on filmmaking are as valuable as Wilder's because, as an actor-writer-director, he understands the role each plays in the creation of a movie.

The following interview took place in Alan Alda's office at Martin Bregman Productions in New York on June 13, 1988:

> DICK: Some writers become writer-directors, or "go hyphenate" as *The Hollywood Reporter* would say, because they want greater control over their scripts. Was that true of yourself?
>
> ALDA: No. I think I became a director because I thought I would love directing; it turned out I did. When I started to direct, I was on *M*A*S*H*. I was eager to direct anything, whether I had written it or not. It would be a chance for me to work under the best conditions, where there were people who could catch me if I fell. Yet I can understand what writers go through when someone else directs their work. Unless a writer and a director are in close touch and are lucky enough to see things the same way, the result may be quite different from what the writer intended. My first *M*A*S*H* script had a very good director, yet the scenes didn't have the point I thought they should; in some cases, the actors didn't get the jokes, and I just had to sit by helplessly. It's a good idea, in general, for writers to direct their own material, and for directors to write their own material—but only if the directors can write. Unfortunately, there are a lot of directors who can't write but who keep doing it. I have great respect for the written word; that comes from having been an actor first. Since I come from the stage, I would never think

Alan Alda on the set of *Sweet Liberty* (1986). *(Copyright © Universal Pictures, a Division of Universal City Studios, Inc. Courtesy MCA Publishing Rights, a Division of MCA, Inc.)*

of changing a word in a script. And I wouldn't do it as a director, either, unless I consulted with the writer.

DICK: You don't believe, then, that the director is the author of the film, as the auteurists do?

ALDA: I have a problem with the auteur theory; the author of the film is the author of the script. I could understand if, by the auteur theory, you mean that the director contributes something to the film. If the director tells the story successfully through the lens, he or she has contributed something the writer couldn't because the writer told the story on paper. John Wayne contributed something unique to his movies, but you don't call a John Wayne film "A Film by John Wayne." After Marshall Brickman finished directing *Simon*, he was asked if he would like it called "A Film by Marshall Brickman." He replied, "No. It's a film by Kodak."

DICK: An editor also contributes something to the film. How much latitude did you allow William Reynolds, who edited *A New Life*?

ALDA: Since we had to get the film out in a hurry, I gave Bill a lot of latitude. As I watched the rushes, I made detailed notes about preferred takes and angles, and how I saw the scenes fitting together. I didn't sit over his shoulder. Actually, I liked the idea of loosening my grip a little. I think I was able to do it on *A New Life* because I was more secure. I told Bill what my ideas were; if he had a better idea or if he felt one of mine wouldn't work, he would tell me and we would proceed from there. I find that editing is like script writing. You refine what you've written and get other ideas. All the cuts have some of my ideas and some of Bill's.

DICK: Did you allow Michael Economou the same latitude on *Sweet Liberty*?

ALDA: No, and I'm sorry I didn't. The fact that I allowed Bill Reynolds more on *A New Life* represents growth on my part. Whether you have tight reins or loose reins, it all boils down to communication. No matter to whom you are talking—the editor, the cinematographer, the actors—you have to be able to describe what you see. You just can't say to someone, "This is the script; you do it." That's not the job of the director or even the producer; that's what the studio does. The studio says, "I like that script; I like that cast. Here's the money. Go make the movie." From that point on, everybody must start communicating with each other. The producer has to say to the writer or the writer-director, "Do you really need that scene? Do you think these lines are clear?" The producer does not do this to achieve the producer's vision, but the writer-director's. And the writer-director tries to get everyone else to realize the vision he or she has.

DICK: Do you have an image in your mind of how the completed film will look?

ALDA: For *Sweet Liberty* I storyboarded. There was a picture of every scene in the movie. An artist I was working with came back with a storyboard that represented the way he thought everything should look. I said, "Thank you, but that's not the point. They hired me to tell the story as I see it." A storyboard conveys a great deal of information; it's supposed to be a visualization of the script as well as an aid to all the departments involved in shooting the script. What I did was draw stick figures and discuss them with the artist so that he could draw the figures properly. Eighty percent of the film looked like the storyboard.

DICK: What about your relationship with the cinematographer?

ALDA: We would discuss what kind of lens, dolly, or crane we would use. I also had a specific shot list. That part of the job was over before I even got to the set, so we didn't have to waste half the morning wondering whether we would shoot this way or that.

DICK: Did you storyboard *A New Life* also?

ALDA: Not as much, since I didn't have an artist. I just drew stick figures.

DICK: Is storyboarding difficult if you're verbally oriented?

ALDA: No. I think in images. I usually start writing when I have a visual image. Novelists do the same, you know. John Fowles had an image of a woman at the end of a jetty, so he wrote *The French Lieutenant's Woman* to find out who she was.

DICK: Did *The Four Seasons* begin with an image?

ALDA: That film came from several sources. First there was Vivaldi's *Four Seasons*. Wouldn't it be interesting, I thought, to make a movie showing the same people on vacation in each of the four seasons? The musical form would dictate the form of the film. Then I had another image: I envisioned three couples getting out of a car. I kept seeing them getting out of the car and walking somewhere, and doing it over and over. It was like seeing a film in a loop. It haunted me. I had to find out more about those people.

DICK: In the film, the car is a very unobtrusive way of starting the film.

ALDA: Yes, in the credits sequence one couple picks up the other couples, so that by the time the actual film begins, you know who everyone is.

DICK: Did you plan to have *The Four Seasons* begin in spring and end in winter?

ALDA: It wasn't until after I had written the film that I realized the whole spring-winter progression corresponds to the four stages of friendship. There's a springtime to a friendship when nobody can do any wrong. In the glare of the summer sun, you see your friends as they are. In autumn, illusions fall away like leaves. In winter, you're "frozen" with your friends; you have to accept them as they are or find new ones who won't be a burden to you because you don't know who they are yet. I think this is what happens in the movie, but didn't understand it until I had written it.

DICK: Do you have a complete script at the time of shooting?

ALDA: Absolutely. I have to, because I haven't got time to rewrite on the set. That's why I go through about a dozen drafts and am overly particular about what I want to shoot.

DICK: When you were in the theater, you did improvisations as a member of the Second City [a Chicago-based improvisational group]. As a film director, do you improvise?

ALDA: If you mean during filming, very little. I may do a bit in scenes where several people are talking at once. In *A New Life*, I improvised a scene in which the character I play is arguing with a lawyer at a party. We did one episode on *M*A*S*H* that was an improvisation. It was called "The Interview" and consisted of someone interviewing the M*A*S*H unit as if for a documentary. Yet it was a highly controlled situation. We rehearsed for weeks by improvising into a tape recorder; the tape was edited by the writer, Larry Gelbart, who added some of his own jokes, and that became the script. But there were also last-minute questions that we had never heard before; that part of the episode was spot improvisation. There's a great difference between a spot improvisation and a script that has been derived from improvisation. When you're improvising, and it works, it is very hard to repeat the improvisation and get the same effect. It may take fifteen or twenty attempts for it to come to life again. If you're working from a script that came out of an improvisation, it's the same as working from any other script. Filmmakers should know that. There is a difference between improvising during rehearsal and improvising whole scenes in front of the camera. But a lot of young directors who have had little experience working with actors think that improvising is a technique that gets the actors to be more truthful. There's a danger that the values of the script will get lost in the improvisation and that nothing will replace them. Also, if the actors improvise in rehearsal, and something exciting happens, the director assumes that if the actors repeat these lines the excitement will recur. The director doesn't realize that it wasn't the lines that were exciting but the creative impulse that inspired them. The first time the impulse passes through the actor is thrilling, yet nobody knows the source of that impulse, and to rediscover it takes several more improvisations. You may or may not get it again.

Directors who feel it's the actors' fault if they improvise brilliantly during rehearsal but can't repeat what they did in front of the camera don't realize it has nothing to do with the actors; it's the way the brain works. Something mysterious might happen during an improvisation that brings the scene to life. What happens is that connections are made and impulses arise that should be explored. The actual words that are said are not nearly so important. Improvisation is useful to find out who the characters are and what their pasts have been, and I've used improvisation during rehearsals for that purpose. Once the actors understand their characters—and improvisation is one way of accomplishing this—they may be able to play the scene with more life. Improvisation also gets the actors to feel comfortable with one another and with the director.

DICK: To make them comfortable, would you change dialogue with which they are uncomfortable?

ALDA: That's a traditional way of making actors comfortable. I do it with caution, but I do it. What is important is what the script is communicating and the truth of the relationships expressed in the script. If changing a word here or there doesn't vitiate that truth, then I'm happy to. But if it wrecks the story, makes it illogical, or denies something truthful about the character, I explain to the actor that I can't. It's the director's job to keep the whole picture in mind. Every department may have a wonderful idea, but it might not fit into the whole scheme of the film. However, an actor may be uncomfortable with a line of dialogue, and after a few days of rehearsal, when the context is clear, the actor is not only comfortable with it but would kill to keep it. Improvisation and changing dialogue are only two ways to make actors feel comfortable. The most important thing is for the actors and director to eat dinner together.

DICK: Is that why food is so important in your films?

ALDA: That happens to be the way I am, the way I run my life. A lot of it is devoted to eating.

DICK: Do you believe in eating with the cast because the meal has always been a symbol of unity?

ALDA: That reason never occurred to me. I think that food is an image that comes to me a lot because I like food.

DICK: Since you've written both teleplays and screenplays, is the basic difference between them that the half-hour teleplay is in two acts, while screenplays are not divided into acts?

ALDA: Actually, a screenplay is divided into acts even though the acts may not be indicated as such in the script. Most screenwriters talk in terms of act one, act two, act three. You introduce the situation, complicate it, and resolve it. George S. Kaufman used to say that in act one you get the hero up a tree;

in act two you throw stones at him; and in act three you get him down. All stories are like that. You introduce the characters in the beginning, along with their goals; then there are complications in their achieving those goals because everyone wants something different. Thus, it won't be so easy for the main character to get what he or she wants because of the obstacles thrown in the way by the other characters. It's what Aristotle in the *Poetics* called "dramatic action"—action in the sense of the characters' trying to achieve something. The resolution is the final working out of their either getting what they want or not, or getting not what they want but what they need. In that case, they experience growth, sometimes tragic growth. They may no longer be able to do what they did in the past, but they have achieved insight. This may not always be apparent in what I write because I stress relationships and internal struggles, but I'm always thinking in terms of action—dramatic action, not car chases. Someone's always trying to accomplish something, even if it's just to understand something.

It's almost impossible for the actor to act unless the character wants something. That doesn't mean the character has to want something external; it can be internal. It may be peace, tranquillity, or self-knowledge. And a director must know what that goal is. Otherwise, if it's a play, you'll just hear a lot of talking, or if it's a film, you'll see a lot of fancy shots.

The writer must give the character a goal, even if it's a limited goal, as it is in *Rocky*. Rocky only wants to go the distance; the fact that he doesn't win is unimportant. He achieved his goal: he went the distance. An actor shouldn't be allowed to go onstage or before the camera if he or she is playing a character without an objective or a goal. If the character doesn't want something, turn the lights out and save electricity. The scene will go dark anyway if the actors are only feeding each other lines so the author can get the exposition out. Shakespeare knew how to handle exposition: in the opening scene of *Othello*, we learn who Iago, Roderigo, Desdemona, and Othello are without one expository line being uttered. Everything comes out of the action. The actors have not been forced to say to themselves, "Well, we just have to say these lines so the audience will get what's going on."

DICK: You have been speaking of writing, acting, and directing as if they were part of the same process.

ALDA: They are. The actors need an objective that the writer provides and that the director achieves. It's painful for me to see writers and actors at odds with each other. The writers complain, "Those damn actors aren't saying my words right." The actors complain, "Who wrote this crap?" They both work the same way, yet they'll never know it unless they sit down and talk with each other. If actors don't speak the dialogue properly, it's probably because they don't understand it. Writers blame actors because they fail to realize an actor must go through a certain process to absorb in a few days what it may have taken the writer two years to create. Being an actor, a writer, and a director, I understand all three.

DICK: If you had to describe the role of a director to someone outside the industry, how would you do it?

ALDA: A director gives direction; it's inherent in the job title. However, it's not a good idea to direct actors down to the last little movement of their pinkie. It's not only a bad idea; it can also wreck the picture. You must find out how you can communicate your vision to each department so that everyone will give you what you want from their heart. What's the point of hiring an art director if you say, "This is what I want—nothing else." All the art director will do is draw the set you designed. You want to be able to get design ideas from the art director, but those ideas must serve *your* vision. All of this is done through communication. You must be able to describe what you see to everyone, and you should be able to compare what you see happening with what you see can happen. But you must understand the specific capabilities of each department, what each can and cannot do. Actors cannot work from results. The first mistake a director makes is to say to an actor, "Be mysterious." That's a result; mystery is what you experience when the actor is doing the scene right. The director has to find out, with the actor, what the actor is trying to accomplish in terms of the action that will make the actor appear mysterious. You have to find the cause that produces the result. Actors can play a state; they can depict a state of drunkenness, for example. But once an actor establishes that the character is drunk, the actor has to achieve something, even if it's trying not to appear drunk.

DICK: Is it possible to learn directing?

ALDA: The only way to learn anything is with a mentor who will go through the steps with you, then let you do it and go over your mistakes. It's like the way my wife and I taught our children to wash their hands. We would put all of our hands under the faucet and rub them back and forth with the soap. Then the kids got the feeling. It's the way an artist guides the hand of a pupil or the way the tennis instructor puts his or her hand over yours on the racket. But you still have to make the shots; still, it's better if you've had hands-on experience with someone who is experienced.

NOTE

[1]The article appeared in *Film Culture* (Winter 1962–1963); it has been reprinted in Leo Braudy and Marshall Cohen, *Film Theory and Criticism*, 5th ed. (New York: Oxford University Press, 1999), 515–35.

Film and Literature

CHAPTER

7

"Film has nothing to do with literature," Ingmar Bergman declared.[1] Yes and No. Like so many dogmatic statements, Bergman's is not entirely true. A film can be subjected to the same criteria as a work of literature, and analyzed in terms of form, rhythm, imagery, and symbolism. A film, however, is not treated like a novel or a poem. A film's rhythm is determined by the way it is edited, not by the variation of stressed and unstressed syllables, as in poetry; or by the alternation of description and dialogue, as in fiction. In film, imagery is visual; in literature, it is verbal.

A film's form derives partly from literature, partly from the visual arts. *Literature* implies something written. A screenplay may be "literature" in the most basic sense (a written text), but rarely in the traditional sense (a literary classic). On the other hand, a film can be a work of cinematic art, while the script would never pass muster as literature. In fact, such film classics as D. W. Griffith's *The Birth of a Nation* and *Intolerance* were shot without a script. While the published screenplays of Ingmar

Bergman, Harold Pinter, and Woody Allen may read like literature (or, at least, like plays), they are not always reliable guides to the actual films. In Bergman's screenplay of *Through a Glass, Darkly*, Martin cuts his finger, which begins to bleed; his wife, Karin, then starts sucking the blood from the cut. From the way the incident is described in the screenplay ("Karin sucks the blood, looks at it, sucks again, is suddenly all enthusiasm"), the reader would assume that Karin is behaving bizarrely. What happens on the screen is far less extreme: Martin cuts his finger, and Karin kisses it. When Bergman wrote the screenplay, he may have envisioned the scene differently. When he directed the scene, he apparently decided to make it less theatrical. Thus, a screenplay may contain material that never reached the screen. Likewise, the film based on the screenplay may—and usually does—include scenes that were never in the screenplay.

A screenplay is like an opera libretto. While there are many great operas, there are few librettos that deserve to be studied as literature. Just as a libretto needs music, a screenplay needs visualization.

A screenplay, as the term implies, is a *play*—a play intended for the screen; thus, a screenplay contains many features of drama. A screenplay is also a form of narrative, sharing certain techniques with fiction. Like a play, a film can have a prologue and an epilogue. In film, however, the prologue can appear as print (an **opening title**) or it can be dramatized as a **credits** or a **precredits sequence**. Opening title and credits/precredits sequences are, of course, peculiar to film; even so, they are prologues—in one case, a prologue involving the written word; in the other, a prologue involving visualized action.

Film also uses many techniques that are found in literature, the most famous of which is the **flashback.**

THE FLASHBACK

In ancient epics, the flashback was the poet's way of incorporating material into the narrative that could not be added in any other way. For example, the *Odyssey* begins ten years after the end of the Trojan War; thus, the only way that Homer could describe Odysseus's postwar adventures was by providing the hero with an occasion—a banquet—where they could be recounted. In the *Aeneid*, Virgil, imitating Homer, also has Aeneas summarize his seven years abroad at a banquet.

The flashback has always been a favorite device of authors who prefer to start in the middle of an action (Milton's *Paradise Lost*) or who choose to work from the present back to the past, as Harold Pinter did in his play *Betrayal* (filmed in 1983), in which he traced the end of an affair between a married woman and her lover from its dissolution to the time it began. In a film, a flashback—which can be introduced by a slow fade-out/fade-in, a dissolve, a wipe, or a quick cut—serves three basic functions: (1) to furnish information that is otherwise unavailable; (2) to dramatize a past event as it is being narrated because the filmmaker has decided that it must be visualized; and (3) to explain the connection between past and present when none of the characters can do so.

The first kind of flashback is the most obvious; for example, without the flashbacks in *Sorry, Wrong Number* (1948), we would never know why a husband has arranged to have his wealthy wife murdered. Tennessee Williams's one-act play *Suddenly, Last Summer* concludes with Catherine Holly's (Elizabeth Taylor) monologue about the death of her cousin Sebastian, whose flesh was devoured by the boys he had propositioned and probably debauched. When Joseph L. Mankiewicz was planning the movie version (1959), he decided to intersperse Catherine's (Elizabeth Taylor) monologue with shots of boys begging Sebastian for food as he sat at an outdoor restaurant with Catherine, the beaches that Sebastian frequented, and Catherine in a revealing white bathing suit that Sebastian made her wear to attract attention. It is an extremely complex flashback. Sometimes Catherine's face, and even her mouth, appear right of frame, as she narrates the details of her cousin's gruesome death. As Catherine does this, what she is narrating fades in behind her—her face appearing in double exposure along with the image.

Not all flashbacks are memory flashbacks. Sometimes we are not within the consciousness of a character but of the camera, so to speak. *The Godfather, Part II* is a flashback film, but not a memory film; no one in the movie is remembering the past, because no one knows enough about it. The purpose of the sequel to *The Godfather* is to integrate the lives of Vito Corleone and his son Michael. Since Vito is dead when the film begins, his story is told in flashback. *Godfather II* is an example of the impersonal flashback, which is not the result of a reminiscence, an inquest, or an investigation but, rather, of the integration of past and present under the supervision of a central intelligence, which might be called the omniscient filmmaker. Stanley Donen's *Two for the Road* (1967) is a good example of the impersonal flashback: a couple's European trip is intercut with incidents from their previous trips. Because past and present are so subtly interwoven, we never ask who is remembering—the wife (Audrey Hepburn) or the husband (Albert Finney). It is established at the outset that the camera is doing the remembering—the same camera that had apparently accompanied them on their former jaunts.

Memory flashbacks, although common, are often poorly motivated. Sometimes a character no sooner says, "It seems only yesterday that . . .," than the present fades out and the past fades in. The best memory flashbacks require an object. In *Kitty Foyle* (1940), a glass paperweight with a girl on a sled is the cue for Kitty's memories; in *Penny Serenade* (1941), phonograph records trigger a woman's memories of her marriage; in *Brute Force* (1947), a woman's picture on a calendar causes four convicts to recall the women in their lives.

THE FLASHFORWARD

A device that enjoyed popularity with filmmakers beginning in the 1960s was the **flashforward,** in which some aspect of an event is shown before it occurs. The flashforward is a distant relative of **dramatic foreshadowing,** a literary device in which one incident presages another, or some indication is given that an event is going to happen before it actually does. But the true ancestor of the flashforward is prolepsis, a rhetorical technique in which a speaker anticipates—and answers—an objection before it has even been raised.

Sometimes what seems to be a flashforward isn't one. During the course of *They Shoot Horses, Don't They?* (1969), the narrator (Michael Sarrazin) speaks directly to the camera—or is he speaking to someone we cannot see? At the end, we discover that he is speaking to a judge, explaining why he shot Gloria (Jane Fonda) at her request. Flashforwards succeed in *Horses* because, from the audience's point of view, they exist in the future; but from the narrator's, they are part of the past. In retrospect, it becomes apparent that the entire movie was a flashback told to a judge.

Because of their anticipatory force, proleptic devices can be quite dramatic. In George Stevens's *The Greatest Story Ever Told* (1965), after Pontius Pilate delivers Jesus Christ to be crucified, an off-camera voice is heard saying, "And he suffered under Pontius Pilate." It is a compelling moment in the film: a historical event has been raised to a Christian article of faith by a quote from the Apostles' Creed, which has not yet been written (but which contains the same phrase). Often a movie's main title has a foreshadowing character. During the credits for *Saboteur,* the shadow of the saboteur moves from the right of the frame into the center. Billy Wilder used the same technique in *Double Indemnity;* in that film the shadowy figure is on crutches, a prefiguration of the insurance salesman's attempt to pass himself off as the man he has just murdered (who had been using crutches because of a broken leg).

Sometimes a shot has the impact of a flashforward although it is really a comment on an earlier incident. Well after the midpoint of *The Story of Adele H.* (1975), François Truffaut inserts a shot of Adele on the Isle of Guernsey, gloriously confident as she prepares to sail for Halifax to reclaim the affections of Lieutenant Pinson. Her voice is equally self-assured: "This incredible thing—that a young girl shall walk over the sea, from the Old into the New World, to join her lover—this, I shall accomplish." Obviously this is an Adele we have not seen before, since the film begins with her arrival in Halifax. The shot is placed where it is to mark the end of Adele's fruitless quest and the beginning of her descent into madness. Had the shot appeared at the beginning, it would simply have been a prologue. Because it appears where it does, it has the force of dramatic irony: Adele did make a journey from the Old World to the New, but it was also a journey from one form of neurotic behavior (obsession) to another (self-inflicted degradation). At the very end of the film, Truffaut repeats the shot, this time drained of its color and looking like a faded photograph. Adele's voyage is now just an item of memorabilia.

POINT OF VIEW

Like a work of literature, a film can be narrated in the first or the third person. A first-person film—one recounted by an "I" in the same way that Dickens's *Great Expectations* is recounted by Pip and Sartre's *Nausea* by Roquentin (that is, an "I" who begins speaking at the outset and continues right up to the end)—is rare. (*Double Indemnity* comes close, with all but the very beginning and the very end narrated by Neff.) What generally happens in film is that the "I" is heard at the beginning and perhaps intermittently thereafter. The semidocumentary may seem to be an exception, since it is first-person narration throughout; however, the narrator is not a character but a disembodied voice. When the voice intrudes periodically, it acts like a fade-out, demarcating the film into narrative blocks.

Something similar happens in *Radio Days*, which is narrated by an adult who is seen only as a child. If *Radio Days* has a distinctly literary quality and seems like a filmed short story, it is because continuous first-person narrative calls attention to itself as narrative. There is also a credibility problem if the "I" relates something to which it would not have had access. Despite the excellence of *Radio Days*, even Woody Allen has difficulty explaining how a grade-school boy can know what he does.

A film need not use "I" narration to achieve a first-person effect without the presence of the narrating "I"; subjective camera can also be used. In subjective camera, the camera doubles as a character so that we are aware of both an "I" and an "eye," as in the slasher movies, when the camera looks in through the window from the outside. There the camera is both an "I" (the predator) and an "eye" (the predator's eye and, by extension, ours).

Thus, point of view in subjective camera is not that of an "it" but of an "I," a definite presence relating something to the viewer as an "I" would relate something to a "you." Sound can also be subjective; when a character hears something, the character is no longer a "he" or a "she" but an "I" telling "us" what he or she is thinking or hearing. In *A Streetcar Named Desire*, Blanche hears a gunshot that no one else can hear. The sound is associated with an incident that she cannot erase from her memory: her husband's suicide. *We* hear the sound because we have been given access to her consciousness.

It is important to remember that voice-over narration does not necessarily mean a first-person film. Since the voice tends to come and go, one soon forgets there is a narrator. Far more important is to see how film emulates first-person narrative through subjective camera and subjective sound.

Omniscient Narrator

In fiction, the **omniscient narrator** tells the story in the third person, moving from place to place, time to time, and character to character, disclosing or concealing details at will.[2] The film equivalent, omniscient camera, is best seen in multiplot films or films that move back and forth in time. When the camera is omniscient, it behaves very much like an omniscient author. The camera in *Nashville* is omniscient. It can leave a freeway crack-up and move on to a hospital to look in on country singer Barbara Jean recovering from one of her breakdowns. It can abandon the Reese home for the local tavern, a nightclub for a smoker, a church for an automobile graveyard.

Omniscient narrators can be intrusive if they pass judgment on what is seen or unintrusive if they suspend judgment. The camera can do likewise because omniscience does not mean impartiality. In *The Day of the Locust*, Homer Simpson (Donald Sutherland) is sitting in a wicker chair in the backyard of his Hollywood home. An orange drops from a bough with the sound of ripe fruit. In the yard above his, a woman looks down on this scene of otherworldly tranquillity. There is ripeness in her face, but it is the overripeness of rotting fruit. The camera has said nothing, but by moving from Homer to the woman it makes its own comment on Hollywood as the earthly paradise for those who bask in the glow of an endless summer and those who decompose in it.

Instead of traveling back and forth among the characters, authors can select one of them as a "center of consciousness," to use Henry James's phrase, or as a "reflector" through whose eyes readers will view the action. In film, the reflector method works well when the script involves a character trapped by his or her fantasies or victimized by some neurosis. In *The Lost Weekend*, Billy Wilder draws us into the consciousness of Don (Ray Milland), an alcoholic. Don becomes a genuine reflector; we share his experiences even when they are portrayed objectively, as they often are.

Early in the film, there is a scene in which Don is attending a performance of Verdi's *La Traviata* and develops an uncontrollable urge to drink during the first-act "Drinking Song." Wilder cuts from Don to the stage, where Violetta and Alfredo are toasting each other, and back again to Don. So far, the camera has been objective: what Don has been seeing on the stage is what everyone else in the audience has been seeing. But not everyone in the audience is an alcoholic; thus, Wilder allows the camera to turn subjective at this point, as Don sees, superimposed against the stage, the checkroom where his raincoat is hanging, with a bottle in one of the pockets. We clearly understand his craving and the effect the "Drinking Song" has had on him.

The Implied Author (Author's Second Self)

Some fiction is written so impersonally that it appears to be authorless. Hemingway's "The Killers" is often cited as the kind of story that seems to have been written by a scientist rather than a novelist. In "The Killers," Hemingway obliterated his actual self and created a second self who mediates between Ernest Hemingway and the story that bears his name. Filmmakers can do likewise; they can suppress or mask their personal feelings so that they do not interfere with the film. This implied author method usually results in an impersonal movie because it does not encourage emotional involvement; as a result, this kind of movie does not reach a high level of emotional intensity.

Barry Lyndon is such a film. First, it is Stanley Kubrick's *Barry Lyndon*, not William Makepeace Thackeray's; and it is Kubrick's film completely: not only did he produce and direct it but he also wrote the screenplay. To say that Kubrick remains aloof from his characters is not the same as saying that he shuns them. The implied author approach is not emotional evasion; it is emotional noninvolvement. Kubrick was more interested in the characters as embodiments of their age than as human beings.

In adapting Thackeray's *Barry Lyndon* for the screen, Kubrick was dealing with a novel written in the nineteenth century but set in the eighteenth. For this reason, the tone had to be Victorian and the atmosphere neoclassical. Kubrick achieved an eighteenth-century air by framing scenes in the style of painters of that era—Watteau, Dayes, and Gainsborough—and by orchestrating them with selections from Bach, Handel, Vivaldi, and Mozart. He re-created a Victorian tone by using an off-camera narrator whose voice was fittingly snobbish.

Seeing *Barry Lyndon* is like viewing a painting. A great painting draws a viewer toward it; but once the viewer is face-to-face with it, he or she instinctively walks backward to see it from a distance. Kubrick uses the same technique. He begins with a close-up; he then slowly zooms out until

The famous *Barry Lyndon* candlelight. All the candlelight scenes were photographed with a special Zeiss lens and entirely with natural light. *(Courtesy Warner Bros., Inc.)*

he is satisfied with the distance between the audience and the image. *Barry Lyndon* is like a tour of the world's great museums. The glow of candlelight is not the smoky haze it usually is in most films; specially created lenses give the candlelight in *Barry Lyndon* the look of melting gold. Light floods a window, not in neat spotlighting cones but in a burst of silver. To achieve such beauty, Kubrick had to sacrifice a certain amount of emotion.

FILM ADAPTATION

One common type of film is the adaptation of a novel, a short story, or a play. The adaptation, however, occasions the greatest amount of criticism because the material has already appeared in another form that becomes the standard against which the film version is compared; hence the often repeated charge, "Well, it wasn't the book [or the play]." There is only one answer to that charge: it wasn't meant to be. The adaptation is *a* version, not *the* version, since there can be several film versions of a particular novel or play. Which *Phantom of the Opera* is Gaston Leroux's novel *The Phantom of the Opera*? The 1925 version, the 1943 version, or the 1962 version?

Adaptation is not as simple as one might think. It is a given that the film version will differ from the original. Why else would a filmmaker

Whoopi Goldberg as Celie in *The Color Purple* (Steven Spielberg, 1986). *(Courtesy MOMA/FSA and Warner Bros., Inc.)*

adapt a work for the screen, and why should audiences be expected to see it if they have read the book or seen the play? The adaptation must be different—but how different? The adaptation may preserve the essence of the original, even though it alters plot details (perhaps even drastically), adds or eliminates characters, and changes the conclusion so that it is the opposite of what it was in the original.

In his 1999 adaptation of Patricia Highsmith's *The Talented Mr. Ripley*, writer-director Anthony Minghella retained the sexual ambiguity of the original (to a great extent, with the casting of Matt Damon as Ripley, who played the part in a teasingly homoerotic way, so that the character seemed to be pansexual). Believing the script needed one final murder victim, Minghella fleshed out a character mentioned only by name in the novel, Peter Smith-Kingsley, whose off-camera strangling is a perfect coda for such a diabolical film. When the movie version of Jack London's *The Sea Wolf* was released in 1941, audiences familiar with the novel were surprised that one of the male leads, John Garfield, played a character who did not exist in the original; that one of the main characters in the novel, the scholarly Humphrey Van Weyden, had been reduced to minor status; and that the journalist Maud Brewster, the only female character in the novel, had been turned into a prostitute, played by Ida Lupino. But at least the captain, Wolf Larsen (Edward G. Robinson), is as sadistic in the film as he was in the novel.

Faithful to the Letter or the Spirit?

When a novel is adapted for the stage, it ceases to be what it once was: a work of fiction. Instead, it has become a work of theater. In the transforming process, characterization has been reduced to dialogue, which is all the playwright has at his or her disposal. Descriptions of places, objects, and attire, if they are to be retained, come under the purview of those who are responsible for the set, the costumes, and the lighting. Interior monologues, if kept, become stage monologues. Playwrights are limited in ways novelists are not. In the theater, the action is advanced through dialogue, embellished by whatever accoutrements (sets, costumes, makeup, lighting) have been chosen for the production, and performed within a space such as an auditorium, an amphitheater, a theater-in-the-round, a loft, or even a parking lot. When Ketti Frings adapted Thomas Wolfe's sprawling novel *Look Homeward, Angel* for the Broadway stage in 1958, she used only one-third of the book, which, she felt, was all that could be dramatized successfully. The play was both a critical and a commercial success. Clearly, it was not Thomas Wolfe's *Look Homeward, Angel*; it was Ketti Frings's.

Perhaps because the theater has such a long and venerable tradition (while movies, on the other hand, date only to the 1890s), purists are less critical of stage adaptations of classics than they are of movie versions. Some literary scholars, for example, take a dim view of film in general, insisting that anything visual can never have the density of a work of serious literature. It would be impossible, they argue, to make a faithful movie version of, say, Thomas Mann's *Death in Venice*, although Luchino Visconti did just that in 1971. *Death in Venice* has so many levels of meaning (art as an obsession, the destructive force of beauty, Platonic love versus physical passion, a plague-ridden Venice that is more symbolic than real) that all a film can do is retain the narrative underpinning (a world-famous novelist's attraction to a Polish boy that eventually destroys him) and perhaps add something meaningful that was not in the original. Thus Visconti's *Death in Venice* is enhanced by Gustav Mahler's music, which captures the novelist's yearning for a perfection that will always elude him.

A filmmaker must regard a literary source as a blueprint that can either be followed closely or radically altered to conform to the filmmaker's vision. Robert Louis Stevenson's novella *Dr. Jekyll and Mr. Hyde* has been filmed many times, but not as Stevenson wrote it. A faithful adaptation would have resulted in a thoroughly uninteresting movie for a variety of reasons. There are no women in the novella, which is really a study in doubles. Not only are Jekyll and Hyde doubles (Hyde being the dark side of Jekyll) but so are two other male characters, Utterson and Enfield: Utterson is a stuffy, conservative lawyer, while Enfield, a "distant kinsman," is his complete opposite—outgoing and pleasure-loving. Jekyll's house also has its double: the façade is pleasant, but the back door, which Hyde uses, is sinister-looking. The last third of the novel consists of two documents, Dr. Lanyon's eyewitness account of the transforming power of the potion Jekyll concocted to turn himself into Hyde, and Jekyll's own "statement of the case," in which he explained the reasons for his experiments (to separate humankind's two natures).

In Rouben Mamoulian's 1932 film version, the best of the lot, Utterson and Enfield are replaced by two women: Jekyll's fiancée, Muriel, and Hyde's mistress, Ivy. Jekyll's valet, Poole, is retained; Carew, one of Hyde's victims in the novel, becomes Muriel's father. The addition of the women allowed Mamoulian and his writers to create a sexual subtext: Jekyll's desire to explore his sexuality, which he cannot do as a respectable physician but can as the disreputable Hyde. Significantly, Jekyll takes the potion after befriending the prostitute Ivy—the image of her leg dangling over the side of the bed lingering in his memory (as the prolonged superimposition of the leg indicates). Faithful to the spirit? Definitely, since it reflects Jekyll's obsession with duality, his experiments to separate the two natures, and the consequences of his folly, which he even admits.

Mary Shelley's *Frankenstein* has also served as the basis of a number of films, the best being James Whale's *Frankenstein* (1931), which has hardly anything to do with the work on which, according to the credits, it

The creature (Boris Karloff) and Maria playing a game that turns deadly in *Frankenstein* (1931). *(Courtesy MOMA/FSA)*

was based. All that was retained was Frankenstein's creation of the monster, which, visually, is the high point of the film. However, there is one incident in the film that is as horrifying as the episode in the novel when the monster strangles Frankenstein's kid brother, William. In the film, the monster comes upon a child, Maria, who, unlike William, shows no fear of him. Maria invites the monster to join her as she throws flowers into the lake. Watching them float, the monster thinks that Maria might float, too, and drops her into the lake. The horror of the scene is not just that Maria drowns but that the monster realizes the enormity of what he has done, and cannot save her. Faithful to the spirit or the letter? Neither. Still, James Whale's *Frankenstein* is an acknowledged masterpiece, as is the sequel, *Bride of Frankenstein* (1935), in which Mary Shelley appears as a character in the prologue (played by Elsa Lanchester, who doubles, uncredited, as the bride), giving us the impression that the monster, who supposedly died at the end of the 1931 movie, didn't and is ready for a mate—meaning that Universal Pictures was ready for a sequel and needed an explanation for audiences that were familiar with the earlier film. *Bride* also takes a few incidents from the novel and completely alters them. Shelley included an episode in which the monster is befriended by a blind man, only to be beaten by the man's son when he finds him in his father's home. In *Bride*, the monster takes refuge in the cottage of a blind hermit, who introduces him to wine and tobacco. The monster believes he has found the friend he has been seeking; the friendship, however, proves to be short-lived when hunters discover his presence. In the novel, the monster demands that Frankenstein fashion a bride for him. After doing so, Frankenstein destroys his creation, fearing that he would be responsible for a race of monsters. In *Bride*, the mate is created, yet even she rejects the monster, causing him to retaliate by destroying the laboratory in which both of them were given life. Faithful to the spirit or the letter? Mary Shelley never wrote a sequel, even though *Bride* implies otherwise. Nevertheless, *Bride* is also a classic that could never have been made without the novel, which it used only as a springboard.

In the 1990s, actor-director Kenneth Branagh decided to make a movie that was, more or less, faithful to the novel. He therefore called his version *Mary Shelley's Frankenstein* (1994), which featured him as Frankenstein and Robert De Niro as the monster. Branagh (who also coauthored the screenplay) may have followed Shelley's novel, in the sense of including the main characters and the major episodes, but his film can hardly be called faithful to the spirit of Shelley's novel. Some of the shots (incisions, the hanging of the innocent Justine, amputations, the monster's cutting out the heart of Frankenstein's wife, Elizabeth, and brandishing it at him, and, worst of all, Robert De Niro's monster makeup) would have appalled the author; today, they elicit two responses: derisive laughter or groans of disgust. Branagh's worst choice was to have Frankenstein restore Elizabeth to life by subjecting her corpse to the same experiment that resulted in the creation of the monster. The result was similarly monstrous (or laughable). Both Frankenstein and the monster fight over Elizabeth, who burns down the laboratory and goes up in flames herself.

Shelley's novel does not lend itself to film, because the early episodes—family history, the adoption of Elizabeth, Victor's education, his teachers at the university, etc.—are really the stuff of fiction, details that fill out a story but that in themselves are not especially interesting. The most important figure in the novel, as in the movie versions, is the monster, whose model apparently was Satan in Milton's *Paradise Lost*, another fascinating figure.

Shelley's *Frankenstein* is an example of an epistolary novel (one told through an exchange of letters): we are actually reading a captain's letters to his sister describing his encounter with Frankenstein and, finally, with the monster who has been following his creator. Epistolary novels are virtually impossible to adapt in their original form. Branagh realized that, and although he retained the captain as a minor character, he dispensed with the letters. In film, even when the contents of a letter are crucial to a particular scene, the complete letter is never shown (unless it is the equivalent of a note) but only the pertinent part, with the rest often masked so that the relevant text stands out.

Because it is an epistolary novel, Alice Walker's Pulitzer Prize–winning novel *The Color Purple* was not easy to adapt for the screen. On one level, it is a novel about written expression and the need to articulate feelings that, if they cannot be expressed orally, must be committed to paper; and that, if they cannot be addressed to the right person, must be addressed to God. Clearly, it would be difficult to present this philosophy on the screen, yet the film repeats the exact words with which the novel opens: "You better not never tell nobody but God. It'll kill your mammy." These words are addressed to Celie, a fourteen-year-old black girl, by her pa. Actually, he is her stepfather, but at this point Celie does not know this. She knows only that Pa, whose real name is Alphonso (in the novel, several characters are not known by their real names), has raped her and that the two children she bore were taken from her shortly after birth.

Forbidden to speak of her suffering and shame to another person, Celie begins a series of letters to God. Thus, *The Color Purple* consists of Celie's letters to God, her sister Nettie's letters to her, and Celie's letters to Nettie.

When Steven Spielberg decided to make the film version of *The Color Purple* (1985), he could not ignore the importance of the letters. Screenwriter Menno Meyjes had to make certain choices, one of which was to give Nettie's letters a purely narrative function so they could fill in details that Celie would not have known. Since Nettie's letters are for the most part nondramatic, Spielberg generates some drama by having them visualized while Celie is reading them. While Celie is on her porch reading Nettie's description of life in Africa, an elephant appears in the background. When Celie is in church reading about the destruction of an African church, a bulldozer comes through the altar of the church where she is sitting. Concurrent visualization at least suggests the effect of language on the imagination, which is one of the novel's main points.

Movies, it should be remembered, originated as mass entertainment for audiences that were considerably less sophisticated than readers and theatergoers. Theatergoers will accept fake scenery, plays performed on a bare stage, such as Thornton Wilder's *Our Town*, and living rooms without a fourth wall—or without any walls in theater-in-the-round. Lovers of theater and serious fiction would feel insulted if a work that was heading toward tragedy suddenly took a detour to happy land; serious moviegoers would feel similarly, except that the industry thought otherwise. The preamble to the Production Code did not equivocate about the function of film being "primarily . . . entertainment without any explicit purpose of teaching or propaganda," although the truth is that movies both taught and propagandized—but they did so entertainingly, which often meant an upbeat ending. In Sam Wood's movie version of *Our Town* (1940), Emily only *dreams* that she dies (in the play, she actually does) and returns to earth to relive one day of her life. When Warner Bros. decided to film Tennessee Williams's *The Glass Menagerie* in 1950, the studio assumed that moviegoers were not ready for the play's downbeat ending, which implied that there would be no more gentleman callers for Laura. The movie suggests otherwise. When the same studio decided to produce the movie version of an even more controversial Tennessee Williams play, *A Streetcar Named Desire*, the ending had Stella leaving Stanley after she learned that he has raped her sister Blanche. The studio felt that audiences would want Stanley to pay for what he had done. However, in the play it is evident that, regardless, Stella and Stanley need each other; and that Blanche's institutionalization will restore their marriage to what it was before she arrived.

David Lean's film version of Charles Dickens's *Great Expectations* has Pip and Estella rushing off together at the end, which is completely contrary to Dickens's intentions. John Ford's *The Grapes of Wrath* scuttles Steinbeck's original ending and instead has Ma Joad extol "the people" for their ability to survive any crisis, including the Great Depression. Yet, strangely, both films capture the essence of their sources but provide more optimistic endings for audiences that could accept the spirit of the novel but not the complete body in which that spirit resides.

One way of coming to an understanding of the nature of film adaptation is to study the novel, then a version of the novel set in the present, and finally a totally faithful re-creation of the novel.

Adaptations of Novels

Emma/Clueless/Emma: Jane Austen from Highbury to Beverly Hills—and Back

Anyone contemplating a screen version of Jane Austen's *Emma* (1815) must deal with the following:

1. A decent but self-absorbed and manipulative heroine, Emma Woodhouse, who lives with her widower father in class-conscious Highbury, not far from London. Emma's social status guarantees her a privileged existence spent, for the most part, in meddling in other people's lives. Emma decides to play matchmaker for the illegitimate Harriet Smith, who idolizes her and never questions her judgment. When a farmer, Robert Martin, shows an interest in Harriet, Emma discourages the relationship. Instead, she steers Harriet toward the vicar, Mr. Elton, who is interested in Emma, not in Harriet. When Elton expresses his true feelings, Emma is shocked. The Emmas of the world do not live in parsonages. Elton eventually finds a wife, who becomes increasingly more overbearing as Emma becomes more understanding after she realizes the consequences of interfering in other people's lives.
2. Emma's foil—her brother-in-law, Mr. Knightley, some sixteen years older than she and capable of seeing her faults as well as reminding her of them. Knightley seems to be the least likely partner for Emma. Austen, however, knows better and artfully brings them together so that the novel can end with their wedding.
3. A world in which men and women eventually make the right match, although it may not have been the one the reader had been expecting. But this is part of Austen's technique: to keep us wondering who will pair off with whom. Harriet—for whom Emma had singled out Elton, and then Frank Churchill—ends up with the man who wanted her from the beginning: Robert Martin. And Frank Churchill, who did not seem especially interested in Jane Fairfax, ends up marrying her. That leaves only Knightley and Emma, whose marriage brings the novel to its conclusion.

For this kind of plot to succeed, each potential relationship must also be probable. One could, for example, imagine the union of Jane and Knightley, or even of Harriet and Knightley; when Elton snubs Harriet at

Alicia Silverstone (left) as Cher, the Emma figure in *Clueless* (1995); and Stacy Dash as Dionne, Amy Heckerling's substitution for Jane Austen's Jane Fairfax. *(Courtesy Paramount Pictures and MOMA/FSA)*

a ball, Knightley saves her from embarrassment by dancing with her. One could also imagine the union of Harriet and Churchill, who rescues her from a band of gypsies. Austen creates situations that are so realistic that any of these pairings is possible; she also convinces us that the marriage partner each character chooses is the right one.

Clueless (1995)

Anyone updating *Emma* will naturally alter, discard, or find equivalents for some of the narrative details or even the characters; still, the adapter must be faithful to the spirit, if not the letter, of the novel by including the following:

1. An affluent and motherless household in which Emma is indulged by her father.
2. Emma's obsession with meddling and matchmaking.
3. Emma's eventual realization that her judgment of others is faulty.
4. A sense of uncertainty on the viewer's part about the resolution of the various relationships.

5. The union of Emma and a family member who is not a blood relative.

Amy Heckerling, who both wrote and directed *Clueless*—an unusually intelligent and occasionally touching version of *Emma*—moves the time ahead to the 1990s and the setting to Beverly Hills. Emma becomes Cher (Alicia Silverstone), who is about five years younger than Austen's heroine and is still a high-school student. Mel, her father, is an affluent lawyer, who indulges Emma's passion for designer clothes and Rodeo Drive shopping sprees. Cher's mother, like Emma's, died soon after she was born; but, unlike Emma, Cher has no sister. She does, however, have a slightly older stepbrother (not thirty-seven but around twenty)—Josh, the son of Mel's second wife from a previous marriage. Although Mel and Josh's mother are divorced, Josh is attending UCLA and often visits with Mel and Cher. Thus Cher and Josh see each other frequently—like Emma and Knightley. Moreover, as the script emphasizes (but not overly so), they are not blood relatives.

Because he is a college student with a social conscience, Josh is the equivalent of Knightley, calling Cher's attention to her shortcomings, which include a total indifference to world affairs. After watching a television news report on the war in Bosnia, Cher remarks that she thought there was peace in the Middle East.

Having chosen to make Austen's three couples—with the exception of Josh—high-school students, Heckerling had to find an equivalent for class-conscious Highbury. For Beverly Hills teenagers, the equivalent would be a high school not unlike the one featured in the television series *Beverly Hills 90210*. No one is poor in this school, but there is the right racial, social, and ethnic mix to suggest a microcosmic society in which distinctions are made according to dress, grades, sexual orientation, and behavior. In this world, which is not that different from the so-called real one, Cher and her friend Dionne, with their fashionable clothes and cell phones, legislate for those who are too insecure to be themselves.

Just as Harriet was unable to assert her individuality in *Emma*, so, too, is Tai, her equivalent in *Clueless*. Tai, the new student—a gawky but sexually experienced young woman who thinks of coke not as a soft drink but as a drug—is the perfect candidate for a Cher and Dionne makeover. Tai becomes their creation, with hairstyle, makeup, and clothes selected by them. Just as Harriet was attracted to the farmer Robert Martin in the novel, Tai is drawn to someone like herself—the class clown and skateboarder, Travis. And, just as Emma discouraged a relationship with Martin and directed Harriet to Elton, Cher steers Tai toward another Elton. Since Heckerling had deliberately chosen the name of Austen's character, she obviously wanted to replicate two scenes from the novel that involve

Elton: one in which he faked concern for Harriet in order to ingratiate himself with Emma; the other in which he shocked Emma by declaring his intentions toward her.

Similarly, Heckerling's Elton is solicitous of Tai because he wants to impress Emma; Heckerling's Elton expresses his feelings for Cher in a car, as his namesake did in a carriage. Cher is so outraged that she bolts from the car and is left in a deserted area, where she is mugged. (A similar incident occurred in the novel when Harriet's purse is taken by gypsies. Heckerling has Cher's mugger take her purse and cell phone.)

Since Austen hinted at a possible union of Harriet and Knightley in the episode in which he dances with her, Heckerling cleverly has Josh dance with Tai when she is consistently ignored. Finally, when Tai has succeeded in ridding herself of any feelings for Elton—realizing that her true soul mate is Travis—she burns mementos of her infatuation with Elton, as Harriet did in the novel.

Heckerling realized that Austen's Jane Fairfax and Frank Churchill, a talented but financially dependent woman and an affluent but self-indulgent man, could never meet in the setting she had created. Instead, she substitutes an African American couple, Murray and Dionne; Murray is a chauvinist who insists on calling Dionne "woman," and Dionne is a feminist who resents sexist language. Murray and Dionne become mirror images of Josh and Cher. Each couple must change, abandoning misconceptions in favor of a deeper awareness of the partner's uniqueness—failings included.

Once Heckerling had substituted Dionne and Murray (who clearly have eyes only for each other) for Jane and Churchill, she could suggest nothing between Tai and Murray. Instead, she created the character of Christian, who dresses like James Dean but whose favorite films are *Some Like It Hot*, which revolves around cross-dressing, and *Spartacus* (1960), in which Laurence Olivier plays a homosexual who does not hide his attraction for Antoninus (Tony Curtis). When Christian shows Cher his *Spartacus* video, his interest is not in her but in the film—particularly the Olivier-Curtis scene. Although Christian could easily have become a stereotype, Heckerling understands that Austen's satire is gentle, not vicious. Austen can poke fun at her characters and reveal their shortcomings, but she does not make them objects of ridicule. In a scene that further reveals Cher's lack of insight, Murray explains to her that Christian is gay, using language that is both street-smart and literary (he explicitly refers to Oscar Wilde). To Heckerling's credit, there is no trace of homophobic contempt in his remarks. Murray—and Dionne as well—can accept what Cher cannot even comprehend.

Any version of *Emma* should include three weddings, which poses a problem if the three heroines are still in high school. Thus, the film cannot end with the marriage of Cher and Josh. But it must end with a wedding. What Heckerling has done is to take two characters—Emma's tutor and Mr. Weston, who have just married as the novel begins—and turn them into two unmarried teachers at the high school: Miss Geist and Mr. Hall, who teach political science and debate, respectively. Motivated partly by her desire to get a better grade in debate and partly by her mania for matchmaking, Cher, with Dionne's help, keeps bringing the two teachers closer together until the inevitable occurs. Present at their wedding are the three couples who will be having their own weddings in a few years.

Clueless offers many rewards for those who are able to view it as less a youth-oriented film than a modern version of a classic that takes liberties with the original but always remains faithful to its spirit.

Emma (1996)

A year after *Clueless* was released, a literal adaptation of *Emma* arrived on the screen. In adapting *Emma*, Doug McGrath, who also directed the film, remained faithful to the novel in both spirit and letter, going so far as to use much of Austen's own language. He has also succeeded—insofar as it is possible for film to do this with a third-person narrative and an omniscient point of view—in re-creating the novel on the screen. Through omniscience, Austen could enter the minds of her characters, noting their moods and actions and commenting on them. Despite the freedom that omniscience gives a novelist, however, Austen used it judiciously in *Emma*, preferring to present as much of the action as she could from Emma's point of view. Heckerling realized this and thus used voice-over narration in *Clueless*—but only from Cher, who becomes the real narrator, commenting on her own behavior and gradually reaching some level of self-knowledge. McGrath also uses voice-over, but he has succeeded in making it more than a film convention; for the most part, voice-over occurs when

Gwyneth Paltrow (Emma) and Jeremy Northam (Mr. Knightley), in *Emma* (1996). *(Courtesy Miramax Films and the Margaret Herrick Library of the Academy of Motion Picture Arts and Sciences)*

Emma (Gwyneth Paltrow) writes in her diary—the closest any adapter can come to evoking Austen's reflections on her characters. Toward the end of the film, in a scene that does not exist in the novel, we even hear Emma's silent prayer in a chapel.

True to Austen, McGrath portrays Highbury as a world unto itself, insulated from anything as mundane as international affairs. Highbury's parochialism is apparent in the credits, during which a planet spins in the galaxy, growing larger as it moves closer into the frame. We soon recognize it as Earth, but not the planet to which we are accustomed. This planet consists of one country, Britain, which is made up of only London and Highbury; soon London disappears, leaving only Highbury.

McGrath also succeeded in having the actors play the potential couples in such a way that any union might be possible. When Frank Churchill joins Jane Fairfax for a duet, he sings with far greater enthusiasm than he did with Emma, who had accompanied him at the piano earlier. On the other hand, when Harriet lies on the ground after being robbed by gypsies, Churchill extends his hand to her; McGrath cuts to a close-up of their clasped hands. Are they clasped because he is literally bringing her to her feet? Or is this a sign of a budding romance? And why does Knightley, who tells Emma that he cannot dance, dance so well with Harriet?

Like Austen, McGrath makes the picnic at Box Hill the turning point. Churchill insists upon a game in which everyone makes one or two witty remarks or three dull ones. When the garrulous Miss Bates jokes that whatever she says will be dull, Emma replies that, at least on this occasion, her dull comments will be limited in number. Knightley realizes the pain that Emma's words have caused Miss Bates and reproaches her for lack of consideration. It is at this point in both the novel and the film that Emma's remorse makes her determined to rise in Knightley's estimation—something one does only if the other party is worth the effort.

But as well written and directed as *Clueless* and *Emma* are, audience reaction depends, to a great extent, on the performances of the leads. Neither Cher nor Emma can be just the typical spoiled brat or "Daddy's little girl," although each is a bit of both. Nor can they be vicious. Glib, insensitive, self-centered, haughty—yes; but deliberately cruel—no. That each moves from the extremes of self-love to love of other is a tribute to the directors and the writers (and in both films the director is the writer) but also to the talents of Alicia Silverstone and Gwyneth Paltrow.

Adaptations of Plays

A play must be "opened up" for the screen; this is particularly important in the case of single-set plays, many of which are among the theater's finest: *The Little Foxes*; *A Streetcar Named Desire*; *Come Back, Little Sheba*;

Who's Afraid of Virginia Woolf?; *Long Day's Journey into Night*; and others. Musicals like *The King and I* and *Gypsy* pose fewer problems because of their multiple settings. Here are some of the traditional ways to open up a play in which the action is limited to one or two places:

Dramatize or visualize material that had to be narrated because it could not be shown on the stage. William Inge's play *Picnic* (1953) takes place in a yard between two houses in a small Kansas town. Thus the Labor Day picnic, which inspired the title (and which is a vital element of the plot), is never seen. Since the play dramatized the way a stranger's arrival on a Labor Day morning altered the lives of all the characters, for the 1956 film version screenwriter Daniel Taradash transferred the most dramatic scenes in the play to the picnic, where the characters revealed their true nature and innermost thoughts. And director Josh Logan used the picnic to provide audiences with a vivid depiction of an end-of-summer ritual in rural America.

    Gore Vidal, who adapted Tennessee Williams's *Suddenly, Last Summer* (1958) for the screen, added more scenes since the play had only one set: a garden. In the play, Catherine Holly had been committed to Lion's View State Asylum because she was considered insane. By showing Catherine (Elizabeth Taylor) at Lion's View, Vidal and director Joseph L. Mankiewicz were also able to portray the horrible conditions that existed there. Since the plot hinges on whether Catherine will be lobotomized, the film opens with a lobotomy being performed in an operating theater. Most important, as Catherine delivers her climactic monologue, in which she recounts the hideous death of her cousin Sebastian, details of the incident and the events leading up to it are shown on the screen.

Visualize symbols so that they cease to be abstract. The "streetcar" in *A Streetcar Named Desire* is both symbolic and real. It is the mode of transportation that takes Blanche DuBois to her sister's home, where she hopes to escape from a sordid and painful past. Film allows us to see the streetcar, which, from the outset, is associated with Blanche, since it was instrumental in bringing her into an environment in which she would eventually be destroyed. In another Tennessee Williams play that became a successful film, *The Night of the Iguana* (1962), the iguana, which is tied to a rope and kept under the porch, could not be seen on the stage; yet it is a symbol of the nonconformist (perhaps the artist), whose movements society tries to restrict because those who deviate from the norm often threaten those who have sworn to uphold it. While it is not really necessary to see the iguana, John Huston, who directed the 1964 movie version, obviously knew that audiences expected it; and seeing the iguana, which does not conform to the traditional notion of beauty, highlights the point that Williams was making.

Move some incidents to other locations to achieve variety. Lillian Hellman had no other choice but to have the villain of her play *Watch on the Rhine* (1941) killed in the living room, since the entire action was set there. The 1943 movie version transfers the murder to the garage. In the play *Streetcar,* Blanche tells Mitch about her husband's suicide after they return from the Moon Lake Casino. The film allows Blanche to tell Mitch at the Casino itself.

Create a character from a name merely mentioned in the play or create a new character to pair off with one who does appear in the play. In the film version of *Tea and Sympathy,* not only does Ellie—who in the play is known only as the prostitute with whom Tom Lee failed so abominably that he attempted suicide—appear as a character but the encounter between her and Tom is depicted as well. At the end of the play *The Little Foxes* (1939), Alexandra knows that her mother, Regina, was responsible for her father's death. When the 1941 film version was released, the Production Code required some kind of retribution; thus the original ending, in which Alexandra stays on to remind Regina of what she has done, might make it seem that Regina has not been punished. In the film, therefore, Alexandra leaves home with a young man, David Hewitt, who did not exist in the play but was created for the film so that Alexandra could be paired off with him—and Regina would be left alone with her guilt.

Not every major play has been adapted for the screen as successfully as *Streetcar, Picnic,* and *The Little Foxes.*

In Marsha Norman's Pulitzer Prize–winning one-act play *'Night, Mother* (1983), a daughter tells her mother that she plans to commit suicide that night. The play observes the three unities of Greek tragedy: unity of action (one main plot), unity of place (one setting), and unity of time (the time covered in the play is identical to the time required to perform it). The plot of *'Night, Mother* is structured in such a way that a film version would also have to observe the unities. In the 1986 film version, the action was opened up a bit, but not enough to keep the moving images from becoming static pictures. Paul Newman's 1986 film version of Tennessee Williams's *The Glass Menagerie* had similar problems. Because of his great respect for the text, Newman scarcely opened up the action at all, and the result was like watching a photographed play.

Thus, strict fidelity to a work of literature does not necessarily result in a good film. Purists may be delighted that the text is intact, but moviegoers expect "moving pictures."

Adapting Short Stories

Short stories are notoriously difficult to adapt because of their brevity. The 1947 movie version of James Thurber's *The Secret Life of Walter Mitty* includes a few of Mitty's fantasies from the original short story, which is about six pages long. The film, which stars Danny Kaye in the title role, runs 110 minutes because more fantasies had to be added, some with musical numbers especially created for Kaye (who came to Hollywood from the musical stage). But at the heart of the film is a real-life adventure that has nothing to do with Thurber's story and is even more surreal than any of Mitty's daydreams. On his daily commute to New York, Mitty encounters a mystery woman (Virginia Mayo) who is pursued by an equally mysterious man. Mitty's efforts to aid the woman involve him in a murder, as a result of which he is pursued by a Nazi-like doctor (Boris Karloff) and a knife-wielding villain, who believe he has a black book that contains information about the location of stolen art. As a Danny Kaye vehicle, *Mitty* succeeds; as an adaptation, it lacks the whimsy and poignancy of the original, in which Mitty is a married, middle-aged fantasist, not a bachelor living at home with his mother. The best movie versions of short stories (for example, Robert Siodmak's *The Killers* [1946] and Hitchcock's *The Birds*) use their sources purely as points of departure.

Daphne du Maurier's "The Birds" and Alfred Hitchcock's *The Birds*

Daphne du Maurier's *Kiss Me Again, Stranger* (1952), a collection of eight short stories, included one called "The Birds." Set in Cornwall, in the extreme southwest of England, where du Maurier spent most of her life, "The Birds" was inspired by two actual experiences in which seagulls attacked the author and her dogs, and later, a farmer as he was plowing.

The story is told from the point of view of Nat Hocken, a farm worker, who lives on an island with his wife and two children. On a day in early December, Nat notices birds circling overhead but pays no attention. That night, they mass at his window, pecking at it—and then at him, when he opens it. One bird even goes for Nat's eyes. They then enter the children's room through an open window, colliding with one another and littering the floor with their dead bodies.

The unprovoked attacks continue, but the official reason seems to be a sudden climactic change that has sent hordes of birds into Britain. Because du Maurier wrote the story in the early years of the Cold War, the townspeople blame the plague of birds on the Russians. Next, a state of emergency is declared in Britain after the birds start attacking RAF planes.

Doubles: The intrusive blonde (Tippi Hedren) serving breakfast to the fearful matriarch (Jessica Tandy) in Hitchcock's *The Birds* (1963), a total reworking of Daphne du Maurier's short story. *(Courtesy MOMA/FSA)*

Isolated in his home with his wife and family, without telephone service or radio reception, Nat lights his last cigarette and waits. "Won't America do something?" his wife asks. The question is never answered, and Nat wonders "how many million years of memory were stored in those little brains, giving them the instinct to destroy mankind with all the deft precision of machines."

In Britain, du Maurier's collection was entitled *The Apple Tree*, suggesting the tree of the knowledge of good and evil, of whose fruit Adam and Eve ate. Obviously, her birds had also tasted of the "fruit of that forbidden tree."

Hitchcock bought the rights to "The Birds" shortly after *Kiss Me Again, Stranger* was published but was interested in only two aspects of the story: the coastal setting, suggesting isolation; and the birds' unprovoked attacks. Changing the setting was easy; it became Bodega Bay in northern California. The attacks were another matter. In the film, they are explained neither scientifically nor politically; Hitchcock would not resort to pseudo-science or Cold War hysteria.

Fresh from making *Psycho*, Hitchcock conceived of a *Psycho*-like plot with an unmarried son, Mitch; his widowed mother, Lydia; and a female intruder, Melanie. It is not coincidental that the women's names, Melanie and Lydia, begin with the same letters as those of the sisters in *Psycho*, Marion and Lila. In both films, a car trip becomes a rendezvous with destiny, a real mother-son relationship replaces a ghostly one, and a female arrives to threaten that relationship.

Visually, Melanie (Tippi Hedren) and Lydia (Jessica Tandy) are doubles, right down to their hairstyles. One could easily see Melanie as a younger version of Lydia; both are born to be grandes dames. Neither can love. Melanie pursues Mitch (Rod Taylor) with a pair of lovebirds, offering symbolically what she cannot give naturally. At the beginning of the film, Mitch is looking for a pair of lovebirds as a birthday present for his kid sister, Cathy. The gift is appropriate. Cathy needs all the love she can get, since she does not receive it from her mother and sees her brother only on weekends. Cathy was a late child. Lydia was so paranoid about being left alone (perhaps because she rightly sensed that her husband would predecease her) that she ignored the basics of family planning and had Cathy some twenty years after Mitch. Cathy, who was six when her father died, has just turned eleven; Mitch is in his early thirties. No wonder Cathy regards Mitch as a surrogate father; it's no wonder, too, that Cathy is attracted to Melanie, who looks more like her mother than Lydia does. Lydia, in fact, could pass for Cathy's grandmother. Similarly, Melanie is attracted to Cathy, in whom she sees herself as a child—a child whose own mother walked out on the family when Melanie was eleven. However, Melanie does not realize that, by pursuing Mitch to Bodega Bay, she will inherit a mother. Lydia, who has sabotaged every one of Mitch's relationships with a woman in order to keep him for herself, has no fears about Melanie. The birds will see to it that Melanie is no longer a threat to Lydia's matriarchy.

If *The Birds* is taken as an allegory, there is no reason to explain the attacks except as an external manifestation of something within the characters. With the exception of Cathy, they are loveless and self-absorbed people, who, had they been birds, would have clawed at each other; had Cathy been a bird, she would have been a lovebird.

It is evident from the film's ironic ending that Mitch, Lydia, and Cathy get—and do not get—what they want. As Mitch, Cathy, Lydia, and the bandaged and traumatized Melanie prepare to leave for San Francisco, conceding victory to the birds, Lydia holds Melanie against her breast. For the first time, Lydia looks benign and strangely happy, knowing that Melanie, who will need plastic surgery, if not psychotherapy, will never marry Mitch. Cathy has a surrogate mother in Melanie, but from the look on Melanie's face, it is hard to imagine her being able to function normally again. Mitch lived up to Lydia's expectations that he act as the "man of the family," like his father, by driving all of them out of Bodega Bay. On the other hand, Mitch and Cathy have both lost: Mitch has lost a potential mate, and Cathy, a mother figure. Lydia, however, has triumphed—thanks to the birds. All that Lydia has lost is her house; she might have to live in San Francisco.

THE NATURE OF SCREENWRITING

If adaptation, which is merely one kind of screenwriting, is difficult, screenwriting in general can hardly be easy. Distinguished authors like William Faulkner and F. Scott Fitzgerald tried to write for the screen, but what they produced pales in comparison with their fiction. Fitzgerald genuinely wanted to write film scripts, but the ones that he wrote either contained dialogue the actors found impossible to speak or were so cluttered with description that they had to be pruned drastically. Fitzgerald's talent lay in fiction, where he could narrate or describe without dramatizing, rather than in screenwriting, where he would have to suppress the urge to tell everything through words and delegate some authority to the camera.

The ideal screenplay advances the plot in two ways: verbally, through dialogue; and visually, through action. If a screenplay were total dialogue, there would be no difference between a screenplay and a stage play. Screenwriters must visualize the action as they write it. When the visual might be more effective than the verbal, the writer must suppress the desire to rely on dialogue and, instead, indicate how the action can be visualized.

Julia has a literate—that is, well written and intelligently executed—script by Alvin Sargent, yet there are parts of the film that contain no dialogue at all. Sargent knew when language was necessary to advance the plot, and when images were. For example, the scene in which Lillian is watching a performance of *Hamlet* in Moscow is crosscut with Julia's murder in Frankfurt. Sargent realized that it would be more effective to have the murder take place without any dialogue at all so there would be a contrast with the performance of *Hamlet*, where dialogue is essential. Thus a further contrast results: verbalized stage violence and nonverbal real violence.

Although it is obvious that a screenplay is intended to be visualized, the consequences of visualization may not be so obvious. One such consequence is the kind of language with which the screenplay is written. Because audiences expect the photographed image to be realistic (as opposed to, say, a painting, which need not be), they also expect the characters to sound realistic. In real life, we point to an object and call it a "this" or a "that." In film, a demonstrative can have a visual antecedent, so that a "this" or a "that" is something the audience sees. When Ellen (Claudette

Colbert) sees the blanket partition that Peter (Clark Gable) has arranged between their beds in *It Happened One Night*, she says, "That makes it all right," glancing in the direction of the blanket. It is the glance that makes the grammar and the line all right, too. A screenwriter who is not thinking visually might have written: "The fact that you've put up a blanket between the beds makes it all right, I presume." That would be stage dialogue, which tends to be more precise and grammatical than film dialogue; it can also turn off moviegoers.

Screen dialogue is often truncated—that is, sentences are frequently left unfinished, and speech is fragmentary. For this reason, screen language is closer to actual conversation than any other kind of dialogue, even that of the most naturalistic kind of theater. An example of stage dialogue is Nick's lines in Lillian Hellman's *The Autumn Garden:* "These are my oldest friends. I think as one grows older it is more and more necessary to reach out your hand for the sturdy old vines you knew when you were young and let them lead you back to the roots of things that matter." Even though these lines are supposed to sound pompous, they would sound doubly so in a film if they were delivered in close-up or even medium shot. The audience might even laugh. *The Autumn Garden* has never been filmed, even though it is considered Hellman's finest play. Yet if it were, and the screenwriter decided to retain these lines, they would have to be changed to something like this: "These are my oldest friends. You might call them the vines that bring me back to my roots."

Movie dialogue is more like the exchange between Butch and Sundance in *Butch Cassidy and the Sundance Kid* (1969):

BUTCH: How long you figure we been watching?
SUNDANCE: Awhile.
BUTCH: How much longer before you think they're not after us?
SUNDANCE: A while longer.
BUTCH: How come you're always so talkative?
SUNDANCE: Born blabby.

To appreciate the way a screenwriter economizes on language, compare the dialogue in a novel with that in the movie based on the novel. Often a screenwriter will incorporate dialogue from the novel into the screenplay if the dialogue is appropriate. However, spoken dialogue is not necessarily the same as written dialogue; screen dialogue has to be made compatible with the rhythms of human speech. In both Raymond Chandler's novel *The Big Sleep* and the 1946 film version directed by Howard Hawks, General Sternwood asks the detective Philip Marlowe about himself. Here is what Marlowe says in the novel: "I'm thirty-three years old, went to college once and can still speak English if there's any demand for it. There isn't much in my trade. I worked for Mr. Wilde, the District Attorney, as an investigator once. His chief investigator, a man named Bernie Ohls, called me and told me you wanted to see me. I'm unmarried because I don't like policemen's wives."

Compare Marlowe's reply in the film: "I'm thirty-eight years old, went to college once. I can still speak English when there's any demand for it in my business. I worked for the District Attorney's office once. It was Bernie Ohls, his chief investigator, who sent me word you wanted to see me. I'm not married." Since Humphrey Bogart was playing Marlowe, the character's age had to be changed from thirty-three to thirty-eight. But the real difference is the succinctness of the screen dialogue, which imparts the same information as the novel but more concisely.

Economy of language, which is at the heart of screenwriting, is not the same as ellipsis, in which words are omitted for the sake of balance or parallelism. Ellipsis is rhetorical rather than dramatic, artificial rather than real. In a scene from Elia Kazan's 1976 movie version of F. Scott Fitzgerald's unfinished novel *The Last Tycoon*, the producer Monroe Stahr (Robert De Niro) watches the rushes of a highly sophisticated 1930s movie in which the hero says to the heroine, "I love you," and she replies, "And I, you." Stahr is furious: "'And I—you!' Who talks like that?" Claudius in *Hamlet* does, for one: "And he to England shall along with you." But that is stage dialogue; in particular, Elizabethan stage dialogue. And nobody talked like that in Elizabethan England, either.

People talk in strands, in words and phrases strung together in a kind of beaded syntax, much the way Neff talks in *Double Indemnity*—in units of thought, where the ideas generate their own rhythm and their own grammar. Sometimes movie characters speak in epigrams, but these are movie, not stage, epigrams. They are memorable because they compress a complex idea into an easily remembered line that is natural for the character to speak and is not merely an occasion for the writer to wax clever. At the end of *Now, Voyager* (1942), Charlotte (Bette Davis) says to Jerry (Paul Henreid), "Oh, Jerry, don't let's ask for the moon. We have the stars." By using images (moon, stars) that everyone readily understands, she sums up with marvelous precision humankind's perennial desire to overreach. Yet what Charlotte says is appropriate to the circumstances: Charlotte is happy just to take care of Jerry's daughter, even though Jerry can no longer be her lover.

Movie epigrams are not stage epigrams, which tell us more about the playwright's gift for language than about the character's motivation or psychology. In Oscar Wilde's *The Importance of Being Earnest*, Lady Bracknell's line "Hesitation of any kind is a sign of mental decay in the young, of physical weakness in the old" is a stage epigram because it functions not so much as dialogue but as an expression of Wilde's wit. While we may enjoy that wit, we sense that we are hearing the author, not the character.

In *All About Eve*, when Margo Channing (Bette Davis) says, "Fasten your seat belts; it's going to be a bumpy night," she is parodying the airline cliché, "Fasten your seat belts; it's going to be a bumpy flight." Margo's line is not a turn of the phrase but a variation on a phrase already turned. Unlike Oscar Wilde's epigrams, which can be quoted out of context and still sound witty, Margo's "Fasten your seat belts" is the closing line of a specific sequence. Realizing that Eve is now her rival, Margo drinks too much at a party and becomes progressively more ill-tempered. Downing one last martini, she sweeps across the room, turns, delivers the line, and exits in the grand manner. The camera, which has been tracking her the whole time, exits in a huff with her. As a curtain line, "Fasten your seat belts" might have fallen flat; as an exit line in a movie, it is ideal, particularly given Bette Davis's memorably corrosive delivery. (Nobody ever says, "Do you remember when Lady Bracknell said, 'Hesitation of any kind is a sign of mental decay in the young, of physical weakness in the old?'" They do say, "Do you remember when Bette Davis said, 'Fasten your seat belts; it's going to be a bumpy night' in *All About Eve*?")

Just as the movie epigram differs from the stage epigram, the movie monologue—an extended speech in which a character reveals important information—differs from the stage monologue. In *All About Eve*, Eve (Anne Baxter) delivers a monologue about her dreary childhood and tragic marriage, playing on the sympathies of her five listeners. Even if Joseph L. Mankiewicz had not directed his own screenplay, a director would have no other choice but to cut to the listeners on certain lines, as Eve either calls her listeners by name or alludes to something about them that causes them to respond. There are some seven cuts in Eve's monologue, yet they are so unobtrusive that by the time Eve finishes speaking the audience feels it has heard a monologue while it has really witnessed a scene. In the theater, the speech could never be a true monologue, since Eve poses rhetorical questions to her listeners or makes references that necessitate a reaction from them, and these reactions demand close-ups. In the movie there is no question that one listener is moved, another is close to tears, a third is attentive, a fourth is concerned, and a fifth is mildly skeptical but ultimately convinced. It is important that we see, and see clearly, each listener's reaction, since Eve is winning each of them over by her tale of woe—a tale that, incidentally, is fabricated.

By its nature, a screenplay is best appreciated after one has seen it brought to the screen. *Patton* (1970) is best remembered for Patton's (George C. Scott) opening monologue; yet, taken simply as a monologue, it is not on a par with such great stage monologues as Hickey's in Eugene O'Neill's *The Iceman Cometh* or Blanche's in *A Streetcar Named Desire*.

However, if, while reading it, you try to imagine Patton growing progressively larger as he becomes more outrageous, which is what happens on-screen, you can then appreciate how the words were translated into images. Patton progresses from a tiny figure against a gigantic American flag to a face that fills the screen to a tiny figure again. It is like watching the ego inflate itself and then lose air.

A novel can span several hundred pages without adhering to a strict code, with the text broken up into chapters or chapter equivalents. Writing a play requires division into acts and, if necessary, scenes within those acts. If the setting changes in a novel, it can be indicated by a phrase ("Meanwhile, in London . . ."); in a play, a change of location is marked by an act or scene change, as in Lillian Hellman's *The Searching Wind:* act 1, scene 1, the drawing room of the Hazen house, Washington, D.C.; scene 2, a room in the Grand Hotel, Rome. In a screenplay, structuring the narrative and designating scene changes are even more complicated.

A screenplay follows a specific format. Every screenplay begins with the same two words in capital letters: FADE IN. Fade in on what? Suppose you wanted to fade in on a cabin in the woods. That would be your first shot. How you indicate it depends on whether you are writing a **spec script** (one for which you have no firm commitment from a studio) or a **shooting script** (one that is being prepared for filming). In a shooting script, shots (or scenes, if they entail more than just a shot) are numbered. So far, we are fading in on a cabin in the woods. But that instruction is incomplete; shots have to be described in terms of place (INTERIOR or EXTERIOR) and time (DAY or NIGHT). Thus, an incomplete opening might be:

FADE IN:
1. INT—CABIN—NIGHT

What is going on in the cabin? Suppose the first shot is to be of Elise, the heroine, standing anxiously at the window, waiting for her husband to return. How is she to be shown? What will be the size of her image: CU, LS, MS? To convey anxiety, a CU is necessary. How will the audience know that she is waiting for her husband? Voice-over narration (V.O.) will be used to reveal her thoughts. In screenwriting, characters' names or designations (ELISE, CROWD), camera movements (PAN TO), transitions (DISSOLVE TO), the words sound (SOUND of laughter), and sound effects (SF or SFX) are capitalized. Thus, the shooting script might begin as follows:

FADE IN:
1. INT—CABIN—NIGHT

CU of ELISE standing anxiously at window. A storm rages outside.

ELISE (V.O.)
John said he'd be back by nightfall, but it's close to midnight.
Dear God, not now . . . please, not now.

To show John, the screenwriter would start a new shot.

2. EXT—MAINE WOODS—NIGHT

ELS of JOHN trudging through snow. SLOW ZOOM IN to reveal face, weather-beaten but confident.

Note, for example, how Alan Alda observes the rules in this brief excerpt from the credits sequence in his *Four Seasons* screenplay:

7. EXT—VILLAGE STREET—DAY

HIGH SHOT—station wagon makes its way down the street. Over this we HEAR:

DANNY'S VOICE
Who ate the bread? What the hell is this?
You started without me?

8. EXT—13TH STREET—DAY

The station wagon pulls up to the curb. CLAUDIA ZELLER is waiting for them, holding a large unfinished painting and a box of supplies. She waves and smiles. Claudia is an Italian from the Bronx. Earthy, intelligent, and strong. She gets in the car with the painting, passing it with difficulty over everybody's head as she gets into the back of the car.

DANNY
You brought your work?

CLAUDIA
It's almost finished. I'm hot. I'm cooking.
I can't stop for a whole weekend.

DANNY
I stopped my work for the weekend.

CLAUDIA
Danny, please, you're a dentist.

DANNY
(to Anne)
You hear this? I can sculpt a bicuspid that would fool God himself, but I'm just a dentist.

CLAUDIA

I'll go out in the fields with the cows.
I'll stay out of everybody's way.

She accidentally sticks the painting in Nick's face. Nick grabs at
his eye and winces.

CLAUDIA (cont'd.)
Oh, Nick, I'm sorry. Are you all right?

NICK

Fine.
(to Danny)
I'm glad you didn't bring your dentist's chair.

JACK
You hear about Janice and Hal?

CLAUDIA

I just got off the phone with her. It's a nightmare.
Drive. Let's get as far away from the whole damn thing as we can.

The station wagon takes off.

CUT TO:

9. EXT—MERRIT PARKWAY—DAY
The station wagon moves down the highway past the greens and reds
and yellows of spring.

SPRING MONTAGE:

Crabapple trees spraying blossoms like fountains.

Lilac branches sagging with purple buds.

Dark rain clouds passing over the sun.

Forsythia shimmering in a spring rain, its buds dropping under the
weight of the fresh water.

Small wet birds in a nest shaking water drops from nearly featherless
wings.

And finally, sunset in the woods. New leaves are everywhere. A rabbit
crawls slowly out of its hole and surveys the place.

10. EXT—THE BARN—NIGHT

In the distance the station wagon pulls up to a barn that has been made into a house.

END OPENING TITLES.

Screenwriting is an art that film history—which emphasizes the development of film as a medium, the studio system and the stars that came out of it, and the role of the director in the filmmaking process—has tended to ignore, perhaps because the script is pre-filmic. Even though most narrative films start with a script, the script recedes into the background as it changes from a verbal to a visual text, so that by the time the film has been completed the words have been translated into images. Thus, moviegoers associate dialogue not with the writer but with the actors speaking the lines or with the scenes in which they are spoken. Understandably, writers bristle at the way films are advertised: "A Film by (director's name)" or "A (director's name) Film" is shown at the beginning, while their names are at the end and generally in smaller type. Nevertheless, anyone who is serious about film will always look for the screenwriter's name in the credits.

NOTES

[1] Ingmar Bergman, "Film Has Nothing to Do with Literature," in *Film: A Montage of Theories*, ed. Richard Dyer MacCann (New York: E. P. Dutton, 1966), 144.

[2] The terms used throughout the rest of this chapter come from Wayne C. Booth, *The Rhetoric of Fiction* (Chicago: University of Chicago Press, 1961).

What Is Film?

8

F ilm provides an experience that cannot be found elsewhere. Film can crystallize an emotion or an idea into a visual image. When language is used, the words are integrated with the images so that they become inseparable. Once we see *Casablanca,* a line like "Here's looking at *you,* kid" is forever linked with the speaker (Humphrey Bogart) and the one to whom it is spoken (Ingrid Bergman). We may not be able to dredge up the exact frame from our memory, but we know that Bogart said it to Bergman, and we remember the look in their eyes.

Films, when remembered, appear as pictures—sometimes pictures without sound; at other times, talking pictures or even musical pictures. Those pictures, with or without sound and/or music, become the touchstone by which we tend to define the nature of film.

One person might say, for example, that the ending of *The Third Man* is the essence of film because it does not rely on dialogue, only on image and sound—the basic elements of moviemaking. Anna (Alida Valli) walks down a Vienna road through a drift of leaves—her face expressionless, her gaze

The ultimate snub: the ending of *The Third Man* (1949), in which Anna (Alida Valli) walks past Martins (Joseph Cotten) without even a nod in his direction. *(Courtesy MOMA/FSA)*

fixed. Holly Martins (Joseph Cotten) leans against a cart and lights a cigarette, waiting to be recognized. As the autumn leaves fall in a silent shower, Anna moves out of the frame—and out of Martins's life—without so much as a glance in his direction. Martins grows progressively smaller, until he is nothing but a tiny figure by the side of a road, ready to disappear like the smoke from his cigarette. The ending achieves what only film can: eloquence without words. Not one line of dialogue is spoken: the zither alone speaks, as it plays with restrained sadness the famous "*Third Man* Theme."

Someone else might argue that, while the ending of *The Third Man* is impressive, it cannot compete with Isak Borg's final vision in Bergman's *Wild Strawberries,* in which Sara, Isak's boyhood love, leads him through a meadow to a bay. Across the bay, Isak sees his mother knitting while his father fishes, apparently with some success, for the rod is beginning to curve over the water. They wave at their son, and he smiles back at them. Isak's vision of his parents has the texture of an impressionist painting. Not only is the shot perfectly composed but it also captures the essence of its subject: eternity objectified as a state into which we do not freeze like figures in a mural but, rather, melt imperceptibly, the way spring softens into summer or summer ripens into autumn.

It is natural to have a favorite scene; yet scenes are parts of a whole, a fact that we tend to forget when we single out scenes for special consideration. What, exactly, is film? Is it just a moment in a movie that crystallizes the film experience? Or is there such a thing as a work that, in its totality—not merely in part—epitomizes the art of film? In other words, a work that could never have been possible, or have reached its level of excellence, in any other medium?

Let us examine four films, the first of which was originally intended for Broadway but found its true niche in Hollywood; the other three resulting from original screenplays.

CASABLANCA
(MICHAEL CURTIZ, 1942)

Before there was a *Casablanca*, there was a play called *Everybody Comes to Rick's* by Murray Burnett and Joan Alison, which Warner Bros. purchased in December 1941; the play, however, never reached Broadway and is rarely staged. Even if the play had managed to open in New York, it would have been poorly reviewed and then forgotten. *Casablanca*, on the other hand, is one of most popular films ever made, even though the plot is not that different from *Everybody Comes to Rick's*. In the play, Rick Blaine is the jaded owner of a café in Casablanca. One evening, a woman from his past, Lois Meredith, arrives at the café with the Czech freedom fighter Victor

Humphrey Bogart and Ingrid Bergman as the legendary lovers in *Casablanca* (1942). *(Courtesy MOMA/FSA and Warner Bros., Inc.)*

Laszlo. Although Rick and Lois resume their relationship, Rick begins to develop a political conscience; realizing that Laszlo must continue to fight fascism and that Lois must go with him, Rick makes it possible for the two of them to fly to Lisbon while he stays behind in Casablanca to meet an uncertain fate at the hands of the Nazis.

Everybody Comes to Rick's furnished the *Casablanca* screenwriters (and there were several) with the main characters and plot points: the African American pianist, Sam, Rick's confidant; the Nazi general, Strasser; Victor Laszlo and Lois (renamed Ilsa in the film); the prefect of police, Reynaldo (called Renault in the film); Ugarte, who traffics in stolen visas and whose letters of transit provide the denouement; and the Bulgarian couple, Jan and Annina, whom Rick helps to leave Casablanca. The Production Code precluded Ilsa's sleeping with Rick as Lois did in the play. The World War II setting dictated the film's ending: Laszlo and Ilsa board the plane, while Rick goes off to join the Free French with Captain Renault, who, like Rick, was once apolitical but now wants to do his part to stop fascism.

If the plot sounds far-fetched, it is. Yet generations have continued to fall under *Casablanca*'s spell because a solid mythic foundation lies beneath a rickety plot. While there is no particular myth to describe the subtext, there is a universal one: the myth of regeneration. *Casablanca* insists that, as long as there are uncommitted people like Rick, who are capable of change, there is hope for the world. And once the uncommitted have changed, they make it possible for the Victor Laszlos to do what most of us cannot: make the world a better place.

We identify with Rick because we, too, may be more concerned about ourselves than about the world; we also identify with Laszlo, because we aspire to his idealism. We even empathize with the patrons of Rick's café, a true cross section of humanity, who show the kind of courage we envy. As the Germans bellow their anthem, the patrons respond defiantly with "La Marseillaise" and drown them out. When Rick tells Ilsa that "the problems of three little people don't amount to a hill of beans in this crazy world," he is admitting that there are times when individual needs must be subordinated to the common good. Yet this is not any man speaking to any woman but Humphrey Bogart speaking to Ingrid Bergman, one icon to another. Each is the perfect embodiment of the character: Bogart, the cynic in need of regeneration; Bergman, the woman with the power to regenerate him.

With two other actors (and others were considered, including George Raft for Rick; Ann Sheridan, Michele Morgan, and Hedy Lamarr for Ilsa; Joseph Cotten and Philip Dorn for Laszlo), the effect would never have been the same. Bogart and Bergman have such powerful screen personae that when they play characters like Rick and Ilsa, a coinciding of persona and character results, so that when one thinks of *Casablanca*, one thinks of Humphrey Bogart and Ingrid Bergman and not merely of Rick Blaine and Ilsa Lund.

THE GODFATHER, PART II
(FRANCIS FORD COPPOLA, 1974)

In the sequel to Francis Ford Coppola's *The Godfather* (1972), the lives of Vito Corleone and his son Michael are interwoven in a way that is truly cinematic. Since Vito is dead when the film opens, Coppola could not crosscut the lives of father and son, so he tells Vito's story in flashback.

The first time the film moves from the present to the past, from Michael (Al Pacino) to Vito (Robert De Niro), Michael is putting his son to bed. Michael's face is to the *left* of the frame. Slowly, the scene dissolves to Vito, his face to the *right* of the frame, as he puts his son Fredo to bed. The transition from son to father, from present to past, is balanced by a movement from left to right. The transition also brings about a corresponding change of rhythm: as the action shifts from 1957 to the turn of the century, the frenetic pace of the present yields to an Old World ease. The color also changes as Lake Tahoe dissolves into Little Italy. Michael's world is dark and forbidding; Vito's is bright and inviting.

The first flashback ends as it began—with a shot of Vito and his son—and suddenly we are in the late 1950s again, with Michael en route to Miami. By ending with a cut instead of another dissolve, Coppola points up the difference between the feverish pace of Michael's life and the tranquillity Vito knew, at least in his early manhood.

The second flashback begins when Michael hears that his wife, Kay, has had a miscarriage, which is later revealed to be an abortion. The scene again dissolves to Little Italy, where Vito is hovering over his son, who is ill with pneumonia. Again, it is a child that effects the transition. Coppola ends the flashback by showing Vito with the young Michael on his lap; then he cuts to a car making its way along a wintry road and proceeding through the forbidding entrance to Michael's Lake Tahoe home. The cut propels us into a present that is so loveless that Kay does not even look up from her sewing to greet her husband.

Coppola could not use a child as a bridge three times in succession. Consequently, the third flashback in *Godfather II* does not spring from a particular image. Coppola merely dissolves a shot of Michael speaking with his mother into one of Vito buying fruit and ends the flashback with the formation of the Genco Importing Company. In the first two flashbacks, it was a cut that restored the action to the present; in the third, it is a dissolve. Just as Vito is about to enter the import business, Coppola dissolves to a congressional investigation at which Michael is being interrogated. By dissolving from the Genco Importing Company to the hearings, Coppola establishes a connection between them. The legitimacy of the Genco Importing Company, the foundation on which Vito built his empire, is now the subject of an investigation. Michael, who has inherited his father's empire along with its foundation, plays the honest businessman who refuses to take the Fifth Amendment, claiming that he has nothing to hide.

The final flashback begins after Kay tells Michael that her miscarriage was really an abortion. Coppola cuts to Vito's return to the Sicilian town of Corleone in order to avenge the murder of his parents, who were victims of Don Ciccio's vendetta. Here the link between present and past is something quite different from a child's being put to bed or the establishment of an import company: the link is death. The admission of an abortion becomes the occasion for a flashback of a mafioso's assassination. It is also death that returns the action to the present. As Vito leaves Sicily after killing Don Ciccio, Coppola dissolves to a casket containing the body of Michael's mother, Mama Corleone.

Godfather II interweaves past and present, contrasting them in a way that's peculiar to film: through variations of rhythm, balance, and color.

RAGING BULL (MARTIN SCORSESE, 1980)

The credits begin with the intermezzo from Mascagni's opera *Cavalleria Rusticana*; it is soothing, tranquil music, coming midway in an opera about betrayal, adultery, and murder. The credits are in color, with the title in flamboyant red. During the credits, a boxer in a hooded robe is seen limbering up in the ring in slow motion. The combination of Mascagni's serene music and the eerie sight of a boxer in an otherwise empty ring, moving with the speed of a puppet, prompts us to wonder if this is the raging bull of the title. And if we know that the film is based on the life of Jake La Motta (Robert De Niro), who lost the title of middleweight champion of the world to Sugar Ray Robinson in 1951 (and who was also known to be ill-tempered and violent), we might also ask why Scorsese has created such dreamlike credits and scored them with music that is similarly restful.

Anyone who has learned to read visuals and correlate them with the accompanying soundtrack would sense that perhaps Scorsese is asking the viewer to feel some compassion for the title character, as one might for a once raging bull that now rages alone because he has become too slow-moving to be a threat.

But poignancy fades as the film begins. Not only does the bull rage but he rages in black and white—and at a pace that is at odds with that of the credits, which look lethargic in comparison. Those who were expect-

Robert De Niro as middleweight champion Jake La Motta in *Raging Bull* (1980). *(Courtesy MOMA/FSA)*

ing a sentimental biopic in color must have been taken aback by the changeover to black and white and the opening shots of pounding fists and battered faces. Scorsese has made four artistic choices: to tell La Motta's story in black and white, the way the great boxing pictures of the past (e.g., *Body and Soul* [1947], *The Set-Up* [1949]) were filmed; to quote as a subtext another movie in which boxing is an important theme (*On the Waterfront* [1954]); to provide a chronological and historical framework through titles introducing each sequence (e.g., "New York, 1964"; "The Bronx, 1941"; "La Motta vs. Robinson, 1943"); and finally to use a framing device, beginning and ending with La Motta, now a nightclub performer capitalizing on his former fame, rehearsing a monologue in his dressing room. Everything else—La Motta's career from 1941 on—is enclosed between the prologue and the epilogue, like a series of texts between two bookends.

Segmenting the action requires variations of rhythm, which poses problems, since Scorsese has to shuttle back and forth between La Motta's professional, domestic, and social life. Yet all of these scenes have one common note: violence. La Motta can be almost as violent at home or in a club as he is in the ring. The turbulence of the first sequence, which includes a bloody fight as well as a riot among the spectators, seems to have abated at the beginning of the second, set in the Bronx, where La Motta and his first wife live. However, we soon discover that only the rhythm is different. An argument over the way a steak should be cooked throws La Motta into such a rage that he almost trashes the kitchen. Violence is violence; the occasion determines the manner in which it is expressed.

Scorsese, with the assistance of his extraordinary editor, Thelma Schoonmaker, varies the rhythm so successfully that no single scene—regardless of where it is set—is the same. When La Motta sees Vicky (Cathy Moriarty), soon to be his second wife, she is at the local pool, looking like a 1940s pinup. The pace slows down, as La Motta fixes his gaze on her. Other men are also aware of her, and Scorsese conveys a men's club atmosphere by having us hear only the men as they speak. Vicky just moves her lips; to the men, she is only an object. They do not hear her because they do not think of women as human beings enjoying the same freedom of speech as men. Women are meant to be silent; if they speak their mind, a slap across the face ends the conversation.

While *Raging Bull* may seem to be sexually explicit, the love scenes between La Motta and Vicky are antiseptic. She behaves robotically, planting kisses on his face or chest and removing articles of clothing as requested. But there is no real passion; the only lust is on La Motta's part, which is short-lived. Because he has a fight coming up, he cools himself by emptying a pitcher of ice water down his shorts. This is clearly a male universe; there is far more affection between the men, who embrace and kiss freely, than there is between the men and the women. When Jake brings Vicky to his apartment for the first time, Scorsese uses a three-shot to illustrate La Motta's hierarchy of love. La Motta, left of frame, and Vicky, right, stand in profile at the dresser, on which there is a picture of La Motta and his brother, Joey (Joe Pesci). The picture stands between them, as does the bond between the brothers after they marry.

Scorsese frequently uses slow motion, but not to give a blow-by-blow breakdown of a fight, as one might expect in a boxing film. Slow motion is used in the fight sequences primarily to reflect the point of view of the boxer, who is so disoriented after a round that nothing looks or moves as it normally would. But Scorsese also uses slow motion outside the ring. When La Motta sees Vicky in a club, it is as if his vision were temporarily altered as she turns into the golden girl of his imagination, moving in a rhythm that is different from that of the real world. It happens again at the Copacabana when she spots some old friends and makes her way to their table.

Segmenting the narrative poses another set of problems: no matter how the rhythm is varied, certain events must be either omitted or telescoped. Scorsese does both. Most of 1944–1947 is reduced to a montage of stills from La Motta's fights and home movies of his and his brother's marriages. But the fact that the films are in color indicates that Scorsese was trying to suggest some of the changes in the media that occurred in the 1941–1964 period—such as color home movies.

The brief switch to color was not accidental, nor were later sequences, set in the 1950s, that showed a television set in La Motta's home. Significantly, the set doesn't work. Jake's days in the ring are over; likewise, sporting events, once available only on radio, can now be seen by anyone who can afford a television set. Jake can afford one, but television will never be his medium, which was evident in 1951 when viewers saw him lose his title to Sugar Ray Robinson.

Like Steven Spielberg and Woody Allen, Scorsese has an astounding knowledge of movie history. Sometimes he refers to past films by evoking an image of the past (e.g., Vicky wearing a white turban and a white two-piece swimsuit, looking like Lana Turner in *The Postman Always Rings Twice* [1946]) or making a direct reference—Terry's (Marlon Brando) famous speech in *On the Waterfront*, in which he chastises his brother Charley for making him throw a fight and thus lose his chance to become a contender ("I could have been somebody. I could have been a contender").

At the end of the film, La Motta, a would-be entertainer, sits at his dressing table, staring into the mirror as he rehearses the speech. He is thinking not of Terry or Charley but of his own brother, Joey, from whom he became estranged when, in a moment of irrational jealousy, he accused Joey of committing adultery with Vicky. In both *On the Waterfront* and *Raging Bull*, the brothers were mirror images—similar and opposite, as reflections are. *On the Waterfront*, then, becomes a subtext for *Raging Bull*—another film about brothers who never saw in each other what they should have seen and therefore could never do more than bond in the most primitive way.

Scorsese does not ask us to sympathize with Jake La Motta; he asks us to view La Motta as we might any protagonist who has experienced a tragic fall. Certainly, none of the classical tragic figures (Oedipus, Hamlet, Lear, Othello) were blameless; frankly, one would not want to be around them very long, given their penchant for rage. But La Motta's fall is as real within the context of *Raging Bull* as Othello's is within that of Shakespeare's play.

The end title is an excerpt from the Gospel of St. John. After Jesus cures a man who was born blind, the Pharisees summon the man a second time, insisting that his sight was restored by a sinner. The man replies that he does not know whether Jesus was a sinner; he knows only that once he was blind and now he can see.

The next title is a dedication: "Remembering Haig R. Monoogian, Teacher, May 23, 1916–May 28, 1980, with love and affection, Marty." This is a personal reference to a professor at New York University under whom Scorsese studied. Perhaps Monoogian encouraged Scorsese to look for qualities in La Motta—or someone like him—that would elude others. The dedication aside, the end title suggests that *Raging Bull* might open the eyes of those who expect to find tragic figures only in the classics but not in everyday life. Perhaps they will say, like the man who was formerly blind, "Now I can see."

With its variations of mood, tone, and rhythm; popular songs as background music, reflecting the changing tastes of the American public over a twenty-year period; intertitles that identify characters and specify time and place; and an end title that exhorts the viewer to see human beings whole before judging them, *Raging Bull* is inconceivable in any form other than film.

THE TRUMAN SHOW (PETER WEIR, 1998)

The Truman Show is a study in media control, depicting the way Christof (Ed Harris), an all-powerful television producer, has managed to turn the life of an ordinary citizen, Truman Burbank (Jim Carrey), into a television series viewed by millions without Truman's being aware of it. For thirty years, Truman's life, including his prenatal state, has been unfolding on television screens. Truman, however, has no idea that Seahaven, the idyllic island community where he lives, is really a set honeycombed with hidden cameras that record his activities (except the most intimate ones); and that everyone, including his wife and his closest friend, are actors. While *The Truman Show* seems to be the forerunner of reality television (e.g., *Survivor, Big Brother*), there is a significant difference: in reality television the performers know they are participating in a narrative that is, to a great extent, their own creation in the sense that their actions constitute the plot; Truman, however, has no idea he is the star of a series created by someone else.

It is easy to imagine the movie's ending with Truman's being killed off the way soap opera characters are when they have served their purpose as plot catalysts and are no longer needed, or when viewers no longer like them. *The Truman Show*, however, does not end with death but with discovery. The faithful viewers (and there seems to be no other kind) long for the day Truman learns the truth, knowing that his emancipation will be theirs. Basically, the viewers look forward to being free to live their own lives without having to tune in to somebody else's.

It is impossible to imagine *The Truman Show*'s being anything other than a movie, even though it is essentially about television. However, the television series portrayed in the film would never have been aired. No network would have authorized a series that violated the Ninth Amendment, which had been extended to include the right of privacy; nor would any network have the technical capabilities to produce such a series. Any-

Jim Carrey as Truman Burbank, whose life has been turned into a television series without his knowledge in *The Truman Show* (1998). *(Courtesy MOMA/FSA)*

one who has ever visited the set of a television show, taken a course in television production, or studied television history would never mistake Seahaven for Mayberry (*The Andy Griffith Show*) or Fernwood (*Mary Hartman, Mary Hartman*). Similarly, anyone who's familiar with film history knows that studios were able to transform their lots into whatever the script dictated. The Twentieth Century-Fox lot became a Welsh village for *How Green Was My Valley*, and the village of Lourdes in *The Song of Bernadette;* it also served as both Yonkers and Manhattan in *Hello, Dolly!* (1969). There is no comparison between the sets of any television series (for example, the Kramdens' Brooklyn apartment in *The Honeymooners*, Frasier's posh Seattle digs in *Frasier,* the *Cheers* bar) and the Seahaven set, which is pure Hollywood. The set in *The Truman Show* allows us to step back and analyze the differences between the two media: television, which can seduce a nation into voyeurism; and film, which is doubly voyeuristic by allowing viewers to watch a movie about a television series watched by others. The film also succeeds in re-creating a world so like our own, yet so different, that we must leave the one before we can appreciate the other.

That is what film does: for a couple of hours we are immersed in a world that has been staged, edited, and musically scored. *The Truman Show* erases the line between illusion and reality. Viewers see a reality that is really an illusion, although the die-hard Trumanians have made it such a part of their lives that they see Truman Burbank as both a real person and a character—in other words, a "real character," the way soap opera fans confuse the actors with their characters, often berating the performers in public for doing something in a particular episode that disturbed them.

Unlike a typical network series, *The Truman Show* dispenses with commercial interruptions. The sponsors' products are incorporated into the scenes, and the commercials into the dialogue. When Truman is gardening, his wife, Meryl (Laura Linney), returns from shopping. "Look at this," she exclaims, holding up one of her purchases, as she looks into a hidden camera lens. "It's a Chef's Pal. Dicer, slicer, and peeler in one. Never needs sharpening. Dishwasher safe." Truman, unaware that his wife has just done a product-placement commercial, replies, "Gee, that's great," sounding like the husband in a typical commercial. Later, Truman's friend Marlon appears brandishing a six-pack, with the beer label clearly displayed.

Although *The Truman Show* demonstrates television's (and film's) ability to create a world that seems as real as our own, it also suggests that it is only by testing the fundamental principles of reality, which we tend to take for granted, that the difference between the artificial and the real can be understood. One of the most extraordinary moments in the film is Truman's discovery that the sky is a cyclorama, which he can actually touch. It is that realization, or epiphany, that frees him from the clutches of Christof, who not only chose Truman for the lead in the series when Truman was in his mother's womb but also adopted him through his corporation, Omnicam.

Some films require a greater suspension of disbelief than others; *The Truman Show*, however, just asks us to accept this premise and not subject it to the rigors of logic by asking such questions as how a corporation was allowed to adopt a child, how Truman obtained a Social Security card, whether his teachers were all actors, and whether the federal government has become a tool of the media, which has now achieved the ultimate in control: complete control of a person's destiny, turning free will into an illusion, life into a script, and relationships, including marriage, into narrative strategies that can be altered whenever the plot needs a new angle or a new character.

These concerns, however, are irrelevant if the film is taken allegorically. Common to allegory are emblematic or transparent names (Christof, Truman, Omnicam, Seahaven) and a two-tiered narrative, which suggest that there is something beyond the literal level of meaning. "Christof" suggests Christopher (literally, "Christ bearer" in Greek), the third-century saint who, supposedly, discovered that the child he was carrying across a river was really Christ. Through his organization, Omnicam ("all camera"), Christof becomes the father or surrogate "bearer" of Truman, the "true man," the only voice of truth in a community built on deception. His surname, Burbank, is a media reference, evoking Burbank, California, the home of NBC-TV, the Walt Disney Studios, and Warner Bros. The true man has been made into a television character because Christof was looking for someone as free of malice as Christ, whom he could protect from the "lies and deceit" of the real world by providing him with an ideal one, where deception is no more harmful than a painted backdrop.

Truman's emancipation leaves him free to pursue a real relationship with the woman who once played a minor character in the series. Her name was Sylvia, although the character's name was Lauren. Sylvia was so determined to alert Truman to the web of deception being spun around him that she forgot her character's name in one episode and used her own. Sylvia was on the verge of exposing Christof's hoax when her "father" arrived on the set and whisked her off in his car, leaving viewers thinking it was part of the plot, while it was really an improvised attempt to keep Truman in a state of ignorance. It is Sylvia to whom Truman rushes when he leaves the fake set, about to emerge into reality. Yet Truman's exit from the world of artifice is not that different from our own departure from the haven of the movie theater. Like Truman, we awaken from the "daylight dream," as the critic Parker Tyler called film, into whatever reality awaits us when the lights come up. The reality to which Truman awakened was the reality of love, based on another equally important reality: truth.

If there is a movie that you believe embodies everything film should be, ask the following questions: Could it have been anything other than a film—a novel, a short story, a play, for example—and still have been as effective; or was film the medium in which it reached its level of excellence? If it is an adaptation of a work of literature, is it so different from its source that, for all practical purposes, it is an original work? If it is a faithful adaptation, does the film version deepen or enhance the source, bringing out details that are only suggested by the author? Or does the adaptation fall so short of the source that it contributes nothing to our understanding of the original? How much of the film is told through images or camera movement, without recourse to dialogue? If everything is conveyed through dialogue, the same effect might have been achieved if the film had been a novel or a play. Do the camera and the script work together, each doing what it does best, so that word and image are allies rather than enemies? What is the subtext, or infranarrative? Without one, a film may exhaust itself in a single viewing. The infranarrative enriches the film, causing a viewer to return to it. If, on the other hand, a film remains entirely on a superficial level, with visuals to match, and whatever it has to offer can be absorbed in one viewing, it is just a diversion.

Film Criticism

Theory and Practice

9

M ost criticism from Aristotle to John Dryden is really the theory of literature. Students reading Aristotle's *Poetics* for the first time may be disappointed if they expect a detailed analysis of a Greek tragedy. In the *Poetics*, Aristotle was practicing legislative criticism. He was setting forth certain principles (art as imitation, plot as soul, the tragic hero as midway between perfect goodness and utter depravity) and establishing various categories and distinctions (the simple versus the complex plot, the kinds of recognition). But he was not explicating a text or exploring its levels of meaning.

In *On the Sublime*, Longinus analyzed one of Sappho's poems, but most of the work is also legislative: how to achieve the sublime, how not to achieve it, what elements of the sublime can be learned, what elements are innate. Horace's *Ars Poetica* also ignores practical criticism, as does Sir Philip Sidney's *An Apology for Poetry*, which by its very title is a defense of an art rather than an interpretation of it.

Descriptive criticism, the analysis of a literary work, is relatively new;

it began in 1688 with John Dryden's *An Essay of Dramatic Poesy*, and not very successfully at that. Dryden was superb when he championed the cause of English drama, but deficient when he tried to analyze a particular English play, Ben Jonson's *The Silent Woman*. The kind of criticism to which most of us are accustomed—where a text is examined in detail—for example, image by image in a poem—started with the New Critics (John Crowe Ransom, Cleanth Brooks, Robert Penn Warren, and others), who focused almost exclusively on the work, ignoring the historical milieu out of which it came as well as the author's biography.

Early film criticism was also theoretical and reflected the basic premises of literary criticism—namely, that criticizing a medium requires a knowledge of what the medium can and cannot do, and that this knowledge is obtained through theory.

THE HISTORY OF FILM CRITICISM

The Russians

Film criticism really began in Russia with the Revolution of 1917. It is true that before that time newspapers had reviewers, that in 1915 Vachel Lindsay published *The Art of the Moving Picture*, and that in 1916 Hugo Munsterberg's *The Photoplay: A Psychological Study* appeared. But no filmmaker attempted to explain the nature of his craft until Lev Kuleshov started writing in 1917. In the famous Kuleshov Workshop at the State Film School in Moscow, which included such pupils as V. I. Pudovkin and, briefly, Sergei Eisenstein, Kuleshov performed various experiments in **montage,** which he defined alternately as "the joining of shots into a predetermined order," "the alternation of shots," and "the organization of cinematic material." To show how editing can alter the face of objective reality, Kuleshov intercut a close-up of an actor's neutral face with three different shots: (1) a bowl of soup, (2) a woman in a coffin, and (3) a little girl with a toy bear. Audiences marveled at the actor's "versatility" in expressing (1) hunger, (2) sorrow at his mother's death, and (3) joy at the sight of his daughter.

Pudovkin continued in his teacher's footsteps. He idolized Kuleshov, and made the extravagant claim that while others made films, Kuleshov made cinematography. Kuleshov was not infallible; although much of his theory still has value, some of it is misleading. His belief that the shot is the equivalent of the word has led to a misunderstanding of what the shot can and cannot say; his comparison between a sentence and a sequence limits the sequence to imparting only the information of which a sentence is capable; his view that the way a film is put together is more important than what it means is equivalent to the fallacy that form is more significant than content.

To his credit, Kuleshov was critical of the way Russian directors shot scenes. A great admirer of American films, he contrasted American "fast montage" with Russian "slow montage." He envisioned a suicide scene in which a despondent man would sit down at his desk, remove a pistol from the drawer, press it to his forehead, and pull the trigger. The American director would fragment the scene by breaking it up into its components: a close-up of the man's agonized face, a shot of his hand reaching into the drawer, an extreme close-up of the man's eyes, and, finally, the firing of the pistol. The Russian director would simply film the scene as if it were taking place on the stage.

What Kuleshov meant by "montage" in this example was nothing other than the editing technique that D. W. Griffith had perfected. Thus, when Kuleshov said montage developed in America, he was speaking the truth. Pudovkin continued to explore the implications of montage, which at this stage still meant editing. He argued that the foundation of film art is editing and that a film is not "shot" but "built" from individual strips of celluloid. Pudovkin was intrigued by what happens when two different shots are combined within the same narrative context. For example, in *Tol'able David* (1921), a tramp enters a house, sees a kitten, and immediately wants to drop a stone on it. Pudovkin reads the scene in this way: Tramp + Kitten = Sadist.

To Eisenstein, Pudovkin was incorrect: the equation was not A + B = C, but A x B = Y. Shots are meant to collide, not join together. With Eisenstein, montage was no longer a matter of combining shots or of alternating them but of making them collide with each other: A x B = Y; fox x businessman = cunning. In *Tol'able David*, when director Henry King cuts from the tramp to the kitten, both the tramp and the kitten are part of the same scene; in *Strike* (1924), when Eisenstein juxtaposes the face of a man and the picture of a fox, the fox is not an integral part of the scene as the kitten is in *Tol'able David*. To King, the kitten is a character; to Eisenstein, the fox is a metaphor.

The Grammarians

As new terms (*montage, dissolve, wipe,* and so on) entered the vocabulary of film, definitions became necessary to explain their functions. In 1935 Raymond Spottiswoode published *A Grammar of the Film*, whose purpose was "to make as precise as possible the language and grammar of film."[1] Spottiswoode was critical of some of the ways in which film expressed itself. He had little use for the wipe because, unlike the cut, which is imperceptible, the wipe calls attention to itself. He believed that while dissolves could be justified, they generally interfered with the film's rhythm because they slurred over the bridge between shots and altered the tone of a scene. Although *A Grammar of the Film* was a serious attempt to analyze film techniques, much of it is outdated by today's standards. We no longer speak of "credit titles," and what were once known as "strip titles" are now "subtitles."

The Apologists

Spottiswoode combined a study of film terminology with a defense of the medium, arguing that movies can become an art only if they first become part of a nation's cultural life and that critics must help film to develop a national character. He was forced to defend film, as Sir Philip Sidney was forced to defend poetry 350 years earlier, against its detractors, who called moviegoers "celluloid nitwits." However, few defenses of the filmmaker are as eloquent as Rudolf Arnheim's in *Film as Art*:

> [The filmmaker] shows the world not only as it appears objectively but also subjectively. He creates new realities, in which things can be multiplied, turns their movements and actions backward, distorts them, retards or accelerates them. . . . He breathes life into stone and bids it move. Of chaotic and illimitable space he creates pictures . . . as subjective and complex as painting.[2]

To Arnheim, the fact that photography is limited is precisely what makes film an art. Because photography is incapable of perfect reproduction, film ceases to be a mere replica of reality and becomes reality's ally or enemy but never its equivalent. Film is the art of partial illusion, the same illusion that exists on the stage, where we accept a room that has only three walls. In a silent film, we accept characters who speak but cannot be heard; in a black-and-white film, we ignore the absence of color.

Because film is capable of distortion, it is not a purely realistic medium. To the doubters who think the camera reproduces the object as it is, Arnheim explains how the camera's ability to approach an object from different and unusual angles creates effects that are ordinarily found in great painting: "Art begins where mechanical reproduction leaves off."[3] And Arnheim had no doubt that film was art.

The Realists

Since the first film critics based their theories on the silents, they were more sympathetic to montage than the critics who came of age with the talkies. Sound brought spoken dialogue, and once the pictures learned to talk, they were not as docile as they had been when they were silent. Russian montage was not well suited to the narrative sound film, in which the combination of happy face and flowing brook could break dramatic continuity or destroy verisimilitude.

"There are cases in which montage far from being the essence of cinema is indeed its negation," wrote André Bazin,[4] whose untimely death in 1958 was an irreparable loss to film criticism. What bothered Bazin about montage was its inability to offer more than a limited and, frequently, distorted view of reality. Bazin discerned two main traditions in film: montage and mise-en-scène, or the cut as opposed to the long take. It was mise-en-scène that he championed, and it was the mise-en-scène directors (Jean Renoir, William Wyler, Orson Welles, and others) whom he favored.

Although mise-en-scène was discussed in Chapter 1, it is worthwhile to review the meaning of a phrase that has now become enshrined in the vocabulary of film. It is impossible to define *mise-en-scène* as succinctly as one would a *dissolve* or a *wipe*. The French expression, which derives from the theater, is difficult to translate because it means staging a film with the same feeling for style and detail that a theater director (*metteur-en-scène*) brings to a play, in the sense that the film director "stages" the action, positions the actors within the frame, sees that they are dressed in costumes typical of the era and suited to the characters, and works with the director of photography and the production designer to create the proper visual style. Mise-en-scène is the result: the blending of all the elements of filmmaking, from acting and makeup to the composition of the shots, into a whole to produce as close an approximation of reality as possible.

Directors who work within the mise-en-scène tradition achieve a high degree of realism by shooting certain scenes in long take. In fact, some of the finest camera work in film is a result of the long take. The opening of Orson Welles's *Touch of Evil* derives its power from being an uninterrupted tracking shot. The long take was particularly evident in *The Best Years of Our Lives* (William Wyler, 1946), a 172-minute movie with 190 shots per hour; the average film has between 300 and 400 per hour. Wyler filmed several scenes without making a single cut, creating action and reaction within the same shot. Bazin justly admired the famous ending: the wedding of Wilma (Cathy O'Donnell) and Homer (Harold Russell). All of the principals are present: Al and Milly Stephenson (Fredric March and Myrna Loy); their daughter, Peggy (Teresa Wright); and Fred Derry (Dana Andrews), Homer's best man. Fred and Peggy are in love, but his inability to find a job has prevented their marriage. As Homer and Wilma exchange vows, Fred turns in the direction of Peggy, who is standing with her parents. At that moment, Wyler brings everyone into the frame. The vows seem equally applicable to Fred and Peggy; the result is

In the celebrated long take from *The Best Years of Our Lives* (1946), William Wyler brings all the principals into the frame for the wedding of Homer (Harold Russell) and Wilma (Cathy O'Donnell). *(Courtesy Samuel Goldwyn Productions)*

the illusion of a double wedding. A cut at any point during the scene would have shattered that illusion.

Another scene Bazin praised was the one in which Fred phones Peggy to terminate their relationship. Fred, Al Stephenson, and Homer are in a bar, where Homer is playing the piano. In one unbroken movement, the camera goes from the piano to the phone booth, pausing only for a quick look at Al. Another director might have used several cuts or allowed us to overhear the conversation between Fred and Peggy. The fact that Wyler did neither reinforces Bazin's thesis that Wyler did not have imitators, only disciples.

Bazin wanted film to encompass as much reality as possible, but mise-en-scène cannot produce realism by itself; it needs **deep focus,** a technique in which background and foreground are in focus at the same time. Thus, mise-en-scène and deep focus are allies. Deep focus has three other advantages for Bazin: (1) it brings spectators into closer contact with the image; (2) it is intellectually more challenging than montage, which manipulates spectators and annihilates their freedom of choice by making

Anatomy of Film

them see only what the filmmaker wants them to see (deep focus, by contrast, presents spectators with the entire image, from which they may choose to see only a part, such as the foreground); and (3) it allows for ambiguity, which is absolutely essential to works of art, whereas montage reduces a scene to one meaning (smiling face + babbling brook admits of only one interpretation).

Bazin never expressed his theory of film in a full-scale critical work, only in the form of essays and articles. Yet it is clear that he was moving toward an aesthetics of realism. Bazin was especially impressed by the neorealistic Italian films that appeared after World War II—for example, Roberto Rossellini's *Open City* (1945) and *Paisan* (1946), and Vittorio De Sica's *The Bicycle Thief* (1947). He saw these films as showing the same respect for reality that deep focus does. Neorealism and deep focus have the same purpose: to keep reality intact. In a neorealistic film, Eisensteinian montage is impossible; nothing can be added to the existing reality. The cutting must follow the script, which cannot tolerate juxtapositions.

Initially, it was film's realism that caused its adversaries to regard it as a copy of nature. To Siegfried Kracauer, film's ability to capture reality, far from being a handicap, is its greatest asset. Just as in the *Poetics* Aristotle determined the nature of art before he discussed the nature of tragedy, Kracauer began his epochal *Theory of Film* not with film itself but with its parent—photography.

Kracauer is unwilling to call photography an art for the same reason that he is unwilling to call film an art: the photographer lacks the artist's freedom to create his or her own inner vision. Both the photographer and the filmmaker are more dependent on the material world than either the painter or the poet. In art, the raw material of nature disappears; in film, it remains.

Kracauer's reluctance to elevate film to an art form inevitably follows from his belief that film is better equipped to record physical reality than any other medium. Consequently, film should stay on the surface of reality, for when it tries to penetrate the surface it becomes uncinematic. Parker Tyler challenged Kracauer's thesis by showing that film has successfully explored such themes as split personality (*Persona* [1967]) and the impossibility of certitude (*Blow-Up* [1969]) by moving from the surface into the realms of human consciousness, where the camera once feared to tread. Kracauer would probably agree with Tyler but then add, "*Persona* and *Blow-Up* are uncinematic," meaning not that they are inferior films (quite the contrary) but that they deal with a form of reality that is better suited to the novel. Kracauer's position is thoroughly classical. Each form reaches its highest stage of development when it accomplishes what no other form can.

To Kracauer, films are either cinematic or uncinematic. The more they reflect the material world, the more cinematic they are; as soon as they forsake physical reality for spiritual reality, they become less cinematic. He would therefore call the following genres uncinematic by nature: (1) the historical film, because it is an artifical reproduction of a bygone age; (2) the fantasy film, because of its otherworldliness; and (3) the literary adaptation, because in a novel or a drama the physical world is not the only one that matters—there is the inner world of the characters, which the camera has difficulty entering.

Because film evolved from photography, it shares four characteristics with this medium: (1) an affinity for unstaged reality, (2) a penchant for the fortuitous and the random, (3) a sense of endlessness, and (4) a preference for the indeterminate. A fifth characteristic is peculiar to film alone: an ability to capture the open-ended flow of life as it appears in the stream of situations and occurrences that constitute human existence. Kracauer is not saying that film must never attempt to stage reality or that it must always deal with such themes as chance encounters and unpredictable events. He means only that film favors nature in the raw and resists the artificial; thus, film balks at being made to resemble a play. As we have seen, shooting a film from the point of view of a spectator in an orchestra seat is entirely different from shooting it from the point of view of the camera eye, which can look up, down, around, over, under, and beyond what it sees. Naturally, photography favors the fortuitous; some of the most memorable pictures ever taken were the result of the photographer's being in the right place at the right time.

When Kracauer says that film has a liking for the fortuitous, he does not mean that the camera will record whatever passes in front of its lens; what he does mean is that a good many movies involve chance occurrences on streets, in the badlands of the West, on ships, in airports, railroad stations, hotel lobbies, and so forth. Film tends toward the endless because physical reality is seemingly without end; thus, in a movie a change of scene may be a change of continent. The filmmaker had to learn how to bridge vast distances by creating such transitions as the fade and the dissolve.

Film is indeterminate because physical reality is indeterminate. The juxtaposition of laughing face and flowing brook evokes the same response the world over. But what of the meal of wild strawberries and milk that Mia offers the Knight in *The Seventh Seal* (1958)? Bergman has not falsified reality by making the strawberries and milk other than what they are. The context of the scene changes the strawberries and milk from picnic food to food for a Eucharistic meal; it also changes those who eat the food into communicants. Reality's indeterminacy is one of the glories of film, in that an object can be both itself and a symbol at the same time. The strawberries and milk never cease to be what they are: a means of sustenance. The scene determines the *kind* of sustenance: spiritual as well as physical.

Toward the end of *Theory of Film*, Kracauer distills the essence of his thesis into a myth. It is not an original myth but the old one of Perseus and Medusa's head. Because the sight of Medusa's head turned men to stone, Athena warned Perseus not to look directly at it but only at the reflection on his shield:

> Now of all the existing media the cinema alone holds up a mirror to nature. Hence our dependence on it for the reflection of happenings which would petrify us were we to encounter them in real life. The film screen is Athena's polished shield.[5]

Hence the complete title of Kracauer's book: *Theory of Film: The Redemption of Physical Reality*. Kracauer does not believe that film deals only with nature in the raw as opposed to nature transfigured. Nature in the raw, of course, is film's starting point, as it must be; for nature in the raw—physical reality—is to film what language in the raw—words—is to literature: the means by which the work comes into being. Yet how does film redeem physical reality? The very fact that Kracauer speaks of holding a mirror up to nature, a polished mirror at that, provides the answer. A polished mirror will not catch a reflection of the physical universe as it is but as something better than it is; it catches a higher form of reality, one that is no less real than what we see around us but is superior to it. How can art imitate nature and improve it? Aristotle never tells us. How can film mirror reality and redeem it? Kracauer never tells us. For the answer, we must examine the works of artists who knew the secret of working within the material universe without becoming mired in it.

The Auteurists

It was in the late 1950s that the cult of the director arose, resulting in a spate of books on great and not so great auteurs. Presently, there is a book, a section of a book, an encyclopedia entry, or a monograph on every director who has made some contribution to the art of film, even if it was only directing a Republic western with verve and style, as Joe Kane did. That contribution might be revolutionary, as in the case of D. W. Griffith, or minor, as in the case of Edgar G. Ulmer. Yet if there can be critical studies of minor authors, there can be critical studies of minor directors. Minor does not mean mediocre; one's influence on a particular art form may not be pervasive, but it can nonetheless be noteworthy.

As we saw in Chapter 6, auteurism is merely *one* way of looking at film. It enables those who need a "handle," so to speak, on film to have one. Certainly it is much simpler to deal with a work of known than unknown authorship; among other things, it affords a sense of control and security. Even though it is common knowledge that Shakespeare wrote *Hamlet* and Dickens wrote *Great Expectations*, we still speak of "Shakespeare's *Hamlet*" and "Dickens's *Great Expectations*." To be able to say "Hitchcock's *Psycho*" means we can approach *Psycho* in the same way we might approach *Hamlet*; just as a literary scholar can discuss *Hamlet* within the broader context of Shakespeare's plays, we can approach *Psycho* within the context of Hitchcock's work instead of viewing it merely as a horror film or as the prototype of the modern slasher film.

There are, of course, drawbacks to auteurism. The auteurist approach cannot be applied unilaterally. It would be something of a joke to write, "Edward Bernds's *The Bowery Boys Meet the Monsters* (1954)," although confirmed auteurists would think nothing of it. Whatever one may think of Edward Bernds (a competent director) or the film, such a designation is bound to strike nonauteurists as laughable.

Auteurists can teach us something about the way directors repeat compositions, framings, and certain types of shots. Frank Capra's love of bells, which ranges from the tolling bells in *Lost Horizon* (1937) to the bell on the Christmas tree in *It's a Wonderful Life* (1946), led to his using the bell as the logo of his short-lived production company, Liberty Films. No doubt Capra associated bells with the spirit of freedom and a feeling of joy. Hitchcock's high shots, or God's eye shots, may be a vestige of his Roman Catholicism or merely an attempt to suggest an unseen, omnipotent presence peering down at the world. At any rate, the high shot is a favorite Hitchcockian device, as is irising in D. W. Griffith, double framing in John Ford, long takes in Orson Welles and William Wyler, and a claustrophobic atmosphere in Edgar G. Ulmer. If writers in the auteurist tradition can deepen our understanding of a director's style, they have served film well. However, auteurism can be considered only as a way of approaching film, specifically of approaching the films of selected directors.

The Mythographers

Parker Tyler was the first film critic to understand how mythic the movies are. In *The Hollywood Hallucination*, Tyler explained the extraordinary appeal of stars like Greta Garbo and Marlene Dietrich: they were mystery women, phantom ladies, moon goddesses like Diana. Their inaccessibility made them more desirable than they really were. If they ever loved a man, they could love him only in myth, where they would never have to yield. Even if a man broke down their resistance, we could never believe these goddesses could offer him anything more than fairy-tale love.

To Tyler, even Mickey Mouse cartoons had mythic underpinnings. Intelligent moviegoers watch an animated mouse without feeling that their intelligence has been insulted because they instinctively recognize some myth, some universal pattern of experience, behind the cartoon. Tyler identified it as the Frankenstein myth, which is based on an even older myth of the artist who creates a human being out of inert matter (e.g., Prometheus, who molded man from earth; Pygmalion, who carved Galatea out of marble). We understand intuitively that Mickey Mouse is someone's creation. Tyler cited other similarities between Mickey Mouse and the Frankenstein monster: both are mechanized beings; both are factory products (Mickey, the product of the Disney factory; the monster, of Frankenstein's laboratory); both obey their masters. There is also a difference between them: in *Frankenstein*, the monster turns on his maker, but Mickey always remains an amiable mouse.

We identify with the underdogs in animated cartoons because they have the same problems we have. We forget that they are ducks, mice, or pigs and think of them as humans, running the same obstacle course as ourselves and encountering the same frustrations. Yet, Tyler asks, is it not the same situation in gangster films? Don't we empathize with the Little Caesars, the Dillingers, the Bonnies and Clydes? Many moviegoers find gangsters sympathetic for various reasons: they are nonconformists who flaunt morality; their lives are colorful; they are upwardly mobile, often beginning at the bottom with petty crime and moving up the ladder of notoriety to bank heists and bloodbaths. Hollywood tends to humanize its gangsters, and to Tyler humanization equals glorification. Interestingly, Tyler made no distinction between Superman and the gangster. Who gave Superman the right to take the law into his own hands? He is only a newspaper reporter, not a police officer. Yet we look the other way when Clark Kent ducks into a phone booth and emerges as Superman; or, rather, our unconscious looks the other way as a reporter becomes a disrupter of the normal order.

In *Magic and Myth of the Movies*, Tyler continued to explore the ways in which the unconscious sees films and to show how we accept certain actions in a movie that we would not tolerate in real life. Physical pain is never humorous, yet we laugh when comics slip on banana peels or get pies thrown in their faces. We do not laugh because we are sadistic; the comics give us the right to laugh by becoming scapegoats for our sake and suffering indignities on our behalf. It is the same with comics who distort their faces and mock themselves: they laugh at themselves first so that we can laugh with them. Yet if we read their actions correctly, the rubber-faced clowns are really asking for our approval, our love. They humiliate themselves in order to win our applause.

Tyler saw the stars of the 1930s and 1940s as gods and goddesses. Because the screen made them immortal, they could not die; they underwent only a ritual death, like the vegetation deities who die in winter and are resurrected in spring. A star can never really die, because divinity makes death impossible. The almost universal interest in films of the past supports Tyler's thesis. Humphrey Bogart will live as long as his films are shown, and there is little likelihood that the world will call a moratorium on movies. To see Bogart in *Casablanca* is to see a man in his prime, not a man who died of cancer in 1957. In *The Happy Ending* (1969), the heroine's husband accuses her of mooning over *Casablanca* whenever it is on television. When he reminds her that practically the entire cast is dead, she replies that Humphrey Bogart, Peter Lorre, Sidney Greenstreet, and Claude Rains are more alive than either of them.

The Semioticians

Semiotics emphasizes the way a film transmits its meaning through signs and codes.[6] Its approach is similar to that of the myth critics, who search out universal patterns and archetypal themes. Semiotics is also the theoretical side of structuralism, which is not so much a new discipline as a new approach to older disciplines such as linguistics, anthropology, psychoanalysis, and rhetoric, disciplines that are more concerned with signs than with objects. Thus structuralists are invariably attracted to myth because myths are the first structures, the first messages of a culture.

But myths are coded; they are invisible patterns, "offstage voices," as French literary critic Roland Barthes might call them. The structuralist tries to bring the voice from the wings to center stage. Myths remain coded until they become transparent; then society discards them as clichés. The reason myths were such unifying forces in ancient societies is that they resisted decoding. Frequently they appeared in binary form, reflecting the dualism inherent in nature (spirit/matter, male/female, life/death) and in culture (urban/rural, endogamy/exogamy, freedom/imprisonment). The great myths are inexhaustibly bipolar; they resist any attempt to reduce them to a single meaning. Oppositeness is at the heart of Greek mythology, which is one reason it is constantly being reinterpreted. The Oedipus myth, for example, embodies the polarities knowledge/ignorance, wife/mother, old order/new order, rationalism/mysticism, sight/blindness. Myths such as this are deathless because they are founded on natural, not artificial, opposites.

It is understandable that semiotics would be in such vogue today. Semiotics is studied in universities and in adult-education centers, where Semiotics for the Layperson teaches students how to translate the signs they encounter in daily life: the TV commercials that promise a world in which young and old, white and black will stand together if they drink Pepsi or chew Juicy Fruit gum; the clothing ads that build sexual potency into their products; the body language that is spoken at parties but not always understood.

In his collection of essays, *Mythologies* (1972), Roland Barthes sees signs everywhere. A person's hairstyle can designate the class and era to which he or she belongs. In Joseph L. Mankiewicz's *Julius Caesar* (1953), the fringed hair of the characters was a sign of their "Roman-ness." Wrestling abounds in signs. The wrestler with the fleshy, sagging body telegraphs certain messages to the spectator: repulsiveness, cruelty, cowardice. The wrestler's body determines the way he acts in the ring. The conventions of wrestling (the armlock, the twisting of the leg) are all parodies of tragedy. Just as the mask of tragedy is an exaggeration of the human face, so, too, is wrestling an exaggeration of human suffering. The opponent who lies flat on his back with his arms outstretched has been crucified. In wrestling, defeat reaches the nadir of humiliation—crucifixion.

Even our detergents speak to us, according to Barthes. Chlorinated detergents proclaim they are absolute; as liquid fire, they blaze a path through the dirt and annihilate it. Powdered detergents are more selective; they liberate the dirt. Foam detergents, on the other hand, are useless; they are luxury items, airy and immaterial, as impractical as bubble bath.

If detergents talk, so does food. Fish-and-chips speaks of nostalgia, of the British bearing up under the Blitz; steak speaks of virility and, if it is served rare and swimming in blood, of an ambrosia that produces godlike strength. (In Jacques Tourneur's *Experiment Perilous* [1944], a woman on a train orders steak for a male passenger because she assumes that steak is a "man's" dish.)

On the surface, semiotics seems rather easy to understand. There is a signifier (say, a gold band) and the signified (marriage); there is **denotation,** by which a word keeps its literal meanings ("He lit the *fire*"), and **connotation,** by which it takes on other meanings ("He was consumed by the *fire* of passion"); there is *langue*, a language system that can be verbal (English, German, and so on) or nonverbal (the "language" of poker, falconry, and so on), and there is *parole* (speech), the actual practice of a language system.

The problems begin when one attempts to apply this terminology to film. In film, what are the signifiers? Can a movie denote and connote, or in film does denotation become connotation? There is also the haunting question: Is film a language system? To Christian Metz, the best known of the film semioticians, film is not *langue*.[7] In language, a word can acquire a different meaning merely by the addition of a single letter—for example, *d* or *r* added to *love*. But film has no words. Metz rightly rejects the shot-as-word theory and compares the shot to the sentence. Like a gifted child, film skipped the parts of speech and moved to a higher grade. But if film has no parts of speech, then it has no grammar. We know that "He see the man" is ungrammatical in standard English; but what is ungrammatical in a movie? Using a dissolve instead of a cut?

Another difference is that in words there is a distance between the signifier and signified. *Sadness* can be broken up into its signifier (the sound *sad-nes*) and its signified (the concept of unhappiness). But in film the signified cannot be disengaged from the signifier. In a movie, sadness is not *sad-nes* but a child weeping, a man wailing, an American secretary sitting alone in an outdoor café in Venice while couples stroll past her. In a movie, sadness is not a concept but an actual situation (a sad family) or an attribute of a specific person (a sad man). For the same reason, denotation and connotation are not distinct in film. A movie denotes and connotes at the same time. When Isak Borg raises a glass of wine in Bergman's *Wild Strawberries*, he is Isak Borg who at that moment is having lunch with his daughter-in-law and some young hitchhikers; he is also Isak Borg the priest figure, officiating at a communion service and elevating not a wineglass but a chalice.

Metz claims that film is "like" language because it communicates. But how does it communicate? In two ways: syntagmatically and paradigmatically. A **syntagma** is a unit of actual relationship; thus **syntagmatic relationships** result when the units of a statement or the units in a filmic chain follow each other in order. If we analyze the way the subplots of *Nashville* interconnect or trace the rise of a character such as Mildred Pierce from housewife to restaurant owner, we are approaching the film syntagmatically.

A **paradigm** is a unit of potential relationship; thus **paradigmatic relationships** are associative, not sequential. They are not concerned with the order of the links in the chain but with the meanings we associate with them. If we associate Frank Serpico with Jesus Christ or the madness that erupted at the Hollywood premiere in *The Day of the Locust* with the outbreak of World War II, we are approaching the film paradigmatically. Because paradigmatic relationships are independent of the order in which the events occur, they can also exist between scenes taking place at different times within the film. Shane's ride of vengeance at the end of George Stevens's film of the same name should, by its horizontal movement, recall the first appearance of Wilson the gunfighter, who also rode horizontally across the frame; yet it also contrasts with the way Shane rode down into the valley at the beginning of the film. If we associate descent with something positive (the desire to reform) and horizontal movement with something negative (the desire to murder), then we have made a paradigmatic connection.

It is not enough for the semiotician simply to isolate syntagmas and paradigms; the movie relays its messages through codes that the filmmaker used and that the semiotician must now reconstruct. There are all kinds of codes: codes of dress, color, lighting, and so forth. In certain simplistic westerns, we may discover that white and black attire mean hero and villain, respectively; in other westerns, the dress code will yield to a landscape code, in which the signifier (Monument Valley) becomes the signified (America in microcosm).

Transportation codes are particularly meaningful in discovering a filmmaker's intentions. Karel Reisz saw the car as a vehicle charged with associations of death in *Isadora* (1969); in *Two for the Road*, the particular car in which the couple is traveling is related to a particular stage in their marriage. In *The Wild One* (1954), the motorcycle is the embodiment of raw virility, fascism, and arrested sexuality; but in *Easy Rider* (1969), the motorcycle epitomizes young, disenchanted America in the late 1960s. The yuppies of the 1980s, however, do not travel by motorcycle; they go cross-country in a motor home in *Lost in America* (1985), in which *Easy Rider* is mentioned so reverentially that the idealistic sixties becomes the yardstick by which to measure the materialistic eighties.

Cigarettes in the movies of the 1930s and 1940s were the epitome of cool and sophistication: Humphrey Bogart in a trench coat and a fedora, speaking with a cigarette between his lips; Bette Davis, brandishing her cigarette as if it were a scepter. The sight of so many stars smoking, which made cigarettes an essential part of one's wardrobe, influenced countless moviegoers to take up the habit.

His Girl Friday is one of the few films in which the cigarette is not just an accessory but a sign of belonging to a special group. The film is a reworking of the famous stage play *The Front Page*, in which a newspaper editor, Walter Burns, resorts to all kinds of devious tactics to keep his star reporter, Hildy Johnson, from getting married. For *His Girl Friday*, Howard Hawks turned Hildy, a male in the play, into a woman (played by Rosalind Russell) with the same name. Although Hawks's Hildy insists that she wants to give up the newspaper business and marry an insurance sales-man, Walter knows otherwise. There are many ways in which Hawks makes it clear that Hildy belongs in Walter's world; her striped suits, for example, which make her look more like a "newspaper man" (which is what she calls herself) than a female journalist. But cigarettes are another sign of belonging. When Walter, Hildy, and Hildy's fiancé, Bruce, are at a restaurant, Hildy and Walter keep blowing their cigarette smoke in his face, making him distinctly uncomfortable. When Hildy interviews a pris-oner, she offers him a cigarette, which the prisoner declines. The prisoner does not belong to the newspaper world, in which the cigarette is almost like a badge or a press card.

Sometimes codes are not quite so easy to decipher. Whenever Mar-lene Dietrich wore a tuxedo in a movie, as she did in *Morocco* and *Blonde Venus*, both directed by Josef von Sternberg, 1930s audiences were taken aback at the sight of such a sensuous woman in men's clothes. A dress code was operating, but what did it mean? In *Morocco*, it meant that a strange

Marlene Dietrich looking androgynous in *Blonde Venus* (1932). *(Copyright © Paramount Pictures. Courtesy MCA Publishing Rights, a Division of MCA, Inc.)*

form of defeminization had taken place by which Dietrich had become the essence of Hollywood Woman (seductive, smoldering) decked out with the trappings of Hollywood Man (debonair, aggressive). Thus the Dietrich figure in a tuxedo became androgynous.

Critics who are influenced by semiotics use a specialized vocabulary. For example, they do not think of film narrative solely in terms of plot. They distinguish between plot, diegesis, and discourse. The **plot,** or what Aristotle in the *Poetics* called the *mythos,* is the ordered arrangement of the incidents in terms of a beginning, a middle, and an end. The **diegesis** is the story that is recounted, embodying everything that pertains to it regardless of how much of it actually appears on the screen. The party in *Notorious* is an all-evening affair, but on the screen it lasts only ten minutes. Thus there is a difference between diegetic time (all evening) and film time (ten minutes). The **discourse** is the manner in which the story reaches the audience. That story includes what is dramatized as well as what is implied; it is based on a script that is brought to the screen by a team that has broken the action down into various codes (color codes, dress codes, lighting codes, codes of manners); it is the result of the interaction between an "I" and a "you," between the one telling the story (the filmmaker) and the one perceiving it (the filmgoer); it is the result of decisions made before, during, and after production. Thus the main title and the end credits would be very much a part of the film's discourse; a credits sequence, which is visualized action, is part of the plot (the film's structure) and diegesis (the film's world).

While semioticians have shown how complex film narrative is, one should remember that it is perfectly possible to write good film criticism without resorting to critical jargon. If it is understood properly, Aristotle's concept of plot is as applicable to film narrative as it is to literary narrative. "Plot is the structure of events," Aristotle wrote. Note that he does not call the plot the story line, as many would, but the *shape* of the story line and the *form* it takes. To Aristotle, the plot is the soul of the work—the source of its life. Remove the plot from a work of fiction and it ceases to be a work of fiction; remove it from a narrative film and it ceases to be a narrative film. Soul is structure; it is the harmony that exists when all the parts work together. Once plot is understood as the nucleus around which the incidents, the characters, the theme, and the setting gather, and the source from which they draw their life, it can then be perceived as the soul of the work and as something quite distinct from the story line, which is a bodily part.

Semiotics is to film what linguistics is to literature. A knowledge of linguistics can be helpful in reading dialect literature or in interpreting poetry, since poets coin new words and use old ones in startlingly new ways. However, literature can be analyzed quite successfully without the terminology of linguistics. Similarly, semiotics can enhance our perception of a film by disclosing the way signs and codes operate in it, yet film can be discussed intelligently without resorting to the vocabulary of semiotics.

Feminist Criticism

Feminist film criticism, whose practitioners include Laura Mulvey, Julia LeSage, Annette Kuhn, and E. Ann Kaplan, is indebted to the work of the French psychologist Jacques Lacan, particularly his theory of the mirror stage of development. Briefly stated, the image a child sees reflected in a mirror produces ambivalent feelings. The child is attracted to the image because it is an ideal image but is repelled by it, too, because the real can never be the ideal; the ideal is *other than* real. The Hollywood studio system, a male-created and male-dominated industry, seems never to have gone beyond the mirror stage, according to radical feminists. In the classic Hollywood film, the separation of real and ideal made woman other, an object rather than a subject. Specifically, the woman was an object of the male gaze; she was an exhibit or a spectacle rendered in terms of anatomy (bosom, legs, mouth, posterior) and fractured representation (close-ups, extreme close-ups). The idealization of woman (soft focus, front lighting, lenses smeared with Vaseline or covered with gauze to give the face a glow) originated in the fear of castration. It was as if the male had unconsciously struck a bargain with the female: if she would not deprive him of his potency, he would glorify her image. In this way, the universe would remain phallocentric, dominated by the symbol of male potency, the phallus, which, according to Lacan, is a signifier. The phallus represents male power as well as male presence, as opposed to female helplessness and female absence. Since the female lacks the organ on which the signifier depends, she denotes absence—the absence of power, authority, and speech. Speech is phallocentric, the prerogative of the male; speechlessness is the state of the female. Thus, even when women speak, they are passive; it might be more accurate to use the passive voice.

Although the woman's film of the 1930s and 1940s placed women at the center of the action, feminists would still argue that, despite the woman's pivotal role, it is the male who sets the plot in motion. *Dark Victory*, a key woman's film, is ostensibly the story of Judith Traherne's acceptance of death from brain cancer. After Dr. Steele, a neurosurgeon, diagnoses Judith's condition, she reluctantly submits to surgery. Later she falls in love with Steele, who cannot bear to tell her that the operation was unsuccessful and her condition is terminal. Judith learns the truth by accidentally coming upon her medical record. Embittered, she turns on Steele, indulges in self-pity and drink, but finally returns to him, begging his forgiveness. Forgiveness for what, one might ask? She is the one who is going to die, not he. Judith even goes to his apartment and admits that she has been a "fool." That visit, however, results in her marriage to Steele, without which the plot cannot be resolved. Judith knows that blindness will precede death. When her eyesight suddenly fails, she does not tell Steele, who must depart for an important medical meeting, but manages to help him pack while continuing to behave normally. The ending of *Dark Victory* would have been impossible without the character of Steele, for it is Judith's marriage to him that gives her the courage to face not just death but death alone.

Like all theories, phallocentrism and the mirror stage cannot be proved scientifically. As a result, they may strike one as either probable or bizarre. One can also argue that women were depicted as goddesses endowed with an aura denied to men because Hollywood believed that attractive women were "good box office." Women liked seeing themselves on the screen, and men liked seeing women on the screen. When moviegoers of both sexes were happy, the studios thrived.

Still, Hollywood's ambivalence toward women cannot be ignored. As Laura Mulvey states in her seminal article, "Visual Pleasure and Narrative Cinema," "woman . . . stands in patriarchal culture as signifier of the male other."[8] Mulvey goes on to argue that the male, trained to avoid gazing at himself (thereby becoming an object), instead makes the female the object of the gaze—the male gaze. Mulvey obviously does not mean that men avoid mirrors or refrain from checking their appearance in them. Her thesis is that the male is expected to be a doer (subject), not a receiver; thus he relegates the receiving or passive role to the female (object). In terms of moviemaking, such transference leaves the male free to control the action, allowing him to become more complete than the gazed-upon female. The screen then replaces the mirror, and just as the ideal ego is conceived in a moment of recognition in front of the mirror, the feminine ideal is conceived on the mirror-screen. However, it is an ideal created by a male, who looked into that mirror and saw not himself but woman and rendered her in accordance with his image. As far as movies are concerned, God may have created the world but it was man who created woman.

When woman is the object of the male gaze, she is given the full treatment; she is exquisitely gowned and impeccably coiffured. Her face is bathed in a light that cleanses it of imperfections. A close-up transforms her image into a portrait. Woman as movie star is Other as Ideal, and the ideal should be idealized. However, other is also not-I, and in a phallocentric world what is not-I is not male. As not-male, woman is often relegated to a subordinate position in the frame. In westerns, she is frequently behind the hero, serving him or standing in the background looking terrified as he takes on the villain. When the hero rides off at the end, she becomes a part of the landscape in the extreme long shot that concludes the film.

Like any theory, Mulvey's is difficult to prove. Men will say they are as concerned with their image as women are, adding that they express this in a different way: shaving, combing their hair, tightening the knot on their tie. Mulvey, however, isn't talking about good grooming but about that stage known as the "mirror-moment" and its manifestation in film. In a typical Hollywood movie, it is generally the male who controls the narrative. In *Vertigo*, the narrative is controlled by Scottie; we see what he sees, and once he makes Judy over into Madeleine we see what he wants to see. It is as if Judy's point of view—or, for that matter, the real Madeleine's—does not exist; or, if it does, it is not worth considering. The real Madeleine isn't even a character; the only time we ever catch a glimpse of her—fleetingly, at that—is when Elster throws her corpse from the bell tower.

Since Hollywood has traditionally been a patriarchy, with comparatively few women ever reaching the executive suite, feminists have wondered if women might have been portrayed differently in the woman's film if the directors—and, ideally, the writers as well—had been female. There have been male directors (for example, George Cukor, Edmund Goulding, Irving Rapper) who were known as "woman's directors" because of their ability to make movies with which female audiences could identify. Cukor's *Camille* (1937), Goulding's *Dark Victory*, and Rapper's *Now, Voyager* may be classics, yet they perpetuate the image of woman as sufferer—a saintly creature who must tolerate abuse, place her lover's happiness before her own, and die nobly when her time comes. We will never know what, if anything, a female director would have done with *Dark Victory*—a death and transfiguration script, in which the protagonist is required to go through a cycle of self-pity and drink before she can accept her terminal illness, after which she has the strength to die alone.

Like *Dark Victory*, *Autumn in New York* (2000) also features a young woman (Winona Ryder) facing terminal illness. Yet anyone looking for a distinctly feminine sensibility in *Autumn*, directed by Joan Chen, that would make it different from *Dark Victory* would be hard-pressed to find it. If Edmund Goulding had the reputation of being a woman's director, it was because he could project that sensibility (the feminine side of himself, perhaps) into the material. *Thelma and Louise* is considered a feminist film; the script was written by a woman, Cali Koury, but directed by a man, Ridley Scott, who also directed one of the most "masculinist" movies ever made, *Gladiator* (2000). Likewise, Penny Marshall showed great compassion for male adolescents (and adolescent males) in *Big* (1988). She showed the same compassion for women in *A League of Their Own* (1992), not only treating each of the women on the baseball team as an individual but also portraying the main male character, an alcoholic ex-ball player (Tom Hanks) as a failure worthy of sympathy rather than contempt. Amy Heckerling has a knack for depicting adolescents of both sexes sympathetically in such films as *Fast Times at Ridgemont High* (1982) and *Clueless* (discussed in Chapter 7). In Gillian Armstrong's remake of *Little Women* (1994), Marmee and her daughters look and act as if they can survive a father's absence. On the other hand, *Julia*, one of the best films ever made about friendship between women, was directed by a man who was also responsible for *The Men* (1950) and *High Noon* (1952): Fred Zinnemann. In *Julia*, Lily (Jane Fonda) and Julia (Vanessa Redgrave) are depicted as women in control of their lives and also of their narrative.

The best one can do is look at two film versions of the same source—one directed by a woman, the other by a man—and try to reach some conclusions. George Kelly's Pulitzer Prize–winning play, *Craig's Wife*, was filmed twice—in 1936 and 1950. The title character is Harriet Craig, whose obsession with making her home into a spotless but lifeless showpiece, alienates everyone around her, including her husband, Walter, who finally leaves her. The play proved enormously popular with women, many of whom sympathized with Harriet, whose need for security began when

John Boles and Rosalind Russell as the Craigs in the first version of George Kelly's play *Craig's Wife* (1936), directed by Dorothy Arzner. *(Courtesy MOMA/FSA)*

her father walked out on his family, leaving Harriet's mother with a mortgage and two daughters to support.

The play's title remained the same in the first version, *Craig's Wife* (1936), directed by Dorothy Arzner, who was known in the industry as a "woman picture director" because the idea of a woman behind the camera was unusual, even though there had been several others before her. The script was also written by a woman, Mary McCall, Jr. The result was a sympathetic portrait of a woman so determined to avoid her mother's fate that she experiences a similar one—the difference being that Harriet was left with a house without a mortgage. McCall structured the screenplay so that the other characters left the house in pairs, until Harriet was completely alone. Rosalind Russell played Harriet in such a way that one pitied rather than despised her, particularly at the end, when, deserted by everyone, she learns of her sister's death.

Although the second version, *Harriet Craig* (1950), took considerable liberties with Kelly's play, the basic theme—a woman's valuing her house over her husband—remained the same. In this version, the director was a male, Vincent Sherman, who specialized in melodrama; the star was Joan Crawford, who excelled at playing tough-minded women; and the script was by Ann Froelich and James Gunn. Froelich, whose sympathy for socialism was well known in Hollywood, could hardly be expected to be sympathetic to Harriet, who represented the worse features of capitalism. Even if the writers wanted to humanize Harriet, they would have had to contend with Crawford's persona: the tough-as-nails woman who fought her way to the top and had every intention of staying there. Crawford's Harriet interferes with her cousin's marital plans, almost manages to convince Walter's boss that her husband is too irresponsible to be sent to Japan (where she could not accompany him), and coldly rejects her next-

The Craigs again: Wendell Corey and Joan Crawford, sporting a severe hairdo and manacle-like bracelets, in the remake, *Harriet Craig* (1950), directed by Vincent Sherman. *(Courtesy MOMA/FSA)*

door neighbor's offer of friendship even after everyone has left her. Harriet gets what she deserves: an empty house. With a script that made it difficult to empathize with Harriet, and a star like Crawford, who made it impossible, no director, male or female, could have won an audience over to Harriet's side. Even if Arzner, who left the industry in 1943, had been coaxed into directing *Harriet Craig*, she could never have accomplished what she did in *Craig's Wife*, where she had the benefit of McCall's script and Russell's subtle acting.

One can only conclude that the script, the subject matter, the actors, and, especially, the director's vision of the material determine how the sexes are portrayed on the screen. The acid test would be to make males, instead of females, the object of the gaze in slasher and exploitation films, directed by both women and men.

Ideological Criticism

This kind of criticism is not quite so simple as interpreting a film as a reflection of the filmmaker's ideology in the sense of a belief system, political or economic, that the filmmaker has embraced and that may be detected in his or her work. If you know that Italian director Gillo Pontecorvo is a committed communist, you might want to approach his *La Grande Strada Azzurra* (*The Wide Blue Sea* [1957]) in terms of his view of capitalism as a dehumanizing force that exploits the masses and creates an underclass whose members might have to break laws in order to survive. While Pontecorvo's radicalism is very much in evidence in the film, it is only one aspect of his art.

The Hollywood product is not quite so radical; still, it is true that many Hollywood movies either have a political subtext or even a political philosophy. Films that glorify empire builders (*Pittsburgh* [1942], *An*

American Dream [1944], self-made Americans (*East of Eden* [1954], *Lucy Gallant* [1955], *Giant* [1956]), pioneers (most American westerns), and rugged individualists (*The Fountainhead* [1949]) are clearly pro-capitalist. Leo McCarey's *My Son John* (1952) is blatantly anticommunist, reflecting the director's own loathing of communism as an insidious force that seduces American intellectuals like the title character.

Other films are more difficult to pigeonhole. Billy Wilder's *The Apartment* is certainly not anticapitalist, although it deals with the way senior executives exploit those under them—a situation that can exist in any profession or in any society. Joseph L. Mankiewicz's *No Way Out* (1950), one of the first films to deal openly with racism in America, is the work of a liberal but not a left-wing filmmaker. Spielberg's *Schindler's List* is anti-fascist, but not left wing. *Reds* (1981), Warren Beatty's three-hour epic about the American communist writer John Reed set against the background of the Russian Revolution, is a sympathetic account of American radicalism but takes a dim view of the Soviet brand of communism. Although you cannot ignore ideology in a film, it would be a mistake to base an entire discussion on it. If you find yourself spending more time writing about ideology than structure, either the film is a political tract, and if so, is propaganda; or you have become so caught up in the filmmaker's ideology that you are ignoring its narrative form.

Analyzing a film in terms of the film's or the filmmaker's politics is only one kind of ideological criticism. Included in the same edition of *Film Theory and Criticism* in which Laura Mulvey's article appeared (see n. 8) is Robin Wood's "Ideology, Genre, Auteur" (668–78), which shows just how complex this kind of criticism can be. Capra's *It's a Wonderful Life* (1946) and Hitchcock's *Shadow of a Doubt* (1943) are two of the most respected films in American cinema. On the surface, they appear to be anything but ideological. *It's a Wonderful Life* seems to be about an archetypal American town, Bedford Falls. Yet there are three communities portrayed in the film: Bailey Park, named after the family that founded the building and loan company where the needy find help because the Baileys believe in people helping people; nearby Pottersville, home of the ogre-like Potter, who wants to get all of Bedford Falls under his control, which he can only do if there were no building and loan company; and Bedford Falls as it might have been if Potter had had his way, as George Bailey (James Stewart) learns when he attempts suicide and is rescued by the angel Clarence (Henry Travers), who shows George what the town would have been like if he had never been born. Bedford Falls would have looked like a film noir set, where harsh lighting exposes everyone's dark side, which is all that is left in the absence of charity and love. This is the Bedford Falls that Potter would have created, a testimonial to his inhumanity. *It's a Wonderful Life* is no valentine to America, despite its frequent appearance on television at Christmastime. It suggests there is the America to which we should aspire, which is Bedford Falls in macrocosm, as opposed to the America that would have resulted if the Potters of the land had refashioned it in their own image.

Wood also reminds us that there are three distinct worlds in *Shadow of a Doubt*, even though the film is a study in doubles, one of Hitchcock's favorite themes. The chief doubles (they are ubiquitous in the film) are an uncle and his niece, who share the same name, Charlie. Uncle Charlie (Joseph Cotten) is a serial killer who preys on wealthy widows; Little Charlie (Teresa Wright) is the one who discovers his criminal past. At the beginning of the film, Uncle Charlie is hiding out in a seedy boardinghouse in a Philadelphia slum. To avoid suspicion, he pays a visit to his unsuspecting sister and her family in Santa Rosa, California. Like Bedford Falls, Santa Rosa seems to be idyllic; like Uncle Charlie, it also has its dark side, which is seen in the Til Two sequence. Realizing his niece has discovered his identity as the "Merry Widow murderer," Uncle Charlie induces her to go into a bar, the Til Two, with him. Til Two is straight out of film noir—dimly lit and sleazily seductive. A waitress, sluggish and zombielike, saunters into view; one of Little Charlie's former classmates, the waitress is shocked to find her in a dive. Is Hitchcock suggesting that the Til Two would have become the norm in Santa Rosa if Uncle Charlie had stayed on, infecting the community with his nihilism? Is Uncle Charlie, who believes "the world's a hell," representative of the Nazis who were making the world a hell in 1943 when *Shadow of a Doubt* was released and who, if they had triumphed, would have reduced it to a film noir nightmare? Although Hitchcock was not a political filmmaker, he always believed that nothing is what it seems to be, including people and countries. America is many things; it is like Henry Jekyll's house in Stevenson's *Dr. Jekyll and Mr. Hyde*, which has a back door that leads to a totally different world.

Approaching a film through the filmmaker's politics is easy. More difficult is finding and resolving the ideological tension that drives the film and gives it a complexity that defies political labels.

Reception Theory

How does an audience "receive" a film in the sense of responding to it? This is the question that practitioners of reception theory, such as Janet Staiger, Timothy Corrigan, and Miriam Hansen, have attempted to answer. According to Janet Staiger's *Perverse Spectators: The Practices of Film Reception*, reception is a complex matter, since the way one reacts to a film or interprets it depends upon a number of factors, including:

1. **Type of film** (action-driven, plot-driven, Hollywood product, international film with subtitles, beginning-middle-end narrative with

closure, open-ended narrative that leaves the viewer with questions about the outcome of the plot or the fate of the characters).

2. **Mode of exhibition** (theater, classroom, tape, DVD, network television, cable television).

3. **The nature of the viewer** (knowledgeable and cooperative/uncritical and indifferent/attentive and quiet/unruly and talkative).

4. **The makeup of the audience** (racially homogeneous/racially heterogeneous—for example, a predominantly black audience with a few whites in attendance at a movie about African American life; a predominantly white audience with a few blacks in attendance at a movie featuring practically no African Americans at all; in general, being a minority member at a movie aimed at a majority, or vice versa).

5. **Level of identification** (the extent to which the audience cannot only differentiate between the characters and their relationship to each other and to the plot but the extent to which they can see themselves or others in these characters).

6. **Ideological perspective** (a feminist at a male-oriented movie where women are demeaned or treated as sex objects; a socialist at a film that extols capitalism/a capitalist at a movie that is sympathetic to left-wing causes; a politically homogeneous audience at a movie that is completely in tune with their beliefs).

7. **Aesthetic considerations** (audiences sensitive to mise-en-scène, appreciative of the artful use of lighting and color and able to see how these elements function in the film, even if the narrative is murky or confused; audiences familiar with the work of a particular director who can see stylistic traces or thematic repetition in the director's latest film; moviegoers who consider a film's technique to be more important than the plot).

8. **Marketing strategies** (newspaper ads, radio and television commercials, and trailers), which can affect audience response positively if there is a correlation between the strategy and the kind of film that the audience has been led to expect; or negatively, if there is none, and the audience feels cheated. Although *Jaws* was an excellent example of commercial moviemaking, it profited from a provocative ad with very little text: "The horrifying motion picture from the terrifying No. 1 best seller" preceded the title, JAWS, followed by "She was the first." Then the image: the "she" was a female swimmer, perhaps even nude, beneath whom lurked a shark with jagged teeth, its beady eyes raised upward as if at the swimmer. The ad promised sex (little) and scares (many) within a PG format. The box office receipts suggested that few, if any, viewers were disappointed.

If *Me, Myself and Irene*, one of the summer of 2000's contributions to gross-out comedy, proved less profitable than *There's Something about Mary*, the answer might be the wholesomely dopey picture of Jim Carrey in the ad, which implied another *Ace Ventura: When Nature Calls* (1995) or maybe an R-rated *Truman Show*.

As movie audiences grow increasingly more diverse, there is little likelihood that there will ever be an all-embracing theory of film reception, only more studies, both sociological and psychological, on spectator response. As Janet Staiger has astutely observed, there is, in addition to the knowledgeable and cooperative spectator, the "perverse spectator," who does the unexpected and is not influenced by hierarchies or criteria created by academics (and who may actually believe a farce is more of a "movie" than a drawing-room comedy); far from identifying with the hero, the perverse spectator reassembles—or maybe reshoots—the film in his or her imagination, making the villain the real protagonist. Such spectators may be experiencing film on a much deeper level than the knowledgeable elites.

The Reviewers

A film reviewer is not necessarily a film critic; few reviewers can be considered critics if by critic we mean a representative of the most insightful approach possible. If Alexander Pope's standards are applied to contemporary reviewers, only a handful would qualify as critics. Pope expected the critic to know everything about the work under evaluation:

> You then whose judgment the right course would steer,/Know well each ancient's proper character;/His fable, subject, scope in every page;/Religion, country, genius of his age:/Without all these at once before your eyes,/Cavil you may, but never criticise.
>
> —*An Essay on Criticism* (I, 118–23)

Film reviewers write for newspapers and magazines or deliver their reviews on television and radio. Film reviewing, then, is a branch of print and broadcast journalism. Movies are a form of news; thus they should be covered. The question is, by whom? Ideally, by someone who is knowledgeable about film. However, it often happens that the film reviewer of a local newspaper is a reporter who was assigned to the movie beat because there happened to be an opening in that department. A major newspaper, on the other hand, is likely to have several reviewers who know film and have a wholeness of vision that is reflected in their reviews. They can relate the film being reviewed to other films of its kind, to the director's or the stars' previous work, to the writer's former scripts. Their reviews are not valentines studded with superlatives; rather, they offer a reasoned and balanced judgment of a film so that if they use words like "greatest" or "best," we know they aren't being hyperbolic.

Television critics are a special breed: limited sometimes to a mere minute of air time, they are almost forced to be glib to keep the viewer from switching channels. Thus, to base one's knowledge of film criticism on television reviewing is to limit criticism to one-liners. If you look at the newspaper ads for movies, you will notice endorsements from so-called critics from entertainment-oriented magazines and the less prestigious newspapers to cable networks, whose function is to promote popular entertainment. Respectable critics can therefore trash a movie, and the distributors will find positive-sounding phrases ("flawless," "unpredictable," "energetic," "hilarious," "dazzling," "two thumbs-up") for a full-page ad.

The best film critics writing today, such as Stanley Kauffman, Richard Corliss, David Denby, David Ansen, and Anthony Lane, write for magazines—Denby and Lane currently for *The New Yorker*. They are essentially essayists, who write reflective pieces and whose reviews never appear on the day that a movie opens (generally, a Friday). Anyone who needs guidance for the movie of the weekend will have to depend on newspaper or television critics. A magazine review may be as late as a few weeks. One reads David Denby not to decide what to see but to encounter a mind at work—a mind that's trying to grapple with what the critic has experienced and hopes to share with concerned readers, some of whom may already have seen the film and want to compare their reaction with his.

Film reviewing in America goes back to the turn of the century, when readers were so hungry for reviews that they even accepted plot summaries and naïve accounts of the wonders of celluloid. By 1904, the *Philadelphia Inquirer* was reviewing movies: its review of *The Great Train Robbery* (1903) was superficial ("There is a great amount of shooting"), but at least it was a beginning. By 1906, the first film journals had been started. In 1909, the *New York Times* ran its first movie review, an archly written piece on D. W. Griffith's *Pippa Passes;* from that time on, film reviewing became a regular department in the *Times*. Since there were no special qualifications for reviewing films, anyone could write about them, and often did. Frank Woods, an advertising salesperson for the *New York Dramatic Mirror*, wrote a movie column in the *Mirror* under the pseudonym "The Spectator" from 1908 to 1912; later, he went on to become a leading screenwriter.

Before he became a major playwright, Robert E. Sherwood served as film critic for *Life* magazine from 1920 to 1928. Men of letters such as Edmund Wilson, Joseph Wood Krutch, and Mark Van Doren also wrote occasional film criticism. However, Wilson, Krutch, and Van Doren made their reputations in literary criticism, not movie reviewing. The first writer to achieve a national reputation for movie reviewing was James Agee, who between 1941 and 1948 reviewed for both *Time* magazine and *The Nation*. In addition to being a critic, Agee was also a novelist, a poet, and a screenwriter; his reviews therefore had a literary tone not usually found in movie columns. Agee could be vicious, but generally he was honest and regarded himself as an amateur conversing with his readers.

Agee's death at forty-five prevented him from leaving behind a fully developed theory of film; yet he demonstrated in outline, if not in detail, what a critic should be. It is clear from his review of Michael Curtiz's *Mission to Moscow* (1943), made when Russia was an American ally, that he sensed the film's importance, not as art but as pro-Soviet propaganda. Although *Mission to Moscow* justified Stalin's purge trials, Agee was unmoved by the film's rationalizations. Instead, he wrote:

> About the trials I am not qualified to speak. On surface falsifications of fact and atmosphere I might, but on the one crucial question, whether Trotsky and Trotskyists were or were not involved with Germany and Japan in a plot to overthrow the government and to partition the country, I am capable of no sensible opinion. I neither believe it nor disbelieve it.[9]

One imagines that Agee would have been the kind of critic who could take a film on its own terms, however political those terms may be. His charge that *Mission to Moscow* indulges its audience is more damning than five paragraphs of invective. Agee was not the kind of critic who catered to prejudices and yearned to make his audience a reflection of himself but, rather, one who believed that readers have the right instincts within them and need only the proper guidance to bring them forth.

Whether Agee would have become an auteurist is problematic. He was certainly conscious of the role of the director, as is evident from his review of Preston Sturges's *Hail the Conquering Hero* (1944). Sturges's mother was a free spirit who gave her son a charmed life: private schools and early exposure to opera, theater, and ballet. His foster father was a down-to-earth Chicago millionaire. Agee saw Sturges as a man torn between his mother's love of the arts and his foster father's love of making money. Thus in his films Sturges was always floundering between art and popular entertainment, tending more toward the latter than the former. Agee realized that he was doing something unusual when he invoked a director's life as background for his films, thus giving us a glimpse into the kind of critic he might have become. Agee understood Sturges's dilemma: does one make movies to make statements or to make audiences happy? In Sturges's *Sullivan's Travels*, John L. Sullivan (Joel McCrea), a liberal director who may well be Sturges's persona, abandons social-consciousness films for comedies because "there's a lot to be said for making people laugh." In *The Palm Beach Story*, Sturges showed his ambivalence toward money, satirizing gold diggers and the frivolous rich alike but resolving their problems before the fade-out.

Agee was not afraid to express admiration for B-films. He must have known that Val Lewton's movies would someday be classics, for he hailed *The Curse of the Cat People* and *Youth Runs Wild*, also a Lewton production, as the best "fiction films" of 1944. He also wrote favorably of Robert Siodmak's *Phantom Lady* (1944), which is now regarded as a model of film noir.

Another important reviewer was Bosley Crowther.[10] Of all the newspaper reviewers of his era, he carried the greatest weight because from 1940 through 1967 he wrote for the *New York Times*. Since Crowther reviewed for the most prestigious paper in America, he did not waste his time on what he deemed to be "junk." Whereas Agee saw more in Val Lewton films than calculated fright, Crowther saw nothing in them. *Cat People*, he felt, was "labored and obvious"; and although he found *The Curse of the Cat People* sensitive, it did not make his Ten Best list.

Crowther wrote for that anomaly known as the *New York Times* reader: someone who was educated but not pedantic, conservative but not a book burner, liberal without endorsing every cause as right, a believer in human values without being a teary sentimentalist. Crowther had these qualities himself. When the National Legion of Decency condemned Roberto Rossellini's *The Miracle* (1948) as an affront to the Virgin Birth, Crowther praised it as a work of art. But in the 1960s his influence began to wane. Movies were changing, and so were audiences. One of the last reviews Crowther wrote before his retirement was of *Bonnie and Clyde*. The review gave no indication of the sane judgments of which he was capable. Unable to see the film as a commentary on the Great Depression, he branded it as cheap, pointless, and marred by violence.

Dwight Macdonald, who devoted more than forty years of his life to movie reviewing, defined the concept of *film critic*: A critic will judge the film's quality, prove its quality, and compare the film with other films, giving it its proper place within the history of motion pictures.[11]

Naturally, not all reviewers can fulfill Macdonald's criteria. Pauline Kael, who, until her retirement from *The New Yorker*, was arguably America's premier film critic, could.

The best of Pauline Kael's criticism has been collected in *For Keeps: 30 Years of Movies*. Because she identifies with the moviegoer, she is sometimes forced to assume an egalitarian, even an anti-intellectual pose. She constantly laments the way film is taught in universities, claiming that an overly scholarly approach will kill "movies" (her favorite term for the medium, because in America we never say "I'm going to the films" but "I'm going to the movies"). She scorns pretentiousness, believing that movies like *Last Year at Marienbad* (1961) can drive audiences away, although that has not happened because there were enough viewers and critics who found its lack of narrative clarity a metaphor for the unknowable. Kael championed American movies, yet she was not chauvinistic; she merely felt that they come closer to what movies ought to be than do most European films. Although she scorned auteurism, she has favorite directors, among them Robert Altman and Sam Peckinpah. Kael may have written for *The New Yorker*, but there is no wordiness in her style; there is wit, however, which may explain her long association with the magazine.

If Pauline Kael sounds like a mass of contradictions, it is because, on the one hand, she writes about an art form that, in its inception, was not taken seriously (movies were "flickers" and nothing more). On the other hand, she is writing about an art form that is now taken seriously and is the subject of undergraduate and graduate study as well. Thus, Kael maintains a "one of the people" stance by addressing the reader as "you," a form of address that David Denby has also adopted. "What you keep reacting to is the film's exuberant doodles," she wrote of *Bull Durham* (1988). Yet, as a critic whose knowledge of the other arts is on a par with her knowledge of film, she is more than just one of the people; she is the people at their most perceptive.

This does not mean that Kael can't make mistakes. No critic is infallible; one should remember that Tolstoy refused to consider Shakespeare a classic, and T. S. Eliot made the extravagant claim that Virgil's *Aeneid* was the only true classic of Western literature. Kael can also be hyperbolic when she feels strongly about a movie: she once compared the evening *Last Tango in Paris* closed the 1972 New York Film Festival with the evening Igor Stravinsky's *The Rite of Spring* premiered, calling each date a cultural landmark. Because she disapproves of auteurism, she set out to discredit Orson Welles as the auteur of *Citizen Kane* in her essay "Raising Kane," which first appeared in *The New Yorker* and then as the introduction to *The Citizen Kane Book*. Subsequent criticism, notably by Robert Carringer, has shown that Kael was not entirely correct in attributing the script wholly to Herman J. Mankiewicz. Kael certainly has her blind spots; she either failed, or refused, to see how Welles impressed his personality on *Citizen Kane* by drawing on his stage and radio experience (especially overlapping dialogue and musical bridges) to combine the best of both media in the film.

To her credit, Kael at least has a philosophy of film: it is a people's art form. Moviegoers loathe sham; they prefer "movies" to "cinema"; they want theorizing kept to a minimum; they cannot bear to see their values mocked. Thus, Kael reacted negatively to *A Clockwork Orange* because it argued that humankind's capacity for evil is never exhausted. Kael, who believes in people (or, at least, in moviegoers), could not accept that. Consequently, she accused Stanley Kubrick of "sucking up to the thugs in the audience."[12]

Pauline Kael wrote what are really essay-reviews. Her method is to reconstruct the film, incorporating her own impressions, comparisons with other films, and frequently comparisons with other art forms. Those who dislike Kael claim that in reconstructing the film she creates an anti-film that bears little resemblance to the original. If Kael does this, and it is not often, readers are at least afforded an X ray of her thoughts so that they can experience what was going on in her mind when she saw the film and later, when she was writing about it. We may not always be able to see every movie we read about. What reviewers as critics can do is suggest how we might have reacted during the film and when reflecting on it. Pauline Kael provides this vicarious experience better than most of her colleagues.

PRACTICAL CRITICISM

If fiction is a house with many windows, as Henry James alleged, then criticism is a house with many doors, each with its own key. No school of literary criticism has a monopoly on interpretation; each offers its own peculiar access to the work. The New Criticism stresses the text; historical criticism places the text within its time; biographical criticism, within the context of the author's life; Marxist criticism, within the framework of the class struggle; psychoanalytic criticism, within the workings of the unconscious; myth criticism, within the universal dreams of humankind.

That criticism is an applied art is evident from the various ways in which a film historian, an auteurist, a myth critic, and a social historian might interpret *Citizen Kane*.

The Film Historian

The history of *Citizen Kane* is filled with so many untruths and half-truths that uncovering the real truth about the film is as complex as the attempt of the reporter, Thompson, to solve the enigma of "Rosebud." The popular assumption that RKO was in such a state of financial instability that its president, George J. Schaefer, wooed Orson Welles, the boy wonder of stage and radio, to Hollywood in the hope of working wonders for the studio, is one such untruth. In "A History of RKO Radio Pictures, Incorporated, 1928–1942" Richard B. Jewell has shown that in 1940, the year RKO signed Welles, its finances were in good shape.[13] Furthermore, the studio had a tradition of hiring stage personalities such as Katharine Hepburn, George Gershwin, and the director Garson Kanin; RKO's hiring of Welles, therefore, was not inconsistent with studio policy, although his being given the right of final cut was inconsistent with Hollywood policy in general.

Although one may never know whose idea it was—Welles's or Herman J. Mankiewicz's—to make a movie based on the life of newspaper tycoon William Randolph Hearst, films about the rise of an entrepreneur from obscurity to renown were not unknown. Since Mankiewicz, who wrote the first two drafts of *Citizen Kane* (which he entitled *American*), had been writing for the movies since 1926, he may well have been influenced by the script Preston Sturges wrote for *The Power and the Glory* (1933), which dealt with a Kane-like railroad magnate. Thomas Garner (Spencer Tracy) in *The Power and the Glory* is as enigmatic as the master of Xanadu. Moreover, there are points of contact between both films: the Horatio Alger theme, the flashbacks following the tycoon's death, violations of chronology, and the extremes of admiration and contempt that both men inspired.

Mankiewicz, however, was not wholly responsible for the script of the film that ultimately became *Citizen Kane*. Pauline Kael's "Raising Kane" is in error on this point.[14] In an attempt to refocus attention on Mankiewicz, whom Welles had eclipsed, Kael downplayed Welles's contribution even to the point of undermining its originality. What other critics consider Wellesian, she attributes to Gregg Toland's cinematography. Kael invites us to compare *Kane* with *Mad Love* (1935), a Peter Lorre "mad doctor" movie, which Toland photographed and which has certain features in common with *Kane*: gothic sets, a physical resemblance between the bald Lorre and the bald Welles in *Kane*'s final scenes, cavernous rooms, and even a white cockatoo.

"Raising Kane," which has occasioned controversy since its publication, has been superseded by what appears to be the definitive work on the subject, Robert L. Carringer's *The Making of Citizen Kane*. Consequently, we now know that "Mankiewicz . . . wrote the first two drafts. His principal contributions were the story frame, a cast of characters, various individual scenes, and a good share of the dialogue. . . . Welles added the narrative brilliance—the visual and verbal wit, the stylistic fluidity, and such stunningly original strokes as the newspaper montages and the breakfast table sequence."[15] Unlike Kael, who exalted Mankiewicz at the expense of Welles, Carringer is perfectly willing to credit Mankiewicz for a contribution of "fundamental importance" but, knowing what he does about the film's genesis, cannot attribute the script solely to him.

Nor can Carringer allow the myth to persist that Gregg Toland determined how *Citizen Kane* would be photographed. Carringer proves that Welles and Toland were in total agreement as to how the film would be shot; it was not to resemble a typical Hollywood movie but, rather, would display all the techniques at which Toland excelled (low angles, deep focus, high-contrast photography, and the like). Deep focus, long takes, and a paucity of close-ups would also serve Welles's purpose. One must never forget that Welles came from the theater; hence deep focus and long takes would be as close as he could come to duplicating stage drama. Since stage actors project more forcefully than film actors, a preponderance of close-ups would reveal their lack of film experience. One must also never forget that the leading roles were played by members of Welles's Mercury Theatre. Finally, it should be remembered that the Mercury Theatre had a weekly radio series, *The Mercury Theatre on the Air*, which Welles hosted and in which he frequently appeared. *Citizen Kane* contains examples of a common radio-drama device, the cross-fade, in which a character begins a sentence in one place and someone else finishes it in another.

Although *Citizen Kane* is not always thought of in terms of RKO, it was an RKO product. As Carringer demonstrates, the glass paperweight that is so crucial to the plot is not that different from a similar paperweight that appeared in an earlier RKO film, *Kitty Foyle*. In both films, the paperweight has a snow motif that conjures up memories of childhood. Since both paperweights were made by the RKO property department, it is unlikely that Mankiewicz or Mankiewicz/Welles hit upon the paperweight idea without some prior knowledge of *Kitty Foyle*.

Knowledge of a film's production history makes it possible to speak authoritatively about the film. Without such knowledge, one runs the risk of crediting the wrong individuals with contributions that others have made.

The Auteurist

Like many a first film, *Citizen Kane* contains within it the director's major themes and preoccupations. Here it is Welles's ambivalence toward wealth and his fascination with corruption. Welles's world is full of potentates, of men who are larger than life: Kane, Bannister of *The Lady from Shanghai*, Gregori Arkadin of *Mr. Arkadin* (1955), and their alter egos in the director's Shakespearean films (*Macbeth* [1948]; *Othello* [1952]; and *Chimes at Midnight* [1967]).

Wealth assumes various forms in Welles's films: Kane's Xanadu, the Amberson mansion in *The Magnificent Ambersons*, the yacht in *The Lady from Shanghai*, the castle of Dunsinane in *Macbeth*, the castle at San Tirso in *Mr. Arkadin*, and Henry IV's court in *Chimes at Midnight*. Conversely, symbols of squalor also recur: Mary Kane's boardinghouse, the boardinghouse to which George and Aunt Fanny retreat in *The Magnificent Ambersons*, the Mexican fleabag in *Touch of Evil*, K's flat in *The Trial* (1963).

There are certain Wellesian artifacts that characterize the rich, the corrupt, and the guilty: mirrors (*Kane*, *The Lady from Shanghai*, *Othello*);

The glass paperweight in *Kitty Foyle* (1940), which probably inspired the one in *Citizen Kane*. *(Courtesy WCFTR)*

corridors (*Kane, Macbeth, The Trial*); staircases (*Kane, The Magnificent Ambersons*); chauffeured cars (*Kane*) and private planes (*Mr. Arkadin*).

Another Wellesian theme is the war of the worlds. The extraordinary world encroaches on the ordinary, and the fortuitous and the irrational confront the stable and the orderly. In *Kane*, Susan Alexander gives up a secure but mediocre existence to enter Kane's erratic world, in which she clearly does not belong. In Welles's other films, the two worlds are reflected in various ways: the automobile confronts the horse and buggy in *The Magnificent Ambersons;* Nazism brings disorder to a quiet Connecticut town in *The Stranger* (1946); an Irish sailor is exposed to the idle but murderous rich in *The Lady from Shanghai;* an ordinary couple is thrown into a nightmarish world of drugs and violence in *Touch of Evil;* the little man is introduced to fascist bureaucracy in *The Trial.* Even in the Shakespearean cycle, worlds collide: Macbeth's and Lady Macbeth's, Macbeth's and Macduff's (*Macbeth*); Othello's and Iago's, Othello's and Desdemona's (*Othello*); Falstaff's and Henry's, Falstaff's and Hal's (*Chimes at Midnight*).

The Wellesian king figure dies as he lived—in style: Kane's arms solemnly folded on his breast, Othello's bier carried aloft, Henry IV expiring on his throne. Even the Wellesian villain goes out in the grand manner: from the top of a tower (*The Stranger*), in a maze of mirrors (*The Lady from Shanghai*), plunging through space (*Mr. Arkadin*).

As Welles's first film, *Kane* represents the beginning of the Wellesian style, which would continue to manifest itself visually (long takes, dichotomy of light and darkness, recurring mirror and snow imagery) and aurally (overlapping dialogue, cross-fades) in his later work. The three-minute-long take that begins *Touch of Evil* had its origin in the camera's moving up the gate of Xanadu at the opening of *Citizen Kane* and in the camera's craning up the billboard advertising Susan Alexander Kane's appearance at El Rancho, moving over to the skylight, then shooting down at Susan seated at a table. Kane's multiple image reflected in the panels of the mirrored corridor anticipates the multiple images of Elsa and Bannister in the climax of *The Lady from Shanghai*. Welles's ambiguous attitude toward light (source of knowledge and sign of its absence; symbol of innocence and illusion as well as the glare of reality) runs throughout his films. Susan, a study in white with her blond hair and gleaming white skin, is a symbol of innocence exploited. The light that floods her face makes her even more pathetic; so does the light that masks the face of the doomed Isabel in *The Magnificent Ambersons*. Conversely, the light that hardens the face of the already hardened (and blond) Elsa Bannister in *The Lady from Shanghai* mocks the symbol of innocence by its profusion.

Like *Kane*, other Welles films open in darkness or semidarkness (*The Lady from Shanghai, The Stranger, Macbeth, Touch of Evil*). Darkness can suggest a womblike withdrawal (the dimly lit Xanadu), as well as a universe unilluminated by grace or providence (*The Lady from Shanghai, Touch of Evil*).

For a true appreciation of *Kane*, one must know how, as the first expression of Welles's visual and aural style, it foreshadowed themes and techniques that reappear in his subsequent films.

The Myth Critic

Every leading character in *Citizen Kane* is the incarnation of a mythological figure. Kane himself is a Zeus type. Zeus, who never had a childhood, was whisked off to Crete by his mother so that his wicked father, Cronos, would not devour him as he had done his other children. Charles Foster Kane was also deprived of a normal boyhood. When he was a child, his mother entrusted him to a guardian so that he could enjoy a lifestyle that she could never give him.

Neither Zeus nor Kane was happily married. Zeus's marriage to Hera may have been made on Olympus, but it was not blessed with tranquillity. Kane's marriage to the cool, patrician beauty Emily Norton was no different. A president's niece, Emily was socially superior to her husband and showed it by her demeanor. Kane therefore looked for love elsewhere, finding it briefly in an aspiring but untalented singer, Susan Alexander. Zeus also sought other women, rarely appearing to them as himself but taking other forms (a bull, a swan, a husband away from the war). Kane also conceals himself by diluting his importance when he describes his job to Susan, preferring that she love him for himself: "I run a couple of newspapers. How about you?"

When Kane tries to make Susan into an opera star, he steps out of the role of Zeus and into that of Pygmalion. But he becomes a Pygmalion in reverse. The sculptor Pygmalion fell in love with his own creation, which miraculously came to life. Welles inverts the myth, making Kane into an anti-Pygmalion who fashions a puppet for himself out of a living woman.

Zeus replaced his father's tyranny with the enlightened rule of the Olympians. Kane must fight his surrogate father (Thatcher, his guardian), who embodies the worst qualities of the privileged class. When Thatcher asks Kane what he would have liked to be, Kane replies, "Everything you hate." In fact, Kane is always fighting Cronos in some form: Thatcher, the elderly owner of *The Inquirer*, which he takes over, the political boss Jim Gettys. When he is not clashing with Cronos, he is battling Prometheus in the person of Leland, who sees him for what he is: "You don't care about anything except you."

Ultimately, Zeus became another Cronos: authoritarian, misanthropic, vindictive, fearful of having his power usurped, and, finally, aloof. Kane gradually grows more and more like Thatcher-Cronos; although he wants to benefit humanity, he has become too corrupted by wealth to do so. In the *Iliad*, Zeus, weary of all the infighting among the Olympians, frequently retires to the topmost peak of Mount Ida; Kane, disillusioned by political defeat, broken friendships, and Susan's failure as an opera star, retires to the seclusion of Xanadu.

If it is viewed as myth, *Kane*'s universality is more evident than it would be if the film were studied as a historical artifact or as the work of an auteur.

The Social Historian

As Machiavelli noted in *The Prince*, half of our affairs are governed by fortune (*fortuna*); the other half, by personal endeavor (*virtù*). It was by pure chance that Mary Kane, the owner of a boardinghouse, acquired the Colorado Lode. A boarder, unable to pay his rent, gave her a deed to an abandoned mine shaft that turned out to be the world's third-richest gold mine. Once fortuna places something in our path, virtù must take over. Unfortunately, Mary Kane's virtù was diseased; married to a failure, she did not want her son, Charles, to become a replica of his father. She therefore entrusted the boy to the care of Walter P. Thatcher, a noted financier; in so doing, she deprived Charles of a normal childhood so that he could enjoy a life befitting a millionaire.

The American dream can become a nightmare. Charles Foster Kane first tries to redeem himself. When he assumes control of the *New York Inquirer*, he begins exposing trusts and slumlords. He tells his guardian, "It is my duty—I'll let you in on a secret, it is also my pleasure—to see to it that decent, hard-working people of this community aren't robbed blind by a pack of money-mad pirates!"

Kane is a principled muckraker. He also refuses to run the newspaper as if it were his private enterprise; instead, he delegates authority. He even writes a Declaration of Principles, promising his readers an honest newspaper. However, while he is writing it, his face is shrouded in darkness. Kane is clearly irredeemable.

There is no salvation for Kane because he is heir to his mother's belief that the purchasing power of money is infinite. Just as his mother bought him a privileged life, Kane buys his second wife an operatic career as well as an opera house, forcing her into a role for which she has no talent. Finally, to achieve the seclusion he requires, he buys a pleasure dome on the Florida Gulf Coast.

Who is Charles Foster Kane? After his death, the press called him a plutocrat; his guardian branded him a communist; the Union Square demagogues labeled him a fascist. Then there is Kane's view of himself: "I am, always will be, and always have been one thing: an American."

The popular conception of Kane, confused and contradictory, is no different from the popular conception of America: the republic to which we pledge allegiance, the democracy we claim we are, the empire others perceive us to be. The three faces of America become Kane's three faces. First, he is the republican editor who delegates authority to his representatives; then, he is the democratic leader, promising in his Declaration of Principles to be a champion of human rights; finally, he is the imperialist, bald and gowned, an Oriental potentate living in splendor at Xanadu. *Citizen Kane* forces us to watch the transformation of the country through the transformation of one man.

While each interpretation is valid as far as it goes, one could easily write an essay combining all of them by recounting details about the film's production history, showing how *Kane*'s visual style is repeated in Welles's other films, relating its archetypal plot to well-known myths, and noting its ambivalence about a society that encourages "rags-to-riches" optimism and places material values before spiritual ones.

GUIDELINES FOR FILM CRITICISM

There is no single way to criticize film. After a lifetime of reviewing, Dwight Macdonald wondered whether the norms that had once served him were still valid. Since Macdonald's guidelines are among the best that a contemporary critic can offer a student of film, it is worthwhile to repeat them here. They represent ways of approaching film, however, not ironclad laws. For this reason, there will be exceptions; some of the guidelines may not be applicable to a particular film, as Macdonald is the first to admit. Still, it is easier to deal with exceptions when one has standards by which to measure them than would be the case if one had no standards at all. The following excerpt from Macdonald's work, *Dwight Macdonald on Movies*, summarizes his guidelines succinctly:

> I know something about cinema after forty years, and being a congenital critic, I know what I like and why. But I can't explain the *why* except in terms of the specific work under consideration, on which I'm copious enough. The general theory, the larger view, the gestalt—these have always eluded me. Whether this gap in my critical armor be called an idiosyncrasy or, less charitably, a personal failing, it has always been most definitely there.
>
> But people, especially undergraduates hot for certainty, keep asking me what rules, principles or standards I judge movies by—a fair question to which I can never think of an answer. Years ago, some forgotten but evidently sharp stimulus spurred me to put some guidelines down on paper. The result, hitherto unprinted for reasons which will become clear, was:
>
> (1) Are the characters consistent, and in fact are there characters at all?
> (2) Is it true to life?
> (3) Is the photography cliché, or is it adapted to the particular film and therefore original?
> (4) Do the parts go together; do they add up to something; is there a rhythm established so that there is form, shape, climax, building up tension and exploding it?
> (5) Is there a mind behind it; is there a feeling that a single intelligence has imposed his own view on the material?
>
> The last two questions rough out some vague sort of meaning, and the third is sound, if truistic. But I can't account for the first two being there at all, let alone in the lead-off place. Many films I admire are not "true to life" unless that stretchable term is strained beyond normal usage: *Broken Blossoms, Children of Paradise, Zéro de Conduite, Caligari, On Approval,* Eisenstein's *Ivan the Terrible.* And some have no "characters" at all, consistent or no: *Potemkin,*

The democratic Kane as Man of the People. *(Courtesy MOMA/FSA)*

Arsenal, October, Intolerance, Marienbad, Orpheus, Olympia. The comedies of Keaton, Chaplin, Lubitsch, the Marx Brothers and W. C. Fields occupy a middle ground. They have "consistent characters" all right, and they are also "true to life." But the consistency is always extreme and sometimes compulsive and obsessed (W. C., Groucho, Buster), and the truth is abstract. In short, they are so highly stylized . . . that they are constantly floating up from terra firma into the empyrean of art, right before my astonished and delighted eyes.[16]

If philosophy begins with wonder, as Plato claimed, so, too, does film criticism—with a sense of amazement that pictures can move, and the desire to explain how the moving picture can be a work of art. Even though you know the pictures do not move miraculously, never lose that childlike sense of wonder that you felt when you saw your first movie. Realize that when you are asked to write about a movie you are sharing in an ancient art, the art of criticism, which goes back to the fourth century B.C. Although film criticism is in its infancy compared to literary criticism, it

The Imperial Kane as Master of Xanadu. *(Courtesy MOMA/FSA)*

works from the same principle: the desire to explain structurally, descriptively, psychologically, or ideologically how a work of art functions. The papers you write will be on limited topics; they always are: "Deep Focus in *Citizen Kane*," "The Chronology of *Citizen Kane*," "Expressionism vs. Realism in *Citizen Kane*." Yet if you peruse scholarly journals such as *Film Criticism*, *Film Quarterly*, and *Literature/Film Quarterly*, you will discover articles by film scholars that are equally specific. One would have to write a book in order to articulate a philosophy of film. Still, when you write your papers, at least try to relate your particular topic to the entire film, showing how deep focus figures in the film's overall meaning, how the alternation between expressionism and realism is part of the film's tension, or how the jumbled chronology reflects the film's attitude toward Kane's life and biography in general.

Think of the parts in relation to the whole. This is what *Anatomy of Film* has attempted to do: to proceed from the components of narrative film to the total film and, finally, to ways of interpreting film. Whether you pursue film criticism professionally or simply as a moviegoer, remember that a work of art possesses integrity, or wholeness. A film is a totality; even if it is approached piecemeal, it does not lose its integrity, although that integrity may be hard to discern unless the parts are reassembled.

Alexander Pope was quoted earlier in this chapter because Pope, who was not even twenty when he wrote *An Essay on Criticism,* formulated principles that are still relevant. As you might expect, he also had something to say about focusing on the whole rather than the parts:

'Tis not a lip or eye we beauty call, / But the joint force and full result of all.
—*An Essay on Criticism* (II, 45–46)

No matter what kind of critic you become or what kinds of critics you read, relate your approach and theirs to the film as a total work of—one hopes—art.

NOTES

[1] Raymond Spottiswoode, *A Grammar of the Film: An Analysis of Film Technique* (Berkeley: University of California Press, 1969), 29.

[2] Rudolf Arnheim, *Film as Art* (Berkeley: University of California Press, 1974), 133.

[3] Ibid., 57.

[4] André Bazin, *What Is Cinema?* Vol. 1, trans. Hugh Gray (Berkeley: University of California Press, 1967), 50.

[5] Siegfried Kracauer, *Theory of Film: The Redemption of Physical Reality* (New York: Oxford University Press/Galaxy Books, 1965), 305.

[6] One of the best general studies of semiotics is Kaja Silverman, *The Subject of Semiotics* (New York: Oxford University Press, 1983); on film semiotics, see J. Dudley Andrew, *The Major Film Theories: An Introduction* (New York: Oxford University Press, 1976), 212–41. Also recommended is the structuralism issue of *College English* (October 1975).

[7] Christian Metz, *Film Language: A Semiotics of the Cinema,* trans. Michael Taylor (New York: Oxford University Press, 1974), 105.

[8] Laura Mulvey, "Visual Pleasure and Narrative Cinema," in *Film Theory and Criticism,* 5th ed., ed. Leo Braudy and Marshall Cohen (New York: Oxford University Press, 1999), 834.

[9] James Agee, *Agee on Film: Reviews and Comments by James Agee* (New York: Grosset & Dunlap, 1969), 39.

[10] On Crowther's career, see Frank E. Beaver, *Bosley Crowther: Social Critic of the Film* (New York: Arno Press, 1974).

[11] Dwight Macdonald, *Dwight Macdonald on Movies* (Englewood Cliffs, N.J.: Prentice-Hall, 1969), 471.

[12] Pauline Kael, *Deeper into Movies* (Boston: Atlantic–Little, Brown, 1974), 378.

[13] Richard B. Jewell, "A History of RKO Radio Pictures, Incorporated, 1928–1942" (Ph.D. diss., University of Southern California Press, 1978).

[14] Pauline Kael, "Raising Kane," *The Citizen Kane Book* (Boston: Little Brown, 1971), 1–84.

[15] Robert L. Carringer, *The Making of Citizen Kane* (Berkeley: University of California Press, 1985), 35.

[16] Macdonald, *Dwight Macdonald on Movies,* ix–x.

APPENDIX

Films Discussed and Directors

Film	Director
Abraham Lincoln (1930)	D. W. Griffith
The Accused (1948)	William Dieterle
An Act of Murder (1948)	Michael Gordon
Address Unknown (1944)	William Cameron Menzies
Against All Odds (1984)	Taylor Hackford
The Age of Innocence (1993)	Martin Scorsese
Alice Doesn't Live Here Anymore (1975)	Martin Scorsese
*All About Eve (1950)	Joseph L. Mankiewicz
All About My Mother (1999)	Pedro Almodóvar
*All Quiet on the Western Front (1930)	Lewis Milestone
All the President's Men (1976)	Alan J. Pakula
Amadeus (1984)	Miloš Forman
American Beauty (1999)	Sam Mendes
*An American in Paris (1951)	Vincente Minnelli

*Films chosen for the Library of Congress's National Film Registry (1989–), created to single out films of historical and cultural significance.

And Now Tomorrow (1944)	Irving Pichel
Angels with Dirty Faces (1938)	Michael Curtiz
À Nous la Liberté (1931)	René Clair
Anywhere but Here (1999)	Wayne Wang
*The Apartment (1960)	Billy Wilder
*Apocalypse Now (1979)	Francis Ford Coppola
Arise, My Love (1940)	Mitchell Leisen
Autumn in New York (2000)	Joan Chen
Avanti! (1972)	Billy Wilder
*The Awful Truth (1937)	Leo McCarey
The Bad and the Beautiful (1952)	Vincente Minnelli
*Badlands (1973)	Terrence Malick
Ball of Fire (1941)	Howard Hawks
The Barkleys of Broadway (1949)	Charles Walters
Barry Lyndon (1975)	Stanley Kubrick
Beauty and the Beast (1991)	Gary Trousdale and Kirk Wise
Beginning of the End (1957)	Bert I. Gordon
Berkeley Square (1933)	Frank Lloyd
*The Best Years of Our Lives (1946)	William Wyler
Big (1998)	Penny Marshall
The Big Carnival (1951)	Billy Wilder
The Big Picture (1989)	Christopher Guest
The Big Sleep (1946)	Howard Hawks
The Birds (1963)	Alfred Hitchcock
*The Birth of a Nation (1915)	D. W. Griffith
The Bishop's Wife (1947)	Henry Koster
The Blair Witch Project (1999)	Daniel Myrick and Eduardo Sanchez
Blazing Saddles (1974)	Mel Brooks
The Blob (1958)	Irving S. Yeaworth, Jr.
Blonde Venus (1932)	Josef von Sternberg
The Blue Angel (1930)	Josef von Sternberg
Bluebeard (1944)	Edgar G. Ulmer
Body and Soul (1947)	Robert Rossen
Body Heat (1981)	Lawrence Kasdan
Bonnie and Clyde (1967)	Arthur Penn
Book of Shadows: Blair Witch 2 (2000)	Joe Berlinger
The Bravados (1957)	Henry King
Breathless (1959)	Jean-Luc Godard
*Bride of Frankenstein (1935)	James Whale
Brief Encounter (1946)	David Lean

Brigadoon (1954)	Vincente Minnelli
Bringing Up Baby (1938)	Howard Hawks
Broken Arrow (1950)	Delmer Daves
Broken Blossoms (1919)	D. W. Griffith
Broken Lance (1954)	Edward Dmytryk
Brute Force (1947)	Jules Dassin
Buddy Buddy (1981)	Billy Wilder
Burnt Offerings (1976)	Dan Curtis
Butch Cassidy and the Sundance Kid (1969)	George Roy Hill
Butterfly (1999)	José Luis Cuerda
The Cabinet of Dr. Caligari (1919)	Robert Weine
Camille (1937)	George Cukor
Cape Fear (1991)	Martin Scorsese
Carrie (1976)	Brian De Palma
Casablanca (1942)	Michael Curtiz
Casualties of War (1989)	Brian De Palma
Cat People (1942)	Jacques Tourneur
Caught (1949)	Max Ophüls
Chimes at Midnight (1967)	Orson Welles
Chinatown (1974)	Roman Polanski
Citizen Kane (1941)	Orson Welles
A Clockwork Orange (1971)	Stanley Kubrick
Close Encounters of the Third Kind (1977)	Steven Spielberg
Clueless (1995)	Amy Heckerling
Colorado Territory (1949)	Raoul Walsh
The Color Purple (1985)	Steven Spielberg
Coney Island (1943)	Walter Lang
The Corn Is Green (1944)	Irving Rapper
Cover Girl (1944)	Charles Vidor
Craig's Wife (1936)	Dorothy Arzner
Creature from the Black Lagoon (1954)	Jack Arnold
Criss Cross (1949)	Robert Siodmak
The Crying Game (1992)	Neil Jordan
The Curse of the Cat People (1944)	Gunther von Fritsch and Robert Wise
Dancer in the Dark (2000)	Lars von Trier
Dances with Wolves (1990)	Kevin Costner
Dark Passage (1947)	Delmer Daves
Dark Victory (1939)	Edmund Goulding
A Day at the Races (1937)	Sam Wood
The Day of the Locust (1975)	John Schlesinger

The Day the Earth Stood Still (1951)	Robert Wise
The Dead (1987)	John Huston
Dead Reckoning (1947)	John Cromwell
Death in Venice (1971)	Luchino Visconti
The Deer Hunter (1978)	Michael Cimino
Detour (1946)	Edgar G. Ulmer
Dog Day Afternoon (1975)	Sidney Lumet
A Doll's House (1973)	Patrick Garland
Double Indemnity (1944)	Billy Wilder
Dracula's Daughter (1936)	Lambert Hillyer
Dr. Cyclops (1940)	Ernest Schoedsack
Dream Street (1921)	D. W. Griffith
Dressed to Kill (1980)	Brian De Palma
Dr. Jekyll and Mr. Hyde (1932)	Rouben Mamoulian
*Dr. Strangelove or: How I Learned to	
Stop Worrying and Love the Bomb (1964)	Stanley Kubrick
Duck Soup (1933)	Leo McCarey
Duel in the Sun (1947)	King Vidor
Easter Parade (1948)	Charles Walters
Easy Living (1937)	Mitchell Leisen
Easy Rider (1969)	Dennis Hopper
Emma (1996)	Doug McGrath
The Emperor Waltz (1948)	Billy Wilder
Empire of the Sun (1987)	Steven Spielberg
*E.T.: The Extra-Terrestrial (1982)	Steven Spielberg
Evita (1996)	Alan Parker
Experiment Perilous (1944)	Jacques Tourneur
Family Plot (1976)	Alfred Hitchcock
Fantasia (1940)	Ben Sharpsteen
Fatal Attraction (1989)	Adrian Lyne
Fedora (1979)	Billy Wilder
The First Time (1952)	Frank Tashlin
Five Graves to Cairo (1943)	Billy Wilder
Fixed Bayonets (1951)	Samuel Fuller
Flying Down to Rio (1933)	Thornton Freeland
A Foreign Affair (1948)	Billy Wilder
Foreign Correspondent (1940)	Alfred Hitchcock
Forever Amber (1947)	Otto Preminger
Forrest Gump (1994)	Robert Zemeckis
Fort Apache (1948)	John Ford
The Fortune Cookie (1966)	Billy Wilder

42nd Street (1933)   Lloyd Bacon
The Four Hundred Blows (1959)   François Truffaut
The Four Seasons (1981)   Alan Alda
Four Weddings and a Funeral (1994)   Mike Newell
Frankenstein (1931)   James Whale
French Kiss (1995)   Lawrence Kasdan
Frenzy (1972)   Alfred Hitchcock
Frequency (2000)   Gregory Hoblit
The Freshman (1990)   Andrew Bergman
Friday the 13th (1980)   Sean S. Cunningham
The Front (1975)   Martin Ritt
The Front Page (1974)   Billy Wilder

The Giant Claw (1957)   Fred S. Sears
Gilda (1946)   Charles Vidor
Gladiator (2000)   Ridley Scott
The Glass Menagerie (1950)   Irving Rapper
The Glass Menagerie (1986)   Paul Newman
The Godfather (1972)   Francis Ford Coppola
The Godfather, Part II (1974)   Francis Ford Coppola
The Godfather, Part III (1990)   Francis Ford Coppola
Gold Diggers of 1933 (1933)   Mervyn LeRoy
Gold Diggers of 1935 (1935)   Busby Berkeley
The Golden Bowl (2001)   James Ivory
Gone with the Wind (1939)   Victor Fleming
GoodFellas (1989)   Martin Scorsese
La Grande Strada Azzurra
  (The Wide Blue Sea [1957])   Gillo Pontecorvo
The Grapes of Wrath (1940)   John Ford
The Greatest Story Ever Told (1965)   George Stevens
Great Expectations (1946)   David Lean
The Great Lie (1941)   Edmund Goulding
The Great Train Robbery (1903)   E. S. Porter
The Green Berets (1968)   John Wayne/Ray Kellogg
The Grifters (1990)   Stephen Frears
Gun Crazy (1949)   Joseph H. Lewis

Hail the Conquering Hero (1944)   Preston Sturges
Halloween (1978)   John Carpenter
Hannah and Her Sisters (1986)   Woody Allen
The Happy Ending (1968)   Richard Brooks
Harriet Craig (1950)   Vincent Sherman
Hello Frisco, Hello (1943)   H. Bruce Humberstone

Hennessy (1975)	Don Sharp
He Ran All the Way (1951)	John Berry
High Noon (1952)	Fred Zinnemann
High Sierra (1941)	Raoul Walsh
High Society (1956)	Charles Walters
Hiroshima, Mon Amour (1959)	Alain Resnais
His Girl Friday (1940)	Howard Hawks
Hold Back the Dawn (1941)	Mitchell Leisen
Hollywoodism: Jews, Movies, and the American Dream (1998)	Simcha Jacobovici
Horse Feathers (1932)	Norman Z. McLeod
The House on Carroll Street (1988)	Peter Yates
How Green Was My Valley (1941)	John Ford
How to Marry a Millionaire (1953)	Jean Negulesco
Humanité (1999)	Bruno Dumont
Hurricane (1937)	John Ford
Hustle (1975)	Robert Aldrich
I Confess (1952)	Alfred Hitchcock
I Married a Monster from Outer Space (1958)	Gene Fowler, Jr.
Indiana Jones and the Temple of Doom (1985)	Steven Spielberg
In the Company of Men (1997)	Neil LaBute
In the Good Old Summertime (1949)	Robert Z. Leonard
In the Mood for Love (2000)	Wong Kar-wai
Intolerance (1916)	D. W. Griffith
Invasion of the Body Snatchers (1956)	Don Siegel
The Invisible Man (1933)	James Whale
Isadora (1969)	Karl Reisz
It Came from Outer Space (1953)	Jack Arnold
It Happened One Night (1934)	Frank Capra
It's a Wonderful Life (1946)	Frank Capra
I Walked with a Zombie (1943)	Jacques Tourneur
Jane Eyre (1944)	Robert Stevenson
Jaws (1975)	Steven Spielberg
Jesse James (1939)	Henry King
Jezebel (1938)	William Wyler
Johnny Guitar (1954)	Nicholas Ray
The Jolson Story (1946)	Alfred E. Green
Jules et Jim (1961)	François Truffaut
Julia (1977)	Fred Zinnemann
Juliet of the Spirits (1965)	Federico Fellini
Julius Caesar (1953)	Joseph L. Mankiewicz

The Kansan (1943)	George Archainbaud
The Kid from Texas (1950)	Kurt Newman
King and Country (1964)	Joseph Losey
*King Kong (1933)	Merian C. Cooper and
	Ernest B. Schoedsack
Kiss Me, Stupid (1964)	Billy Wilder
Kitty Foyle (1940)	Sam Wood
Knock on Any Door (1949)	Nicholas Ray
Kundun (1997)	Martin Scorsese
Lacombe, Lucien (1974)	Louis Malle
L.A. Confidential (1997)	Curtis Hanson
The Lady and the Monster (1944)	George Sherman
Lady Be Good (1941)	Norman Z. McLeod
*The Lady Eve (1941)	Preston Sturges
The Lady from Shanghai (1948)	Orson Welles
Lady in the Dark (1944)	Mitchell Leisen
Lady in the Lake (1946)	Robert Montgomery
Lady in White (1988)	Frank LaLoggia
The Last Emperor (1987)	Bernardo Bertolucci
*The Last Picture Show (1971)	Peter Bogdanovich
Last Tango in Paris (1972)	Bernardo Bertolucci
The Last Temptation of Christ (1988)	Martin Scorsese
Last Train from Gun Hill (1956)	John Sturges
The Last Tycoon (1976)	Elia Kazan
L'Atalante (1934)	Jean Vigo
A League of Their Own (1992)	Penny Marshall
*Letter from an Unknown Woman (1948)	Max Ophüls
A Letter to Three Wives (1949)	Joseph L. Mankiewicz
Lifeboat (1944)	Alfred Hitchcock
Little Big Man (1970)	Arthur Penn
The Little Foxes (1941)	William Wyler
Little Women (1994)	Gillian Armstrong
The Locket (1946)	John Brahm
Long Day's Journey into Night (1962)	Sidney Lumet
Look Who's Talking (1989)	Amy Heckerling
Lost Horizon (1937)	Frank Capra
Lost in America (1985)	Albert Brooks
The Lost Weekend (1945)	Billy Wilder
Love in the Afternoon (1957)	Billy Wilder
M (1931)	Fritz Lang
Macbeth (1948)	Orson Welles

Mad Love (1935)	Karl Freund
*The Magnificent Ambersons (1942)	Orson Welles
The Major and the Minor (1942)	Billy Wilder
Malcolm X (1992)	Spike Lee
The Man from Laramie (1955)	Anthony Mann
Manhattan (1979)	Woody Allen
Manhattan Murder Mystery (1993)	Woody Allen
The Man Who Shot Liberty Valance (1962)	John Ford
Marnie (1964)	Alfred Hitchcock
Married to the Mob (1988)	Jonathan Demme
Mary Shelley's Frankenstein (1994)	Kenneth Branagh
*M*A*S*H (1970)	Robert Altman
The Matrix (1999)	Larry and Andrew Wachowski
McCabe and Mrs. Miller (1971)	Robert Altman
Medium Cool (1969)	Haskell Wexler
Meet John Doe (1941)	Frank Capra
*Meet Me in St. Louis (1944)	Vincente Minnelli
Meet Nero Wolfe (1936)	Herbert Biberman
The Merry Widow (1934)	Ernst Lubitsch
Metropolis (1926)	Fritz Lang
Midnight (1939)	Mitchell Leisen
*Mildred Pierce (1945)	Michael Curtiz
The Miracle (1948)	Roberto Rossellini
The Mirror Has Two Faces (1996)	Barbra Streisand
Mission to Moscow (1943)	Michael Curtiz
*Modern Times (1936)	Charlie Chaplin
Monkey Business (1931)	Norman Z. McLeod
Moon over Miami (1941)	Walter Lang
Moonstruck (1987)	Norman Jewison
*Morocco (1930)	Josef von Sternberg
Mr. Arkadin (1955)	Orson Welles
Mr. Deeds Goes to Town (1936)	Frank Capra
Mrs. Doubtfire (1993)	Chris Columbus
Mrs. Miniver (1942)	William Wyler
Mr. Skeffington (1944)	Vincent Sherman
*Mr. Smith Goes to Washington (1939)	Frank Capra
Mulholland Falls (1996)	Lee Tamahori
The Mummy (1932)	Karl Freund
Murder on the Orient Express (1974)	Sidney Lumet
*My Darling Clementine (1946)	John Ford
My Life (1993)	Bruce Joel Rubin
My Little Chickadee (1940)	Edward Cline

My Man Godfrey (1936)   Gregory La Cava
My Reputation (1946)   Curtis Bernhardt
My Son John (1952)   Leo McCarey

The Naked City (1948)   Jules Dassin
The Naked Dawn (1955)   Edgar G. Ulmer
The Naked Spur (1953)   Anthony Mann
Nashville (1975)   Robert Altman
Natural Born Killers (1994)   Oliver Stone
A New Life (1988)   Alan Alda
Night and Day (1946)   Michael Curtiz
A Night at the Opera (1935)   Sam Wood
A Night in Casablanca (1946)   Archie Mayo
'Night, Mother (1986)   Tom Moore
The Night of the Hunter (1955)   Charles Laughton
The Night of the Iguana (1964)   John Huston
The Night Porter (1974)   Liliana Cavani
Ninotchka (1939)   Ernst Lubitsch
North by Northwest (1959)   Alfred Hitchcock
No Sad Songs for Me (1950)   Rudolph Maté
Now, Voyager (1942)   Irving Rapper
Nurse Betty (2000)   Neil LaBute

O Brother, Where Art Thou? (2000)   Joel Coen
Of Mice and Men (1939)   Lewis Milestone
Old Acquaintance (1943)   Vincent Sherman
The Old Maid (1938)   Edmund Goulding
One Flew over the Cuckoo's Nest (1975)   Miloš Forman
One True Thing (1998)   Carl Franklin
One, Two, Three (1962)   Billy Wilder
Only You (1994)   Norman Jewison
On the Town (1949)   Gene Kelly and Stanley Donen
On the Waterfront (1954)   Elia Kazan
Othello (1952)   Orson Welles
Our Town (1940)   Sam Wood
Out of the Past (1947)   Jacques Tourneur

Pale Rider (1987)   Clint Eastwood
The Palm Beach Story (1942)   Preston Sturges
The Passenger (1974)   Michelangelo Antonioni
Paths of Glory (1957)   Stanley Kubrick
Patton (1970)   Franklin Schaffner

Pearl Harbor (2001)	Michael Bay
Peggy Sue Got Married (1986)	Francis Ford Coppola
Penny Serenade (1941)	George Stevens
The Perfect Storm (2000)	Wolfgang Petersen
The Petty Girl (1950)	Henry Levin
The Philadelphia Story (1940)	George Cukor
Phone Call from a Stranger (1951)	Jean Negulesco
Picnic (1956)	Joshua Logan
The Picture of Dorian Gray (1945)	Albert Lewin
Pinocchio (1940)	Ben Sharpsteen and Hamilton Luske
Platoon (1986)	Oliver Stone
The Player (1992)	Robert Altman
Pleasantville (1998)	Gary Ross
Postcards from the Edge (1994)	Mike Nichols
The Postman Always Rings Twice (1946)	Tay Garnett
Potemkin (1925)	Sergei Eisenstein
The Power and the Glory (1933)	William K. Howard
The Preacher's Wife (1996)	Penny Marshall
Pretty Woman (1990)	Gary Marshall
Priscilla, Queen of the Desert (1994)	Stephen Elliott
The Private Life of Sherlock Holmes (1970)	Billy Wilder
Psycho (1960)	Alfred Hitchcock
The Purple Heart (1944)	Lewis Milestone
The Purple Rose of Cairo (1985)	Woody Allen
Pursued (1947)	Raoul Walsh
The Quiet Man (1952)	John Ford
Radio Days (1987)	Woody Allen
Raging Bull (1981)	Martin Scorsese
Raiders of the Lost Ark (1981)	Steven Spielberg
Rebecca (1940)	Alfred Hitchcock
Rebel without a Cause (1956)	Nicholas Ray
Red River (1948)	Howard Hawks
Reds (1981)	Warren Beatty
The Red Shoes (1948)	Michael Powell
Rhapsody in Blue (1945)	Irving Rapper
The Roaring Twenties (1939)	Raoul Walsh
Romeo and Juliet (1996)	Baz Luhrmann
Rope (1948)	Alfred Hitchcock
The Runaway Bride (1999)	Gary Marshall
Run Lola Run (1998)	Tom Tykwer

Saboteur (1942)	Alfred Hitchcock
Sabrina (1954)	Billy Wilder
Sahara (1943)	Zoltan Korda
Saving Private Ryan (1998)	Steven Spielberg
Scarface (1932)	Howard Hawks
Schindler's List (1993)	Steven Spielberg
Scream (1995)	Wes Craven
Scream 2 (1997)	Wes Craven
Scream 3 (2000)	Wes Craven
The Searchers (1956)	John Ford
The Secret Garden (1949)	Fred M. Wilcox
The Secret Life of Walter Mitty (1947)	Norman Z. McLeod
September Affair (1950)	William Dieterle
The Set-Up (1949)	Robert Wise
The Seventh Seal (1957)	Ingmar Bergman
The Seven Year Itch (1955)	Billy Wilder
Shadow of a Doubt (1943)	Alfred Hitchcock
Shadow of the Vampire (2000)	E. Elias Merhige
Shakespeare in Love (1998)	John Madden
Shane (1953)	George Stevens
She Wore a Yellow Ribbon (1949)	John Ford
Shock Corridor (1963)	Samuel Fuller
The Shop around the Corner (1940)	Ernst Lubitsch
Show Boat (1936)	James Whale
Singin' in the Rain (1952)	Gene Kelly and Stanley Donen
The Sixth Sense (1999)	M. Night Shyamalan
Sleepless in Seattle (1993)	Nora Ephron
Snow White and the Seven Dwarfs (1937)	Ben Sharpsteen
Soldier Blue (1970)	Ralph Nelson
Some Like It Hot (1959)	Billy Wilder
The Song of Bernadette (1943)	Henry King
Sorry, Wrong Number (1948)	Anatole Litvak
The Spanish Earth (1937)	Joris Ivens
Spartacus (1960)	Stanley Kubrick
Spellbound (1945)	Alfred Hitchcock
The Spirit of St. Louis (1957)	Billy Wilder
Stagecoach (1939)	John Ford
Stage Fright (1950)	Alfred Hitchcock
Stalag 17 (1951)	Billy Wilder
A Star Is Born (1954)	George Cukor
A Star Is Born (1976)	Frank Pierson
Star Spangled Rhythm (1942)	George Marshall

Star Wars (1977)   George Lucas
The Steel Helmet (1951)   Samuel Fuller
Stella Dallas (1937)   King Vidor
Stepmom (1998)   Chris Columbus
The Story of Adele H. (1975)   François Truffaut
The Stranger (1946)   Orson Welles
A Streetcar Named Desire (1951)   Elia Kazan
Suddenly, Last Summer (1959)   Joseph L. Mankiewicz
Sullivan's Travels (1941)   Preston Sturges
Sunset Boulevard (1950)   Billy Wilder
Sweet Liberty (1986)   Alan Alda
Swing Time (1936)   George Stevens

Take a Letter, Darling (1942)   Mitchell Leisen
The Talented Mr. Ripley (1999)   Anthony Minghella
A Tale of Two Cities (1935)   Jack Conway
Tarantula (1955)   Jack Arnold
Taxi Driver (1976)   Martin Scorsese
Tea and Sympathy (1956)   Vincente Minnelli
Tell It to the Judge (1949)   Norman Foster
Terms of Endearment (1983)   James L. Brooks
That's Life! (1985)   Blake Edwards
Thelma and Louise (1991)   Ridley Scott
There's No Business Like Show Business (1954)   Walter Lang
There's Something about Mary (1999)   Bobby Farrelly,
     Peter Farrelly

They All Kissed the Bride (1942)   Alexander Hall
They Died with Their Boots On (1941)   Raoul Walsh
They Shoot Horses, Don't They? (1969)   Sydney Pollack
They Were Expendable (1945)   John Ford
The Thing (1951)   Christian Nyby
The Thin Man (1934)   W. S. Van Dyke
The Third Man (1949)   Carol Reed
This Island Earth (1955)   Joseph Newman
Through a Glass, Darkly (1962)   Ingmar Bergman
Till the Clouds Roll By (1946)   Richard Whorf
Time after Time (1976)   Nicholas Meyer
The Tin Star (1956)   Anthony Mann
Tol'able David (1921)   Henry King
Tootsie (1982)   Sydney Pollack
Tora! Tora! Tora! (1970)   Richard Fleischer
Touch of Evil (1958)   Orson Welles
The Truman Show (1998)   Peter Weir

Twelve O'Clock High (1949)   Henry King
Two for the Road (1967)   Stanley Donen
The Two Mrs. Carrolls (1947)   Peter Godfrey
Two Rode Together (1961)   John Ford
2001: A Space Odyssey (1968)   Stanley Kubrick
Two Weeks in Another Town (1962)   Vincente Minnelli

Ulzana's Raid (1972)   Robert Aldrich
The Umbrellas of Cherbourg (1964)   Jacques Demy
The Unbearable Lightness of Being (1988)   Philip Kaufman
Une Femme Douce (1969)   Robert Bresson
Unforgiven (1992)   Clint Eastwood
The Uninvited (1944)   Lewis Allen
An Unmarried Woman (1978)   Paul Mazursky
The Untouchables (1987)   Brian De Palma

The Vagabond King (1956)   Michael Curtiz
Vertigo (1958)   Alfred Hitchcock
Victor/Victoria (1982)   Blake Edwards
Viridiana (1961)   Luis Buñuel

Wabash Avenue (1950)   Henry Koster
Wagonmaster (1950)   John Ford
Wag the Dog (1997)   Barry Levinson
A Walk in the Sun (1945)   Lewis Milestone
War of the Worlds (1953)   Byron Haskins
Watch on the Rhine (1943)   Herman Shumlin
Waterworld (1995)   Kevin Reynolds
When Willie Comes Marching Home (1950)   John Ford
While You Were Sleeping (1994)   Jon Turteltaub
White Heat (1949)   Raoul Walsh
Who Framed Roger Rabbit (1988)   Robert Zemeckis
The Wild Bunch (1968)   Sam Peckinpah
The Wild One (1954)   Laslo Benedek
Wild Strawberries (1957)   Ingmar Bergman
Witness for the Prosecution (1957)   Billy Wilder
The Wizard of Oz (1939)   Victor Fleming
The Wolf Man (1941)   George Waggner
A Woman of Affairs (1928)   Clarence Brown
Woman of the Year (1942)   George Stevens
Women in Love (1970)   Ken Russell
The Wrong Man (1957)   Alfred Hitchcock

X-Men (2000)	Bryan Singer
You've Got Mail (1998)	Nora Ephron
Ziegfeld Follies (1946)	Vincente Minnelli

Sample Student Papers

Art vs. Violence in
A Clockwork Orange

DAVID GOULDSTONE

Stanley Kubrick's adaptation of Anthony Burgess's novel received the New York Film Critics award for the best film of 1971. It was acclaimed as much for its aesthetic qualities as for the moral questions that it raised. Kubrick incorporated music from various classical compositions at critical moments in the film to highlight the tensions and ambiguities that he wanted to illustrate. He used the music of Rossini and Beethoven (which inspire Alex's dreams of mayhem and destruction) as a background for the senseless violence that Alex and his friends commit.

When Alex and his clique fight a rival gang, the violence of both groups is given a perverse beauty through stylish choreography and music from Rossini's "Thieving Magpie." Consequently, the audience is torn between the viciousness of the fight and the beauty of its visualization, experiencing a sense of uncertainty and ambiguity. This is intentional on

Kubrick's part; it is his attempt to estrange the audience from the victims of the encounters. Perhaps he is using this tension to illustrate the variety and contradictions of human nature. While society may condemn acts of violence, there is, nevertheless, an innately aggressive aspect of human nature. Kubrick's use of music, therefore, retrieves this tendency from the audience's unconscious, thereby causing moral uncertainty.

Thus, we don't know whether to sing along with Alex to the music of "Singin' in the Rain," kicking our feet in time with his, or to be repelled by his brutality. Kubrick even has the kindness to remind us of our uncertainty at the end, leaving "Singin' in the Rain" resonating in our ears and forcing us to choose between memories of the fleet-footed Gene Kelly dancing across the puddles and of Alex's cruel feet stomping his victim.

Interestingly, Kubrick plays with our attitude toward Alex in a similar way. First he incites our contempt as we witness Alex's relentless cruelty; then our sympathy as he is betrayed and spiritually crucified; and, finally, our uncertainty as he "rises" again. We can detest his adoration of "ultra-violence," yet the undeniable charm of his Elizabethan dialect and his love of "Ludwig van" prevent us from rejecting him completely. Alex is, paradoxically, a cultured barbarian, which is, perhaps, what Kubrick is accusing us all of being.

The film exudes aesthetic appeal. As one critic wrote, "Mr. Kubrick constantly uses . . . a wide-angle lens to distort space relationships within scenes," contending that the director intends to separate people and images from the environment and emphasize their distinctions (Canby 193). Kubrick creates a surreal, dreamlike atmosphere from the start. First, we are greeted by the face of Alex (one eye ringed with fake lashes); then we take in his environment. Kubrick may have used this surreal technique to represent the drug-induced vision of Alex and his gang when they are at the milk bar. Kubrick reverts to a realistic style when they are not high—for example, during the day or when Alex is sent to prison.

On the surface, the film is futuristic, but, in truth, it is a critique of contemporary society. The clothes and the setting have a futuristic look, but Kubrick refuses to comfort the audience by implying that the events are in the distant future.

Alex's final line, "I was cured, all right!" mocks the therapy that society prescribed for him. Alex has returned to his old self with the help of the very people who tried to destroy his soul and his freedom of choice. It is an ironic redemption for Alex, who has risen, fallen, and risen again in a world that is no less sick than he is. Consequently, it is impossible for such a society to offer Alex any salvation. Therefore, when he once again dreams of rape and violence to the music of Beethoven's Ninth Symphony, we accept the fact that he is back to "normal." Quite simply, it was futile to expect that the cause of his condition—society—could also be his cure.

Works Cited

Canby, Vincent. "'A Clockwork Orange' Dazzles the Senses and Mind." Review of *A Clockwork Orange*. *New York Times,* 20 December 1971. Reprinted in *The New York Times Film Reviews (1971–1972)*. New York: *New York Times* and Arno Press, 1973. 193.

A Clockwork Orange. Directed by Stanley Kubrick. With Malcolm McDowell, Patrick Magee, and Adrienne Cori. Warner Bros. 1971.

Run Lola Run:
Running to Stand Still

PAUL BELL

"Love can do everything." A statement that is simple, yet strong and direct, as is Tom Tykwer's *Run Lola Run* (1998). The line is spoken less than five minutes into the movie, yet it remains a constant throughout. In what may start a resurgence in the German cinema, *Run Lola Run* is one of the few German films that have succeeded in the American market. It has a strong yet simple screenplay that has been transformed into an amazing film.

The film begins with Manni (Moritz Bleibtreu), a low-tiered criminal, calling his girlfriend, Lola (Franka Potente), from a pay phone to ask why she has failed to pick him up. After learning that her moped has been stolen, Manni explains that he has lost the money he was carrying, leaving him with only twenty minutes to come up with 100,000 DM (roughly $55,000); otherwise, he will be killed by the mob.

What follows are three different versions of the couple's quest for the money. In the first, when Lola fails to get the money from her banker father, Manni attempts to rob a supermarket with Lola's belated help. The robbery almost succeeds, until they turn a corner and are caught. A police officer accidentally shoots Lola, whose refusal to die results in a cut to Lola's hanging up the phone twenty minutes earlier.

In the second version, Lola holds her father at gunpoint while she robs the bank. Although she is able to catch up with Manni before he tries to rob the supermarket, he carelessly walks out into the middle of the street and is struck by an ambulance. This time it is Manni's refusal to die that triggers the third version, in which Lola just misses her father at the bank and instead goes into a casino, where she wins enough to save Manni. However, at the same time, Manni stumbles upon the vagrant who originally stole the money, which he is then able to give back to the mob boss.

The film ends with Manni's asking Lola what she has in her bag, which we know is the extra 100,000 DM.

The film's main theme is that even the smallest events can have major consequences. The best example occurs in the telephone conversation between Lola and Manni. As Lola is hanging up, Tykwer cuts to a television screen where we see a domino chain in action. There is no clearer example of causality than dominoes. The seemingly irrelevant incident that sets the chain of events in motion is a man with a dog, attempting to trip Lola as she races down the stairs of her apartment building. As she continues to interact with the other characters in her quest for money, the camera will focus on them and then cut to snapshots of them in the future.

One such character is a woman pushing a child in a stroller. Lola nearly collides with the woman, and in each of the three versions they cross each other's path. In the first, the woman becomes destitute, her child is taken from her, and she steals someone else's child. The second imagines a future in which the woman plays the lottery and strikes it rich. In the third, she finds religion.

The fate of the man on the bike, too, differs in each version. The first two versions have him trying to sell the bike to Lola. In the first scenario, the man, after being beaten up by thugs, finds a woman whom he marries; in the second, he becomes a drug addict. The third is tricky: instead of witnessing the man's future, we see him selling the bike to the vagrant who stole Manni's money.

Every character in the film is subjected to different scenarios, including Lola's father, his lover, and the bank's security guard. The lover is pregnant with her husband's child. However, in each version Lola's father does not get the full story. Twice, the lover is only able to admit that she is pregnant before she is interrupted. The second time, her full account precipitates an argument between her and Lola's father just as Lola walks in; in the third version, the lover is cut off again before she can tell Lola's father that the child is not his.

Different scenarios also create different consequences for the security guard, who suffers a heart attack in the third version. In an interesting scene, in which Lola holds the guard's hand, doing her part to resuscitate him, the viewer is left to wonder if the guard, with whom Lola has had many strange altercations, is her real father.

Run Lola Run has moments when dialogue is important, such as the scene in which Lola's father claims that he is not her real father and that he is leaving Lola and her mother to have a child with his lover. These moments, admittedly, are few and far between; but when they occur, Tykwer focuses completely on the conversation. Unnecessary background movement and sound come to a halt, so the viewer can pay attention to the dialogue, despite the fact that the film is primarily visual.

Tykwer's creative use of the medium—for example, the alternation between film and video—is what makes *Run Lola Run* so impressive. Any scene involving Manni or Lola is shot in 35 mm. Those in which they are not involved are shot in video, suggesting that there are two different worlds. In Manni and Lola's world, the real one, "miracles can happen just like in the movies" (Tykwer). Then there is the other world, the synthetic one, which changes to the real one when Lola comes running into it, and Tykwer switches back to 35 mm.

Tykwer's camera not only zooms in on the characters but also moves around them. Lola is constantly in pursuit of the money for Manni. Even when she is standing still, her mind is moving as fast as she is running. The camera is rarely still; it is a constant reminder that Lola has a time limit, and that, as each second ticks by, Manni is closer to dying.

Tykwer uses a variety of film techniques, including animation, perhaps to create a surrealist effect (for example, when Lola runs down the stairs of her apartment building); split screen (Manni on the left waiting for Lola/Lola on the right, waiting to catch up with him before he tries to rob the supermarket); color symbolism (red filter for the love scenes between Lola and Manni); human sound (Lola's scream, which occurs during moments of helplessness and represents her inability to control her destiny); and a musical soundtrack that complements the action (urgent in the first version, more intense in the second, optimistic in the third).

The ending may seem confusing. Tykwer wants us to understand that Lola has gone through all three scenarios, not just the last one. Rather, she has experienced all three, taking a little bit from each with her. For example, she knew the man with the dog was going to try to trip her. How is this possible? Love can do everything: "It is this woman's passion alone that brings down the rigid rules and regulations of the world surrounding her (Tykwer)." Love can move mountains—and does.

Works Cited

Run Lola Run. Directed by Tom Tykwer. With Franka Potente and Moritz Bleibtreu. Sony Pictures Classics. 1998.

Tykwer, Tom. As quoted on *www.spe.sony.com.classics/runlolarun.*

APPENDIX

Video and DVD Rental and Purchase Sources and Web Sites

III

Mail-Order Sources

Students who are interested in purchasing or renting tapes or DVDs should consult the latest edition of Leonard Maltin's *Movie & Video Guide* (New York: Signet), which is updated annually and includes a complete list of mail-order sources. Two of the best are **Critics' Choice Video** <www.criticschoice.com> and **Facets** <www.facets.org>. Another is **Movies Unlimited** (1-800-4MOVIES), or <www.moviesunlimited.com>.

Web Sites

Just as books can go out of print, Web sites can disappear from the Internet. The newest and the best are presently listed on <www.digital-librarian.com/movies.html>. Another site, which boasts 25,000 links, is <www.cinemedia.org>. Since the information superhighway has so many detours and exit ramps to strange locations, you will waste less time (and are less likely to get lost) if you have a specific destination or goal in mind. For example:

Ratings

The outcry of parents over the PG-13 rating for *Nutty Professor II, The Klumps* (2000), which made *There's Something about Mary* seem PG, proved that the ratings are not always reliable. You might want to consult <www.filmratings.com>, which tries to be as objective as possible about sex and violence ("graphic violence," "strong sexuality"), but such descriptions tend to be relative. Your best bet is a reliable newspaper critic or the Weekend edition of the *New York Times*, which features a column on recent releases and their suitability for children, including age levels. Anyone who is concerned about subject matter can also log on to <www.critics.com>, which includes reviews that are quite specific about the amount of obscenity, sex, and violence found in new films.

New Films

Usually the Web site is some variation on the title. For some films, only the title is needed: <www.castaway.movie>. Others, like *Chocolat*, require the studio's name as well: <www.miramax2000.com/chocolat>. To be certain, check the movie ads in a major newspaper like the *New York Times*, preferably Sunday's Arts & Leisure section, for specific Web addresses.

Studio News

The studios also have Web pages. Again, the designations vary, but generally it is <www.studio.com> (for example, <www.warnerbros.com>). Some Web pages are more informative than others. **Fox Searchlight** (<www.foxsearchlight.com>), which has distributed such unusual independent films as *The Full Monty* (1997) and *Quills* (2000), and **Paramount** (<www.paramount.com>) are among the better ones. Students who are planning to work in the film business should consult the Paramount Web page, which also lists employment opportunities at the studio.

Casts and Credits

The **Internet Movie Database** (<http://imdb.com>) is a good place to start, although it is not always as complete as one would like. Another site is the **All Movie Guide** (<www.allmovie.com>). Most of the time you can get what you need from the Internet Movie Database, which is worth perusing for a variety of reasons, one of which is the comments section; there, you'll find responses ranging from the knowledgeable to the uninformed. If you need a vital piece of information that you cannot find on the Web, you might have to write to or call the Academy of Motion Picture Arts and Sciences' **National Film Information Service (NFIS),** the Center for Motion Picture Study, 333 S. La Cienega Boulevard, Beverly Hills, CA 90211-1972 (310-247-3000).

The Library of Congress

Although you may not associate the Library of Congress with films, you will if you log on to <http://lcweb.loc.gov/film>. Go into **Film Preservation and Cultural Organization** (<http://lcweb.loc.gov/film/orgs.html>), where you will discover links to the National Film Registry, the Academy of Motion Picture Arts and Sciences, the American Film Institute, the British Film Institute, Film Festivals, Film Archives On Line (FAOL), and The Silent Movie Theatre, among many others.

Directors' Sites

These continue to multiply. You might try <www.director's name.com> or <www.director'snamefilms.com>—for example, <www.hitchcock100.com> for Alfred Hitchcock, the "100" referring to the centennial of his birth (1999). Whether the addition of "100" will be necessary in the future is unknown. As of 2001, you can obtain a great deal of information about Hitchcock, but even more about Universal, the studio where he ended his career. Stanley Kubrick has a fairly direct site <www.kubrickfilms.com>, while Steven Spielberg's and Woody Allen's sites are not: Spielberg's is <www.lochnet.net/bozweb/sp>; Allen's, <www.geocities.com/sunsetstrip/club/9542/woody.html>.

While the great (and not so great) films last regardless of, or despite, technological innovation, Web sites do not. *Close Encounters of the Third Kind* will never undergo a change of title, but there is no guarantee that Steven Spielberg will always be at the same Web address. Many Sunday newspapers carry an informative supplement called *Access: America's Guide to the Internet* (<www.accessmagazine.com>), which includes Web site reviews.

Use technology, but watch movies—and treasure them.

Glossary of Motion Picture Terms

actual sound Sound from an identifiable sound source, either on- or off-screen.

ambient sound Noise.

American montage See **montage.**

anthology film A feature film consisting of (1) several short, self-contained films or vignettes based on short stories (*O. Henry's Full House, Trio, Quartet*); (2) interrelated narratives with a common theme (*Tales of Manhattan, Flesh and Fantasy*); or (3) excerpts from various films (e.g., the musical sequences from MGM's *That's Entertainment* and *That's Entertainment II*).

A-picture The main attraction on a double bill during the studio years (1930–1960); the second feature is termed a **B-picture** because it cost less to make.

archetype A universal theme (quest, odyssey, revenge, love, death), setting (cave, desert, the other world), or character (savior, sorcerer, knight-errant, imperiled maiden) found in the myths and literature of all peoples.

art director Originally the individual responsible for the design and construction of the sets in accordance with the screenplay and the director's interpretation of it. Presently, someone working under the **production supervisor (designer),** who is responsible for the film's "look."

aspect ratio The ratio of image width to height, formerly 4:3 or 1:33:1 (resulting in an image $1^1/_3$ times wider than high) and now approximately 1:8:1.

asynchronous sound Sound related metaphorically or contextually to the next image that we see (for example, the mother calling to her child in *M*, followed by shots of various objects, but not of the child, who is dead).

auteur French for "author," a term applied to directors such as Hitchcock, Ford, and Welles, whose films are so distinctive that they are regarded as having been "authored" and are designated accordingly (John Ford's *Stagecoach*, Orson Welles's *Citizen Kane*).

auteur theory (auteurism) The philosophy that the director is the central intelligence behind a film and deserves authorial status and possessory credit

(Alfred Hitchcock's *Psycho*). The theory has proved quite controversial, although it can be justified when applied to the work of such auteurs as Billy Wilder, Joseph L. Mankiewicz, John Ford, Hitchcock, and others capable of leaving their personal imprint on their films.

back lighting Lighting from behind the subject to create a sense of depth.

best boy Assistant to the **gaffer** (chief electrician).

biopic A biographical film such as Spike Lee's *Malcolm X* (1992).

bottom lighting Lighting from below the subject, leaving part of it in shadow.

B-picture The second, less expensively made film (*B* for budget) on a double bill during the studio years (1930–1960), when many theaters featured two movies. Some B-movies are now acknowledged masterpieces (e.g., *Cat People, I Walked with a Zombie, Detour*).

canted shot An angled shot, resulting in an asymmetrical, lopsided image to suggest that something is amiss. Also known as a Dutch-angle shot.

close shot (CS) A head-and-shoulders shot as opposed to a **close-up,** to which it is so similar that the two terms are often considered synonymous.

close-up (CU) Literally, a shot in which the camera is or appears to be close to the subject (e.g., a shot of the human head).

colorization Computer-created addition of color to a black-and-white film without the consent of the filmmaker, who is usually dead.

commentative sound Sound from a source outside the physical setting, such as background music.

composition (composing a shot) The act of planning a shot or a series of shots as an artist might the details of a painting, with close attention to such matters as lighting, color, camera angles, and spatial relationships.

connotation The metaphorical meaning of a word ("he was *consumed* with hatred") or, in film, an image (the numerous reflections of Eve's successor at the end of *All About Eve*, implying that there will always be newcomers waiting to replace the stars).

continuity editing The arrangement of the shots in accordance with the director's visualization of the material, resulting in a natural flow of the action and a beginning-middle-end plot.

contrast cut A transition from one shot to another that is so radically different from the first that it calls attention to the disparity between them.

crane shot A shot taken when the camera is mounted on a crane (a mechanical arm attached to a trolley, similar to the cherry picker used by utilities crews), enabling the camera to engage in ascending, descending, and lateral movement.

crawl Credits or **titles** that move from the bottom of the screen to the top, and occasionally vice versa. Also known as a **roll-up title.**

credits The names of the film's creative personnel (actors, writer, production designer, costume designer, director of photography, editor, producer, director), which usually—but not always—appears at the beginning of the film as part of the **main title.**

credits sequence A narrative segment of the film that unfolds during the credits, often functioning as a prologue and imparting information that is necessary to an understanding of the plot.

crosscutting Switching back and forth between two actions taking place at the same time but not necessarily and, in fact, rarely in the same place. Also called **parallel cutting.**

cut (1) The joining of two separate shots so that the first is replaced by the second; (2) the joint connecting two shots; (3) a director's signal ("Cut!") to terminate a scene; (4) a version of a movie (**rough cut, director's cut, final cut**).

deep focus A type of photography in which foreground, middle ground, and background are clearly visible.

denotation The literal meaning of a word; in film, the image independent of its symbolic, or **connotative,** meaning (white attire as a mode of dress and not the sign of a white knight).

diegesis Greek for "narrative" and used by some academics to mean the world of the film, including what happens both on- and off-screen as well as past events that have not been dramatized.

digital cinema Film created to be computer-readable, shot in digital video with the information stored on a hard drive, and edited digitally with transitions such as **wipes** and **dissolves** (which can be added or deleted without affecting the original footage).

director The individual ultimately considered responsible for the visualization of the screenplay, although the actual making of the film was a collaborative activity.

director's cut The film in the form in which the director has envisioned it.

discourse In linguistics and **semiotics,** speech as personal expression, either verbal or nonverbal; in film, the way in which the story reaches the audience, including all the narrative strategies that have been used, both visualized and implied.

dissolve A transition in which one shot fades out as another fades in, sometimes with the two shots overlapping (called a lap dissolve).

distribution The second phase of moviemaking, after **production,** which involves the manner in which a film is marketed and released.

documentary A nonfiction film.

dolly shot A moving shot taken on a dolly (a wheeled platform or cart).

dramatic foreshadowing Early indications of events or actions that will happen later.

editing The arrangement of the shots in such a way as to create the film's narrative, rhythmic, and tonal structure so that there is variety of image, size, mood, color, texture, and pace.

end credits A list at the end of the film of virtually everyone, from the stars to the caterer, involved in the production.

end titles Text that appears at the end of the film and provides the audience with vital information, such as the fate of the characters.

epistolary voice Voice-over narration accompanying the reading or writing of a letter.

establishing shot (1) Generally a **long shot** identifying a location, such as a shot of the New York skyline; (2) a long shot (for example, a family gathering) that becomes the basis of closer shots of the various components (individual family members).

exhibition The third phase of moviemaking, after **production** and **distribution,** which refers to the showing of a film in a theater or an auditorium.

extreme close-up (ECU) A shot in which the camera is so close to the subject that only some aspect of it can be recorded, such as an eye or a monogram.

extreme long shot (ELS) A shot in which the camera is so far away that the result is a broad, panoramic view.

fade-out/fade-in The image either disappears as the screen goes dark (**fade-out**) or materializes out of a dark screen (**fade-in**).

fiction film See **narrative film.**

fill light An auxiliary light placed opposite the **key light,** in conjunction with which it eliminates shadows and produces a uniform image.

film infranarrative The film's **subtext,** consisting of the various associations made while watching the film (for example, associating the characters with mythic types and archetypal figures, the actors with their previous roles or with other actors with whom they share common traits, and so forth).

film noir French for "dark film," meaning a film with a discernible dark look characterized by **low-key lighting, high-contrast photography,** rain-slick streets, flashing neon signs, smoke-filled bars, mirrored cocktail lounges, sunless living rooms, femmes fatales, and easily ensnared males.

final cut The version that audiences eventually see, except for some last-minute fine-tuning, generally of the soundtrack.

flashback A segment of a film, brief or extended, that dramatizes what has happened in the past.

flashforward A shot or series of shots depicting an event that will take place at some point in the film but not at the point at which either appears.

focal length The distance from the center of the lens to the point where the image is in focus.

Foley artists Sound effects personnel, named after Joe Foley, who synchronize the appropriate sound with the on-screen image (creating the sound of footsteps on a pavement with a shot of someone walking along the pavement, for example).

form cut A cut from one object to a similarly shaped one (for example, from the wheel of a moving vehicle to a spinning roulette wheel).

form dissolve A dissolve from one object to a similarly shaped one (for example, from the figure of a ballerina on a music box to a young girl in a ballerina's costume).

frame (1) A single photograph on a strip of film; (2) the borders enclosing the photographed image as if it were placed within a picture frame.

framing The act of composing a shot after the filmmaker has decided on its visual form.

freeze frame A form of stopped motion, in which the image is reduced to a still photograph.

front projection Photographing live action in front of a screen, with some kind of background, still or moving, projected onto the screen from the front; the opposite of **rear projection,** in which background is projected from behind the screen.

full shot See **long shot.**

gaffer The chief electrician.

genre A literary form or type of film in which recurring motifs, stylistic conventions, characters, and plot devices have become so familiar that the work or film is relegated to a category such as tragedy, comedy, or lyric poetry in literature or screwball comedy, horror, or science fiction in film.

God's eye shot A shot taken from above the subject. See **high shot.**

graphics Any combination of print and image, such as a film's **main title.**

grip The individual who oversees everything—props, mostly—except for what falls under the jurisdiction of the gaffer.

handheld camera Filming with a portable camera that is either held or attached to the cameraperson.

high-angle shot A shot in which the camera is positioned *above* (**high shot**) or at an angle *above* the subject (**high-angle shot**). See also **God's eye shot.**

high-contrast photography Sharp contrast between the bright and dark areas of the image; in film noir, a white image against a black background.

high-key lighting Lighting that produces uniform brightness (ideal for musicals and comedies) resulting from a low contrast of **key** to **fill light.**

iconography Re-creating an image so that it evokes a traditional or familiar pictorial representation, such as a well-known painting or sculpture.

independent film (indie) (1) A movie made without a studio affiliation; (2) one made by a producer whose production unit is based at a studio that has provided some form of financing and functions as the film's distributor; (3) one distributed through a studio's specialty unit, such as Sony Classics, Fox Searchlight, or Paramount Classics.

insert A shot, such as a written text (for example, part of a letter), that is edited into the film, not photographed during the particular scene but inserted later.

intercutting Similar to crosscutting, except that in intercutting switching back and forth from one location to another results in a complete scene (the attempt to sabotage the launching of the battleship in *Saboteur*, for example).

intertextuality Inserting references to other works within one's own, often as a way of acknowledging influences, paying homage, or answering predecessors. Brian De Palma's *Obsession* is a tribute to Hitchcock's *Vertigo*, and Peter Bogdanovich's *The Last Picture Show* pays homage to Howard Hawks's *Red River.*

intertitles Text that appears on the screen periodically to provide some kind of information; a common technique in silent films. See **titles.**

iris-in/iris-out The circle-enclosed image keeps expanding until the image is in full view (**iris-in**); the shot seems to close down as the image is reduced to a circle, which then disappears from the screen (**iris-out**).

iris shot A shot in which the image is enclosed within a circle, although rectangular and lozenge-shaped shots also fall under this category.

jump cut An abrupt transition from one location or time frame to another, sometimes for effect but often because of mediocre editing.

key grip The head grip, who supervises the others.

key light The primary source of illumination, usually placed above and to the side of the subject.

Logo A studio's trademark (e.g., MGM's lion, Universal's globe).

long shot (LS) A shot in which the camera appears at a distance from the subject (the complete person with some background visible). Also known as a **full shot (FS).**

long take A take that lasts at least a minute, although there have been instances of shots lasting as long as ten minutes (the eight ten-minute, or thereabouts, shots in Hitchcock's *Rope*). See also **sequence.**

low-angle shot A shot in which the camera shoots up at the subject from below, making the subject larger than it actually is.

low-key lighting The result of a high-contrast ratio of key to fill light, producing dark, shadowy images that are ideal for horror and film noir.

main title The film's title and opening credits, often creatively designed and an artistic creation in itself.

masking Altering the shape of the frame so that it can assume a particular shape (a keyhole, peephole). The frame is considered to be **masked** when everything is blacked out except the shape in which the image will appear.

match cut A transition from one shot to another that is related to it contextually but is often spatially and temporally distinct from it, done so smoothly that there is no break in continuity.

matte shot A shot created by masking out part of the frame, clearing that area for the insertion of another image. In *King Kong*, the scene in which Fay Wray is terrorized by a prehistoric creature is a matte shot; the image of the creature was matted onto the shot of Wray screaming in fear.

medium close-up (MCU) Midway between a close-up and a **medium shot** (chest-to-head).

medium long shot (MLS) Midway between a medium shot and a long shot, providing less detail than a long shot.

medium shot (MS) Midway between a close-up and a long shot (waist up).

metonomy The substitution of one term for another to which it is closely related ("crown" for "royalty," "chair" for "chairperson").

miniature rear projection A technique in which live action (not live actors) is projected onto a screen, in front of which is a scaled set with model figures (for example, a bust of King Kong) whose movements are correlated with the live action through **stop-motion photography.**

mise-en-scène A French theatrical term meaning the staging of a production; in film, composing a shot or a sequence with the same attention to detail (set, lighting, costumes, makeup, positioning of actors within the frame, etc.) that a stage director lavishes on a play.

mobile camera A general term for the camera in a moving state.

montage (1) Editing in the sense of assembling the shots to create the complete film; (2) a series of shots that appear in rapid succession; (3) a series of shots linked by **dissolves** and wipes to collapse time, often indicated by newspaper headlines or calendar pages dissolving into each other (also known as **American montage**).

morphing Suggested by "metamorphosis" and referring to a computer-created transformation of one image into another (for example, human into animal or vice versa, a fictional character into a historical figure).

Motion Picture Production Code See **production code.**

myth A timeless narrative that expresses universal truths about life and death, fate and nature, and the divine and the human.

narrative film A film with an invented plot. Also known as **fiction film** and **story film.**

negative cost All the expenses incurred in producing the original negative from which positive prints are struck.

New Wave (French New Wave, *la nouvelle vague*) A movement in French cinema that began in the late 1950s, when film critics such as François Truffaut, Jean-Luc Godard, and Claude Chabrol became directors who broke with the past, used improvisation, filmed on location (streets, bistros, apartments), deliberately paid homage (*hommage*) to their favorite American directors by repeatedly evoking their films, and upgraded the director from foreman to auteur or surrogate author of his or her films.

omniscient narrator A third-person storytelling technique in which the narrator knows everything about the plot and the characters, including their unconscious desires and innermost thoughts.

opening title Text that appears at the beginning of a film and provides some kind of background information.

optical printer A camera interlocked with a projector to re-photograph images from the original film, so that optical effects such as wipes, dissolves, fades, and freeze frames can be added.

outtakes Shots eliminated from the final version but sometimes included in the end credits.

overlapping dialogue (1) Dialogue in which actors speak over each other's lines, supposedly to sound more realistic; (2) dialogue that carries over from one scene to the next.

overlapping sound Sound that carries over from one scene to the next or anticipates a new scene by starting at the end of the previous one.

pan shot A shot in which the camera rotates horizontally on a fixed axis. Not properly a **moving shot** because the camera itself does not move, only the camera head.

paradigm In **semiotics**, a unit of potential relationship; **paradigmatic relationships** are associative, not sequential, and are concerned with meaning rather than order (for example, associating a scene of fictional violence with a historical incident that resulted in a similar bloodbath).

parallel cut A transition from one shot to another occurring at the same time. See also **crosscutting.**

plot A work's narrative structure—not the story line but the arrangement and order of the episodes that make up the work.

point-of-view (POV) (1) A shot from the character's point of view—what the character sees; (2) a shot representing what the character experiences—in a reverie, a memory, a dream—so that we momentarily become the character. See also **subjective camera.**

postproduction The stage following the completion of a film, including the editing, the addition of **transitions** and **visual effects,** and musical scoring.

precredits sequence A segment of the film that occurs before the credits come on and often contains information that is vital to an understanding of the plot.

preproduction Everything that precedes the actual filming (for example, the preparation of the script, casting, selection of a director and the creative team).

producer The individual who "puts the package together" (cast, writer, director, and so forth) and oversees the entire production from its inception to its completion and, in some cases, its marketing, while also making sure that the film stays within budget.

production The first phase of moviemaking, followed by distribution and exhibition, and denoting everything involved in the making of the movie prior to its being edited.

production code (Motion Picture Production Code) A self-regulatory policy created in 1930 in response to public pressure to "reform the screen" and replaced in 1968 by the **rating system.** Unacceptable screen content and language included nudity, homosexuality, drug-taking, vulgarity, obscenity, and blasphemy. White slavery (enforced prostitution) and interracial relationships were cautioned against; crime could not pay, nor could adultery be justified. Rape and seduction could only be suggested.

production designer (production supervisor) The person responsible for the film's "look" as determined by the script and the director's vision of it.

product placement Placing a brand name in a prominent position in the shot so that audiences cannot help noticing it.

rack focus The shifting of focus from one character or area within a shot to another by reducing the character or area to a blur, until such time as the indistinct section is restored to focus.

ratings (the Motion Picture Rating System) A system of rating films inaugurated in 1968 by the Motion Picture Association of America (MPAA) after it became evident that the production code was outdated. The categories, which are now considerably different from those of 1968, presently consist of G (general audiences), PG (parental guidance), PG-13 (parental guidance for children under 13), R (restricted to those 17 or older unless accompanied by an adult), and NC-17 (no children under 17). The R category is especially problematic, since such films as *Schindler's List* and *Saving Private Ryan* have been classified as "R."

rear projection Projecting background footage (for example, a ski slope, a city street) onto the rear of a screen in front of which live action is photographed, so that the characters appear to be skiing or driving down Broadway though they are really in a movie studio.

reflexivity The self-conscious attempt by a novelist, playwright, or filmmaker to call attention to his or her work as a novel, a play, or a film, so that we are reading a novel about the writing of a novel, watching a play about theater, or seeing a film about movies. Sartre's *Nausea* is a novel about the complex process of creating a novel, Jean Anouilh's *Antigone* calls attention to itself as a modern version of Sophocles' tragedy, and Woody Allen's *The Purple Rose of Cairo* makes it clear that it is about movies as the "daylight dream."

roll-up title See **crawl.**

rough cut An early version of the film as the director had planned it but that is not yet ready for release.

screwball comedy A type of romantic comedy that is noted for witty dialogue, oddball characters, a battle-of-the-sexes plot, and a happy ending in which such barriers as class and profession vanish in the face of true love.

self-reflexive See **reflexivity.**

semidocumentary A fiction film based on fact, photographed and acted in such a way that it resembles both a fiction film and a documentary.

semiotics The study of signs and codes to determine their meaning, especially in such matters as food, color, gesture, dress, and body language.

sequence A segment of a film that, when excerpted, makes a certain amount of narrative sense (*Psycho*'s famous shower sequence).

shallow focus Rendering the foreground with greater clarity and sharpness than the background; the opposite of **deep focus.**

shooting script A script prepared for filming, with the scenes numbered and designated in terms of interior/exterior, place, and day/night (INT: Cabin—Day), the camera positions indicated, the transitions marked, and the proper spacing observed.

shot What is recorded by a single, uninterrupted run of the camera. See also **take.**

shot/reverse-shot Switching back and forth between two characters in conversation so that each one's reaction can be seen.

side lighting Lighting from either side of a subject, leaving it half in light and half in shadow.

special effects See **visual effects.**

spec script A script that is written without any studio commitment and submitted without any guarantee of sale.

Steadicam A camera that is attached to the operator's body, enabling him or her to move easily into, out of, or around areas that cannot accommodate a dolly.

stop-motion photography A type of photography often used in animation in which the camera operates one frame at a time so that objects can be adjusted between frames, thereby "coming alive."

story film See **narrative film.**

straight cut The immediate transition from one shot to the next.

stream of consciousness The flow of thoughts, memories, and associations, both conscious and unconscious, within a character's mind.

subjective camera A technique in which the viewer stands in for the character, experiencing what the character would have experienced. See also **point-of-view** shot.

subtext See **film infranarrative.**

subtitles Print that appears at the bottom of the screen to provide information such as a translation from a foreign language. See **titles.**

swish pan An unusually rapid pan, sometimes resulting in a momentary blur.

synecdoche Similar to **metonomy,** though usually restricted to the substitution of the part for the whole ("law" for "police officer," "deck hands" for "crew").

syntagma In semiotics, a unit of actual relationship; **syntagmatic relationships**

are those in which the narrative units follow each other in order, allowing the viewer to connect them in a meaningful and coherent pattern.

take Theoretically, the same as **shot,** except that several takes may be necessary before the right one is achieved.

theatrical film A film made for exhibition in a movie theater.

three-point lighting The standard lighting scheme involving some combination of back, key, and fill lights.

three-shot A shot with three characters.

tight framing Confining the image, usually a character, within the frame lines to suggest entrapment.

tilt shot A shot in which the camera rotates vertically on a fixed axis.

titles Any printed text in a film.

top lighting Lighting from above the subject, capable of producing a glowing effect.

tracking shot A moving shot, originally with the camera on tracks but now referring to any shot taken when the camera is on some sort of moving vehicle or mechanism, such as a dolly, crane, car, or truck—or even held by or strapped onto a person (e.g., a Steadicam).

transitions Devices used for bridging scenes, such as fades, dissolves, wipes, and irising.

two-shot A shot with two characters.

virtual reality A computer-simulated environment, which those who have access to it can alter as they wish.

visual effects (special effects) Effects achieved through special optical and mechanical processes (wipes, dissolves, freezes, matte shots, stop-motion photography, miniature rear projection, etc.).

voice of God Omniscient off-camera narration.

voice-over Off-camera narration either by a character or a commentator.

wide-angle lens An angle that has a short focal length.

wide-angle shot A shot taken with a wide-angle lens, which, though it can offer a broader view and provide more visual information, also makes the foreground and whatever is in it seem unnaturally larger than the background.

wipe A transition in which a line appears to move vertically, horizontally, or diagonally across the screen, causing one shot to disappear or close down and another to materialize. Wipes can also appear in the form of clocks, fans, and spirals.

zoom lens A lens of variable focal length, allowing the filmmaker to create the illusion of movement by changing the focal length to move into (**zoom in**) or out of (**zoom out**) a scene.

Index

Motion Picture Production Code, 13, 137, 150, 165, 166, 207, 260, 268, 283

movie, use of the term, 2

movie time, 10–11

moving shots, 73–75

Mr. Arkadin, 325

Mr. Skeffington, 85, 210

Mrs. Miniver, 84, 145, 221

Mr. Smith Goes to Washington, 82, 88

Mulholland Falls, 143

Mulvey, Laura, 311, 315

Mummy's Curse, The, 169

Murder, My Sweet, 46, 139

Murder on the Orient Express, 52

Murdoch, Iris, 9, 158

musical associations, 209–17

musicals, 120–27

  animated, 126

  comedies with music, 121

  dance, 123–25

  dramas with music, 121

  integrated, 120

  operettas, 121

  revues, 120–21

  show-business (backstage musicals), 121–23

My Darling Clementine, 56, 107, 127, 128, 131, 134, 229

My Life, 168

My Little Chickadee, 154, 155, 156

My Reputation, 165

myth (mythic associations), 181–90, 327–28

  concept and definition of, 181–83

mythographers, 302–304

Naked City, The, 49

Naked Dawn, The, 56

Naked Spur, The, 134

Naremore, James, 8

narrating "I," 46–48

narration, voice-over, 44–49

narrative film, 5

  history and, 11–15

Nashville, 11, 252, 306

National Lampoon's Animal House, 155

Natural Born Killers, 101, 139

Nausea, (Sartre), 158

neorealism, Italian, 299

Net, The, 39

New Faces of 1952, 121

New Life, A, 81, 240, 241, 242, 243

New Wave, 200

New York, New York, 121

New York Times, 319, 321

Nicholson, Jack, in *One Flew over the Cuckoo's Nest*, 193–96

Nickelodeon, 11, 40, 91, 162

'Night, Mother, 268

Night and Day, 13

Night at the Opera, A, 153

Night in Casablanca, A, 153

Night of the Hunter, The, 161

Night of the Iguana, The, 267–68

Night Porter, The, 212

Norman, Marsha, 268

North by Northwest, 73, 89, 102, 161, 229

  associative sequence in, 81

  dissolves in, 86

No Sad Songs for Me, 163

Nosferatu, 162

Notorious, 10–11, 55, 308

  associative sequence in, 80–81

  fades in, 84–85

  key sequence in, 77, 78

novels, adaptations of, 261

Now, Voyager, 274, 312

Nurse Betty, 29

Nyoka and the Lost Tablets of Hippocrates, 159

objective shot, 58

O Brother, Where Art Thou?, 161, 162

Odyssey (Homer), 132, 161, 190, 248

Of Mice and Men, 30

Old Acquaintance, 164, 167

Old Maid, The, 164

omniscient narrator, 252–53

One Flew over the Cuckoo's Nest, 193–96

O'Neill, Eugene, 75

One True Thing, 168

One, Two, Three, 227

Only You, 150

On the Town, 120, 125

On the Waterfront, 67, 166, 286, 288

opening titles, 33–34

operettas, 121

Ophüls, Max, 51, 74–75, 86

optical printer, 113

Othello, 326

Our Town, 260